Praise for
Our Fermented Lives

"This book shows us how countless generations before us have made meaning with their food, and how we can continue that tradition and make new meanings, stories, and traditions of our own."

—from the foreword by Sandor Ellix Katz, *New York Times* best-selling author of *The Art of Fermentation*

"Julia's deep knowledge and reverence for the craft of preserving food makes my life as a forever student all the more joyful."

—Cortney Burns, chef and author of *Nourish Me Home*

"The recipes are fabulous, and by setting microbes in their historical and social contexts, Skinner makes this book a unique addition to the literature on fermentation."

—Ken Albala, professor of history, University of the Pacific

"Skinner weaves together ancient history with modern conversations about food security, inequality, and appropriation. In doing so, she has created a rich tapestry that illuminates fermentation's place in the human experience—one that encompasses food preservation, flavor, health, and the intersection of human and microbial cultures."

—Kirsten K. Shockey, coauthor of *Fermented Vegetables* and cofounder of The Fermentation School

"Skinner has brilliantly combined practical, hands-on knowledge with historical context and anthropological themes for this treasure trove!"

—Jenny Dorsey, chef, writer, and founder of Studio ATAO

Our Fermented Lives

A HISTORY

*How Fermented Foods Have
Shaped Cultures & Communities*

JULIA SKINNER

Foreword by Sandor Ellix Katz

Storey Publishing

The mission of Storey Publishing is to serve our customers by publishing practical information that encourages personal independence in harmony with the environment.

Edited by Sarah Guare Slattery and
   Carleen Madigan
Art direction by Ash Austin
Book design by Stacy Wakefield Forte
Text production by Jennifer Jepson Smith
Indexed by Christine R. Lindemer,
   Boston Road Communications
Illustrations by Karl Fröhlich, from
   Karl Fröhlich's *Frolicks with Scissors
   and Pen* (R. Worthington, 1879) from
   www.oldbookillustrations.com
Backgrounds by Annie Spratt (cover and
   title page)

Storey books are available at special discounts when purchased in bulk for premiums and sales promotions as well as for fund-raising or educational use. Special editions or book excerpts can also be created to specification. For details, please call 800-827-8673, or send an email to sales@storey.com.

Storey Publishing
210 MASS MoCA Way
North Adams, MA 01247
storey.com

Printed in the United States by Lakeside Book Company
10 9 8 7 6 5 4 3 2 1

Library of Congress Cataloging-in-
   Publication Data on file

To Dave Skinner, who showed me that
better worlds are always within our grasp,
if we are only just willing to reach out our
hands to touch them.

To Danielle (Doc) Holliday, whose friendship and conversation inspired many parts
of this book, though they did not get to see
it to completion. I love you to the moon and
all the way past the stars.

CONTENTS

FOREWORD

BY SANDOR ELLIX KATZ, *NEW YORK TIMES* BEST-SELLING AUTHOR
OF *THE ART OF FERMENTATION*

There's no doubt about it, our lives *are* fermented. Whether or not you've
ever given a thought to fermentation, the phenomenon has played an
immense role in your life. From the very beginning, in our deepest evolutionary past, the earliest life-forms were fermentative, in the biologist's
sense of the word, meaning that their metabolism was anaerobic. Only
after some of the descendants of these earliest organisms began producing oxygen via photosynthesis did aerobic life-forms such as ourselves
even become possible. We are descended from bacteria, we have never
lived without them, and we are utterly dependent upon them. The trillions
of bacteria each of us is host to are integral to our functionality. The soil,
plants, and animals that give us our food are host to their own microbial
communities, similarly essential to their well-being.

We are only beginning to grasp the complexity and importance of these
organisms. Yet somehow, without specifically knowing about them, people
everywhere, thousands of years ago and ever since, have developed methods for working with microbes in varied contexts, including agriculture,
fiber arts, medicine, energy production, and most prominently, food and
beverage fermentation. Fermented foods and beverages are present in
cuisines everywhere, generally not in incidental ways but rather as foun-
dational elements: bread, cheese, yogurt, vinegar, soy sauce, wine, beer.
Almost certainly, you—like almost everyone else everywhere—eat or drink
products of fermentation every day.

I first took note of flavors of fermentation as a New York City kid who
loved pickles. As a young adult experimenting with a few different dietary
ideas, I learned that some people ascribed digestive, immune, and other
health benefits to live fermented foods, and started eating them regularly
as a health practice. Later, when I took up gardening, it was the practical
aspect of preserving the crop that got me to investigate how to make sauerkraut. Sauerkraut was my gateway, and three decades later, not only do
I continue an avid fermentation practice in my kitchen, but fermentation
has become a central focus in my life. Almost every day I think and talk

about fermentation, and frequently I read about it, write about it, and teach about it.

I think that what has kept fermentation so endlessly fascinating to me is how incredibly multifaceted it is. The products of fermentation can be scrumptiously delicious, and there is a long list of practical benefits of fermentation—including food preservation, improved digestibility and nutrient bioavailability, and probiotics. But there is so much more to fermentation than even that. Fermentation is an inevitable manifestation of the biodiversity of life. Far from a unified set of techniques, fermentation is an extremely varied constellation of interventions. People have conceptualized and practiced fermentation in many different ways, in response to different conditions and different available food resources, yet it is integral to cultural traditions everywhere. Fermentation is thoroughly enmeshed in the human story. It has inspired ritual, ceremony, poetry, and song. People have worshipped fermentation deities, and ferments have been flashpoints in wars and political disputes. The practical delicacies that are the products of fermentation are further enhanced by the profound meanings that human cultures have ascribed to them and to the process itself.

The stories and the significance associated with fermentation and its products are Julia Skinner's central focus in this book. This is not exactly a traditional history book. It contains many fascinating historical tales, drawing from very eclectic sources and traditions, spanning the globe and all of recorded history (and beyond). There are recipes as well, which look wonderful. Some are Julia's takes on classics, or her interpretation of historic ferments; others are quite inventive. The stories and recipes are interwoven into broad narrative themes. As Julia tells us at the outset, she's "itching for some big conversations."

Fermentation is a prism that Julia Skinner deftly uses to illuminate diverse aspects of culture and history. For fermentation enthusiasts and afficionados, this book will expand the context for understanding some of your most beloved foods and beverages and introduce you to new ones. But most important, this book shows us how countless generations before us have made meaning with their food, and how we can continue that tradition and make new meanings, stories, and traditions of our own.

PREFACE

This book began to ferment in my own mind when I was accepted into a weeklong residency with Sandor Katz. Sandor is one of my food heroes and also one of my greatest models for how to teach with empathy, compassion, and a focus on process over results. The experience was absolutely transformative, not only for my food but for my whole life path. I learned about all sorts of ferments I had never played with before, in a space where everyone was learning from each other. I got to hear about fermentation successes and failures from a ton of perspectives. That residency also came at a critical juncture for me, at a time when I was seeking to rekindle my self-acceptance. In this space, with this group of people, I found that I could simply be me and didn't have to hide certain identities (queerness and paganism in particular) that I've often been asked to tamp down elsewhere in my world. Working with ferments in this liberating environment gave me a special affinity for them (though I'd been fermenting for a decade or more already), and as I've grown more fully into myself, I've grown more and more fascinated by ferments, too.

After my residency with Sandor Katz, I returned to the restaurant world as a fermenter at a local restaurant in Atlanta. I had worked in restaurants before, but not as a fermenter specifically. To my knowledge, I was the first dedicated fermenter at any restaurant in the city. It was exciting to share my work, and it was an invigorating reminder of the passion and enthusiasm I love so much about my industry colleagues. But I realized I wanted to do something bigger: I wanted to share the ferments I make more broadly, and I was also itching for some big conversations. And so I decided to write this book and found my company, Root, which is centered on food history and fermentation. I do everything from consulting with restaurants about food waste to doing set design for independent films to teaching and writing.

I started writing this book at a time when my own world seemed to be falling apart, and I found that fermentation (and food history) was the glue that held it together. As I coped with multiple losses and huge waves of change (both good and bad), ferments offered me a grounding space to go back to. Each morning when I woke up, the first thing I did was check on my ferments. Watching them develop, growing from whatever humble ingredients I tossed into a crock into something delicious, felt amazing. I realized that if I could facilitate such a wonderful transformation with these microbes, I could facilitate a great change inside myself and the world around me as well.

Learning to ferment food, and later learning the history of the foods I ferment, has been one of the most impactful and important experiences of my life. While I can't assume that will be the case for everyone, I hope the deep love I feel for these foods comes through in my research and my recipes, and that it inspires you to find your own home with ferments, too.

The Intertwinings
of Humans and Microbes

This book is an exploration of fermentation's path through human history. Within it, we see that fermentation's history and our own are absolutely inextricable, from our very biome to the flavors we seek out to the ways we've made our food safe to eat over the centuries and even the ways we come together with our communities to celebrate milestones or to ensure everyone is fed.

In my work as a food historian, I have found that many people are eager to know about the history of fermentation. Countless colleagues, students, and friends have asked me about the history of particular ferments as much as they ask about the process of creating them. Folks from the most novice cooks to professional chefs all feel pulled to learn more about ferments, and I hope this book is a helpful accompaniment to the many incredible volumes out there that teach fermentation methods.

This book is not an encyclopedia. There would be no way to cover the history of every fermented food in depth (at least not within one author's lifetime). It does, however, have a global reach: I have tried to account for fermented foods found across as many cultures as I could.

Whenever possible, I have talked to or read the works of people who actually make these ferments, and I have shared with you what they say. I think it is critically important, particularly as someone with relative privilege, not to overshadow others' stories with my own words and perspectives. Instead, I share the words of those creators who are steeped within the cultures from which these ferments come, and in so doing I hope to foster a deeper understanding of the foods we're talking about and offer a platform for each fermenter I speak with to share the significance of their work with you.

Culture and Relationships

Fermentation trains us in seeing the ground as inherently shaky. It makes visible the invisible potential of those things that seem still.

—MERCEDES VILLALBA, *MANIFIESTO FERVIENTE*

Every fermentation enthusiast remembers their first ferment. Maybe they don't remember the first time they ate fermented food, but each person I've spoken to has a story of what they made and why, and ultimately how that one simple step into the world of fermentation launched a lifetime of experiments—both beautiful and maddening (or both)—and opened up a world of new flavors and textures to explore.

For years, I thought that sauerkraut was the first fermented food I had ever made. In my early 20s, running into the age-old problem of what to do with a garden of produce that ripens all at once, I turned to sauerkraut as the answer, upon the advice of a farmer friend. Soon whatever container had been empty in my kitchen was filled with living foods, all bubbling away on the counter. Those I didn't refrigerate fresh and eat soon were canned and given away as gifts or consumed later, stretching my meager food budget.

As it turns out, that sauerkraut was my introduction to *lacto-fermentation* (when the naturally occurring lactobacilli bacteria on a plant convert the sugars in the plant into lactic acid; we'll talk more about this on page 38), not to fermentation as a whole, because I had, unknowingly, been making ferments my entire life. My actual first ferment was Amish friendship bread, a sweet quick bread that is similar in texture to banana bread. Friendship bread starters—zippered baggies of pungent, runny batter—and a set of directions are passed from friend to friend. Each recipient cultivates more starter, divides it, and shares it, using the remainder to bake their own bread.

Friendship bread is a great example of the ways in which our cooking intersects with fermentation much more often than we might think. I never thought my family made anything fermented: We never had crocks of vegetables bubbling away, or homemade beer or wine. But we did have friendship bread, and I always giggled with delight when a new starter appeared in our home. And that starter? It's fermented.

Friendship bread, it turns out, was the perfect introduction to the craft of fermenting because it speaks to how fermentation cultures shape and are shaped by our communities. The bread brings friends and family together in the sharing of it, and the bread's starter quite literally picks up a bit of each place it's been, making the microbial community within that culture representative of the human community it is passed through. (See page 272 for my own friendship bread recipe.)

Knowing where food is from and how we use it in our communities to feed and celebrate each other is a central theme in my writing. I also believe in using the simple fermentation methods our ancestors would have used, and you'll find that this homespun approach permeates my recipes. I tend to focus on wild fermentation (which uses naturally occurring microbes in the environment, rather than a purchased culture) both because I appreciate the spontaneity it offers and because it is what our ancestors often did. When I can't use a wild starter, I prefer to use a whole-food starter (such as the sauerkraut juice from the last batch) rather than a commercially available starter. In some cases, I do use purchased starters (like koji), but when we get to talking about those fermentations, I will tell you what the starter is, where to get it, and why I'm using it.

I learned about fermentation the way my ancestors would have: through trial and error, through advice from more experienced community members, and through lots and lots of practice. I like to think of women (and some men) in earlier generations using the same foods as me to feed their families and communities: wild-fermented foods with simple, local ingredients, and foods that use up every scrap of the raw ingredients we can find.

Fermentation equals community, both in a microbiological sense and through the human connections built by this style of preparation. Fermentation relies entirely on relationship: the relationship between the maker and the microbe, and between the microbes themselves. Fermentation can be a long process, taking up to a year or more. And while not every ferment needs constant attention, you can't set it and forget it. In order for a ferment to be successful, you must create a selective environment that makes the microbes you work with happy and healthy. Ferments need to be smelled, stirred, wrapped, unwrapped, lightly heated, slightly cooled, and gently nurtured into life. Just like our human relationships, ferments require our love and attention to grow.

You put your trust in microbes to do the work of creating the result you want, and, just like with human relationships, this succeeds the vast majority of the time. And when you don't get the expected result—when there's a need you didn't realize you had to meet— the project is resigned to the compost heap or, on the opposite end of the spectrum, it exceeds your wildest dreams.

Perhaps it is because fermentation necessitates this relationship between microbe and human that people are drawn to it—and drawn to others who are fermenting. More than any other preparation method I've engaged in, fermentation builds a community of enthusiasts who are curious and hungry for new knowledge—and hungry not only to learn but to learn from each other.

Working on a ferment is an act of cocreation with the microbes you're coaxing to grow, as well as with whomever you are fermenting. Some of my most precious fermentation memories are of foods I made with someone else, or shared with someone else once the ferment was finished. I hope that as you read this book, you get a sense of not only the centrality of ferments in our human history more broadly but the centrality of ferments in human relationships as well. From communities coming together to make kimchi to the alcohol served at a feast, ferments have long had a place at the tables we set for those we love. I hope that when you learn about this history, you're inspired to create your own ferments to feed and learn with others.

After my early forays into fermenting, I found that I couldn't help but make more and more fermented foods, filling up much of my free time and every available square inch of counter space in my home with veggies packed in brine, vinegar made from my autumn apple scraps, and bottles of kombucha. But while I made ferments frequently, it wasn't until relatively recently that I started making a wide variety of them. Truth be told, I still found a lot of ferments to be intimidating, and while I dreamed of a root cellar brimming with living foods and homemade beverages, I was worried I would somehow mess up and ultimately fail at my most ambitious projects.

As so often happens in life, the worry was worse than the failure. I realized, "So what if I do fail?" I've definitely made plenty of mistakes in fermenting, as has every other fermenter (don't let anyone tell you otherwise!). All fermentation asks of you is that you show up with an open heart, creative mind, and hands ready to work. If you do, it will reward you either with a lesson or with something delicious—possibly something delicious beyond what you ever imagined.

Fermentation has taught me a lot about letting go, trusting the process, and giving my heart to projects no matter how they turn out. In return, those projects have fed me in all the ways I need, from physically nourishing me to helping me grow as a cook and a teacher. Today I finally have my little root cellar, just as I dreamed of years ago.

A Few Favorite Recipes

Here, as at the end of each chapter, you will find a collection of fermentation recipes. The recipes that follow are some of my favorite simple ferments to make.

The sauerkraut and cultured butter are among the first ferments I learned, and they offer an easy and approachable way to dip your toes into the world of fermentation.

The horseradish paste is one of the most versatile ferments in my repertoire. I also make ginger and garlic paste. I started down this particular fermenting path a couple of years ago, and I fell in love with the deep flavors that develop in each paste as well as all the ways these simple ingredients can be used in everyday cooking.

The corn beer is a historical recipe that was shared with me by a friend who sells rare books, and it is the first of many historical preparations this book explores.

I round out this recipe collection with two of my favorite ways to use honey: in a delicious and healing turmeric ferment, and in a basic mead recipe. Both are gently sweet and wonderfully customizable, offering a great first foray into a style of cooking that is inherently slow, exploratory, and playful.

SAUERKRAUT

This is the way I learned to make sauerkraut more than a decade ago. The person who taught me made it in jars, rather than a crock, to keep their small apartment from smelling like cabbage, and I find this method to be so easy (and to work so well in small spaces) that it's become a go-to for me when I teach fermentation classes.

You'll need two pint jars with lids and bands for this method.

MAKES
2 PINTS

1 head cabbage

Sea salt

Spices (such as caraway, fennel, juniper berries; optional)

1 Remove the outer two layers of leaves from your cabbage and set them aside. Quarter and core the cabbage, then thinly shred it.

2 Add the shredded cabbage to a bowl and sprinkle liberally with salt (I use about 1 teaspoon). Toss together and allow to sit for 10 minutes.

3 Massage the salt into the cabbage until the cabbage releases enough liquid to form a brine (you'll know it's ready when it releases a thin stream of liquid when squeezed). If it doesn't seem like the cabbage is releasing liquid, add a bit more salt and keep massaging.

4 Give the brine a quick taste: You want it to taste salty like the sea. If it seems like the brine needs a bit more salt, you can always add more and massage it in, though I've rarely found that the salt needs adjustment at this point. If you're using spices, add them now.

5 Pack the cabbage tightly into glass pint jars. Using your hand—either flat or balled into a fist—or the back of a ladle, or a wooden sauerkraut pounder, press your cabbage down firmly to release any air bubbles and to ensure that the brine will cover it. If your cabbage is not completely covered, add more brine. If you find there are still air bubbles, gently slide a chopstick or knife down the edge of your jar to release them.

6 Fold over one of the outer cabbage leaves you set aside earlier and place it on top of the shredded cabbage in the jar. This top leaf keeps the shredded cabbage in the brine. Make sure the leaf itself is also submerged in the brine.

Recipe continues on next page. >

7   Place the lid on each jar and set the jars on a baking sheet or plate. Allow to ferment out of direct sunlight for 2 to 3 weeks (or longer, if desired, which will soften the cabbage and make it more sour). Loosen each lid and check your ferment at least every couple of days, making sure all the cabbage stays submerged in the brine. If you need to add more brine, use a solution of 1 teaspoon salt dissolved in 2 cups water.

8   Once your kraut is as sour as you'd like, store it in the fridge in an air-tight container (such as the jars you fermented it in), where it can keep for several months if it stays submerged in brine. One note: When storing ferments with metal rings in the fridge, it can be helpful to put a piece of parchment or waxed paper between the top of the jar and the lid to prevent corrosion. Just make sure the paper doesn't come in contact with the ferment itself.

CULTURED BUTTER

Cultured butter is easy to make and delicious, and it's a great way to sneak some extra live cultures plus a boost of savory and tangy flavor into your meals. Because it creates a selective microbial environment wherein beneficial microbes outnumber (and thus outcompete) harmful ones, culturing has been used historically to prolong butter's shelf life. It also leaves you with two endlessly useful products: a fresh, delicious butter and some buttermilk full of active cultures that can work as a leavener and flavoring in baked goods.

MAKES ABOUT 1 POUND

1   **quart heavy whipping cream** (not ultra-pasteurized)

1   **tablespoon plain yogurt** (see note)

NOTE When selecting a yogurt to use, look for an unflavored variety, preferably organic, with live and active cultures. If you like the way it tastes, you can use it to start your own yogurt, too, and never have to worry about buying yogurt again! There are many resources out there for learning to make yogurt, and you can find instructions online or in fermentation books such as Sandor Katz's *The Art of Fermentation* or Gianaclis Caldwell's *Homemade Yogurt & Kefir*.

1   Combine the cream and yogurt in a nonreactive mixing bowl and whisk
    together. Cover with a clean cloth or towel, and allow to rest at room
    temperature overnight.

2   Using an electric mixer, beat the cream until it forms butter, 5 to 10 min-
    utes. Initially you'll get a thick whipped cream and might think you're
    done. Keep going! You'll know you have butter when the buttermilk and
    butter separate.

3   Pour off the buttermilk into a separate container and store in the fridge.
    Use within 2 to 3 days for the freshest flavor, though it will keep for up
    to 1 week.

4   Gently massage the butter under cold water until the water runs clear to
    remove the excess buttermilk. This will prolong the life of your butter.

5   Transfer the butter to a jar or other lidded vessel and store in the fridge.
    Like your buttermilk, cultured butter tastes best when used relatively
    soon after making, though it can keep in the fridge for 2 to 3 weeks.

BUTTER CULTURE VARIATIONS

You can make cultured butter using all kinds of ferments beyond yogurt.
I was inspired to jump down this rabbit hole by chef and fermenter Sean
Doherty of Cera restaurant in Maine, whose experiments culturing butter
with blue cheese (which is so good) inspired me to start my own. Each
ferment imparts its own unique qualities to butter, giving you another
layer of flavor when you use that butter in dishes or as a spread.

The process is the same as above; just substitute another ferment for
the yogurt. For most, I use between 2 and 4 tablespoons of ferment per
quart of cream. This is a great space to play around and see what tastes
best to you. In all cases, make sure you're using live cultures.

My favorites include:

- crumbled blue cheese

- unpasteurized fire cider

- live-culture pickle brine

- unpasteurized banana or strawberry-jalapeño vinegar

- unpasteurized honey vinegar or mead

CORN BEER

Corn beer, which is made from just corn, molasses (a common beer ingredient through much of American history), and water, was once a common beverage in the South, but few contemporary recipes exist. I share two recipes below. The first, published in the 1863 *Clarke's Confederate Household Almanac*, was printed in Vicksburg, Mississippi, just months before the Union army's victory in the city. It is a reminder of the myriad social contexts with which our food intersects.

The second is a recipe that I devised. For my recipe, you will need a 1-gallon carboy, an airlock, and a carboy bung (see the Appendix). You'll also need a length of sturdy thread and a needle to go with it.

This beer makes use of a starter culture, which in this case is a handful of corn kernels threaded onto a piece of string. This is added to the molasses and water mixture, and as it ferments, the kernels (and the string as well) pick up the microbial cultures developing in the mixture. When added to future batches, the kernels serve to speed up the fermentation process by introducing the desired microbes to the ferment.

I was admittedly skeptical about the flavor of a beer made from just molasses and water (and corn on a string), but it's actually quite good, especially in fall and winter when dark, flavorful brews are particularly welcome. I don't love it warm (a suggestion in the original recipe), but you might, and because you'll have a whole gallon lying around, it's worth trying at least once. Play around with the ratios as you make this (something I'll tell you again and again). I like a 3:1 ratio of water to molasses, but there's plenty of room to adjust for a milder or more flavorful brew.

THE ORIGINAL RECIPE

Corn Beer — A Good Drink — Boil a small teacupful of corn till soft and string it like beads to prevent pouring it out of the bottle. Put this into a thick, strong bottle, which fill with molasses-sweetened water—rather sweet to drink. With a long smooth cork of soft white pine, cork airtight.

Keep the bottle at a temperature of 60 to 80 deg., and before using set the bottle in cold water.

The first preparation may require several days, before fit for use. If it sours, replenish the sweetened water. The corn will last for several months without change, and even then a few of the old grains should be retained for a nucleus.

It does not require to be warmed; and if warmed it has a fine flavor.

When once it is under way it can be made in three to six hours.

This beer is superior to any Beer or Cider I have ever drank; innocent for a child, if taken so soon as the gas forms and not permitted to sour.

From some cause, I cannot tell what, when the old corn is lost and you begin entirely with new corn, it may be days and perhaps weeks until it gets right, and then no trouble.

It can be made with ginger, sassafras, &c. Don't allow it to acidify, or it affects the head as does hard cider or vinegar.

MY CORN BEER RECIPE

MAKES 1
GALLON

½ **cup fresh corn kernels**

5½ **cups blackstrap molasses**

Scant 1 gallon of water

Flavorings (such as ginger, sassafras root, or spices; optional)

1 Boil the corn kernels until they are just soft. Let cool.

2 Thread a needle with sturdy thread. Gently pierce the kernels with the needle and thread them, leaving some space between each one. Tie a knot on each end of the thread.

3 Stir the molasses into the gallon of water in a large mixing bowl. Funnel the mixture into the carboy.

4 Gently add your threaded corn to the carboy, along with any flavorings (if using), and seal.

5 Check your ferment daily, and pull it when it is good and bubbly and has developed a flavor you enjoy.

6 Store the finished beer in the fridge. Keep your threaded corn starter in the brew until you're ready to make a new batch.

the history of corn beer

This beer is one example of a food created through lack. According to Don Lundgren, my friend and the owner of Rabelais: Fine Books on Food & Drink, corn beer was made in Civil War POW camps, and the publication of the recipe on page 8 in *Clarke's Confederate Household Almanac* shows that it existed outside that context as well. This makes sense, as shortages of food and supplies existed for households on both sides of the war, and we see many recipes from that era filled with substitutions or creatively reusing food scraps to help stretch what little was available (the same thing happened during World War I and World War II).

Other historians and fermenters have suggested to me that this beverage was invented by, or at least also made by, enslaved and free Blacks in the South, too. I have not yet found this reflected in the historical record, though that is unsurprising given whose history was considered "worth" recording at this time. It also underscores a point you'll see repeated elsewhere in this book: Many ferments are passed on through oral tradition and through learning by doing, and those that are recorded speak to what history's gatekeepers (or those writing the primary source documents later generations refer to) wanted to record. Finding and recording the stories of those whom history has overlooked is an empowering act. By doing so, we preserve and pass along those stories to future generations of family and scholars, filling gaps in our knowledge and ensuring that we have a more complete picture of a time and place, culture and tradition, and how foods fit within those stories. When I say that recording fermentation history is vital, the story of corn beer is a good example of why.

HORSERADISH/SCALLION PASTE

Stir this paste into mayonnaise, yogurt, or sour cream to make a horseradish sauce (highly recommended on baked potatoes!) or into mustard for an extra kick. Stir it into soup stocks, work it into meat rubs (for beef especially), use it to add some extra depth and kick to your borscht, mix it into salad dressings, or even add a dollop to your scrambled eggs. The possibilities are endless!

MAKES ABOUT 1 PINT

4	teaspoons sea salt
1	quart water
1	horseradish root, sliced
3–5	whole scallions

QUICK FERMENT

1   Dissolve the salt in the water to make a brine.

2   Put the horseradish root and scallions into a 1-quart jar, add enough brine to submerge them completely, cover, and let ferment for 2 to 3 days.

3   Transfer the ferment to a blender or food processor and blend to desired consistency. Store in the fridge, where it will keep for at least 1 month.

LONGER FERMENT *(more savory)*

1   Dissolve the salt in the water to make a brine.

2   Put the horseradish root into a 1-quart jar, add enough brine to submerge it completely, cover, and let ferment for 7 to 10 days.

3   Add the scallions to the jar and let ferment for another 2 to 3 days.

4   Transfer the ferment to a blender or food processor and blend to desired consistency. Store in the fridge, where it will keep for at least 1 month.

TURMERIC, LAVENDER, AND HONEY FERMENT

Turmeric has a long history in human culture; it's been used in India for more than 4,000 years as medicine, as food, and in religious ceremonies, and it is common in cuisines across the world, particularly those of the Middle East and Southeast Asia. Lavender has been used as both an aromatic and a healer for millennia; it's commonly used to treat gastrointestinal distress, depression, and anxiety and as an antiseptic, and it was even used in the ancient Egyptian mummification process. Honey also has a long history of use in health care, helping to heal everything from wounds to sore throats.

Together, turmeric, lavender, and honey create a wonderful floral, sweet, and slightly tangy flavoring. I ferment this mixture for only a couple of days, just enough to begin softening the turmeric and developing its flavor. Even a short ferment like this helps ingredients open up and taste more fully like themselves, while also delivering a boost of nutrients.

The fermented blend can be used in two ways: as a spice paste that you can incorporate into sweet and savory dishes (it's equally as wonderful in muffins or cake as it is in a curry or dressing) or as a dehydrated seasoning (it's great tossed with roasted vegetables or as a replacement for plain turmeric powder in golden milk).

2 cups sliced organic turmeric root (organic is important, as it means the root has retained its beneficial microbes, unlike some conventional roots that have been irradiated)

1 sprig fresh lavender or 1 scant teaspoon dried lavender flowers

¼ cup honey (raw, local honey is best)

1 Place the turmeric, lavender, and honey in a quart jar.

2 Add enough water to cover the ingredients. Place the lid on the jar and shake thoroughly to dissolve the honey.

3 Allow to ferment for 3 to 5 days, or until the mixture develops a flavor you're happy with.

FOR PASTE

MAKES
ABOUT
1 PINT

Remove the turmeric and lavender from the jar, transfer them to a food processor or blender, and add a drizzle of the liquid from the jar. Pulse or blend until the mixture reaches the desired consistency, adding more liquid as needed. (You can use any left-over liquid as a component in desserts or dressings, or just as a turmeric-heavy mead.) Store your liquid in the fridge, where it will keep for at least a week.

FOR POWDER

MAKES
ABOUT
¼ CUP

1   Remove the turmeric and lavender from the jar and arrange them in a dehydrator. (It may be helpful to cut the turmeric into smaller pieces.)

2   Set the dehydrator to 130°F/54°C and dehydrate the plant material for 12 to 24 hours or until it is completely dry to the touch.

3   Transfer the dehydrated turmeric and lavender to a coffee grinder (I have one I use just for spices, so all my spices don't taste like coffee) or a mortar and pestle and grind to the desired consistency. If you find your turmeric powder still has moisture in it, put it back in the dehydrator until completely dry to the touch. Store in an airtight container at room temperature, where it will keep for at least a month.

MY BASIC FRESH MEAD

Mead is one of my all-time favorite drinks (it is also one of humankind's most ancient foods, which is something we'll get into in the next chapter). I love the flavor of honey in just about anything, but I find many commercial meads to be cloyingly sweet, so I often make my own. That allows me to add whatever I like to my mead, and I usually forage ingredients from around my home so that my mead reflects the season and landscape in which it's made.

I encourage you to take this basic recipe and run with it. Play with the ingredients, flavoring your mead with fruits, shoots, nuts, leaves, and more (some good standbys include blackberries, fresh herbs, and warming spices such as cinnamon). Play with the amount of honey and the length of time you ferment it. Over time, you'll learn what works best for you, in your season and place, giving you a mead that's all your own.

MAKES
ABOUT 2
QUARTS

2 **cups honey** (raw, local honey is best)

2 **quarts room-temperature water**

Flavorings of your choice (optional)

1   Stir the honey into the water until dissolved.

2   Transfer the mixture to a fermentation vessel. I typically use a wide-mouthed crock, but a large glass jar or other food-safe container also works.

3   Add your desired flavorings (if any) and stir to distribute. Cover the fermentation vessel with a tea towel or cheesecloth (held in place with a rubber band, if needed) to keep insects out.

4   Let the mixture ferment, stirring it several times a day. After 3 or 4 days, start tasting it once or twice a day. When the mead is good and bubbly and has the flavor you want, 4 to 7 days, pull out the flavorings (the herbs, spices, or whatever else you added at the beginning). You can compost these, or you can get creative and try chucking them in a dehydrator (like the turmeric and lavender in the recipe on page 13) or in whatever you're making for dinner or dessert (berries that have been used to make mead make a fantastic sauce for ice cream).

5   You can drink the mead at this stage, which was the most common choice historically, and certainly the easiest method. Just store any unused portion in the fridge to slow further fermentation. If you would like to make a mead with a higher ABV, or one that is carbonated, there are a lot of great resources out there with specifics on how to do so, including Jereme Zimmerman's *Make Mead Like a Viking*, Sandor Katz's *The Art of Fermentation*, and Christopher and Kirsten Shockey's *The Big Book of Cidermaking*.

1

FERMENTS FOR LIFE

If you've ever tucked a vegetable into a jar of brine, you're probably aware of the fact that fermentation makes food last longer and taste better. But our relationship with beneficial microbes doesn't end there: We coevolved with fermentation microbes, making them fundamental not only to our food but to human life as well.

What Is Fermentation?

What do you think of when you hear the word *fermentation?* The answer to this question may depend on where you're from, what your interests are, and what kinds of foods you eat. For a brewer it might mean beer, and for a baker it might be bread, but for people who are only vaguely familiar with the concept, it may be hard to think of any particular fermentation. I teach classes on fermentation, and when I ask this question of my students, I get an incredible range of answers, from "I have no idea!" to specific types of food (such as sauerkraut) or processes (such as making alcohol). However, most people don't realize how broad the term actually is, or that it encompasses more than just food.

Fermentation can best be described using Sandor Katz's definition: It is "the transformative action of microorganisms." These microorganisms— such as yeast, bacteria, and fungi—transform our food, our bodies, and our environment.

Their transformative processes give us many of the foods we eat and beverages we drink, including yeasted bread, alcohol, cheese, black tea, sauerkraut, miso, pickles, yogurt, and more. We may ferment these foods using wild yeast and bacteria from the environment around us, or we might use a starter culture of specific yeast and/or bacteria, depending on what we're making. After we have made and eaten these foods, those same microorganisms will join with the microbial community in our gut to help us digest them.

Fermentation has been a part of human history since its earliest stages. Biologically speaking, our bodies coevolved with the microorganisms on this planet, offering them safe harbor while they offered us a strong immune system and an intimate physical connection to the geographic spaces we occupy. Fermented foods are a part of every human culture; they are central to community life (bread, wine, and beer are an integral part of many celebrations), and they play an important part in preserving our harvests, offering nourishment for future meals. Through both necessity and curiosity, we invented a wide range of ways to collaborate with the microbes all around us, and by manipulating environmental conditions, we have learned to create environments that favor certain beneficial microorganisms and discourage the growth of others.

classifying ferments

The classification of ferments broadens, narrows, or changes focus depending on whom you ask. For example, some people focus on the substrate (dairy, vegetables, meat, and so on) when classifying their ferments, while others focus on the microbial processes. In a 1997 paper released one year after his *Handbook of Indigenous Fermented Foods*, microbiologist Keith Steinkraus offered a classification scheme in which home-fermented foods from around the world were divided into seven basic categories:

- **TEXTURED VEGETABLE PROTEINS** are made from legumes and/or cereals (for example, tempeh and oncom from Indonesia).

- **AMINO SAUCES AND PASTES** include plant-based foods such as miso and shoyu as well as fish sauces. These all tend to be high in salt and aged for an extended period of time (though not always, as with young misos). I would also classify other meat-based amino sauces, such as my recent experiments with rabbit garum (see page 316), in this category.

Fermentation has numerous benefits beyond food preservation. Probiotic foods, meaning foods that have live, active cultures of beneficial microorganisms, help support our intestinal microflora by both introducing new microbes and positively influencing the health of existing colony members. Fermentation also makes nutrients more bioavailable (that is, usable by the body)—for example, by breaking down trypsin inhibitors and phytates that inhibit our access to minerals and proteins in cereals and legumes. Fermentation can also increase the nutritive value of our food—for example, by increasing the amount of some B vitamins.

- **LACTIC ACID FERMENTATIONS** include lacto-fermented vegetables (sauerkraut, kimchi, and so on), dairy (such as yogurt), grains (such as Indian idli), and meat or fish (such as Filipino balao balao).

- **ALCOHOL FERMENTATIONS** include all the various forms from wine and beer to mead, sake, Thai rice wine, and Indian jackfruit wines.

- **ACETIC ACID FERMENTATIONS** include both vinegars and kombucha. (Steinkraus did not, however, suggest that vinegar and kombucha are the same, which is the subject of much debate. Though both have similar properties, microbially they are different.)

- **ALKALINE FERMENTS** include natto, which is perhaps the most famous, but other representatives are Nigerian dawadawa and sumbala from Côte d'Ivoire and elsewhere in West Africa.

- **YEAST-LEAVENED BREADS** are made using wild (sourdough) or commercially manufactured yeasts. These breads can be various shapes and sizes, from a French baguette to naan from India to a fluffy loaf of sandwich bread in the United States.

And the process itself is easy, inexpensive, low tech, and very safe. When we make our own ferments, we can experiment with different ingredients and flavor profiles and end up with a result that is superior to what we could buy in the store. Finally, fermentation offers a way to connect to our cultural food history, which is both grounding and fulfilling.

Fermentation History Is Human History

Looking back through the mists of time to write about the history of food is often a challenge. The archaeological record shows us only slivers of the whole picture, and written documentation, which existed only in more recent millennia, is sometimes damaged and lost (and, of course, subject to human error and bias, just as writing is today). All of this requires us to have astute powers of observation, a critical reading of historic sources, and a bit of luck, but the quest is not as dire as it might seem. In the case of fermentation, at least, the story isn't just written in the artifacts we leave behind; it's written in our cells themselves.

Bacteria were the first inhabitants on our planet, and all modern-day cells, including our own eukaryotic cells, evolved from a common bacterial ancestor. Their presence and proliferation in these first years of life on Earth reshaped the planet's surface and atmosphere, creating an environment where all that came after them could emerge. As other single-celled life-forms emerged, they developed symbiotic (and sometimes predatory) relationships with bacteria. And modern evolutionary theories suggest that as cells became more complex, they incorporated bacteria in a symbiotic relationship that resulted in our cells' mitochondria and chloroplasts. These more complex eukaryotic cells, in turn, make up plants and animals (including us).

Bacteria are so central to the processing of nutrients that all organisms on Earth have coevolved with them. In our own bodies, they outnumber our DNA and influence gene expression, support our immune function, protect reproductive organs, assist with digestion, and more. Microbes are found on every surface of our bodies, and their biodiversity is mind-boggling: More than 700 species of microbes can be found in a healthy person's mouth alone. As Sandor Katz says, "The importance of bacteria and our bacterial interactions cannot be overstated. We could not exist or function without our bacterial partners."

While we've had a happy relationship with beneficial microbes for a long time, archaeological evidence of intentional food and beverage fermentation dates back only 9,000 to 10,000 years. Since that time, we've developed an endless array of sour, pungent, salty, and fragrant goodies (and some mildly flavored ones, too), all using the magic of microbes.

To know the history of fermentation is to know ourselves, and understanding ancient fermentation processes is more than just a flight of fancy. Knowing them helps us more accurately interpret the evidence left behind from these cultures and, in so doing, better understand where we come from and who we are. For example, recent examinations of remains from Pompeii have challenged long-standing notions that the Vesuvius eruption happened in August. This revised interpretation was due in part to archaeological evidence of winemaking on the site, showing that the grapes (a crop harvested in autumn) had already been crushed and that Pompeiians had begun turning them into wine, a process that would have been impossible to complete in summer.

The First Ferments

There has been a long-standing debate about whether bread or beer came first, and while we may never have an exact answer, we do know that they started to be made at around the same time, coinciding with the rise of agriculture and with more reliable access to stores of grains. We also know that these two types of fermentations were heavily intertwined; they originated not only at around the same time but also in the same locations, and their methods are related.

ALCOHOL

Humans began to (intentionally) ferment alcoholic beverages around 9,000 years ago (though herbalist Stephen Harrod Buhner, author of *Sacred and Herbal Healing Beers*, suggests that mead brewing goes back perhaps even 35,000 years ago). However, we started consuming alcohol even earlier: Researchers studied a digestive enzyme called alcohol dehydrogenase 4 (ADH4) that is capable of metabolizing ethanol efficiently, allowing modern humans to consume alcohol (in moderation) without getting sick. They examined the enzyme throughout the roughly 70 million years of primate evolution until they located a variation occurring around 10 million years ago that resulted in the ethanol-metabolizing enzyme we have today. The researchers pointed out that the change coincided with the era in which primates adopted a terrestrial lifestyle (that is, living on the ground rather than in trees). Fruit collected from the forest floor was more likely to have begun fermenting (in comparison to fruit, even ripe fruit, on trees, which would have lower concentrations of fermenting yeast and alcohol), the researchers noted, which meant that primates with ADH4 would have had a biological advantage over those who lacked it. In other words, our bodies became able to metabolize alcohol well before we were brewing it.

Human-directed alcohol fermentation began in the Neolithic period (which lasted from roughly 10,000 BCE to around 4500 BCE, though the dates are debated). We see evidence of alcohol ferments in that time in the archaeological record from around the ancient world, crossing continents and millennia to show up in indigenous American communities as well as in the Middle East, China, and elsewhere.

In China, a chemical analysis of jars from the Neolithic village of Jiahu shows that a beverage made from rice, honey, and either hawthorn fruit or grapes was being made as early as the seventh millennium BCE, followed by beverages brewed with cereals in the second millennium BCE, which were preserved in sealed bronze vessels from the Shang and Western Zhou dynasties. Elsewhere, we see arguments that mead was the first fermented beverage, predating both wine and beer: The Khoisan people of modern-day South Africa, for example, are believed to have started drinking mead around 15,000 years ago. In the Fertile Crescent, we find evidence of brewing, including the presence of oxalate salts (the principal molecules in beer stone, a grayish brown scale that forms on the inside of beer-brewing equipment and containers), from 9,000 to 10,000 years ago. By 6000 BCE, we see evidence that the Sumerians valued beer enough to use it as currency.

All alcohol is made by the same basic principle: A sugar solution (be it fruit juice, honey in water, granulated sugar in water, or malted grain cooked in water) is allowed to sit (stirred regularly) until it starts to ferment. The earliest alcoholic beverages were made with whatever sugar source was available—grain, honey, and fruits such as grapes, pomegranates, and more. As a result, flavors and alcohol content varied considerably.

BEER

Traditionally, beer was made from either cooked grains or leftover bread. In ancient Egypt, beer was such an important resource that it was used as currency for laborers, and there were legal penalties for brewers who made and shared a bad batch. It was brewed in large, single-fired terra-cotta vessels that were watertight but unglazed. These vessels wicked heat, helping brewers maintain a desirable brewing temperature.

Beer was very popular in ancient Egypt, even making its way into the provisions for the dead in the afterlife, as evidenced by numerous vessels of the brew found in tombs. Ancient Egyptian temple art seemed to show a brewing process that involved crumbling stale bread with water in a brewing vessel, but this was not the only brewing technique that was used. In 1996, archaeologist Delwen Samuel published a study showing evidence that some ancient Egyptian beers, at least, were brewed using a mixture of malted and unmalted grains, and that dates were often added, most likely as a source of yeast. Samuel went on to publish numerous other studies about ancient grains and the archaeology of brewing in ancient Egypt. In 2018, food historian Tasha Marks, along with brewers Michaela Charles and Susan Boyle, made a batch of beer with the same techniques and ingredients as the ancient Egyptians, based on archaeological evidence from the British Museum and Samuel's findings. They discovered that Egyptian beer was actually quite similar to the beers of today. (This is part of why I share recipes with you at the end of each chapter: The best way to learn about this stuff is by doing it!)

which came first: beer or bread?

In the 1980s, anthropologists Solomon H. Katz and Mary M. Voigt hypothesized that barley domestication grew out of early beer brewing, thus leading to the development of Neolithic agriculture. This hypothesis generated a lot of curiosity. After all, isn't it just thrilling to think that our whole modern system of feeding ourselves grew out of a desire for booze? Since that time, researchers' more nuanced findings have tempered this titillating proposition.

As anthropologist Joy McCorriston noted in 2000, grain domestication may have come before brewing, as brewing requires the use of pottery (which, she notes, appeared after cereal domestication), and one must be sedentary, rather than nomadic, to brew beer, because the logistics of hauling around vats of fermenting liquid would be a considerable challenge. She argued that evidence from Mesopotamian clay tablets tells us that early beer was made from bread, not from malt (that is, sprouted barley), and that beer making may have emerged as a result of bread fermentation. Later research suggests that beer was developed as a way to use up leftover bread.

Some other researchers suspect (and I count myself among them) that brewing and bread making developed concurrently with grain domestication, perhaps by accident and perhaps not, as people developed ways to manipulate grains and thus learned the different ways in which these grains develop into usable foodstuffs as they ferment. Bread developed from the dried and ground grains, and beer from grains that had sprouted (perhaps accidentally during storage), first driven by experimentation or happenstance.

Things are even further confused by the fact that modern terminology for alcoholic beverages is different from historic terminology. This complicates our attempts to understand what people were drinking, and when, because we must attempt to view food and drink through the eyes (and language) of our ancestors. Classicist Max Nelson notes in his book *The Barbarian's Beverage*:

> By far the most popular fermented beverages in ancient Europe were those made from fruits, from honey, or from malted cereal, that is, wine, mead, and beer, respectively. . . . These designations are of course modern, and though ancients did differentiate drinks that were, for instance, grape-based from others that were honey-based or barley-based, it is fairly clear that there were no terms directly equivalent to our generic terms "alcohol," "wine," or "beer."
>
> What makes the situation even more complicated with regard to nomenclature is that the Europeans, from very early times, were particularly apt to make fermented beverages from a variety of sugars and thus for the most part there did not exist the rigid categories of alcoholic beverages so familiar to us today. Indeed, it seems to have been only under Roman influence that more rigid categorization of beverages came to be developed.

Did someone experiment with brewing prior to the movement from nomadic to settled communities? Maybe so. Was malt, and its subsequent use in brewing, discovered by accident? Most likely. We may never know the full history of beer brewing, but asking questions, and thinking about possibilities, is half of what makes the history of fermentation so fun.

Our understanding of ancient Egyptian brewing continues to evolve as more archaeological evidence surfaces and more studies are completed. One year after Marks's experiment, scientists Mohameg A. Farag, Moamen M. Elmassry, Masahiro Baba, and Renee Friedman tested archaeological samples using infrared and mass spectrometry, confirming Samuel's

alcohol and safe drinking water

Prior to modern sanitation technologies, many people lacked access to clean drinking water. Fermentation, however, creates a selective environment wherein beneficial microbes thrive and dangerous ones are crowded out. In addition, alcohol itself is antimicrobial, making it even harder for harmful microbes to take up residence. For this reason, it was often safer for people to consume fermented alcoholic beverages rather than water. Alcoholic beverages were not only safe to drink but also offered calories and nutrients (such as B vitamins) to hungry populations.

Depending on where you were, you would make either beer or wine in large batches for your family or buy it from a neighbor or a town shop. Beer was common in the British Isles, whereas wine was more likely to be found in the Mediterranean region, where grapes were abundant. Both were a critical part of the common people's diet, and both were consumed throughout the day by all members of the family, even young children (although those beers were often lower in alcohol than most of the stuff you find on tap today). Writing in 1615, Gervase Markham described beer as the drink "by which the household is nourished and sustained."

arguments about the presence of dates and malt. They also found evidence of the use of phosphoric acid (used as a preservative in modern beverages), suggesting that ancient Egyptians had brewing technologies sophisticated enough to brew at scale and for storage as well as for fresh consumption.

As time went on, people began to produce a wider variety of beers. They added ingredients such as hops to increase shelf life, experimented with flavorings ranging from fruits to toasted grains and foraged botanicals, and used a variety of aging times and conditions. One example is the "March Beer" recipe from 1615, which would sit for an entire year. This recipe comes from Gervase Markham's *The English Housewife*, a cookbook geared toward the rural gentry. Unlike some other cookbooks at the time, Markham's cookbook emphasized the economical use of resources and the reduction of waste, and it included an entire section on brewing.

Individual taste likely played as much a role as availability of ingredients in the increased variety. Even in the earliest known archaeological evidence of alcohol production, we see the addition of fruits to a fermented rice beverage. This evidence comes from a dig in Jiahu, China, led by archaeologist Patrick McGovern (sometimes called "the Indiana Jones of Ancient Ales, Wines, and Extreme Beverages"). Their analysis found evidence of rice wine brewed with grapes, hawthorn, and herbs in the seventh century BCE. McGovern's later research, this time in modern-day Georgia and the South Caucasus, also found evidence of grape wine going back to the early Neolithic period (6000–5800 BCE). Fruit, in that time, may have been added to brews to introduce the yeast on their skins, but it's also very likely that they were added to make the brews a little more delicious. Our ancestors, just like us, wanted food that tastes good.

Hops have been used in European beer for about eight hundred to a thousand years, though they have been a part of our landscapes and diets for much longer. In ancient Rome, hops were said to grow "wild among the willows like a wolf among sheep," according to author Helen Bateman, and were called *lupulus,* or good wolf. Indigenous communities and colonists in North America used them as an aid for sleep and digestion and to help heal wounds and toothaches.

In the year 768, during the reign of Pepin the Short (Charlemagne's father) over the Frankish empire, the king gifted hop gardens to the abbey of Saint-Denis. Thereafter, the hops cultivated in those gardens began to show up in the monastery's beer. And while the hops added a bitter flavor, they also added shelf life: Beer with hops lasted up to 6 months (much longer than beer without them), meaning it could be preserved for local use or shipped over longer distances than it could before.

In the twelfth century, Saint Hildegard von Bingen mentioned the use of hops in beer for medicinal purposes, suggesting that by this time their use was relatively widespread. However, hops continued to face pushback during the next few centuries, including by King Henry VIII, who tried to stop their use to maintain the integrity of "good old English ale." Other herbs, such as mugwort, were still commonly used for bittering in beers called "gruit" beers, or those brewed with botanicals other than hops. Ironically, maritime England came to fully embrace hops to preserve beer on long voyages, adding hops with a heavy hand in the hope of ensuring the beer's longevity. This gave us India pale ales, so named because the East India Company commissioned the heavily hopped beers for their ships in the 1800s.

While we have records of kingly opinions (and others) about large-scale beer brewing in the early modern period (from around 1500 to 1800 CE), we don't always have an insight into how it was made by most people at home. This may be because women were traditionally the brewers in the home. In his introduction to the reprinted version of Gervase Markham's *The English Housewife*, Michael Best writes:

> The absence of treatises on malting earlier than Markham's, like a similar absence of works on the brewery, the dairy, the preparation of hemp and flax, and the bakehouse, may indicate that, as women's work, it was a subject of little interest to male writers. The literature of the period, however, is rich in reference to malting and brewing. However much Markham may have regretted the mass production methods of "men maltsters" turning the malt with a shovel rather than by hand . . . the malt man was well enough established that he could appear as a character in a popular song.

In English literature and popular culture (such as the ballad "John Barleycorn," from this same period), we hear most about the roles of men in brewing. Where we do hear about women, either the records are sparse or (as in the end of "John Barleycorn") the important role of women in brewing was acknowledged, but with a warning:

All you good wives that brew good ale,
God turn you from all tears;
But if you put too much water in,
The Devil put out your eyes.

Admonishments from English ballads aside, women were, and are, a critical part of the history of brewing. Women brewed beer for their families, as well as for neighbors or to sell in shops. In ancient Egypt, brewing was a domestic chore assigned to women and overseen by the goddess Hathor. We'll explore women's roles in brewing more in Chapter 5.

As Christianity spread and large monasteries sprouted up, men began to take over brewing processes. Of course, women were brewing in convents as well, though their contributions have not received as much attention—with the exception of Hildegard von Bingen, who after her death became the patron saint of brewing.

MEAD

Mead, a fermented honey beverage, is said to be the world's oldest fermented beverage. Many cultures claim it as a gift from the gods, given to humans for ritual and nourishment. The first European meads are attributed to the Picts and Celts around 4,000 years ago in the British Isles, and to residues on ceramics from the Bell Beaker culture (roughly 2800 to 1800 BCE), which was distributed across western Europe (including Britain). Early Celtic meads were made using simply heather honey and water. Later, some meads would be a hybrid fermentation of honey and other sugar sources, such as barley.

Ethiopia's tej is the most famous mead from the vast and diverse African continent, but it is not the only one. Karri, brewed by the Khoisan people of southern Africa, is thought to date back 15,000 years. According to legend, many millennia ago the Khoisan found a fermented beverage bubbling in the hollow of a karri tree, perhaps as some honey dripped from a beehive and mingled with recently fallen rain. With trepidation, the people reached out, dipped their fingers in the brew, and gave it a taste, perhaps feeling a mixture of curiosity and concern. Ultimately they were taken with the sweet brew, and the beverage was named after the tree where it was first found. Through trial and error, Khoisan honey gatherers were able to replicate the beverage they had found. Today, karri is harder to find, perhaps because imported European beverages took precedence under colonialism, indigenous plant populations have declined due to colonialism and urbanization, and traditional knowledge has been lost between generations. But it is still available and made the same way today as it has been for centuries, using water and honey. The Slow Food Foundation says

heather honey

Heather honey has an incredibly thick, viscous texture thanks to its high protein content. This makes it hard to extract from the comb, and so brewers would often throw the whole comb into the ferment, including, as Stephen Harrod Buhner says, its "angry bees, propolis, pollen, royal jelly, honey, and wax." The high protein content (and the myriad other nutrients introduced by that particular medley) makes for a formidable mead. A moss, colloquially known as fogg, often coats heather stems and is thought to be both mildly narcotic and hallucinogenic, potentially adding to the brew's intoxicating effects. Heather mead was possibly the source of two similar ancient sayings: the Scottish "mead drinkers have as much strength as meat eaters" and the German *Bienen kommen eben so weit als Bare*, or "mead is as strengthening as meat."

that karri, like all natural meads, has "terroir-based flavours unique to their respective regions."

Mead was very popular in the ancient world and remained popular until the middle of the nineteenth century, when it fell considerably out of favor. It remained a little-known drink through much of the twentieth century, but it has increased in popularity in recent years.

Honey has numerous advantages as a food source, including that it maintains its vitamin content indefinitely, is easily digested, and improves health (a couple of studies have shown that regular honey consumption helps with hemoglobin production and energy levels). It also has benefits when used topically: It is a fantastic wound treatment and has helped heal infected wounds that were not responding to antibiotics.

It is harder for yeast to consume the fructose in honey than it is for them to eat the sugars in other foods, which means that it takes longer to make mead than to make beer. Unlike with beer, when a mead stops foaming during fermentation, it only means that the yeast has consumed the glucose in the honey, not that it has finished fermenting. Meads vary considerably in their flavor, ranging from sweet to dry, as well as in their nutritional makeup. Mead brewed with heather honey, for example, has a higher protein content than mead brewed with other honeys.

WINE

Wine is simply fruit juice that has been fermented. While we tend to think of it as fermented grape juice, historically wine has been made from a range of fruits, sometimes with added ingredients (such as sugar). Wine, like beer, was a safe alternative to water for hydration, but it also provided a practical and delicious way to put up a fruit harvest.

The history of wine stretches back as far as brewing history itself: The oldest known fruit-based brew found to date is a grape or hawthorn wine, from the burial site in Jiahu, China, mentioned earlier. This early example shows how our tipples (mead, wine, and beer) often share ingredients, and have done so since the beginning. This particular wine was brewed from a blend of fruits, rice, and honey, placing it at the intersection of wine (fruit), beer (grains), and mead (honey). That creative flourish suggests that the practice of winemaking itself stretches back even farther.

The oldest winery in the world is thought to have been founded in a cave in Armenia around 4100 BCE, and winemaking in some form or fashion has a long history on every continent but Antarctica. Most people think of wine as a beverage made from grapes, but the term *wine* refers to any fruit-based alcoholic drink. There are many non-grape examples worldwide, from pineapple-based tepache in Central America to banana wine in western Africa.

Historically, the privilege of wine consumption depended on either geography or social standing. In medieval Ireland, for example, winemaking was not a major industry and imports were expensive, so only the wealthy could enjoy wine. In ancient Greece, on the other hand, where grapes were common and winemaking a household task, wine was a normal part of the diet and could be found at various grades and price points. In ancient Egypt, wine and beer existed in tandem, and though beer was often brewed by women and seems to have been more of an everyday drink, winemaking was carefully controlled and only directed by men.

Because the basic principles of fermentation have not changed over time, it makes sense that winemaking recipes from home cookbooks written from about the 1600s to the 1800s look remarkably similar to those for the small-batch wines we make today. In one manuscript recipe dating from roughly 1700 (author unknown), black cherries are bruised by hand and mixed with water that has been boiled and cooled. The cherries are soaked for 3 days, and stirred every day, and then are strained. The fruit is pressed to remove excess juice. Sugar is then added and the juice is put in the cellar for about 3 months before the lees are drawn off, a bit more sugar is added, and the juice is bottled. However, the bottle was kept uncapped (as the original recipe says, "You must not stop ye vessel, till it hath done working"), which tells us that the goal was to continue the fermentation of sugar into alcohol, but without carbonation.

TEA AND COFFEE

Not all of our fermented beverages are alcoholic. Tea and coffee are also derived from fermentation. Like alcoholic beverages, they have a long history of popularity and were at times a safe alternative to potentially contaminated drinking water (though not from the fermentation of the liquid but from the boiling of the water to steep the leaves or beans).

According to legend, Emperor Shennong of China discovered tea around 2700 BCE when leaves from the tea plant fell into water he was boiling. The earliest reliable references come from the third or fourth century CE, when tea cultivation (rather than foraging) was becoming more common. All types of tea (black, green, white, oolong, and pu-erh) come from the same plant: *Camellia sinensis*. The difference between them lies in how the leaves and buds are treated. Black tea is fully fermented: The green leaves are rolled, allowed to oxidize, and then dried. Oolong is semifermented, meaning it is only partially oxidized, and green and white teas aren't fermented at all—the young leaves are just picked and dried. For pu-erh tea, the leaves are dried, then steamed and formed into cakes. The cakes ferment as they age, sometimes for 50 years or more.

Coffee was discovered in the land of Abyssinia (modern-day Ethiopia), though as with tea we don't know exactly when it first came into use in human society. One legend tells us that a goatherd discovered it when finding his goats dancing among coffee bushes after snacking on the berries. Early uses involved chewing the berries and leaves, but then more creative methods of preparation emerged, including steeping them into tea or fermenting them into wine. Eventually our ancestors learned to ferment the beans; microorganisms help degrade the pulp around the bean during fermentation, which reduces the drying time and develops flavor and aroma. The fermented beans are then dried, roasted, ground, and steeped to make the beverage we are familiar with today.

GRAINS

Humans were consuming wild grains long before the rise of agriculture. Archaeological evidence shows that people living at Ohalo II, a former village on the shore of the Sea of Galilee in present-day Israel, were eating wheat and barley at the peak of the last ice age, more than 10,000 years before those grains were domesticated during the agricultural revolution. And archaeologists have evidence of Neanderthals eating barley and other grains 40,000 years ago, as well as evidence that hominids have been cooking (plants as well as meat) for 700,000 to 800,000 years. Food historian Rachel Laudan argues that by the time humans began tackling grains as food around 20,000 years ago, "they were smart experimenters" who had been "surveying the earth for things to eat for thousands and thousands of years." Our early ancestors employed techniques from hearth and pit cooking to pounding, grinding, and more, along with fermentation.

Across ancient communities, grain ferments were the result of experimentation with a variety of methods (such as boiling and grinding). They allowed people to make a replicable product—a food that can be prepared using the same method repeatedly to achieve similar results. After all, if you make a great beer once to serve your family, it doesn't do you much good if you can't make it again the next time you need a safe drinking source.

Our ancestors used the grains that were available to them, just as many people today do. Barley, for example, grew in Central Asia and Europe and was used in those regions in brewing, bread making, and other food productions. In many areas of the African continent, in contrast, sorghum and millet were common, used in making beers and porridges (such as the sorghum beer of Zulu communities of southern Africa). Around the world, many other grains were eaten in both fermented and unfermented forms, such as rye, corn, and wheat.

With baking, as with brewing, our ancestors adapted their techniques to different tastes and interests. While early breads were unleavened flatbreads, there still was room for variety; different grains were used to create different textures, for example. Modern studies have shown that early humans were making these breads from wild grains about 4,000 years before grains were domesticated, with the earliest known breads coming from modern-day Jordan. However, humans soon began to experiment with leavening, and it is widely believed that the ancient Egyptians were the first to make leavened breads regularly, though there is also archaeological evidence of sourdough bread in Switzerland dating back to around 3700 BCE.

One of the most famous early breads is the Greco-Roman panis quadratus (or kodratoi), so named because of four cuts made across the top of the loaf, yielding eight similarly sized sections. Excavations in Pompeii,

Herculaneum, and neighboring settlements destroyed during the eruption of Mount Vesuvius in 79 CE have unearthed loaves of this bread, carbonized by the intense heat, which offer incredibly valuable insight into the diet of that time. The excavations have revealed that Pompeii had a large number of bakeries (35) for its population (about 12,000), which speaks to the importance of bread to this early culture. Bread was baked at home, but more often it was made in one of these bakeries, which were run by a powerful trade union and consumed incredible amounts of resources (grain for the bread, wood for fires, and so on) in order to provide what experimental archaeologist (someone who does hands-on experiments to test our understanding of ancient techniques and technologies) Farrell Monaco calls "the backbone of Pompeii's daily diet."

what we ferment impacts what we grow and eat

Our ancestors' fermentation practices had an impact on which grains came under cultivation and how they evolved over time. In Europe, for example, prehistoric peoples favored "naked" barley, which required more irrigation but had an easier-to-remove chaff and hull, suggesting the grain may have been used for flour in addition to other uses. During the first millennium BCE, as the expansion of the Roman Empire resulted in a shift toward wheat-based breads, barley became a more common ingredient for brewing. As a result, the hulled varieties, which required less irrigation and whose harder chaff was not an issue for brewers, became more popular.

Of course, commercial yeast packets were not available at this time, so these loaves would have been made with sourdough starter, which would have been maintained and used daily. Sourdough starters use wild yeast, so the taste and texture of the loaves would have varied by location, as would have the process for making the breads. In many cases, however, the basic steps would have been the same: Establish the starter by combining flour and water and letting it sit out to become populated with wild yeasts, carefully feed the starter more flour and water until the wild yeasts are fully established, and then take some of it to make bread, replenishing the starter with flour and water to keep the yeast thriving.

The type of flour used to make the starter and the loaves would have varied depending on what was available, social class, and personal taste. Pliny the Elder, who died in 79 CE, the same year that Mount Vesuvius erupted, wrote *Naturalis Historia* (*Natural History*), a massive undertaking of 37 books meant to cover the history and present state of the entire natural world. In this work, he describes several different ways of making leaven (or starter), including with millet and grape juice, as well as with barley. It is unclear how professional bakers came to be in ancient Rome: Farrell Monaco says they did not exist until the second century BCE, perhaps because Greek bakers were employed (Pliny mentions the skills of Greek bakers with leaven) or perhaps because of the conquest of Macedonia, where baking was better established than in Rome.

However they came to be, these bakers were skilled and the iconic round loaves they made were beautiful, and, if modern re-creations are accurate, they were delicious as well.

In addition to these daily breads, our ancestors began making specialty breads to mark certain occasions, such as religious festivals. One example is prosphora, the bread offered at the Orthodox Christian Eucharist. Modern prosphora is made by taking two separate rounds of dough, putting one atop the other, stamping the dough, and baking it.

*   *   *

Bread and beer (as well as mead and wine) were so important to early humans that they took up central roles in myth and legend as well as daily life. Many rituals were devoted to honoring the production and consumption of ferments—and, of course, their sometimes intoxicating effects. Grains and honey, in particular, held our early attention and are cited in religious texts as well as inventories from around the ancient world. To my view, one of the most beautiful quotes about grains comes from the Atharva Veda, a Hindu scripture written some 3,000 years ago:

Rise up, become abundant with thine own greatness, O barley.

I find both the poetry of the words and the potential within those little grains to be beautiful. Whether through bread or through beer, fermentation helped unlock the greatness of grains so that they could be used to nourish and sustain our ancestors with foods that were not only more nutritious but also more delicious.

Of course, civilization wasn't built on bread and drink alone. Even as bread was being baked, porridge stirred, and beer brewed, other foods were being made alongside them.

DAIRY

One of the most critical macronutrients the human body requires is protein, and dairy was a significant source of protein in many ancient communities. However, milk spoils quickly when warm, naturally giving rise to many fermented products.

We see legends from the Middle East, Central Asia, and the Balkans that share a common theme: Either a nomadic tribe, or a solo traveler, brings milk along in an animal skin flask to fuel their journey. The day was warm, and by the time the milk was poured out, it had curdled and soured, likely thanks to the lactic acid bacteria on the animal skin. We'll never know if this origin story is true, but however it happened, at some point milk was exposed to wild lactic acid bacteria, causing it to sour and thicken. Humans, being curious (or hungry), gave it a shot and liked it. They started intentionally letting their milk sour in animal skins and then eventually cultivated yogurt starters, some of which are passed down even today from generation to generation.

One of my favorite examples of milk "spoiling" into something tasty is clabbered milk. The English word *clabber* derives from the Gaelic word *clabar*, meaning "mud." And that Gaelic term is evocative: When milk clabbers, the milk fats and solids come together in a thick, slightly sour sludge, separated from a thin whey. In his book *The Art of Fermentation*, Sandor Katz shares a recipe from his father's friend Ray Smith, who used to eat clabber when visiting North Carolina (clabber became part of southern Appalachian food culture due to the heavy Scots-Irish presence in the region). Smith's aunt recalled that "back in the old days you simply set some milk aside and sooner or later it clabbered by itself. . . . In this day of pasteurized milk, I guess you would need a starter." This is due to the fact that pasteurization kills the good bacteria naturally present in milk, rendering it sterilized and thus unable to support its own souring. If you've ever left out pasteurized milk by accident, you know that the sour result you get isn't at all good for eating.

Sour cream, like the name suggests, is cream that has gone sour, similar to clabber. Cheese in its many forms comes from milk that has been curdled and then treated in numerous ways, including being aged, pressed, shaped, or pulled. Both have been around since ancient times. Yogurt, which relies on lacto-fermentation, also has an ancient history: It has been consumed in Anatolia (modern-day Turkey) for thousands of years and is a critical part of the diet in that region to this day. (We'll go into more detail about fermented dairy on page 64, in Chapter 2.)

FRUITS AND VEGGIES

Fruits and vegetables are important sources of dietary fiber, which fills and fuels our bodies, as well as vitamins and minerals that help our bodies perform a whole range of functions—from helping our organs run efficiently to helping our bones heal. But many fruits and vegetables have short shelf lives, meaning we need to preserve them while they are in season in order to access these nutrients continuously. Fermentation provides added nutrition (we'll talk more about fermentation and vitamins on page 172) while also extending the shelf life of these foods.

Lacto-fermentation happens when lactobacilli bacteria (specifically, *Lactobacillus plantarum* and *L. brevis*) acidify a brine (salt and water) by consuming the starches in whatever plant is being fermented. This creates an optimal environment for beneficial microbes to thrive and inhibits the growth of harmful microbes. It preserves the food being fermented and provides minerals (from the brine) as well as nutrients. Humans have been lacto-fermenting vegetables and fruits for millennia, in great variety and to delicious effect. Records indicate that macerated, salted vegetables were consumed in Korea as early as the third or fourth century. This preserving method was likely implemented for the same reason I started fermenting vegetables in my own home years ago: Everything turns ripe at the same time, far more than can be eaten fresh, and it needs to be put up so it can be eaten later and not wasted. Likewise, fruits (such as plums) have a long history of being pickled in brine to extend their shelf life, in addition to being fermented into alcohol and vinegar.

An important part of lacto-fermentation is salt. In some methods, salt is massaged into the vegetables, causing them to release their juices and form a brine (such as when making sauerkraut). In others, it is combined with water to make a brine, which is then added to the vegetables (such as when making pickles). The salinity of the brine (ranging between 2 and 5 percent) prevents many harmful microbes from growing and provides a place for lactic acid bacteria to flourish. These microbes acidify their environment, making it safe for vegetable storage. In addition, vegetables that are kept submerged in brine are kept away from air and thus away from harmful microbes (such as some molds) that require oxygen to survive.

Humans have been salting their food since at least the Neolithic period, from around the same time that we see the emergence of other early ferments such as mead, beer, and bread. However, we are not sure when brine fermentation began. Our ancestors were most likely packing excess crops in salt water around the time of the agricultural revolution, when some communities began to raise domesticated crops and livestock in lieu of a nomadic hunter-gatherer life. I think it's also likely that humans were packing their foraged fruits and vegetables in salt water prior to the development of agriculture.

There are a million examples worldwide of lacto-fermented veggies, but sauerkraut and kimchi are perhaps some of the oldest. They also offer us a bit of insight into how we ferment one humble vegetable: the cabbage. Cabbage has had staying power in many communities around the world because it's easy to grow, easy to store, nutritious, and filling.

SAUERKRAUT

Sauerkraut is typically associated with eastern Europe, where cabbage has been a staple crop for centuries. The process of making sauerkraut, however, is thought to have originated farther east in China, where, for about 2,000 years, laborers regularly ate shredded cabbage fermented with rice wine. Mongols introduced fermented cabbage to the rest of Eurasia after they invaded Russia in 1237. The rice wine, which was not common in Europe, was then replaced with salt and sometimes spices, creating a new but similar dish. Because cabbage had already been a staple in Russia and across eastern Europe, sauerkraut caught on quickly and spread throughout the region.

While the term *sauerkraut* (sour cabbage) is German, shredded and fermented cabbage has appeared across numerous global cuisines. Cabbage was common in both Greek and Roman gardens, for example, and was considered a general cure-all, and the Roman author Pliny the Elder (first century CE) was perhaps the first to describe the fermentation of salted cabbage in earthen vessels.

There are approximately 400 species of cabbage, and there are at least as many different kinds of sauerkraut. The taste of sauerkraut can vary based on how long it ages and the kind of cabbage used, but it also varies based on the flavorings used with it, which traditionally have included everything from juniper berries and caraway seeds to citrus peels and fresh spring herbs. Hearty, dense cabbages (sometimes called "hard headed," rather than the loose-headed cabbages such as Savoy) are typically used, and they seem to have been cultivated primarily in northern Europe, where they grew best, as opposed to the looser-headed varieties that thrived in the European south. Some researchers have suggested that this type of cabbage was first developed by the Celts and grown in Germany since ancient times before spreading to Russia, England, and Scotland. Perhaps the story of sauerkraut is, like many food stories, one of cross-cultural contact, where the Chinese method of preserving vegetables came in contact with this particular veggie, and a new food emerged.

KIMCHI

Kimchi originated 2,500 to 3,000 years ago in Korea as a preparation of salted vegetables made during harvest season to prevent food waste and keep the family fed in winter. According to food scientists Kun-Young Park and Hong-Sik Cheigh, the first record of kimchi appears in 289 CE in the *Koguryojon*, a Chinese text that also notes that the Korean people "are skilled in making fermented foods such as wine, soybean paste, and salted and fermented fish." According to Park and Cheigh, we see later references in a text called the *Kapoyukyong* (part of the 53-volume *Dongkukisangkukjip* from 1241), which refers to white radish leaves put up in soy paste, differentiating them from jangajji (vegetables pickled in soy paste or sauce). This same volume mentions autumn kimchi-making gatherings, called kimjang, telling us that kimchi has been an important part of feeding communities en masse for centuries (we'll talk more about kimjang in Chapter 5, page 226).

The earliest kimchis were made primarily with radishes, though they also might include cucumber, eggplant, and scallions. A range of imported ingredients was introduced during the Choson dynasty (1392–1600), resulting in a wider variety of kimchis, including ones made with red peppers, which were first mentioned in 1715. More and more ingredients came to be used, and napa cabbage became a central component in many versions, alongside daikon radish.

While we have seen that there is a tremendous variety of sauerkrauts, there is an even larger variety of kimchis. The *Umshikdimibang* (a Korean recipe book from around 1670) shows 7 different kinds, the *Jungbosallimkyongje* (1776) describes 41 different kinds, and the *Imwonshibyukji* (1827) describes 97 varieties. Modern kimchi recipes are incredibly diverse, varying by region, season, and even family. Preparations vary—sometimes the cabbage is fermented whole and stuffed with other vegetables, for instance—as does the aging process, which can range from about a week to a year and take place anywhere from a glass container on the countertop to a clay vessel buried in the ground.

Kimchi is often referred to as the backbone of Korean cuisine (modern Koreans consume roughly 1.5 million tons of kimchi per year). It appears at every meal, whether as an ingredient (as in kimchi jigae, a soup with kimchi and pork belly) or as a condiment. We see kimchi's importance to Korean cuisine in its centrality in banchan, the variety of side dishes that appear on the table at each meal. They are meant to be nibbled on throughout the meal to help provide a diversity of flavors to the palate. Even in times of economic depression, such as in the post–Korean War period of the 1950s, when food was scarce and starvation an imminent risk, Korean families strove to put kimchi on the table, even if there were no other sides to go with it.

* * *

To sum up, our ancestors developed fermentation practices to survive: Alcohol provided calories and was safe to drink at a time when water was not, dairy ferments preserved scarce animal protein, and fermented vegetables, grains, and fruits provided fiber and micronutrients. Even without having the information we have today about health and nutrition, our earliest ancestors knew what their bodies needed and were able to seek it out.

As far as we can tell, fermentation developed in multiple cultures at the same time, before those cultures mingled. Certainly fermentation processes and dishes spread between communities, but in many places a regular fermentation practice has existed since at least ancient times. This speaks to the power of fermentation: It is a practice that is literally embedded in our cells, and our ancestors knew to harness it to feed themselves. That knowledge is still there for us today, and looking to the foods of the past is one way to unlock it.

The Influence of Place and Trade

How did our ancestors find these ingredients to ferment in the first place? Did they forage by trial and error? Once they learned a plant was edible, how did they learn what to do with it to make it taste good or to preserve it? Our ancestors likely looked to the world around them for clues (they would have noticed, for example, which plants the birds and other animals were eating and which plants they were avoiding), and their preparations of those foods almost certainly involved not just observation but experimentation, as well as some happy accidents.

It is important to remember that humans evolved *from* something else (our hominid ancestors), and that those ancestors had many millennia of experience in foraging and hunting for food and a keen sense of what they could and could not eat. As humans evolved, we brought this wisdom with us. And as we developed new techniques for surviving and thriving (cooking with fire, using salt, domesticating plants and animals, and so on), we were able to add to this wisdom and apply what we already understood in new ways.

As time went on, we began to create dishes with flavors unique to where we lived, so the dishes had a strong sense of place. When there was little variety in basic ingredients, flavorings were a way to wake up the palate. And when new foods were introduced, flavorings were a way to add a familiar note.

While the earliest ferments relied upon those ingredients immediately available in the local environment, as trade between communities grew (first between immediate neighbors and then farther and farther afield until we developed our modern global system of trade), people could access and use foods in ever greater variety. We do not always know how a particular food entered a culture, but in the cases where we do know, it was usually through trade or immigration.

When early European colonists (namely, the Dutch, Spanish, English, and French) came to the Americas, they forcibly took land, spread disease, and drastically reshaped entire ecosystems. This was among the most terrible and widely impactful events in human history. As settlements grew, enslaved people were brought from Africa or captured from local populations and forced to raise and process crops both imported to and indigenous to the continent. This had a profound impact on countless lives and on food cultures. Global foodways changed dramatically, and incredibly quickly compared to the pace of change across earlier human history. Many ingredients that have now become central to European and Asian fermented dishes—including peppers, tomatoes, and corn—did not appear in those cultures before this point. Try to imagine Korean food without peppers today, or Turkish food without tomatoes. These crops were not part of either culture for millennia, but they are absolutely ingrained in them today. At the same time, as global trade took root and grew at an accelerating pace, new ingredients, foods, and flavorings from other parts of the world—from Asia, Africa, the Middle East, and beyond—spread in all directions.

This movement of products, plants, animals, and people (willingly and forced) has completely altered our world. Our crops, for example, are often nonnative plants, grown in places that colonial administrators and botanists decided, at varying points and for varying reasons, should be grown in different regions. Acres upon acres of land were cleared for tea plantations in India and Sri Lanka, for example, as well as for cloves, cinnamon, nutmeg, and countless other crops that appear in our ferments and other dishes.

Living Cultures

Because ferments are such an important part of global foodways, both past and present, it makes sense that we find records of them not only in archaeological evidence and recipe books but also in songs, stories, and traditions. Fermentation does not exist in isolation, and so it's important we acknowledge that each food we discuss is itself a living entity, and that it is part of a living and breathing (and growing and changing) human culture.

While the focus of much of this chapter has been on the history of ferments as a means of preservation and survival, the title of this chapter, Ferments for Life, also refers to the life of a human culture. By fermenting foods, we carry on long-standing food traditions that might otherwise be lost to the ages. Salt-rising bread and acarajé are two examples of traditional foods that very nearly went extinct, but thanks to the growing interest in fermentation and foods that connect people to their ancestors, they are seeing a resurgence.

SALT-RISING BREAD

Salt-rising bread is a wild-fermented bread developed in the early days of European settlement in Appalachia. It was made in various pockets in the southern Appalachians and in the coal belt of Pennsylvania, but it was especially prevalent in Virginia and West Virginia. There are many parts of the Appalachians where it was *not* made, too, and where people tend not to be familiar with it—an important reminder that the cuisine of this region is not a monolith.

Salt-rising bread has a unique cheesy aroma and dense texture. Due to its temperamental nature and to modern work schedules, which no longer easily accommodate watching a dough that requires almost 2 days to make, salt-rising bread fell out of favor over the years. Now, however, many bakers and chefs are regaining an appreciation for its dense texture and funky flavor.

There are a few theories for the bread's name, including that it is a corruption of *salaterus*, an old name for potassium bicarbonate (the precursor to sodium bicarbonate, or modern baking soda). Both potassium bicarbonate and sodium bicarbonate are naturally occurring compounds that react with acidic ingredients (such as buttermilk or cream of tartar) to produce leavening through chemical means rather than fermentative ones. While salt-rising bread is wild fermented, it often relies on baking soda for its texture. Another theory holds that the name stems from the tradition of placing the bowl of starter inside a larger bowl of warmed salt. Salt-rising bread likes to be toasty warm at each stage of the baking process, and salt that had been warmed and placed in a bowl made an excellent insulator for the starter as it sat overnight.

We see examples of salt-rising bread throughout historic and modern texts, including in the oldest known cookbook by an African American woman, *A Domestic Cook Book* (1866) by Mrs. Malinda Russell, who was born a free woman in Tennessee. Russell's life was one of hardship and adaptation, and food weaves itself throughout her personal narrative as a grounding force and a source of income. Russell was an entrepreneur and single mother who ran a successful pastry shop and a boardinghouse before being forced to flee her home in Greeneville, Tennessee, for Michigan in 1864. She published the book to support herself and her son, hoping to make enough money with the book to fund their return home to Greeneville. Her book, which is today recognized as a pivotal piece of African American culinary history, was published only several months before the town of Paw Paw, where Russell lived, burned almost entirely to the ground. There is no trace of Russell after that time.

The book opens with Mrs. Russell's autobiography, immediately followed by this recipe:

SALT RISING BREAD

To a half pint warm water, a pinch of salt; stir to a thick batter and keep warm until it rises. To one pint of this rising add three pints warm water, a little salt, and a small piece of lard. Knead the dough until smooth, make into rolls, keep warm until it rises; bake quick, but do not scorch.

The remainder of her bread recipes are largely quick breads (such as gingerbread), which rely upon chemical reactions from baking soda or baking powder to produce results, although there are a few yeasted breads and sweets in the mix. Her decision to open the book with salt-rising bread shows that she brought her Appalachian heritage with her to Michigan, and that she considered the recipe to be an important one.

BRAZILIAN ACARAJÉ

Acarajé (see the recipe on page 57), a fritter made of fermented black-eyed peas and onion, offers an especially powerful example of how a ferment can both preserve and share cultural heritage. Originating in the state of Bahia and sold as street food throughout Brazil, it is an iconic part of regional cuisine as well as of Afro-Brazilian culture as a whole.

Acarajé has strong African roots, from the ingredients used (black-eyed peas are an African import) to the dress of the *baianas de acarajé* (the traditionally female acarajé sellers who wear clothing rooted in African aesthetic practices). Acarajé is almost identical to West African akara, which is also made with onion and fermented black-eyed peas. How did the West African dish travel to Brazil? Oral histories from the region note that the myriad of practices around the dish—from ingredients to dress—derive from Candomblé communities, a diasporic religious group that emerged in Brazil in the nineteenth century as a combination of West African, Roman Catholic, and indigenous Brazilian spiritual traditions. While the dish itself is not inherently religious, it is sometimes given as an offering to gods, and vendors selling this traditional food are often Candomblé practitioners, whose religion and wares reflect the intersection of cultures.

In 2005, Brazil's National Institute of Historic and Artistic Heritage designated the fritters and the work of the baianas de acarajé as part of Brazil's intangible national heritage. However, acarajé was not always recognized so highly, which we see in the first known mention of the dish from the early 1800s. Luis dos Santos Vilhena, a Portuguese colonial bureaucrat, said, "It is common to see eight, ten or more slaves coming out of the most opulent households . . . to sell on the streets the most vile and insignificant foods," among which he goes on to include acarajé.

As a food of the enslaved, acarajé would not have been preserved nor shared with the larger culture had not those making the dish consistently and intentionally done so. The work done by Africans and their descendants to preserve their cultural heritage, particularly in places where those in power did everything possible to destroy it, speaks to their incredible strength and their belief in the importance of tradition. This veneration for cultural food traditions is something the general populus in the United States is only starting to understand, thanks to the work of researchers, historical interpreters, and others.

Ferments and Identity

Fermented foods can tie us to culture and place; through eating a food from a particular tradition, we can reconnect with that culture or place, even if we are far away from it. Food can be especially important to diasporic communities, separated from their mother culture. "It's the last vestige of culture that people shed," says Jennifer Berg, director of the graduate food studies program at New York University. "There's some aspects of maternal culture that you'll lose right away. First is how you dress, because if you want to blend in or be part of a larger mainstream culture, the things that are the most visible are the ones that you let go. With food, it's something you're engaging in hopefully three times a day, and so there are more opportunities to connect to memory and family and place. It's the hardest to give up." Journalist Amy S. Choi writes, "For me, a first-generation Korean-American, comfort food is a plate of kimchi, white rice, and fried Spam. Such preferences are personally meaningful—and also culturally meaningful. Our comfort foods map who [we] are, where we come from, and what happened to us along the way."

Because ferments are such a central part of our daily lives, it makes sense that they show up in myth, story, and discussions of the human psyche. Clarissa Pinkola Estés, whose wonderful and compelling book *Women Who Run with the Wolves* sits at the intersection of storytelling and psychoanalysis, states:

> Putting a veil over something increases its action or feeling. This is known among women far and wide. There was a phrase my grandmother used, "veiling the bowl." It meant to put a white cloth over a bowl of kneaded dough to cause the bread to rise. The veil for the bread and the veil for the psyche serve the same purpose. There is potent leavening in the souls of women in descent. There is a powerful fermenting going on. To be behind the veil increases one's mystical insight. From behind the veil, all humans look like mist beings, all events, all objects, are colored as though in a dawn, or in a dream.

Estés articulates the significance of our seemingly small daily rituals around those fermentation tasks that keep us fed. This framing reminds us of the power within those daily tasks: Far from being mundane, veiling the bowl is an offer put forth to us to encounter the divine.

Estés's words remind me of son-mat, the Korean concept roughly translated as "the taste of one's hands." In a figurative sense, it's the understanding that we each make food that tastes like our own, and no one else's, and in Korea, where so much of food production is hands-on, there is also a literal sense. As Korean food blogger Grace Meng says, "The best cooks don't become that way through formal training or expensive equipment, but by the heart and spirit they bring to their food." To some, it can also refer to cooking without a recipe, instead eyeballing measurements and working from experience—a not-uncommon practice in Korean households. Over time, the culinary concept of son-mat has become deeply embedded in Korean culture as a whole. In fact, it was made manifest in Jiwon Woo's 2017 series called *Mother's Hand Taste (son-mat)*, comprising blown-glass objects that were created based around the living microbiome (yeasts and bacteria) from the hands of the artist's mother.

In the world of food and beyond, some artifacts are consistently a part of a culture (such as kimchi), some have a popularity that ebbs and flows (such as salt-rising bread), and some fade away almost entirely (such as garum). In ancient Rome, garum (fish sauce) was an absolute staple, used in place of salt both in cooking and in seasoning food tableside. However, today garum has fallen out of favor. Salt is cheaper and easier, and Italian cooks are more likely to reach for salt than for a fragrant bottle of fish sauce.

As we've seen, a culture's food traditions are determined by the foods that culture had access to, shaped by the ways the culture found to best engage with those ingredients. However, these food traditions are anything but static: People move, new ingredients are introduced, old ones sometimes go way, and tastes change. Our understanding of the role of foods in our culture can change, too. Here in the United States, for instance, yogurt was once mainly used as a component in or a condiment for other dishes. Now modern marketing efforts have reframed yogurt as a healthy, protein-rich, probiotic stand-alone snack. However, while plain yogurt is indeed healthy, most of the "healthy" flavored versions contain loads of sugar, colorings, and other add-ins. Despite this, many Americans think that these commercial flavored yogurts are just as healthy as their plain, unflavored counterparts.

Ferments and Modern Life

Much of the fermented food we enjoy today came out of the need to preserve fresh foods while they were available so we could have them for sustenance and flavor when options were more limited. People in much of the world take for granted that food will always be available in stores or restaurants (whether or not all of us can access that food is, of course, a very different issue). During the past couple hundred years, new technologies for food preservation (such as canning and refrigeration) and transport (such as railroads) have emerged, alongside changes in agriculture that favor monocultures and cheap prices. This has resulted in a greater variety of shelf-stable, cheap foods, but this convenience has a price: We are more disconnected from the foods we eat, both because they offer minimal nutrition and subpar flavor, and also because we will never feel as connected to food from a package as we will to food made by hand.

In the last decade or two, there has been a considerable resurgence of interest in ferments in Western markets. Of course, some of us have been fermenting for decades, whether from economic necessity, a desire to remain connected to food traditions, or just practicality. But even people who have access to other food options, and perhaps do not grow any food of their own at all, are enthralled with fermentation.

As we'll see throughout this book, the stories of food offer endless examples of human ingenuity in overcoming struggle and scarcity, historically and today. Each step in the preparation of a dish, from the ingredients we start with to the spices we add and the way we cook it, is informed by thousands of versions of that dish that were made before. We don't have to look to an idealized version of the past to learn about the history of the human diet; we just have to look at what's right in front of us, on our plates and the plates of our neighbors around the world.

BASIC EGYPTIAN BEER

This simple recipe, inspired by the research of Delwen Samuel and brewing experiments from Tasha Marks, brings together several of the ancient brewing traditions discussed in this chapter, using standard kitchen equipment. Like ancient Egyptian beer, it uses both malted (sprouted) and unmalted grain; emmer and kamut would be historically accurate, but barley and wheat berries work fine. You can bottle and carbonate the beer, if you wish, but it's delicious however it's served.

Like historical brews, this beer relies on wild yeast for fermentation, which means there's a lot of room for variation in flavor. Any plant material will work as a yeast source; just make sure that it's organic. I often use whole dates, which add a bit of sugar, but I've also used rose petals from my garden, which provide both wild yeast and flavoring. It's okay to use dried dates, but with herbs and flowers, it works best to use fresh. If you wish to jump-start the microbial activity of your ferment, you can add a splash of finished beer or a little sourdough starter to your wort after it has cooled and before it starts fermenting.

You can make this beer with minimal flavorings, or you can add any range of flavors from the traditional to the uncommon. I like using pistachio, green cardamom, and rose, or herbs such as chamomile, and have seen a similar beer made with roasted pistachio, sesame, coriander, rose, and cumin. And I once made this brew with purple barley, dates, and a ton of foraged spiderwort and ended up with a delicious (and purple!) beer. The only limit is your imagination!

MAKES
ABOUT
1 GALLON

1 **quart barley** (I used unhulled, which takes longer to cook but is a more historically accurate choice)

2 **gallons water**

1 **quart emmer, kamut, or wheat berries**

Yeast source (4 dates, 1 cup rose petals or other herbs, or similar)

Other flavorings (optional)

Recipe continues on next page. >

1   Malt your barley: Pour it into a large container, add just enough water to slightly moisten the grains, and cover. Check the grain a couple of times a day, gently rolling or stirring the container to redistribute moisture.

2   Depending on the ambient temperature, among other factors, the barley will begin to sprout in about 2 days. Once it has begun to sprout, pour half into a large bowl and set aside.

3   Combine the remaining malted barley with 2 cups of the whole grains (emmer, kamut, or wheat berries) in a large pot, and add 1 gallon of water, or enough water to cover the mixture. Cook over medium heat, stirring occasionally, until it has a thin porridgelike consistency (not a thick paste; you still want liquid in there), which signals that the starches have broken down into fermentable sugars. Depending on how tough your grains are, this might take a bit (usually about an hour), and you may have to add more water partway through. Just remember the final texture you're going for and you'll be fine!

4   Meanwhile, add the remaining 2 cups of whole grains to the reserved bowl of malted barley, and add 1 gallon of water or enough to cover. Let soak while the hot mash cooks.

5   Once the mash is cooked, and while it's still warm, stir in the uncooked grains and their soaking water.

6   Once the mash cools to room temperature, use a mesh sieve to strain it into a wide-mouthed fermentation vessel. Gently push down on the mash left in the sieve with a wooden spoon to extract all the liquid.

7   Add the yeast source to the fermentation vessel, along with any additional flavorings you might desire, and stir to distribute them. Cover the vessel with cheesecloth secured with string or a rubber band to keep out bugs. Let sit at room temperature to ferment.

8   This beer will ferment quickly, so keep an eye on it. Daily drinking beers in Egypt were usually lower in alcohol, and if you want to re-create them, I suggest using a nonsugary starter (for example, rose petals instead of dates) and pulling it after perhaps a day or two, or whenever it just begins to taste like beer rather than sugar. Ultimately, as with any ferment, this is about making something you want to drink and that you're happy with, so there's no right answer beyond what your palate tells you! Store the finished beer in the fridge, where it should be consumed within a week.

MILLET OGI

Nourishing and easy to make, fermented grain porridges are staples in West Africa, Kenya, and elsewhere in Africa. They can vary considerably based on the availability of ingredients and preparation method. Millet, sorghum, and cornmeal are the traditional base. Some porridges are fermented for days on end, and others are barely fermented—if at all. Some are thick and rich, while others are thin and drinkable.

The names differ, too. In Nigeria, *ogi* can refer to a thick cornstarch-based porridge served with evaporated milk, whereas elsewhere the term simply refers to a millet or sorghum porridge.

This recipe and the Multigrain Uji on page 54 are based on what I have learned from friends who grew up eating the porridges and from my own research, but bear in mind that a continent as large and diverse as Africa produces many, many variations on such recipes. As such, there are many rabbit holes for you to jump down and explore as you play with different grains and preparations to find what you like best.

You can customize the flavor with a range of add-ins, including sweeteners (honey and coconut sugar are the two I've seen most often) or coconut oil, sour cream, or evaporated milk to add richness.

MAKES ABOUT 4 SERVINGS

1¼	**cups whole millet grains**
1½	**quarts water**
	Salt
1	**tablespoon coconut oil or butter**

1   Combine the millet and water. Let soak for 1 hour, then run through a blender until the millet is as smooth as you'd like. (Alternatively, you can use a grain mill to grind the millet and then add it to water, if you prefer.)

2   Pour the mixture into a nonreactive bowl and let sit at room temperature to ferment anywhere from overnight to several days. The longer it sits, the more sour it becomes.

3   When it's time to cook your porridge, combine the grain ferment, salt, and oil in a saucepan and heat over medium heat. Simmer, stirring frequently, until it has the consistency you'd like, 15 to 20 minutes. Serve warm.

MULTIGRAIN UJI

In Kenya, *uji* refers to a porridge made of sorghum, millet, and corn. As with Millet Ogi (page 53), have fun customizing your flavor with sweeteners and milk.

MAKES ABOUT 4 SERVINGS

2 **tablespoons sorghum grains**

¹/₂ **cup millet grains**

1¹/₂ **cups cold water**

2 **cups corn flour or cornmeal**

1 **quart room-temperature water**

Sweetener to taste (optional)

Evaporated milk, sweetened condensed milk, or coconut oil to serve (optional)

1   Combine the sorghum and millet grains with the cold water. Let soak for at least 1 hour to soften, then run through a blender until smooth. (Alternatively, you can use millet and sorghum flours, in which case you can omit the soaking step. Simply whisk your flours with the water.)

2   Pour the mixture into a nonreactive bowl, add the corn flour, and stir to combine. Let sit at room temperature to ferment anywhere from overnight to 4 days. The longer it sits, the more sour it becomes.

3   When it's time to cook your porridge, bring the room-temperature water to a boil in a saucepan, adding sweetener if desired. Add your grain ferment and simmer over medium heat, stirring frequently, until it is as thick as you'd like, 15 to 25 minutes. In Kenya, uji is often somewhat thin, but I've also seen thicker versions, so let your own taste preferences be your guide.

4   Add the milk or oil, if using, and serve.

TARHANA

Made from a mixture of grains, vegetables, pulses, and yogurt that is fermented and then dried and powdered, tarhana is often rehydrated into a nourishing soup in Turkey and elsewhere in the Middle East. With its long history of traditional use, it offers an excellent example of how fermentation has supported us throughout human history, in this case offering

 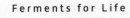

nutritional sustenance (with protein and carbohydrates, as well as B vitamins and minerals) that is portable and has a longer shelf life than the fresh ingredients.

Modern recipes for tarhana vary considerably. Some include only aromatic vegetables and yogurt, for example, while heartier versions include grains and pulses as well. My version here is meant to serve as a jumping-off point; you should customize your version as you wish.

The key to success is finely grinding the dried tarhana. This gives you a smoother texture and shorter cooking time when you're making it into soup.

MAKES
ABOUT
1 QUART
TARHANA

6 **cups plain Greek yogurt** (try to find one that does not have added thickeners) **or strained homemade yogurt**

12 **fresh Roma tomatoes, diced**

3 **large red bell peppers, diced**

2 **cups dried chickpeas**

2 **cups uncooked bulgur wheat**

1 **cup dried split peas**

3 **cups roughly chopped fresh greens** (my usual mixture is 1 large bunch parsley, 4 sprigs basil, several large scallions, 1 large bunch oregano, and 2 large sprigs mint)

2 **cloves garlic, minced**

¾ **cup unrefined salt**

¾ **cup all-purpose flour, plus extra as needed**

1 Combine the yogurt, tomatoes, bell peppers, chickpeas, split peas, bulgur, greens, garlic, and salt in a large nonreactive bowl. Mash together with your hands to create a uniform mixture.

2 Sprinkle the flour over the mixture and mash again, thoroughly combining until you have a loose but cohesive mixture. (If your yogurt and veggies have a lot of liquid in them, the mixture may be watery. If so, just add a bit more flour.)

3 Cover the dough with a tea towel to keep out bugs and set aside at room temperature to ferment, stirring daily, for 7 to 10 days. The

Recipe continues on next page. >

finished dough should have a slightly sour but still pleasant smell. When it smells good to you, it's ready to go.

4   Roll the fermented dough into small balls about the size of a quarter, and place on a parchment-lined baking sheet. Allow to sit out in the sun until they begin to dry, about 12 hours. Turn the balls over and allow to continue drying until they feel dry to the touch, 12 to 24 hours longer. (Alternatively, you can dry them in a dehydrator set to 135°F/57°C, turning after 8 hours and checking them again after another 8 to 10 hours.)

5   Break the balls apart by hand. If you notice that the mixture still feels a bit wet, place it on a parchment-lined baking sheet and gently dry it in an oven on the lowest setting or in a dehydrator set to 135°F/57°C. Note that most ovens do not go down to 135°F/57°C, which means that your tarhana will not have active cultures. If you put it in the oven, be sure to check it regularly so it doesn't burn!

6   Grind the pieces using a food processor, coffee grinder reserved for spices, or mortar and pestle. You'll end up with a fragrant, nutritious dry soup powder. Store your powder in an airtight container at room temperature and use within a month.

TO MAKE A BOWL OF SOUP

1   Place the desired amount of tarhana in a bowl and sprinkle with water (I usually use about 1 tablespoon tarhana per 1 cup finished soup). Let sit for about 1 hour.

2   Melt a little butter in a pan over medium heat. If desired, sauté veggies, such as onion and bell pepper, and minced or finely diced beef in the butter. Then add the tarhana powder and cook for just 15 to 30 seconds.

3   Add about 1 cup stock or water and gently bring to a boil over medium heat (use more stock for thin soup, and less for a thick and flavorful stew). For a thicker-bodied soup, whisk in a bit of tomato paste.

4   Garnish with chopped herbs, if desired, and serve hot.

ACARAJÉ

Acarajé is an Afro-Brazilian dish of fermented legumes that are formed into balls and fried. It is based upon West African akara, which was brought to Brazil by enslaved Africans. The two dishes are nearly identical—both being made with black-eyed peas, onion, and salt, as they have been for centuries—but they can differ in toppings. Traditionally, acarajé is served with vatapa, a shrimp and coconut milk stew. Akara's toppings depend on where you are: In Senegal, for example, tomato sauce is common when akara is served on a baguette as a sandwich.

In 2005, the Brazilian government passed a resolution stating that acarajé and the fillings put inside the fritters could be made only with traditional ingredients, and those selling acarajé had to wear the traditional style of dress. While I am not aware of any similar resolutions in West Africa, there are still expectations that akara be made properly—for example, by pulling the "eyes" off the black-eyed peas with your thumbnail to make the batter smooth. I have most often seen akara fermented, but it isn't always: Food historian Michael Twitty, for example, offered a nonfermented version, inspired by the cooking of an enslaved man named Hercules who worked under George Washington, for the *First Chefs* exhibition at the Folger Shakespeare Library in 2019.

MAKES
ABOUT
A DOZEN
SMALL
PATTIES

2 cups dried black-eyed peas

1 teaspoon sea salt

1 medium yellow onion

Red palm oil, for frying

1   Combine the beans and salt in a large jar or other lidded vessel and add enough water to cover. Seal, shake, and allow to ferment for 2 to 4 days, stirring daily. If the beans absorb all the water and you need to add more, add salt, too, at a ratio of 1 teaspoon salt per 1 quart water.

2   When the peas are slightly sour smelling and the skins separate from them easily, they're done fermenting. Rub the peas gently between your hands to remove their skins. For the smoothest batter, also pull off the "eye" from each pea with your thumbnail. The more skins you can remove, the smoother your batter will be later.

Recipe continues on next page. >

3   Combine the peas and onion in a food processor and process until the batter is as smooth as possible, about 10 minutes. Then use a hand or stand mixer to beat the batter for 2 minutes on medium speed, then for 3 to 8 minutes on medium-high, scraping down the sides at regular intervals, until the batter is smooth and fluffy with a velvety texture. It's critical to remove as many chunks as you can so the batter holds together when you're frying the fritters.

4   Heat about ¼ inch of palm oil in a cast-iron skillet over medium-high heat.

5   Oil your spoon, then drop spoonfuls of batter into the hot oil (or gently pat out silver dollar–size patties with your hands). Fry until lightly golden, about 3 minutes per side. Gently place on a paper towel to drain.

SENEGALESE TOMATO SAUCE FOR AKARA

In West Africa, street vendors sometimes sell akara nestled into a baguette and topped with tomato sauce for a filling and delicious lunch. The sauce is easy to make and full of flavor. Thank you to Abdala Faye for teaching me how to make it.

MAKES ABOUT 2 CUPS

Ghee or vegetable oil

1   **onion, minced**

2   **habanero peppers, minced**

2   **cloves garlic, minced**

½   **cup tomato paste**

Salt and freshly ground black pepper

1   Warm a spoonful of ghee or a splash of vegetable oil in a skillet over medium-high heat. Add the onion and sauté until it just starts to become translucent, about 10 minutes. Add the habaneros and garlic, reduce the heat to medium, and cook until fragrant, 1 to 2 minutes.

2   Deglaze the pan with a splash of water, then add the tomato paste and stir to combine. Add more water, if needed, to create a thick sauce. Season the sauce to taste with salt and black pepper.

3   Cook for 5 to 10 minutes, adding more water if the sauce becomes too thick. Serve warm, on top of or alongside akara.

POZOL

Pozol is a fermented corn beverage from pre-Columbian Mexico (not to be confused with pozole, a hominy stew). Historically, it was used to sustain travelers on long journeys.

Pozol is an incredibly important part of the daily diet in southeastern Mexico. It derives its nutrition both from fermentation and from nixtamalization, which is the process of adding lime to corn while boiling. Nixtamalization increases the available protein as well as calcium and other nutrients in the corn. Pozol can be consumed plain or flavored. My favorite flavoring is cacao, and cinnamon and hot peppers are common, as are sweeteners. There are a couple of ways to make pozol: The more traditional method nixtamalizes fresh corn, and a modern method uses masa. The modern method is less time intensive but still tasty (though admittedly not as tasty, as the flavors don't have a chance to develop). I've provided both below. Feel free to experiment with the fermentation time; I've seen anywhere from 3 hours to more than a month.

MORE TRADITIONAL POZOL

3   cups dried corn kernels

1   tablespoon Cal Mexicana (powdered calcium hydroxide, a.k.a. lime, available at many Latin American grocery stores or online)

1/2   cup cacao nibs, ground to powder

Banana leaves or corn husks (optional)

Other flavorings (sugar, honey, spices, hot peppers, and so on; optional)

1   Place the kernels in a pot with enough water to cover by 2 to 3 inches and bring to a boil. Once the water is boiling, add the Cal Mexicana and stir. The corn will change color and texture rather quickly. Cook, stirring occasionally, until the skins easily peel off the kernels when rubbed between your fingers, about 1½ hours.

2   Thoroughly drain and rinse the corn, then rinse twice more, using your hands to rub the skins off the kernels as you do.

Recipe continues on next page. >

3   Place the corn kernels into a grain mill or food processor and grind to a paste. Add the cacao and mix until evenly distributed.

4   Roll the dough into palm-size balls. Wrap the balls in banana leaves or corn husks (you can also use plastic wrap, though I prefer the leaves) and tie closed.

5   Let the dough ferment at room temperature for 1 to 3 days, away from direct sunlight, until it is slightly sour and a bit dry but still smells sweet.

6   To serve, pinch off a big piece of dough and, breaking it apart with your hands, drop it into 2 quarts of water. Stir until it dissolves. If you'd like, you can sweeten or flavor the pozol with sugar, honey, spices, or hot peppers. You can also add ice to serving glasses to make it more refreshing. Store any unused dough in an airtight container in the fridge, where it will keep for 1 week.

NOT-SO-TRADITIONAL POZOL

1   **cup masa flour**

2–3 **tablespoons cocoa powder** (depending how cocoa-y you like things; optional)

Corn husks, banana leaves, or plastic wrap, for wrapping

Other flavorings (sugar, honey, spices, hot peppers, and so on; optional)

1   Place the masa and cocoa powder (if using) in a bowl. Mix in just enough water to form a stiff but still pliable dough.

2   Roll the dough into palm-size balls. Wrap the balls in corn husks or banana leaves and tie them closed, or wrap them in plastic wrap.

3   Let the dough ferment at room temperature for 1 to 3 days, away from direct sunlight, until it is slightly sour and a bit dry but still smells sweet.

4   To serve, pinch off a big piece of dough and, breaking it apart with your hands, drop it into a pitcher of water. Stir until it dissolves. If you'd like, you can sweeten or flavor the pozol with sugar, honey, spices, or hot peppers. You can also add ice to serving glasses to make it more refreshing. Store any unused dough in an airtight container in the fridge, where it will keep for 1 to 2 weeks.

2

PRESERVATION

Food preservation, in practical terms, means extending the shelf life of foods so that they can be kept and used outside their growing season. It also often aims to use up every part of our food that we can, turning what otherwise might be wasted into a source of nutrition.

Both aspects of food preservation have been critical through much of human history, when our diets were limited by the seasonality of food availability. Today, people in affluent industrialized areas such as the United States can find food year-round at big-box grocery stores; they don't have a seasonal way of eating, like our ancestors did. Our ancestors used a whole range of preservation methods to put up their food, including drying, smoking, salting, quick pickling, and burying. But key among these methods worldwide was fermentation.

Food Preservation Is Food Security

For early humans, food insecurity was a very real concern. Though trade existed in ancient times, goods from elsewhere did not account for the bulk of most anyone's diet. When most or all of the food you consume is produced nearby (whether cultivated or gathered), dealing with the seasonality of your diet becomes paramount. For example, if all your crops ripen in summer, what do you eat once winter hits? Or, in warmer climates, what do you eat if a natural disaster destroys the food sources you usually rely on? Preserving what you have, when you have it, then becomes a matter of life or death.

Many studies have looked at how Neolithic societies formed social groups and argued that food preservation is a critical piece of the puzzle. Anthropologist Ian Kuijt argues that "storage represents a critical form of risk management. This relationship is a clear one: in general, the more food people were able to store, the better off they were. In contexts of high resource variability, people will attempt to minimize risk in multiple ways, including stockpiling food in case of repeated crop failures."

God made yeast, as well as dough, and loves fermentation just as dearly as he loves vegetation.

—RALPH WALDO EMERSON

Those with more shelf-stable food, then, potentially had greater food security and better nutrition than those who didn't. Many scholars have argued that preservation of food exacerbated or even created social hierarchies:

Those with access to more food and with more preserved food put away, including food preserved through fermentation, were able to wield greater power than those who didn't have preserved food on hand.

However, to say that food preservation caused social hierarchies to develop is an oversimplification. Neolithic people had complex and nuanced needs and desires, just as we do, and the reasons behind increasingly complex societies are incredibly varied. Preparation resources were shared, for example, suggesting the possibility of shared food stores between families or other groups. Inheritance is another consideration, as an initially small bequest can be compounded over the generations with the addition of more goods and property.

The ability to preserve food and build food security also impacted the movement of people: If you are able to carry your food and beverages with you and they will keep for some time, then you can travel farther and be away from food and water sources for a longer period. This may be one reason why ferments have stuck with us over human history, and why we see so many even today in the modern world. For example, researcher Hamid Dirar has documented more than 80 fermented foods and beverages presently in use in Sudan alone, including a variety of porridges, breads, beers, wine, mead, dairy and meat ferments, fish sauces, and plant-based ferments. These traditional ferments include some utilizing food scraps (such as bones), which help stretch food supplies, as well as those introduced from other countries, showing the movement of people and their fermentation traditions. As we saw with tarhana (see the recipe on page 54), travel-friendly ferments and other preserved foods are nothing new.

The ability to preserve food is critical in the face of climate change, too. In Europe, the Little Ice Age began around 1150 and the climate continued to cool until 1460, and then the climate became very cold between 1650 and 1850. This had all kinds of impacts, including on growing seasons (during the coldest points, England's growing season was shortened by 1 to 2 months) and on what could grow in increasingly cold, wet weather. Crop yields were particularly poor in some years (for example in 1816, "the year without a summer"), and livestock were hard to sustain, resulting in famine and malnutrition. Winemaking, once common in England, nearly ceased in that country as temperatures cooled.

With shorter, darker, and colder days, diminished crop yields, and fewer livestock, the need to preserve food became acute and urgent. Multiply that over the course of multiple generations and you have a need that becomes ingrained in the culture. It is hardly surprising that fermented vegetables and other preserved foods (such as smoked and cured fish) are common in northern Europe, if you consider the food needs that existed during this long, cold period.

Even in tropical climates, where bitter cold was not an issue during the Little Ice Age, food preservation was (and is) still important as a means of establishing food security, making sure no food goes to waste, and extending the availability of seasonal produce. By preserving their foods, people living in the tropics could get the diversity of flavors and nutrients that their palates and bodies needed, even if faced with larger shortages. So, as in cold climates, the need to preserve food in warm climates led to the development of fermentation practices that persist to this day.

While we preserve our food to make it last longer, there's an added benefit: We get an entirely new product from the original harvest. Oranges become marmalade, cabbage becomes sauerkraut, sprats become fish sauce. Through necessity, we have built new flavors, textures, and even nutrients into our diets, giving us a range of comestible experiences throughout the year.

Preserving Dairy

When humans started to keep livestock 10,000 to 15,000 years ago, they suddenly had consistent access to milk, and they were eager to preserve this nutrient-dense food rather than let it go to waste. People in the Middle East, Africa, South Asia, and Europe learned to turn milk from cattle, goats, sheep, and camels into fresh and aged cheeses, yogurts, cultured cream, cultured butter, and more. In Sumeria, for example, recipes for fermented milk go back to at least 2000 BCE; clay tablets from that time outline multiple cheese recipes using multiple methods.

Milk, no matter which animal it's from, spoils quickly. The discovery of dairy fermentation was a boon to preservation and to our health, too, as fermentation drastically reduces the lactose content of milk, making this nutrition source available to people even if they have trouble digesting lactose. It appears that through most of history, adults mostly got their dairy fix through fermented milk, and very rarely through consuming it raw. Many cultures used lactic acid fermentation to produce yogurt, and our ancestors made cheese by employing a range of plants and animal products as curdling agents.

Livestock were introduced to the British Isles around 3500 BCE, and evidence suggests that they gave a generous supply of milk to use for butter and cheese. The Celts used plant rennet (such as that from wild thistle, nettle, or lady's bedstraw) to make cheese; as the writer and historian Colin Spencer notes, the ability of certain plants to curdle milk was "perhaps discovered by accident when stirring warm milk with a stem or twig of one of these plants." By the time the Roman occupation of Britain had ended, the ancient Roman writer Columella tells us, people in Britain were also using lamb or kid rennet in cheesemaking. The ancient British peoples also made butter, and in areas with peat bogs, "bog butter" (butter that has been buried in a peat bog for long-term preservation) is still sometimes found. Even after thousands of years it remains a viable product, though from what I've read, it tastes very, very cheesy.

Of course, in any time or place, the types of cheeses that were produced would depend on the type of milk that was available (different milks have different butterfat content and different properties), the type of salt that was used, and the amount of cheese to be made. A Great Depression–era bulletin from the US Department of Agriculture (USDA), for instance, advised farmers making small amounts of cheese not to use the milled-curd method (where the curd is formed into loaves and then cut to facilitate even salting, a process used to make many forms of cheddar cheese). This particular method was considered too complicated for the small-scale producer using home equipment. Instead, the USDA recommended the stirred-curd method, where the cheese is curdled and then the curds are stirred and pressed (a process used to make farmhouse cheddar as well as some soft cheeses such as mozzarella). This method was used by many generations of home cooks, and today it is also used by many commercial-scale producers.

historic cookbooks and other ferment sources

The written history of fermentation is incomplete, and some of it will unfortunately never be recovered. This is in part due to what humans have chosen to record (both in terms of what processes and foods were considered important and whose stories were considered important), as well as which records survive. We can look to a variety of resources for information about the history of our food, including cookbooks.

Historian Ken Albala has authored more than 25 books on food, and he told me that reading between the lines to find missing information is part of what interested him in making ferments: "It was working with cookbooks and making historic recipes and then realizing that some of the most important foods weren't covered in them. They were made by professionals other than chefs. So bakers, butchers, cheesemakers, winemakers, and I wanted to know what they were doing, too, since these were such a large part of the diet. So I had to start winging it, not using modern protocols or equipment but hints I could find in old texts, intuition, and guessing."

To learn about what kinds of ferments our ancestors made, we can turn to many different written sources, from receipts for grain to handwritten feast menus. One of our richest sources of information, particularly as printing became more prolific and books cheaper to produce, is cookbooks. Manuscript cookbooks (simply a handwritten book of recipes rather than a published book with multiple copies) and recipe boxes have been around for a long time, but printed ones have been around for only 500 years or so. Cookbooks give us a small window through which to view the culinary landscape of time and place. As author Cynthia Bertelsen says, "Cookbooks mirror the political and social climates surrounding their authors, in addition to matters of food and cookery and health."

This small window into the past, however, is hardly the whole picture—particularly when it comes to fermentation. It's important to consider which people in any particular culture would have had the time and enough education to enable them to write cookbooks, and how that informs the traditions we have. Many fermentation recipes, for example, have been passed on orally and so do not appear in cookbooks from the era in which they were common.

Commentary about food (such as Jean Anthelme Brillat-Savarin's classic *The Physiology of Taste*, first published in France in 1825) complements didactic manuals, providing context and food for thought. These help us further understand the dialogue around cooking and eating, including around ferments; for example, Brillat-Savarin's opinions on wine and digestion (see the sidebar on page 206) are quite illustrative.

Western recipes written before the end of the nineteenth century are different from recipes written today. Those older recipes were narrative paragraphs of information; the ingredients and instructions were not broken up into discrete sections. Recipe formats changed in 1896 with Fannie Farmer's publication of *The Boston Cooking-School Cook Book*. This book was used to teach cooking in a more classroom-style, standardized way, and it radically transformed how we use and present recipes.

For example, a sauerkraut recipe from a couple hundred years ago was simply a small block of text meant to guide the reader as though they were working alongside the cook in the kitchen. Measurements and instructions were not precise. Current-day precision can help new fermenters find their footing, but our modern recipe style lacks something, too: a sense of play and of familiarity with our food. We have less courage to change a recipe or perhaps even toss it out entirely. I have included a combination of both recipe styles, so that you can have the benefits of each.

A major byproduct of cheesemaking is whey—it accounts for 85 to 90 percent of the original volume of milk. Whey has a ton of nutrients and can be used in many ways, from feeding it to livestock and using it to add nitrogen to garden soil to adding it to soup stocks and using it as a liquid for baking. Perhaps the most famous use of whey is in making ricotta, which is made by cooking down the whey to get the remaining solids from the milk.

Scandinavians make toasted whey cheeses called gjetost, brunost, mysost, and numerous other names depending where you get it, the depth of color, and the type of milk that was used. Like ricotta, these cheeses are made by cooking the whey, but unlike ricotta the whey is cooked down until most of the liquid is evaporated and the sugars in the milk begin to caramelize. This results in cheeses that range from a light caramel color to a deep chocolate brown, reminiscent of the range of colors and flavors you can get when making roux by cooking down butter and flour. We do not know where and when these Scandinavian cheeses were first developed, but one dairy producer claims that they were

whey cheese in the scandinavian kitchen

Whey cheese is a part of kveldsmat, a nighttime snack-meal that journalist Rebecca Dinerstein calls "an edible lullaby, usually consisting of a slice of bread with either brown cheese or wild-strawberry jam *and* brown cheese." And it is a part of skive: open-faced sandwiches, often with brown cheese, on dense multigrain bread. The experience is hard to replicate elsewhere. As Dinerstein notes, "When I later tried to recreate a *skive* in the States, it didn't work. Our bread tasted synthetic and floppy, our butter failed to spread, and our cheese was merely cheesy—it had no secret kick."

invented in 1863, after a Norwegian named Anne Hov was given toasted whey cheese and liked it so much that she made her own, adding cream for a richer texture, which is how many of them are made today. (And if this story is true, of course, it means toasted whey cheese was already around by that time.)

In Italy, cheese is so prized that even the scraps are preserved. For example, formadi frant (fragmented cheese) from the Carnia mountains is made by blending the last remaining bits from multiple blocks of cheese (some many months old and some only a few weeks) with milk, cream, salt, and pepper, then pressing the result and aging it. Formadi frant is typically aged in a glass jar, though there is a similar cheese aged in stone, called formai del cit, from the Val Tramontina.

Preserving Meat

Fermentation was part of a larger suite of methods our ancestors employed to preserve meat, including drying, smoking, and salt curing. The type of method used depended on the type of cut, the desired shelf life of the meat (a short-cured ham versus a piece of jerky, for instance), and the intended culinary use. Naem (fermented Thai pork sausage), discussed in Chapter 3 in terms of its flavor, is not solely an endeavor in flavor enhancement: Fermentation also helps the pork last longer in the hot and humid Thailand weather.

People have been fermenting meat for millennia. In the fifth century BCE, for example, Babylonians pickled fish (including salmon, catfish, and sturgeon) and poultry. For them, as was the case for many ancient peoples, one goal of meat preservation may have been not just to make meat last longer but also to extend their salt stores. Salt was precious, and fermentation offered extra oomph to dishes, so that less salt was needed to make them taste good.

Changes in agricultural technologies had a big impact on what and how meat was preserved. Food systems and agriculture in Great Britain are well documented and well studied, and this gives us the opportunity to see how technological change impacts preservation. Up through the eighteenth century, seasonality governed the diet of people in Great Britain. Colin Spencer says, "From November to April there was no pasture, and the little hay that could be cut had to be saved for the draft animals, the warhorses, and the breeding stock. Thus, most of the animals were slaughtered before the winter began." If the British people wanted that meat to last through winter and spring, they would have to come up with ways to preserve it. And they certainly did, employing curing, drying, and smoking, among other methods. Even the offal was preserved, pickled in spiced ale to make "umble pie" for Christmas.

Later developments during the eighteenth century, such as selective livestock breeding and planting higher-yield crops, meant that farmers no longer had to slaughter animals at the beginning of winter. But those developments also resulted in the British Enclosure Acts, which removed public access to common lands, cutting off many rural people from their livelihoods. The combination of loss of livelihood with changes in food availability impacted Britons' dietary habits dramatically. Many moved to cities to find work, and in some cases whole villages became ghost towns. As a result, many of the preservation techniques that had been critical before fell out of use, in part because people were buying their food from others instead of raising it themselves, and they no longer had to process and preserve a whole animal's worth of meat. As Colin Spencer reflects, "Within a generation, cooking skills and traditional recipes were lost forever, as the creative interrelationship between soil and table (the source of all good cuisine) had been severed."

FISH FERMENTATION

SURSTRÖMMING has a long history in Sweden. According to legend, surströmming, or fermented herring, was the accidental discovery of Swedes trying to conserve salt. They had the same motivation as the people who first made garum (the fish sauce used in ancient Greece and Rome), soy sauce, or fish sauces in East and Southeast Asia—to add a big dose of umami to their food while using less salt. In the seventeenth century, surströmming was part of army rations during the Thirty Years War, and even today its production is still regulated by a royal ordinance dating back to the Middle Ages. According to this ordinance, herring used for surström-ming must be caught in April and May, just before the fish spawn. The head and entrails are removed but the roe is kept intact. The fish are then put in barrels of lightly salted brine; each barrel holds about 200 pounds of fish. They ferment for 10 to 12 weeks in cool temperatures (54–64°F/12–18°C), and finally, on the third Thursday in August, producers are allowed to sell them. These days, the fermented herring are often removed from the barrels and canned in July, but in the old days they'd be kept in their brine and sold straight from the barrel.

FISH SAUCE appears to have originated in China and then spread throughout the ancient world, like many other salt-based sauces and pastes. Sprinkling salt directly on food was, historically, a rarity. According to Mark Kurlansky in *Salt: A World History*, "Fish fermented in salt was one of the most popular salt condiments in ancient China. It was called *jiang*. But in China soybeans were added to ferment with the fish, and in time the fish was dropped altogether from the recipe and jiang became *jiangyou*, or, as it is called in the West, soy sauce."

GARUM or liquamen was made in ancient Greece and Rome by salt-ing whole fish in a vessel, sometimes alongside additional fish guts. Sometimes the fish were of a single species, and other times they were a mix. The salty mixture was then set in the sun to ferment, and some recipes suggested frequently shaking it, too. The heat from the sun (as well as the enzymes in the intestines) broke down the fish, and once a good bit of liquid had seeped out, the entire thing was strained through a basket into a vessel below. The solids left behind were often pressed again to make a cloudy sauce that was cheaper than the more desirable clear garum, and the solids themselves were also used as a seasoning.

WHOLE ANIMAL PRESERVATION

Preserving animals whole, as well as the use of organ meat and scraps in fermentation, offers creative ways to get the most out of our meat without anything going to waste. We see examples around the world of different ways animals and scraps and organ meat make their way into our ferments.

KIVIAK is a traditional dish of the Inuit people and an incredible example of culinary ingenuity. It's made by stuffing whole auks (a type of seabird) into a gutted seal carcass, burying the carcass, and allowing it to ferment until the birds are almost liquid. Though the origins of the dish aren't clearly documented, given the long winters and lean resources in the Arctic, it seems highly likely that kiviak was created out of the necessity to preserve food for an extended period.

SALAMI was traditionally made in Italy with ground pork, cubed fat, seasonings, and salt. It (along with other cured, ground meats) sometimes included organ meat or scraps, in addition to being stuffed inside intestinal casings. The name *salami* comes from the Italian *salare*, "to salt." Salami

the nomenclature of preserved meats

As we've seen with the changes to British agriculture and diet, the history of fermentation exists in a larger changing context, and that is reflected in our descriptions of our food. The terms we use to describe our fermented meats are often time-based.

Writer and certified Master Food Preserver Christina Ward notes, "Often, a food is called by a different name based on the length of fermentation. Scandinavian gravlax only becomes that after the prepared salmon cures for the prescribed time. A shorter cure time, and it is surlaks. And of course, gravlax is similar to lox. In fact, many revered local culinary delicacies are often related to other items from different areas. Slight variations in spice and technique are often the only difference."

And just as the process influences language, the language influences the process as well. As Ward says: "Fluid word and similar cured meats are fermented with nitrates, which inhibit harmful microbial growth. Humans have historically used celery powder, which naturally contains nitrates, in cured meats, and even today celery powder is used in organic cured meats, which forbid the use of industrially produced nitrates. Saltpeter, traditionally made by scraping potassium nitrate crystals from manure, appears in recipes going back to the Middle Ages—including a recipe for preserving a whole deer by covering it with saltpeter and burying it. Ken Albala theorizes that nitrates may possibly have been already present in the locally mined salts ancient peoples were using to preserve meats, allowing them to cure the meat in salt without having to add any other nitrates.

meanings also influence our preservation methods. Often, the word 'cure' is used interchangeably with the word 'ferment,' especially when talking about meat and dairy products." What we end up with is a spoken and written language about our food that intersects with the olfactory language of experiencing that food. Writer and sustainable food expert Meredith Leigh offers an example in describing the experience of eating bacon (admittedly not a fermented food, but a salt-cured one): "When we experience really good bacon . . . our eyes see beautiful striations of velvet-white fat and deep red lean; our mouths water as we imagine the taste; our ears hear the crack of fat in the pan; and our noses twitch at the smell of smoke and salt and pork. What we taste is history, as well as hickory, the inevitable morning mist on a farm, the memory of fire. What we taste, if it is really good, will be recorded for later, and not just filed into our intestines . . . ."

Lacto-Fermented Fruits and Vegetables

For as long as we've been fermenting vegetables, we've had salt to do it with. Salt, as we discussed in Chapter 2 (see page 39), enables lacto-fermentation. We don't know how the first lacto-fermented vegetables came about, but as with other ferments, they were either an accident or a preservation experiment (I would personally guess the latter). Perhaps an enterprising Neolithic human packed some veggies in seawater and,

preservation in the southern appalachians

The southern Appalachians are home to many rich and varied food preservation traditions from a cross-section of cultures, including indigenous communities, enslaved Africans, and European settlers. However, the area has until recently largely been overlooked and understudied. As a result, eaters outside the region are only beginning to learn about the considerable variations in cuisine and culture in this mountainous region.

While some of these ferments (for example, sauerkraut) originated in Europe, Appalachian ferments are not simply European ferments mapped to a new space. An entire rich community lived in the area prior to Europeans ever being there. While many indigenous communities in the Southeast preferred smoking and drying to fermentation, the Eastern Band of Cherokee made ferments from corn, a staple crop in the region. These included sour corn as well as a sour corn drink called sofkey.

Current research shows only a handful of examples of fermentation practices in indigenous communities in the United States, but it seems extremely likely that there are others not documented observing that they soured but didn't rot, started to refine the process. This is one of the frustrations and beauties of looking at the historical record around food: It is incomplete, allowing for imagination and conjecture.

Salt, a critical component in the lacto-fermentation of fresh produce, naturally occurs in many places around the globe. It's in the sea, of course, but it is also in landlocked saltwater lakes, such as Lac Rose in Senegal, and in underground deposits. Humans have found ways to collect it since prehistoric times, from gathering dried deposits on seashores to digging it out of the earth. With salt and time, they could use lacto-fermentation to preserve all sorts of fruits and vegetables.

in studies. The subsequent centuries of genocide and cultural disruption led to the loss of traditional knowledge on many fronts, including knowledge about food production and foraging, as well as the loss of seed varieties and the land itself. Today, numerous people and organizations are working to reclaim and share this knowledge and indigenous heritage, including Mariah Gladstone of Indigikitchen, chef Brian Yazzie, and Sean Sherman of The Sioux Chef and the North American Traditional Indigenous Food Systems (NATIFS) organization.

Enslaved Africans also had an enormous impact on the food of the southern Appalachians, and of the South as a whole, bringing certain crops (such as okra and watermelon) and production methods to the New World with them. While pickled okra and watermelon rind are now common outside African American communities, their similarity to West African dishes speaks to their origins on the African continent. If you are interested in learning more about African American foodways, I highly recommend Michael Twitty's work, as well as that of Leni Sorensen, Toni Tipton-Martin, Jessica B. Harris, and Adrian Miller.

Which fruits and vegetables were preserved depended, of course, on what was available. Until relatively recently, people were primarily reliant upon the foods that grew in their immediate vicinity. Over time, as cultures shared, borrowed, and stole plants, methods, and techniques from each other, some fruits and vegetables diversified, while others fell out of fashion. Let's look at some specific examples.

CHOW CHOW

Chow chow is a sour (or sometimes sweet and sour) relish often containing cabbage, green or red tomato, bell pepper, and/or mildly spicy chiles such as banana peppers. It can be fermented or quick-pickled, and its exact contents can vary with the seasons. In an interview with Wren Awry, West Virginia chef Mike Costello describes how chow chow speaks to preservation and place:

> If there's one dish that means the most to me as a cook from West Virginia, it might be chow chow. Sure, chow chow isn't found *only* in Appalachia, but it embodies so much of what we talk about when we discuss food from the mountains reflecting a place-based culture. I've heard from so many of my dinner guests that chow chow is strongly symbolic, representing hard times, of which they'd rather not be reminded. Yet when you open a jar of this fermented or vinegar-pickled relish, you're exposed to layers of saltiness, sweetness, a sharp tang with subtle bitter, sometimes smoky notes. Its unexpected layers of complexity bring out reactions of surprise, similar in a way to those I've witnessed when people hear unfamiliar stories about the mountains at the dinner table, when shameful narratives about desperation and poverty become proud stories of creativity, thrift and ingenuity.

FERMENTED BRASSICAS

Throughout the world, people have preserved brassicas (plants in the mustard and cabbage families) via fermentation for generations. Cabbage is lacto-fermented into various types of sauerkraut in a wide range of cultures, as we saw in Chapter 1 (page 40). Similarly, radishes have been pickled in East Asia for thousands of years, though it's hard to tell where this practice originated. Turnips, though indigenous to the area between the Baltic Sea and the Caucasus (and still found wild in eastern Europe and Siberia), spread across Europe, and we see evidence of them being pickled and fermented going back thousands of years. First-century Roman writer Columella gives a recipe for pickling turnips in mustard and vinegar, while the *Apicius*, a first-century collection of Roman culinary recipes, recommended mixing them with myrtle berries and preserving them in vinegar and honey. The fourteenth-century chronicle *The Four Seasons of the House of Cerruti* noted that turnips could be preserved for up to a year provided they were soaked in vinegar or brine.

GUNDRUK, a blend of brassica greens that are fermented and then dried, "occupies an eminent place in the Nepalese diet and is eaten with great relish" according to researcher Tika Karki. It is made by setting out hearty greens (typically leaves from radishes, cauliflower, cabbage, kale, and mustard, including the lesser-used outer leaves) in the sun, turning them frequently so different parts of the leaves are exposed to sunlight, until they wilt. The wilted leaves are then squeezed and massaged to make a juice, packed into a container, fermented, and then dried. Gundruk was traditionally made in earthenware jars, which were set in the sun during the day and by the fire at night so that the ferment could be kept warm enough to facilitate microbial processes. Unlike the vast majority of vegetable lacto-ferments, no salt is added to this ferment: It simply uses the liquid produced by the wilted leaves. A similar Nepalese ferment called sinki uses sliced radish root instead of the green tops.

CUCURBITS

The Cucurbitaceae plant family features heavily in global pickling and fermenting traditions. Cucurbits encompass a wide variety of plants, including melons, watermelons, cucumbers, gourds, pumpkins, and squash, and native varieties can be found from tropical and subtropical Africa to Southeast Asia and the Americas.

Some cucurbits, such as winter squash, can be stored for some time before going bad and lend themselves to being dried in strips, but others are watery and quick to spoil. Cucumbers in particular are infamous for their short shelf life, and as a result they have been the subject of many preservation methods, perhaps most famously the fermenting of a barrel of sour cucumber pickles.

The cucumber is believed to have originated in India and to have been cultivated for at least 3,000 years before spreading to Greece and Rome and later to China, Russia, England, and the Americas. Food studies researchers David Maynard and Donald N. Maynard note the wide variety of uses for cucumbers in the East: "They are generally eaten fresh or pickled and are particularly important in the diets of people living in Russia and East, South, and Southeast Asia, where they may also be served as a fresh or cooked vegetable. In India, the fruits are used in the preparation of chutney and curries." Watermelon, too, is quick to spoil and thus eaten relatively soon after harvest, and while the fruit is typically eaten fresh, the rinds are typically pickled (see the recipe on page 276).

It is believed that the fermented cucumber pickle emerged from the Baltic region and then spread throughout eastern Europe. As immigrants moved to the United States, these traditions evolved into the American versions of full sours (strong, sour fermented cucumber pickles) and half sours (fermented for less time than full sours and thus less sour and more crisp).

Preserving Grains

Once harvested, grains are relatively shelf-stable: Provided they are stored properly and are free from mold and pests, grains can keep for months. Fermenting grains into bread was (and is) one of our primary ways of turning these shelf-stable grains into nourishing food. Most breads are eaten fresh (or relatively so), but some, such as thin flatbreads and crackers, are prepared with minimal moisture so that they will keep for some time without becoming moldy (hardtack is an infamous example). What to do with stale bread is an age-old question, especially for people, such as our ancestors, who were dedicated to minimizing food waste and stretching resources, and one solution was often to work it into other ferments.

Fermenting grains preserves something else, too: cooking fuel. When fuel had to be gathered by hand and fires built and tended, people were mindful of how much of their limited fuel supplies could be devoted to a meal. Fermented grain porridges let the fermentation process, rather than the fuel, do the bulk of the cooking: The softened grains needed to be boiled for significantly less time.

GRAINS AROUND THE WORLD

J. M. J. de Wet's study on sorghum reminds us that "cereal domestication is a process, not an event." Domestication does not mean simply gathering seeds from a wild plant and sowing them in a field; it is a process of gathering seeds from plants with appropriate attributes, planting them, and continuing that pattern over many generations. Our domestication of cereal crops has resulted in grains that differ greatly from their wild ancestors—but feed us well.

RICE. The rice genus *Oryza* includes 20 wild species and 2 cultivated species scattered across all continents except Antarctica. The two cultivated species are commonly called African rice (*O. glaberrima*) and Asian rice (*O. sativa*), and the production method for both is similar, relying on standing water in the fields (sometimes called rice paddies) to promote cultivation. But the plants themselves are a bit different: *O. glaberrima* has wider leaves that help shade out weeds and is more disease- and pest-resistant. African rice is considerably harder to find in the West (even in African markets) than Asian rice varieties, which are commercially grown in 112 countries. There have been long-standing arguments about whether *O. sativa* originated in India or in China. Recent research suggests there was a common ancestor for all the subspecies, domesticated around 8,200 to 13,500 years ago. Fermented rice products include rice wine as well as rice vinegar and rice beer. Rice vinegar, in particular, was a shelf-stable product used to preserve other foods through pickling.

WHEAT AND BARLEY. These grains have been grown in what we now call the Fertile Crescent and along the Mediterranean coast of North

Africa since at least the fifth century BCE. Wheat was central to the diet in many cultures, including that of the ancient Egyptians, who preserved it by baking it into bread and brewing it into beer, along with barley and dates. Wheat was so prolific in this area that Egypt served as the imperial granary during the Roman period (30 BCE–395 CE).

Barley seems to have been used primarily for brewing, and this is not unique to ancient Egypt: In the Middle Ages in England, wheat was cultivated for what Colin Spencer calls the "fine white bread of the nobility," while barley was grown for brewing (and if you weren't rich, you were probably eating rye and "lived off . . . daily pottages, supplemented by curd cheese, eggs, and whey").

OATS. Oats thrive in cooler weather, and as a result almost all oat production takes place in the Northern Hemisphere. As cereal crops go, oats are a relative newcomer on the scene, having been domesticated only about 4,000 years ago. Like wheat and barley, oats were domesticated in the Middle East, and archaeological evidence shows that this grain was actually first a "weed" in wheat and barley fields before being recognized for its nutritional value and put into cultivation. Trade and the growth of the Roman Empire spread oats across Europe. They were heavily used for livestock feed and became a staple in some human diets, too, including in Scotland and Scandinavia. Scottish colonists brought oats with them to North America in the 1600s, and they remained a popular crop until the 1920s, when horsepower began to be replaced by machines and the crops that fed those animals were replaced by other crops that were considered more profitable. Oat fermentation has a fascinating history, as we'll see in the discussion of sowens on page 84; the hulls, often a by-product of oat processing, were fermented into an important food source.

SORGHUM. Along the African savanna, sorghum, along with millet and finger millet, was among the first grains to be domesticated. While sorghum is native to Africa, it is now also widely grown in India, the Americas, and China.

Bicolor sorghum is a major food source of the Chari-Nile–speaking peoples of the Sudan, Chad, Uganda, northeastern Nigeria, and Cameroon. It's a relatively new species developed sometime between 350 and 900 CE. Bicolor sorghum is a striking example of the archaeological record showing the cohabitation of human and plant and the subsequent human-directed evolution of said plant. Botanists Ann B. L. Stemler, Jack R. Harlan, and J. M. J. de Wet's research on sorghum found that the distribution of cultivated sorghum so closely mirrored that of Chari-Nile–speaking people that a causal relationship between the two seemed probable. They also noted that the sorghum had been selectively bred to "produce a large amount of grain under adverse conditions with a minimum amount of care." While sorghum is used in a variety of ways (particularly for porridges and sour beers) in many parts of the African continent, this is the only example I know of a sorghum variety directly reflecting the geographic footprint of a people. The grains are typically ground into a flour and the flour is then fermented into porridge. However, in Nigeria, bicolor sorghum is grown for the production of malt to use in the brewing industry.

grains, pulses, and nuts

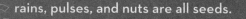 rains, pulses, and nuts are all seeds.

- **GRAINS** are small, dry seeds (sometimes with a hull/fruit layer, sometimes not). While the term *grains* typically refers to cereals, or the seeds of grasses (such as wheat, corn, and rice), it can also refer to the seeds of other plants such as amaranth and buckwheat.
- **PULSES** are the edible seeds of legumes (plants in the Fabaceae family), which include peas, lentils, and beans.
- **NUTS** are seeds encased in an inedible hard shell. They have been critical to human survival since prehistoric times, and they were among the first crops we cultivated.

BREAD

Making bread with yeast, whether wild (sourdough) or commercial yeast packets, is a form of preserving grains through fermentation. And the history of bread making is closely intertwined with our own.

Flatbreads—something akin to naan or crackers—were almost certainly the first breads that our ancestors made and ate, and they have remained

active dry yeast

The introduction of commercial yeast starters in the late 1800s changed the landscape of modern bread fermentation, as bakers were then able to bake loaves quickly and without having to maintain an active starter culture. Though it is much less flavorful than its wild yeast counterpart, active dry yeast is convenient, which has made it popular.

Commercial yeast was first produced in Europe. In 1871, the Austrian baron Max von Springer had the idea to extract yeast from brewing wort and sell it to bakers. The following year, the French yeast company Lesaffre opened its first yeast plant and began commercially producing the yeast (Lesaffre remains the largest yeast producer to this day).

In the United States, the first commercial yeast was Fleischmann's. It was introduced to the public at Philadelphia's Centennial Exposition in 1876 and later refined at the company's Peekskill, New York, research laboratory that opened in 1900. This early commercial yeast was initially sold in blocks and lost its viability after only a few days at room temperature. In the 1940s, new manufacturing methods produced dry yeast granules, like the packets we get today, which are shelf-stable for a longer period due to their lower water content. The 1980s saw the introduction of finer-grain dry yeast, which rose faster than its larger-grained predecessor.

with us for centuries. Injera, a spongy flatbread made from teff, is fermented and is similar in shape to a pancake or crêpe. Teff has been grown in the Ethiopian highlands for more than 2,000 years, and evidence of teff as a food source goes back to at least 3550 BCE, marked by its presence in Egyptian pyramids. Some researchers argue that injera itself has been around since 100 BCE.

In Ethiopian cuisine, Yohanis Gebreyesus, author of *Ethiopia: Recipes and Traditions from the Horn of Africa*, tells us, injera "holds another crucial dimension, one that conveys a positive human energy through a powerful saying 'enebla.' *Enebla*, in Amharic, translates to 'let us eat' and our staple food *injera* is made in a way that invites more than one hand to the meal. It is a moment of sharing, of caring and of showing respect for one another."

Injera batter is typically allowed to sour for several days before being used, whereas loaves of European-style sourdough bread are typically fermented for 24 to 48 hours. Breads made with modern commercial yeast are often ready for baking in less than a day, and some recipes call for just barely fermenting the grains. (At the turn of the twentieth century, for example, French chef Auguste Escoffier made jam-filled Viennese fritters that rose for only half an hour before being fried.) And breads, once baked, can be preserved in a variety of ways to keep them from being wasted—for example, as a starter for beet kvass (see the recipe on page 213), crushed and added to other foods such as tarhana (see the recipe on page 54), or brewed into beer.

FERMENTED OATS

Fermented oats have been eaten in porridges all across Europe for hundreds of years. In the British Isles, flummery, a fermented oatmeal, was eaten in the early modern period. (After that point, the meaning of *flummery* shifted to refer to a custard-based dessert, which was popular through the Victorian period.) In eastern Europe, fermented oats were once a large part of the diet. In the Caucasus region, Circassians ate bexhin (or baxhin), a cold fermented oat soup. Examples of sour oat porridges have also been found in Belarus, and one study suggests they may have existed in Hungary at one point.

While fermented oats (and oats in general) are eaten in many Celtic areas, including Wales, Ireland, and Brittany, their popularity there pales in comparison to the Scots' obsession with this grain. Oats have long been a critical part of Scottish culture, so central that they merit their own vocabulary within the country. Journalist Waverley Root explained: "Corn, which stands in English-speaking areas for the most-used grain in each, means oats in Scotland. The stick with which the batter for oatcakes is stirred is known as a spurtle and the utensil on which they cooked is not a griddle but a girdle. The bannock is an oatcake too large for convenient handling by a single eater, so it is broken into quarters known as farls. Brose is raw or toasted oatmeal over which some boiling liquid is poured. Oatmeal, naturally, goes into haggis."

Though not native to Scotland, the grain was introduced by the Romans, becoming one of the few nonnative crops that thrived in Scotland's cool, wet climate. As oats adapted to Scotland, so did Scots adapt to the oat, taking lessons from the harvest process to create a uniquely Scottish dish called sowens, which, while hard to find today, was at one point a staple.

THE SOWENS-MAKING PROCESS. Sowens (sometimes called sowans, sughan, or suans) is a traditional Scottish porridge made by soaking and fermenting oat kernels after they have been removed from the grains by threshing. It is a wonderful example of taking a byproduct that might normally be considered "waste" and creatively reshaping it into a nutritious food resource. Rather than throw away the kernels, millers would sift these so-called "sids" from the oats and reserve them. Because milling was an imperfect process, the kernels would have some of the oat kernels stuck to them, meaning that when they were fermented, the hungry microbes would have starches to consume.

Sowens were fermented in a container called a sowens-bowie or sowan-bowie, essentially a narrow wooden tub that looked like a small barrel, and would be left to sit for about a week or so until sour. The sowens-making process results in several different products:

- **THE KERNELS** are strained out of the fermentation and used as livestock feed (my chickens love them).

- **THE SOWENS,** a thick, sour paste left in the bottom of the fermenting vessel, can be consumed as a porridge or a drink or added to baking for scones. Like the fermented ogi and uji porridges in Chapter 1 (see pages 53 and 54), sowens is typically served with just a few simple toppings, if any, such as milk or currants.

- **THE SWATS** is a nourishing, sour liquid that separates from the sowens during fermentation. In some cases, the swats is fermented for longer than the sowens.

This is, of course, in addition to the oats themselves, which, once removed from their hulls, can be used in all the ways you normally would use oatmeal.

HISTORICAL REFERENCES TO SOWENS. The first known written reference to sowens in Scotland is found in George Ridpath's *An Answer to the Scotch Presbyterian Eloquence* from 1693, where it is described as a good food for both body and soul. Ridpath simply describes them as good for health without defining them or encouraging the reader to give them a try. This suggests they had been a part of the culture for some time beforehand—long enough for them to become part of common parlance.

Prior to the rise of industrial agriculture, tenant farmers were required to bring their processed sids and oats to a victual house (storehouse). However, some farmers would try to sneak some of the sids back for themselves. In December 1736, the records of the Barony of Kintore dictate that tenant farmers must sufficiently sift their sids, noting that "if any quantity of sids happen to be found among the ferms [farms] after they are brought to the victual house, the owners of the said ferms shall be ordained to forfeit double the weight of the said sids and meal." This shows us the value of sids, and by extension sowens and swats, to Scottish culinary culture.

Scottish folklorist and writer Scott Richardson-Read points out that sowens were a critical food for maintaining health even a century after they first appeared in Ridpath's writing; they were listed as one of the foods given to patients at the Dundee Royal Infirmary in 1798. The 1812 *The Healthful Cookery Book* also lists sowens (spelled *sowins* in this case) under "diet drinks for the sick," along with other porridges.

Sowens are said to be easy to preserve long term. William Leslie's *General View of the Agriculture of the Counties of Nairn and Moray* (1813) describes how sowens were often made in huge batches, then dried to make them shelf-stable and easier to ship:

> In this country sowins are prepared at short intervals of about a week. In Caithness more art is displayed, the whole stock for half a year or more being made up at once; and similar to starch, is preserved, instead of the bran, in the form of dry paste; in which state it is sent to families resident in Edinburgh.

Sowens can also be preserved for months (without being dried) simply by pouring off the swats and adding fresh water.

While the swats were, as far as I can tell, poured or gently scooped off the sowens and largely enjoyed as is (they make a lovely and nourishing sour beverage), sowens had several versatile applications. Depending on where you went in the country, sowens might be served in different ways. According to Richardson-Read, sowens porridge was called brown plate sowens in Caithness, and while "gain-'e gither" sowens refers to porridge, a lighter, thinner sowens made by adding water and butter was called "douchrea." The creamy sowens paste was also used to make scones.

Scottish folklorist and author F. Marian McNeill suggested the following method for serving them: "Use a gill (five fluid ounces) with twice as much water (2 gills or ten fluid ounces) per person (for Americans I think this is roughly half a cup to a gill) and boil it until it's like a thick cream (roughly ten minutes)."

"Drinking sowens" (fermented porridge that was warmed and sweetened with molasses) was a traditional winter holiday treat. In Aberdeen, Christmas Eve is also called Sowens Nicht (Sowens Night) in anticipation of it. In some places, the sweetened porridge was called Yule sowens, but whatever name you use, it was for many centuries inextricably linked to wintertime celebrations.

Sowens was consumed both on Christmas Eve and on Christmas morning. An 1832 issue of the *Scots Weekly Magazine* sets the scene in a Highlands household, which the night before had been party to games and revelry in celebration of the holidays, but this morning is a site of nervous anticipation and breakfast in bed:

> As soon as the brightening flow of the eastern sky warns the anxious housemaid of the approach of Christmas-day, she rises full of anxiety at the prospect of her morning labours. The meal, which was steeped in the *sowens-bowie* a fortnight ago, to make the *Prechdachdan sour*, or *sour scones*, is the first object of her attention. The gridiron is put on the fire, and the sour scones are soon followed by hard cakes, soft cakes, buttered cakes, brandered bannocks, and pannich perm. The baking being once over, the sowens pot succeeds the gridiron, full of new sowens, which are to be given to the family, agreeably to custom, this day in their beds. The sowens are boiled into the consistence [sic] of molasses, when the *Lagan-le-vrich*, or yeast bread, to distinguish it from boiled sowens, is ready. It is then poured into as many bickers as there are individuals to partake of it, and presently served to the whole, old and young. It would suit well the pen of a Burns, or the pencil of a Hogarth, to paint the scene which follows. The ambrosial food is dispatched in inspiring draughts by the family, who soon give evident proofs of the enlivening effects of the *Lagan-le-vrich*. As soon as each dispatches his bicker he jumps out of bed—the elder branches to examine the ominous signs of the day, and the younger to enter on its amusements.

If Yule sowens don't appeal to your taste, William Watson's *Glimpses o' Auld Lang Syne* (1903) offers another way to use them:

> It was then quite a common practice to go with a pailful of sowens, and with a white-washing brush "sklaich" the doors and windows of dwelling-houses after the inmates had retired to their beds. The houses selected for "sowening" in this way were usually those of the "near-b'gyaun" and unsociable folks, who never gave nor accepted of invitations for "Yule sowens."

The poet Robert Burns also links luxurious buttered sowens to an evening of merrymaking on Halloween:

> Till buttered so'ns wi' fragrant lunt,
> Set a' their gabs a-steerin';
> Syne, wi' a social glass o' strunt,
> They parted aff careerin'
> Fu' blythe that night.

But sowens weren't all fun and games. They would also be enlisted to help in the very serious task of seeing the future. On Halloween/Samhain (as well as sometimes Yule), objects might be hidden in sowens food (and various baked goods) and portions served out randomly. The object a person found in their portion was said to predict their future—for example, a coin for wealth or a ring for marriage.

* * *

By 1871, sowens scones were popular in the north of Scotland. Unfortunately, there was less and less mention of sowens as the twentieth century opened and rolled on, perhaps in part because industrial agriculture moved many away from relying on local farms and millers. Anecdotally, I have spoken with a few Scottish friends whose parents have a vague memory of having sowens as children in the 1950s and 1960s, though no one I know personally, at least, grew up with them. Both sowens and swats are absolutely wonderful, though, and I hope to see them become popular once again.

CORN

Originally from Central America (its closest wild relatives grow in Mexico and Guatemala), corn has been an important cereal crop in the Americas for millennia. After European colonization of the New World in the sixteenth and seventeenth centuries, corn was introduced to Europe, Asia, and Africa, where it also became an important crop. By the end of the seventeenth century, corn was a regular part of enslaved Africans' rations in the United

States. It was also given to South African mine laborers under the British, and shortages in maize supplies were one of the reasons behind the miners' uprisings against perilous working conditions and limited food.

As we've already mentioned (see page 74), the Cherokee used lacto-fermentation to make a dish called sour corn. On the other side of the world, after corn was introduced to New Zealand (said to have happened in 1772), the Māori incorporated the grain into their diet, including through fermentation. They prepared a fermented corn dish called kaanga kopuwai (or kaanga pirau or kaanga wai), also known as "rotten corn," by soaking unhusked corn in water (usually in a basket set in a stream) for about 3 months and then preparing the soft kernels as porridge.

Preserving Pulses and Nuts

Like grains, pulses are relatively shelf-stable once dry. The fermentation process softens them, so fermented pulses take less time to cook and are more flavorful and nutritious. Easy and inexpensive to grow, store, buy, and prepare, pulses have formed the backbone of the diet of the working classes and enslaved people worldwide for thousands of years. They're often eaten with a grain (for example, the various forms of rice and beans), and they provide the basic building blocks of nutrition.

Turkish tarhana (see the recipe on page 54) is one example of fermented pulses forming the backbone of a food staple. It combines grains, dairy, veggies, and pulses to create a balanced nutritional source for ready-made meals that can be enjoyed even when ingredients are out of season and fuel is in short supply. Southern Indian idli and dosa are other good examples of the ways humans have combined pulses and grains for nutritional oomph. Both are made from a batter of ground rice and split peas, which is then fermented before being steamed in molds to make spongy idli or fried to make a crispy pancake (dosa). The rice and peas are traditionally ground using a stone grinder, called a quern, whose use dates back 10,000 years. (And you can still buy a quern, whether manual or electric, today.)

Making tempeh by fermenting soybeans with rhizopus molds is a process unique to Indonesia. Originating in Java, the ferment became popular throughout Indonesia in the twentieth century as a way to extend the shelf life of and add flavor to soybeans.

Elsewhere, nuts were fermented, then brewed into drinks or ground into flour. *Pawcohiccora* (sometimes spelled *powcohicora*) is an Algonquin word that refers to hickory trees (it's where we get the English word for hickory). It also refers to a beverage and a soup made from hickory nuts and/or a blend of native North American tree nuts that the Algonquin people have been making since precolonial times. They would extract the nutmeat from the shells, then boil it down and squeeze it to make a milky beverage, which could then be fermented. The pulp could be used for numerous purposes, including in baked goods or soups.

Fermented acorns were a common food in precolonial Turtle Island (modern-day North America). The indigenous people would bury the acorns in mud or soak them in water for months, then roast them. Ken Albala says, "I like to think that people learned this trick from birds and squirrels—those they forgot about naturally sprouted and grew into trees."

Alcohol as Preservative

Alcohol (all of which comes from fermentation) has a long history as a preservative. Food was stored in alcohol (called an infusion), and food scraps and large harvests alike were used to make alcohol.

Alcohol is a wonderful preservative for fruits and herbs. For example, an abundance of fresh herbs might be packed into a jar, covered with alcohol, and left to steep, imbuing the alcohol with their flavors. Fruit could be treated in the same way, not only flavoring the alcohol but also yielding boozy preserved fruit to consume later.

Of course, foods can be preserved not only by putting them in alcohol but by using them to make alcohol in the first place. When an overabundance of fruit turns ripe all at once, alcohol production is a good way to preserve large quantities of it. Overripe fruits and fruit scraps that would otherwise be wasted can also be turned into alcohol.

FRUIT WINES. In southwestern Nigeria, wines are made from overripe bananas and plantains. Throughout Europe and North America, country wines are made from all manner of fruits—from plums to strawberries to peaches—depending on what is in season and needs to be put up at a given moment. Fruits in particular are easy to turn into alcohol (as we saw in Chapter 1, they do it on their own if you let them!) because they don't require malting (the process of germinating barley in water) or the addition of sugar, which is helpful when time or resources are limited. Fruit wines were a boon during harvest season, when fruit positively drips from the trees and must be put up with some haste lest it rot on the ground. And because alcohol production does not rely on the whole fruits, blemished fruits or those that needed to have bruised bits cut out were still perfect candidates.

APPLE CIDER. This is an excellent example of a ferment that could be made quickly and in bulk when the short harvest season is afoot. Apple

cider starter culture

If you make wild cider, play around with different apple varieties, as different varieties yield big differences in the type and depth of flavor (or lack thereof) in the finished cider. Cider maker David Buchanan notes that "typical dessert apples like McIntosh and Cortland don't make very good cider. They're fine for fresh juice, but after fermenting not much taste and depth remain."

You can experiment with your yeasts, too. Even prior to the development of modern commercial yeast, our ancestors kept starter cultures going to get flavor profiles they liked, as well as to jump-start the fermentation process with beneficial microbes before any other microbes had a chance to open up shop. Wild yeasts are found everywhere—from flowers to fruits to vegetables—so there is plenty of room to get creative.

cider is simply the unfiltered juice of pressed apples that, when fermented, becomes a tart/sweet alcoholic beverage that highlights the flavors of the apples. In the most basic form of cider making, wild yeasts in the air and on the apples do the work of fermentation for us. Wild ciders are less consistent than those made with commercial yeasts, but they are no less delicious.

TEPACHE. This is a delicious Mexican beverage brewed from the skins and cores of pineapples. It is a great example of using every last bit of food, including the scraps. Its roots go back to pre-Columbian Mexico, encompassing several cultures dating back around 20,000 years and up until Spanish colonization in the 1500s. Traditionally, the pineapple skins and cores are fermented into a light, refreshing drink that, depending on how you make it, can be alcoholic or nonalcoholic. Because it relies on wild yeasts, the flavors can vary considerably between batches. Today it is also made with spices such as allspice and cinnamon.

APPLE BEER. A lesser-known fermented fruit beverage, apple beer is actually not really beer but more like a mock apple juice. To make it, the 1972 edition of *The Foxfire Book* tells us, "peel your apples and dry the peelings in the sun or by the stove. Put them in a crock and add enough boiling water to cover. Cover the crock and let it sit for one to two days, until all the flavor comes out of the peelings. You may add some sugar if you want." Because the juice is sitting out for a bit, it will begin to ferment. However, it won't be alcoholic (that takes a bit longer).

PRESERVING THE BYPRODUCTS OF PRESERVATION. In most cultures, the byproducts of alcohol production would be put to use as well. For example, the leftover grains from brewing beer could be fed to livestock or wildlife or baked into bread. In England, barm (the foam skimmed off vats of fermenting beer and wine) was used to leaven bread.

Preserving Alcohol

What kind of alcohol our ancestors kept around often depended on how long it could be preserved. Wine, being more shelf-stable than beer, was a sought-after commodity in many regions. In early medieval Ireland, for example, where wine production was not established, the "great families" (those with the most political control) traded salted meat, hides, hunting dogs, and enslaved people for wine. They kept wine for feasts and also to dispense at just the right moment for political advantage.

PRESERVING WINE. Wine will turn into vinegar if given the chance, so most modern store-bought wines contain sulfur, which stops the fermentation process and thus the conversion of wine to vinegar. For the home fermenter, the best way to keep alcohol from turning into vinegar is to keep it away from air.

Acetobacters, the bacteria that convert alcohol into vinegar, are aerobic, which means they need oxygen to do their thing. By minimizing the amount of air in contact with your booze, you reduce the likelihood of it going sour. Some practical ways to do this are to siphon it into bottles (rather than pour it through a funnel), fill your bottles up close to the top so there's very little air in them, and keep a tight lid on your bottles so air can't get in.

PRESERVING BEER. Beer is interesting from a preservation perspective because, unlike wine, the products from which it's made (grains) are relatively shelf-stable and do not need to be fermented to extend their shelf life. However, beer has at various points in time been made with stale bread or brewed with perishable foods such as fruits and herbs, and thus in both cases becomes part of a larger food preservation strategy. Like wine, most beers, save for those with very little alcohol, will turn into vinegar if exposed to air. In fact, malt vinegar has become a staple condiment in geographic areas where our ancestors drank more beer than wine; English fish-and-chips, for example, aren't the same without it.

In some cases, the infusing herbs themselves were preservatives. Food historian Ivan Day notes that in medieval and early modern Britain, brewers added several herbs to beer to help it keep longer:

> Ground ivy, clary, mugwort, tansy, maudlin and costmary were all found to act as preservatives. Iris roots hung in ale were said to prevent it turning sour. The success of some very old methods of preservation depended on a certain amount of divine intervention, since it was thought witches and evil spirits were capable of

spoiling ale. One Anglo-Saxon recipe advises: "If the ale be spoilt, take lupins, lay them on the four quarters of the dwelling, and over the door, and under the threshold, and under the ale vat, put the herb into the ale with holy water."

DISTILLATION. Distillation is the act of purifying a fermented liquid through heating and cooling; it is a process that is historically interconnected with alchemical work. Distillation is used to make higher-proof spirits as well as to make essential oils and hydrosols. In the case of alcohol, the alcohol evaporates before the water, allowing you to separate it from water through heating followed by cooling and condensation. The resulting high alcohol content of the distillation inhibits microbes, making it shelf-stable.

The Sumerians are the first people known to have experimented with essential oil and hydrosol distillation, dating back to around 3500 BCE, and there is evidence of distillation in China from around 2000 BCE as well. Distillation flourished in Alexandria during the time of the Roman Empire, and the devices that were used were often kept secret, known only to priests and temple servants. Alcohol distillation came later to the game and was embraced as a part of medieval medical and alchemical practices. There is evidence of crude spirits being distilled in China around 800 BCE, and later on in ancient Greece. In the eighth century CE, Abu Musa Jabir ibn Hayyan designed the alembic pot still, which was more effective at distilling alcohol than earlier stills. For the next handful of centuries, distillation was considered a strictly scientific endeavor: Records, including those from a twelfth-century Italian medical school and Hieronymus Brunschwig's *The Virtuous Art of Distilling*, published in 1500, all describe its use in terms of scientific and ritual purposes. It wasn't until a century later, with the 1618 publication of a travelogue titled *The Penniless Pilgrimage*, that distilled spirits make an appearance as a recreational beverage (they were called aqua vitae, an early euphemism for distilled drinks).

Throughout history, distillation technologies have allowed us to make potent alcohol, medicine, mediums for fruit storage, and more from the plants we wish to preserve. Sometimes those uses overlapped, and some of the botanical spirits we drink today (such as gin) started their lives as medicinal infusions. In the eighteenth century, "brandy fruits" were, as the name suggests, fruits packed in brandy and served at the end of a meal. German rumtopf was simply fruits preserved in a crock of sugar and rum, served alongside dessert. Fruits could also be juiced and added to alcohol for a ready-to-go tipple, such as cherry bounce, which was popular in the eighteenth century.

ALCOHOL AND PRESERVATION IN THE TWENTY-FIRST CENTURY

In the twenty-first century, we can draw on historic lessons when we make our alcohol. It isn't just for fun: When done right, alcohol is part of a sustainable food system. Food and drink writer Alicia Kennedy reminds us, "All alcohol is an agricultural product, and it should be regarded as such. It's easy to forget this, because that's what the major brands would like you to do, and also because alcohol is about release, thoughtlessness, a party. Alcohol consumption is also moralized, stigmatized, nothing to be taken seriously lest you look like some sort of deviant. But it's also an essential component of a functioning food system."

Liquor was first developed as an agricultural byproduct. Distillation offered a way to use up excess grain, creating a product that was portable, intoxicating, and delicious.

While many spirit brands are opaque about their sourcing, processing, and labor, there is an increasing interest in, and presence of, craft brands that push toward transparency in labeling regarding ingredient sourcing, labor, and additives. As Kennedy says, "Basic information would go a long way in terms of educating drinkers, reminding them that despite being called *spirits*, they are not created from thin air."

If we view alcohol in its historic context, we can better appreciate and enjoy the role it plays in our world. Ken Albala and Rosanna Nafziger Henderson encourage us to step away from some of the stigma that Kennedy described:

Social lubricant, a means of winding down after a long day at work, or the perfect accompaniment to a meal, alcohol is inextricably entwined with civilized life. Scientists have also discovered that it not only does not kill brain cells but in a certain sense clears out the stuffed mental filing cabinets crammed with minutiae, letting us focus on the important things in life. Most cultures have used alcohol in celebratory rituals because it brings us closer to divinity, helping us loosen those tight coils that bind us daily to rush and riot, effacing a sense of self and ultimately uniting us with the gods. What better way to honor the deities than letting natural processes transform simple fruits into a substance that is truly magical?

Vinegar

The word *vinegar* comes from the French *vin aigre*, "sour wine." As the name implies, it is simply alcohol (wine, cider, beer, or mead) that has been left to sit out; the ethanol in the alcohol is metabolized by acetic acid bacteria, producing acetic acid, which gives vinegar its sour flavor. There are records of vinegar production going back to Babylon in 5000 BCE. The Babylonians of this period already had experience making wine, and vinegar may have been a happy accident: Someone left a batch of wine to brew a bit too long, and voilà! A new food appeared.

Vinegar is a boon to food preservation. You can make vinegars out of food scraps, and you can make them from those less-than-drinkable alcohols that might ultimately taste better in a salad dressing than in a cocktail glass (I make vinegar from the trimmed-off tops of jalapeños and strawberries regularly, though truth be told it tastes great in both places). In addition, you can use vinegar to preserve other foods.

Vinegar production starts with an alcohol of between 4 and 15 percent alcohol by volume (ABV); an ABV higher than 15 percent and your acetobacter won't be able to do their work, which is why distilled spirits do not turn into vinegar even when left out for years. Some people add a vinegar mother (a gelatinous mass of acetic acid bacteria) to the alcohol, but it's not necessary—a fermenting alcohol will make a mother on its own. As the alcohol sits, the acetic acid bacteria do their work, creating a delightfully tart and sour vinegar.

Vinegar is a powerhouse for using up food waste and has been used as such for thousands of years. You can make vinegar from leftover alcohol, as well as juices and other sweet liquids. Scraps, such as those strawberry and jalapeño tops, can be added to sugary liquid and fermented to make a flavorful vinegar. And even the waste left over from making alcohol (for example, pomace, the pulp left after apples are pressed for cider) can be used for vinegar making. In fact, records show that in the sixth century CE, Chinese brewers repurposed wine lees or "sour or damaged" wines that were otherwise unusable by fermenting them as vinegars.

QUICK PICKLES

Most quick pickles are made by pouring a brine of vinegar, water, and salt over the fruit, vegetable, or other substrate being pickled. The brine is instantly acidic—there's no need to wait around for lactic acid bacteria to acidify the brine over the course of the fermentation process.

Examples of quick pickles abound across global history. Records show that they were made in China during the Tang dynasty (618–907 CE); there, the brine was sometimes flavored with acidic kumquat leaves and was used to preserve duck eggs as well as an entire host of vegetables and meats. Indian food historian and food scientist K. T. Achaya points out that in 1594, one text describes at least 50 kinds of pickles, including raw mango, citrus, onion, chile, wild boar, prawn, and fish.

The watermelon rind pickles on page 276 are a great example of what I call a hybrid quick pickle, which are pickles made by soaking or fermenting a food before pickling it in a vinegar-based brine. This hybrid method is a great way to ferment tough food scraps (such as watermelon rind) that otherwise might not be the most enjoyable to eat. Watermelon rind pickles are common in the American South (though perhaps not as common as they once were), and like many foods in this chapter, they were developed as a way to get every usable bit out of every piece of food.

Quick pickling also allows you to use up unripe produce—perhaps produce that has to be brought in before a frost or before pests eat it (or just because you have so much). Green tomatoes, a staple in the South, are often pickled or used in making chow chow, for example. Similarly, picalilli often includes green pepper, cabbage, celery, spices, vinegar, green tomato, and sugar, and like chow chow can be adapted to use whatever overabundant produce is on hand. Picalilli is a transplant from England, where it was created to mimic Southeast Asian chutneys and pickles. Unlike the American Southern version, the English recipes I've encountered have been mustard- and turmeric-heavy.

Quick pickles are also a way to use up surprise vinegars made, for example, by leaving cider out too long. They turn what could be called a "mistake" into something delicious.

The kinds of pickles we see at particular locations and times depend, of course, on the types of foods that were grown or imported there. In colonial-era North America, for example, apples were prevalent, resulting not only in lots of cider for drinking but also in a bounty of cider vinegar for preserving food. According to writer and historian Erika Janik, "Cider vinegar proved essential to food preservation, used to pickle fruits and vegetables. So plentiful was cider that barrels of it became its own barter currency, traded for everything from clothes to livestock to a child's education. An account book from New York lists 'one half-barrel of cider for Mary's schooling.'"

Preservation Technologies

Modern-day fermenters have access to a variety of technological innovations—from specialty fermentation chambers to measurement instruments—to help them more easily achieve specific, consistent results. There is considerable magic in ferments that *aren't* consistent across batches, too. These ferments take on the character of the moment in which they're created, and in the hours thereafter as they develop. In the Appendix (see page 318), I share with you the go-to tools that I use.

One thing I love about studying the history of food is seeing the ways our ancestors employed the tools around them. For fermentation, we see people worldwide using something as seemingly simple as a crock or hollowed-out log or as complex as specialty barrels or temperature-stable underground spaces, such as root cellars or caves.

In some cases, these technologies are still very much a part of our lives. Fermentation crocks, for example, are easy to come by and relatively affordable. In other cases, the technology has become obsolete—fallen out of use as a particular food has fallen from popularity or as people's living situations have shifted, perhaps leaving them with less workable space to keep large vessels. The wooden sowens-bowie, for example, that was a part of many rural Scottish households for centuries is now an uncommon sight, in part due to changes in oat processing that reduced the availability of starch-covered hulls for making sowens.

CONTROLLING TEMPERATURE

Temperature and time are the two major factors that we can manipulate to impact a ferment's outcome: A higher temperature means that fermentation will happen more quickly, and a longer time means that more fermentative action will take place. However, raise the temperature too much (or let it fluctuate) and your ferment might fail. To address the issue of temperature control, people have harnessed various techniques, including the material used for making the fermenting vessel.

In ancient Egypt, for example, we know that the clay vessels used to ferment beer were single-glazed, which means that they were watertight but still able to wick heat. Around the world, people have buried fermenting foods in the ground to keep them cool or kept them in caves or root cellars to regulate temperature and protect them from the elements. The Japanese barrels used for shoyu, sake, miso, and a range of other ferments, called kioke, are made of wood, which maintains a steady temperature and humidity while also housing beneficial microbes from previous batches that help start a new ferment. The trays used for fermenting koji, called kojiban, are made from wooden slats to help regulate temperature. They are also shaped in such a way that the rice can be spread out flat and run through with furrows to increase the surface area and keep it from overheating.

WEIGHTS

In order to make an *anaeorobic* ferment (one that doesn't require oxygen) in brine, it is important to keep whatever you're fermenting fully submerged to prevent the growth of mold and other unwanted critters such as kahm yeast (which is harmless but throws off the flavor). To do this, you can use a weight or other covering, and people have employed a wide range of materials over the years. Some examples include a layer of cabbage leaves over the top, perhaps with another weight on top; smooth river stones, boiled to clean and sterilize them; specially sized weights to fit inside crocks; and a plate or bowl pressed on top of the ferment. Japanese kioke barrels have round wooden covers set inside the barrels. In some cases of miso production, the covers are piled high with stones to evenly compress the miso as it ages.

USING HOG BLADDERS AS LIDS

Through the ages, people have used all kinds of lids and seals to close their fermentation vessel, everything from a square of fabric stretched across a crock and tied with twine to a custom-size crockery or wooden lid. One fun, but now uncommon, sealing tool is a hog's bladder. In western Europe and the colonial United States, it would be stretched across the top of a pot or crock and tied, so it would be taut like a drum. In this case, the act of preservation is twofold: People would make use of a scrap part of an animal (thus preserving resources) to help preserve other food.

A bladder serves a similar function as a modern screw-top lid: It keeps out some of the air (and bugs and dust) so anaerobic ferments can do their thing. It's important to note that a bladder and a lid do not keep out all the air, like an airlock does, so you can still get kahm yeast and the like on your ferment's surface if you don't weight it down. In the course of writing this book, I ran a series of experiments using different types of hog bladders to cover my sauerkraut, pickled carrots, and mead. I was curious about the flavor and microbes they would impart, as well as the success rate of using hog bladders as a lid.

EXPERIMENT 1 was with imitation hog's bladder, which you can purchase online. Synthetic bladders are essentially sheets of thick collagen that you hydrate in a bowl of warm water and then stretch across the mouth of the fermentation vessel. Stretching a "bladder" is much easier to do in theory than in practice without a second set of hands, and I resorted to using about a dozen rubber bands to hold it in place while I secured it with the more aesthetically pleasing butcher's twine. One issue with the synthetic bladders is that you don't get the added "microbial funk" that you would get with real bladders. Ken Albala pointed out to me that, due to their lack of microbial oomph, synthetic bladders might be functionally akin to using plastic wrap.

FOR EXPERIMENT 2, I tracked down fresh hog's bladders (you may be able to get them from local hog farmers or online from Craft Butchers' Pantry) and got to work. Compared to the synthetic ones, the fresh bladders were an absolute joy to work with. I rinsed the salt off them and they easily slid onto my fermentation vessels without hassle. I was able to press the fresh bladders along the edges of the jars and they stayed in place, drying tight like a drum—no string required. They did, however, make my hands smell like hog bladders, much to the delight and confusion of my cats.

EXPERIMENT 3 was with dried hog bladders, used in the same way you would use the imitation bladders: by rehydrating them and stretching them over the top of the vessels. This yielded results in between the fresh and synthetic bladders. The ferments had a bit of the flavor from the dried bladders, but the bladders were as difficult to wrangle onto the vessels as the synthetic bladders had been.

The sauerkraut I made for the experiments was just a basic salt-and-cabbage affair, kept simple to allow me to compare the flavor across the different bladder "lids." As I suspected, the synthetic bladders added no flavor at all, the dried bladders added a bit of flavor (mostly just to the top half of the ferment), and the fresh bladders added a lot of flavor—the whole jar of kraut tasted strongly of hog bladder, which was memorable (and pungent). The kraut covered with the fresh bladders seemed to ferment a bit more quickly, too, which isn't terribly surprising given how many extra critters those bladders probably brought to the party.

I made two containers of carrots for each of the bladders: one container that I fermented for a week (in each, they retained their crunch pretty well) and one container that I fermented for a month. Interestingly enough, the carrots didn't absorb the characteristic funk of the fresh hog bladders to the extent that the kraut did, perhaps because the carrots had less surface area than the shredded cabbage did. Because I purposefully didn't weight these carrots in order to see how much air the bladders would let in, the monthlong ferment got squishy and developed some mold on top in all three cases, indicating to me that the lids were airtight (like a jar lid, almost), but too porous to serve as an actual airlock.

To confirm the porous nature of the bladders, I used them to cover narrow-necked bottles of mead. I made two identical meads for each kind of bladder: one I carbonated in a bottle with a screw-top lid, and the other I tried to carbonate in an identical bottle sealed with a bladder. None of the bladders were able to keep enough CO_2 in my ferment to carbonate it, though the mead sealed with the dried bladder did get a tiny bit fizzy. As an aside, drinking mead that has been aged under a hog's bladder is a . . . singular flavor experience.

What did these experiments teach me about how people fermented historically? First, they showed me that there is a place for both fresh bladders (easier to use) and dried bladders (less flavor), and I would suspect that given a choice, both may have been used to cover fermentation vessels based on the desired flavor outcome. It also confirmed for me that human ingenuity for harnessing what's in the environment is almost boundless. We see this with the bladders, but also with the various leaves, stumps, rocks, and other natural materials employed in fermentation practices.

While many peoples used these natural materials because they were available and they worked, they also had another effect: By creatively using what was around them, our ancestors were able to connect more deeply with their environment and with the plants and animals that fed them.

MAKING MEANING IN OUR OWN KITCHENS

Our ancestors used the materials around them to make their ferments, shaping the clay in the ground into pots and crocks, taking the wood from the trees to make their barrels, and hauling the water from the well or creek to make their brines. In the process, they added meaning to their worlds by literally shaping into existence the tools they needed to create foods that would keep them fed far into the future.

You can do this, too. Using objects from your environment in your preservation endeavors is a fun and rewarding practice, and it's a great way to connect with your place. Wildcrafting is the practice of harvesting and working with wild, rather than cultivated, plants. I enjoy using environmental materials found around me in tandem with my wildcrafting practice to connect to the place I am and appreciate all the land has to offer.

For example, if I dig up particularly tempting flat, round stones, I'll boil them and use them as fermentation weights. If my neighbor's tree sheds bark into my yard, I see if I can fashion it into some sort of a lid or even a makeshift bowl or plate. After my grandma passed and left me her stunning array of shells, I use the largest ones as plates, ladles, and cups (they actually get more use than much of the china they sit next to in my china cabinet). There are plenty of folks out in the world doing this, too: Writer and creator Miss Wondersmith (as she has named herself) and wild food expert Mallory O'Donnell are some examples, but undoubtedly there are people in your own wildcrafting, herbalism, and culinary communities experimenting with this stuff as well. Spend a day wandering your environment and ask yourself what humans through most of history have: What can I use from the environment immediately around me to help me survive?

Jarod K. Anderson, who creates the scripted fiction podcast *The CryptoNaturalist*, has this to say about meaning:

> The world has clay.
> People make pottery.
> The world has happenstance.
> People make meaning.
> Meaning is a craft, not a found thing.
> Build what you need.

From this perspective, when we craft something to ferment in, we are not simply creating a vessel, we are creating a delineation of what is important to our culture: how and what we eat, how much, and with whom (and for whom). The useful objects we shape to hold our food hold meaning, just as our food itself does.

When I think of the title of this chapter, "Preservation," the word does not simply mean to make food last longer. It means all the ways in which we preserve our relationship to food—through kitchen equipment, written records, oral history, our own memories, and each dish we craft with our hands.

One of my favorite concepts is *traces of use*. In the study of material objects in archaeology and book history, this refers to the physical evidence left behind by human interaction with an object. In relation to our fermentation vessels, we can look to the archaeological record to find these traces (for example, the winemaking sediment in ancient Greek amphorae). In our own kitchens, we may have a favorite crock with stains from an old batch of sauerkraut, or a beloved wooden spoon with just a bit more wear on the handle than the others.

But we can also look to our records *about* what we cook as well. The next time you pull a cookbook off your shelf or open a box of recipe cards, give them a look. Each page that's dog-eared or that has a bit of extra wear, a stain, or a tear is one that was used a bit more often than others. The paper clip or little sticky note set on a recipe card to make it easy to grab signals its favor. The notes in the margins speak to our inventiveness and play and to our efforts to adapt someone else's culinary experience to our own context.

Looking at the recipes and tools we most value tells us a lot. Do we want recipes for easy, quick meals, or do we only bust out the cookbooks when entertaining? What kinds of dishes do we make, and for whom? Which ingredients are our favorites? How do we adapt the knowledge of others to our own kitchens?

What we choose to preserve, be it a jar of sauerkraut or a handwritten recipe, is a tangible map of what we hold dear. When we look at the landscape of culinary practices we already have, it becomes easier to read this map and to imagine where we would like to grow and expand our practice next.

Ferments and Food Preservation Today

As I've mentioned, one important aspect of food preservation is using up every part of our food that we can. When we examine what this means for us today, we see that fermentation can be used to tackle two major modern problems: food waste and food insecurity.

FOOD WASTE

The scale at which food waste is currently taking place is truly a modern phenomenon (not that our ancestors didn't waste food—sometimes in considerable amounts—but not to the extent that we do now). Americans waste roughly 40 percent of all fruit and vegetables they buy. Europeans throw out about 90 million tons of food a year. Fermentation is a powerful way to help us waste less.

When we undertake a fermenting project, we are more mindful of what we are making and how; we can preserve large harvests that may otherwise have gone unused, and we can use fruit or vegetable scraps that may have otherwise gone to the compost heap. Many dishes we see in this book are the product of our predecessors' efforts to ensure nutrition and food security, and we can adapt them to the food scraps we encounter (for example, adding carrot tops to a ferment). In so doing, we can engage with the mindset of those who came before us who *didn't* have supermarkets, while also reducing the waste we produce.

The history of our food is something we can see and taste and experience in the world around us, and the stories we learn are ones we can use to enrich our world and to work to improve it—in this case, through saving and reusing food to delicious effect. This can involve small and simple changes. For example, when making the tarhana recipe on page 54, you can add pepper stems and seeds rather than throw them away. It also can involve larger and deeper changes, such as thinking seasonally and long term, rather than assuming every item we need will always grace our supermarket shelves.

FOOD INSECURITY

Here in America, people who are able to afford to put a roof over their heads and food on their tables often seem to take it for granted that everyone else can, too. However, food insecurity is a very real issue. The hunger-relief organization Feeding America estimates that in 2019, one in eight Americans were food insecure. Given growing wage gaps and rising housing prices, these problems are likely to get worse before they get better.

The number of food-insecure Americans grows larger when we have a natural disaster because our food production systems do not have "extras" built in. Food historian Rachel Laudan wrote at the start of the COVID pandemic that our production and distribution systems rely on so-called "just in time" logistics to move products to stores based on existing data about shopping trends, with the goal of having enough product to move off the shelves, with some (but not too much) in back stock. With unforeseen events such as pandemic-induced stockpiling, this system falls apart, and we get a small glimpse into the hardships of the past. Just a few decades ago, for example, seasonality played a role in what was available, meaning produce in particular was limited in early spring. In 1969, the author Georgina Horley said that March is "still a problem month in the kitchen" for finding green vegetables, and even potatoes are "down to the oldest and most battered." This was after modern logistics networks and the dominance of supermarkets were well established. If fruits and vegetables were in short supply then, imagine how critical it would have been to preserve your fruits and vegetables in the years before that!

Fermentation isn't the magic bullet to fix widespread societal problems, of course, but it can serve as a tool to help people stretch their food resources. I'll offer myself as a case study: About 20 years ago, I relied almost entirely on everything from soup kitchens to food banks to put food on my table. This was before I took up gardening and, later, fermentation (it was also before I started driving buses, which paid me enough to afford the luxury of paying rent *and* every single bill in the same month).

Had I been able to ferment the half-rotten produce I got from the food bank each week, I would have eaten much better than I did (I remember one week, for example, that my groceries from the food bank consisted of a loaf of bread and a single box of mac 'n' cheese—nary a veggie in sight). By the time I was on food stamps, I had developed an interest in cooking, and food assistance along with my burgeoning gardening habit helped pay for some of my early fermentation projects (and by extension, my blossoming career in food).

Once I knew how to ferment my veggies, the health issues I experienced in my earliest adulthood (most likely from my not-so-balanced diet) cleared up, and I always had a rich pantry of food from which to choose. Now when I think there's nothing to eat, all I have to do is open my fridge to find a cornucopia of probiotics and good flavors. However, many people are not so fortunate. Reincorporating a range of ferments into our diets is one way to help people with limited access stretch what they have, and help all of us reduce waste (it does not, however, absolve us of working to minimize larger cultural issues around food insecurity).

Here are some of the ways I've used fermentation to stretch food stores and to get creative with rethinking food waste. While this is not an exhaustive list, it may offer a jumping-off point for you to discover your own methods or to find inspiration to rethink your own food consumption habits.

USE FOOD SCRAPS. Fermentation is a wonderful way to save food scraps and get creative in the kitchen at the same time. For example, instead of throwing away the stems from the broccoli you made for dinner, shred them, throw them in brine, let them sit for 24 hours, and put them on a salad. If you have apples that are getting soft, throw them in with some sugar and water to make apple scrap vinegar. There are as many possibilities here as there are stars in the sky.

USE FERMENTATION SCRAPS. The scraps from fermentation can be used to create entirely new products. For example, leftover chiles or apple scraps from making vinegar can be chucked into a dehydrator (or dehydrated in your oven), then ground up by hand or in a food processor to build a seasoning blend that rivals anything you buy in the store. If you made wine and don't like the results, it might make a good vinegar.

If you fermented something in brine, you can use the brine to add an extra punch (and extra nutrition) to soups, stews, and marinades without using extra water or buying extra flavoring ingredients. You can even cook your rice and pasta in it!

If you're making alcohol, vinegar, or liquid fermentation, you can save the fruit and vegetable scraps you use in making it for other uses. You can throw fermented vegetable scraps in a blender with stock (or water) and a bit of fresh vegetables, then heat it up for an easy soup. Or mix fermented fruits with fresh fruit to make a compote that can top your cake, pie, ice cream, or other desserts.

ENGAGE IN COMMUNITY. Become part of a community garden and take a community fermentation class. As anyone who gardens knows, you often have a long period of waiting followed by an abundance of a certain food. Sharing knowledge about how to preserve fresh food through fermentation provides a way to prolong that harvest and help food-insecure gardeners and cooks put food on the table for longer.

SEEK OUT SUSTAINABLE, WILD FOODS. Foraging is increasing in popularity, and some well-known foragers (for example, Pascal Baudar) place an emphasis on foraging for wild invasives (such as kudzu in the South or garlic mustard in much of the country) as a way to control the spread of invasive plant populations while feeding hungry people and preventing overharvesting. Foraged edibles are a great option for everything from fermented pestos to seasonal meads and vinegars to fermented whole vegetables and fruits. For those who hunt, curing wild meats can offer richness to your dining table. Foraged and fermented plants also are used in numerous herbal medicinal applications. Sustainable wildcrafting is rewarding on many levels. As chef and fermenter Mara King, cofounder of the fermentation company Ozuké and cohost of the video series *People's Republic of Fermentation*, says, "If we understand the methods and means of the visible and invisible worlds around us we can find symbiosis, we can dance along with the seasons and enjoy everything nature has to offer without doing harm. In fact by working and practicing new and inherited cultural techniques we will make more robust structures for the future of humankind."

As with any worthwhile foraging directive, the following rules apply:

- **LEARN YOUR STUFF.** Work with someone knowledgeable or a good guidebook to learn how to make proper identifications of wild edibles. Also learn about proper, sustainable harvesting: For example, if you must harvest wild ramps rather than grow them yourself, just cut off the tops and leave the roots intact.

- **DON'T PICK THE RARE STUFF.** Steer clear of endangered and threatened wild populations (a famous example in my neck of the woods is ginseng). One good rule of thumb used to be to take 1 out of every 10 plants; however, with the popularity of wild foods growing, I now recommend gathering much less than this. If you're eager to try out a rare food, consider sourcing seeds or seedlings and growing your own. You'll be helping native flora and fauna by providing food, shelter, and other good things (such as nitrogen fixing, depending on the plant), and you'll leave wild populations to thrive.

- **GO WILD, BUT NOT TOO WILD.** Foraging wild edibles is incredibly rewarding and it offers an abundance of free food, but remember you aren't the only one eating it. Birds, insects, and other wild populations rely on the plants you pick to sustain themselves. Make sure you leave enough for them.

SOWENS

Sowens is a comforting and nourishing sour oat porridge made in Scotland from the bits of starch left clinging to oat kernels after milling. Though not as popular as it once was, it is an especially welcome treat on cold winter mornings.

This recipe requires a burr grinder (similar to a hand-cranked coffee grinder), mortar and pestle, or metate for grinding the oats. If you aren't able to grind your own oats, you can experiment with making sowens using a mixture of oat bran and rolled oats (I usually do two-thirds bran to one-third oats ground together, but there's room to experiment, as always). In the traditional method, you use only the kernels of the oats for sowens, so as an added bonus, if you mill your own you get fresh, delicious oats that are way better than the canisters of stale oats from the store.

Some people lightly toast their groats prior to milling them, but I've found that doesn't make much of a difference in the flavor or how easy the oats are to hull.

> Measure out 2 cups of oat groats. Run the oats through a burr grinder or grind them with a stone mortar and pestle or metate until the kernels are broken from the grains. Do not use an electric coffee grinder or a food processor, as they will grind the whole grain, kernel and all, into a powder (which can still be used for sowens, so it is not a total loss if this happens—you just won't get oats out of it, too).
>
> Put your ground oats in a fine-mesh sieve over a mixing bowl. Gently tap the sieve and stir the oats to allow the ground kernels to fall into the bowl below. Make sure you keep the sieve relatively close to the bowl, especially if you're working outside, so the oats don't blow away.
>
> Once you've separated the oats and kernels, pour the oats into a jar and seal with an airtight lid. Because these are fresh grains, they tend to keep best in the fridge. I always use them within a month.
>
> Leave your kernels in the bowl and add enough water to completely cover them (I usually add enough water to go an inch or so above the hulls once they settle). Whisk everything together and

MAKES
ROUGHLY
1 QUART SIDS
AND 1 CUP
SOWENS

pour the mixture into a jar, leaving a bit of space at the top so the hulls have room to expand as they hydrate. Seal the jar with a lid.

Let ferment for about a week in warmer weather or 10 to 12 days in cooler weather, shaking your jar a couple of times a day to disrupt the surface and prevent mold growth. As always, feel free to experiment (I've seen recipes range between 2 and 14 days of fermentation time).

Taste the liquid at the top of the container every couple of days. Once it is sour, it's time to strain your sowens!

To do this, *gently* pour off the liquid (swats) from the starch that has accumulated at the bottom (sowens), being careful not to disrupt the settled starches. Both can be stored in the fridge until you're ready to use them. Swats can be consumed as a chilled beverage.

When you're ready to cook your sowens, heat the starchy mixture to a gentle simmer in a saucepan until warm and steamy. Depending how thick the sowens is, you may need to add a bit of water or milk to achieve a porridgy consistency. Just as with any other porridge, you can mix in additional goodies to taste. Milk and butter are common, and it's also good with a bit of cinnamon or dried fruit.

SIDS

Sids are the inner husks of the oat grain that are used to make sowens. This hull, when ground away from the endosperm or the edible grain itself, contains traces of starch from the oats. It is an excellent example of our ancestors squeezing every last drop of nutrition that they could from their food.

PICKLED GREEN BEANS

This recipe is adapted from the 1976 book *Cabbagetown Families, Cabbagetown Food*, which contains recipes and recollections from residents of the Cabbagetown neighborhood in Atlanta in the late nineteenth to mid-twentieth centuries. Many of them had come down from the Appalachian Mountains to work at the nearby textile mill, bringing their recipes with them. Not surprisingly, many of their recipes are remarkably similar to those found in other Appalachian sources, such as the 1972 edition of *The Foxfire Book*. This particular recipe was inspired by a recipe from Lila Brown Brookshire, a Cabbagetown resident who shared her pickled bean recipe in the 1976 book.

MAKES
ABOUT 3
PINTS

1   **pound fresh green beans**

4   **tablespoons sea salt**

2   **quarts water**

1   Snap the beans in half and place them in a crock or jar, pressing them down slightly.

2   Mix the salt into the water and stir to dissolve. Pour the brine over the beans.

3   Place a weight on the beans to hold them under the brine. Cover the crock or jar with cheesecloth or a dish towel and allow to sit out at room temperature.

4   Check the beans each day, and when they have developed a level of sourness you like, put them in the refrigerator or can them following guidance in a reputable source such as *The All New Ball Book of Canning and Preserving*.

CHOW CHOW

Chow chow is a pickled relish that is popular in many parts of the southern Appalachians. It is often made as a quick pickle, with the flavor of a sweet-and-sour relish, but I also enjoy fermented versions, which have the sour taste of a lacto-ferment. I've included both the fermented and the quick-pickled versions here. The fermented recipe was inspired by two of my favorite Appalachian recipe sources: the 1976 book *Cabbagetown*

Families, Cabbagetown Food and my grandfather's copy of the 1972 *Foxfire Book*, which sits in a place of honor on my kitchen shelf. The quick-pickle version is a staple in my home during early summer, when fresh green tomatoes and cabbages are both to be had.

Some chow chow recipes call for other ingredients such as onion, garlic, and corn, but this simple version below is the way I've had it most often. For that optimal relishy consistency, the key to success is to finely shred your cabbage and finely dice your tomatoes and pepper.

Chow chow has a comforting, bright flavor and reminds me of a vastly superior version of the jarred relishes we ate when I was growing up. If you make your own vinegar, this is a great place to experiment with different flavor profiles!

FERMENTED CHOW CHOW

MAKES ABOUT 2 PINTS

- **½ head green cabbage**
- **½ tablespoon finely ground sea salt**
- **1 banana pepper** (or other pepper of your choice)**, diced**
- **2 large, firm green tomatoes, diced** (you can substitute firm red tomatoes if green are unavailable)

1 Core and finely shred the cabbage.

2 Transfer the cabbage to a large bowl and sprinkle with the salt. Lightly massage the salt into the cabbage until the cabbage releases enough liquid to form a brine. Stop while the cabbage still has some crunch to it.

3 Give the brine a quick taste: You want it to taste salty like the sea. If it seems like the brine needs a bit more salt, you can always add more and massage it in.

4 Pack the cabbage into a jar or crock. Top off with the brine, completely covering the cabbage (you may need to add water to do this). Press down on the cabbage to release any air bubbles. Then weight it to keep the cabbage submerged.

5 Let the mixture ferment at room temperature, checking it every day. Once it has the taste you'd like (chow chow is usually sour but not as

Recipe continues on next page. >

lip-smackingly sour as, say, a long-aged kraut; mine usually takes about a week), mix in the diced pepper and tomatoes and allow to ferment a day or two longer.

6   Store your finished chow chow in the fridge, where it will keep for at least 3 weeks.

Note: You can also experiment with adding the pepper and tomatoes at the beginning of the fermentation, or at the very end if you want them to be extra firm (just let the chow chow sit in the fridge for a day or two before serving to let the flavors blend). As always, use your intuition and let your taste buds guide you!

QUICK CHOW CHOW

4   **large green tomatoes, diced**

1   **fresh banana pepper** (or other pepper of your choice), **diced**

3/4   **cup vinegar**

Pinch of salt

1/2   **head cabbage, finely shredded**

1   Combine the tomatoes and pepper in a pan over medium heat and bring to a simmer.

2   Add the vinegar and salt, stir, then add the cabbage. Cook until the desired texture is reached, 10 to 20 minutes.

3   Store in the refrigerator.

SOUR CORN

Corn has been cultivated in the southern Appalachian Mountains by the Eastern Band of the Cherokee and other indigenous communities since precolonial times. It is used for a whole range of dishes.

You can ferment the whole cobs, you can cut the cobs into a few pieces, or you can strip the kernels from the cobs and ferment them (you can then save the cobs to simmer for corn stock or slice them, dry them, and then grind them to make flour). Sour corn ferments relatively quickly: I find that mine is usually ready in less than a week (sometimes in only a few days), so it's a great choice if you're looking for a ferment with a minimal time investment.

If you have a large crock or barrel to play with, it can be fun to ferment the whole cobs. Simply shuck your corn (remove the husks and silk) and pack it into a large crock. Alternatively, cut each corncob into rounds and stack them in a container, or remove the kernels and just ferment those. (To remove the kernels, place each corncob upright in a bowl and carefully run a knife from top to bottom to cut the kernels from the cob. The bowl will catch the kernels, and you can set the cob aside for other uses.)

Mix up a 4- to 5-percent salt brine (see page 327) with unrefined salt and room-temperature water. Pour it over your kernels or corncobs, completely covering them. You can add in other ingredients, too; I often throw in a handful of shredded carrot and diced green bell pepper, but sour corn is amazing all on its own.

Put a weight on your corn, or be ready to give it a stir a couple of times a day to keep yeast from growing on top of the brine.

Cover with a cloth or lid and let ferment at room temperature. Check daily. Once the corn tastes as sour as you'd like (usually a few days in warm weather and 5 to 7 days in winter), store it in the fridge.

BANANA VINEGAR

This is quite possibly the easiest recipe out there. And banana vinegar is a great way to turn too-ripe bananas into something useful—a nod to our ancestors' resourcefulness if ever there was one. Use it to add some tang and fluff to banana bread and baked goods, to lend an unexpected sour note in dressings or fruit salad, or to culture butter (see the cultured butter recipe on page 6).

Very ripe bananas

Unpasteurized vinegar or a vinegar mother (optional)

Recipe continues on next page. >

STEP ONE: MAKE ALCOHOL

1   Mash a banana (or several) in a jar until it's thoroughly and completely mashed up.

2   Let the mash sit in a jar covered with a lid or with a tea towel secured with string or a rubber band, stirring once a day, for 15 to 20 days, or until it becomes liquid, bubbly, and alcoholic. It may still have small pieces of banana in it. That's okay! It will still be alcoholic enough to become vinegar.

STEP TWO: IT'S VINEGAR TIME!

3   For a speedier fermentation, add some unpasteurized vinegar or a vinegar mother (about 2 tablespoons raw vinegar to 1 cup banana alcohol). Or you can just let the alcohol turn to vinegar naturally.

4   In order to turn alcohol to vinegar, acetobacters need access to oxygen. Pour the banana alcohol into a nonreactive bowl, crock, or other vessel with a large surface area, then cover with a cloth to keep out bugs while allowing air to circulate. Whatever container you use, make sure you fill it only half full or less to maximize the surface area.

5   Let the liquid ferment at room temperature out of direct sunlight for anywhere from 2 to 4 weeks, or until the alcohol has turned to acetic acid. At this point, it's time to test your vinegar. You can buy chemical titration kits to test whether or not any alcohol is left, or you can test it the old-fashioned way: by smell and taste. If it smells and tastes like vinegar, it's vinegar, and if you like the taste, go ahead and pull it. If it's not very sour yet, try letting it go a bit longer. And if it's too sour, you can dilute it a bit before use.

INJERA

Injera is a flavorful, slightly spongy flatbread from Ethiopia and Eritrea that is easy to make and a dietary staple in both countries. If you have an existing sourdough starter (or some injera batter from an older batch), you can add some to this batter to speed things up a bit, but you don't need to.

In Ethiopia, a large, flat skillet called a mitad, usually about a foot in diameter, is used to cook the injera. The mitad is sometimes an electric skillet or simply a flat surface set over a fire, but any large, flat skillet will do.

For a traditional Ethiopian dinner, injera is placed flat on a plate and topped with piles of stews, veggies, and sautéed meat. It can also be torn into pieces and used to scoop up bites of food.

MAKES ABOUT 20 6-INCH INJERA

2	**cups teff flour**
4	**cups water, plus more as needed**
¼–½	**cup sourdough starter or injera batter** (optional)
	Unrefined salt
	Clarified butter or vegetable oil, for cooking

1 Whisk together the teff flour and water in a large, nonreactive bowl. Then whisk in the sourdough starter or injera batter from your last batch, if using.

2 Cover the bowl with a clean cloth and set aside out of direct sunlight. Allow to ferment until the batter is bubbly and active and has a sour taste, 4 to 5 days if you did not add starter and 2 to 3 days if you did. It will have brown liquid on top—that's totally normal!

3 Pour off the top layer of liquid, then add salt to taste. Whisk the batter, then add enough water to give it the thin consistency of crêpe batter.

4 Heat a large, flat skillet over medium heat. Pour the batter into a large liquid measuring cup.

5 Coat the surface of the skillet with a tiny bit of clarified butter or oil (quickly wiping the pan with an oiled paper towel or cloth works well). Then pour a thin, even layer of batter into the pan. To make injera properly, you pour the batter in a spiral from the outside inward, with the goal of getting the edges of each ring to touch without overlapping.

6 Cook for several minutes, until bubbles form on the surface. Then cover the pan with a lid and allow the injera to steam until the edges curl, the top is dry, and the bread releases from the bottom of the pan, 3 to 5 minutes. (Don't flip your injera.)

7 When it's ready, gently remove the injera from the skillet with a thin spatula and transfer to a basket or a plate lined with parchment paper. Repeat the cooking process until you have used up all the batter. Allow each injera to cool for a few minutes before you stack any others on top of it.

3

FLAVOR

Our ancestors didn't create food solely to survive. Like us, they were driven by the human desire to be not only nourished but *fed*, eating food that brings joy and pleasure as well as sustenance. They, too, had taste buds, personal preferences, and the ability to discern high-quality ingredients, layer flavor, and plate up a dish with flair.

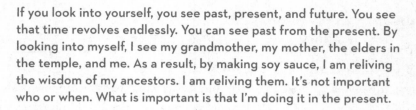

If you look into yourself, you see past, present, and future. You see that time revolves endlessly. You can see past from the present. By looking into myself, I see my grandmother, my mother, the elders in the temple, and me. As a result, by making soy sauce, I am reliving the wisdom of my ancestors. I am reliving them. It's not important who or when. What is important is that I'm doing it in the present.

—JEONG KWAN, KOREAN BUDDHIST NUN AND CHEF

So much of what informed the development of our culinary traditions was a discovery of what met our needs but also *tasted good*.

If we look to records of past ferments and contemporary research about them, we find a world of flavor to explore. Local aromatic plants were used to scent and flavor dishes. Fermented porridges were (and are) nourishing, delicious, and flavorful—anything but a bland and runny gruel. Bread and beer offered flavor and nutrients, and fish sauces, as well as amino sauces and pastes, flavored meals for millennia.

"Good Food" Is Subjective

The "goodness" of a ferment exists in context: Each time you step into the kitchen and begin to cook, you bring with you an entire host of familial, historical, cultural, and personal factors that inform your impressions of what you are making. As Buddhist nun and chef Jeong Kwan does with her soy sauce, we connect past, present, and future each time we prepare a ferment.

We also bring our own uniqueness as individuals to what we make; that is, when we ferment food, we cook into it our own "flavor." Here in the United States, we describe this as "made with love," whereas in Korea it is *son-mat* (hand taste). In Hawaii, it's seen in the saying "good hands make good poi." Across all these traditions, there is the concept of being one with the food you're creating: Who you are shapes the food you make. This is connective, healing magic in the truest sense, making the experience of flavor about far more than our biological response to the compounds in our food.

WINE AND POWER

Sometimes, what constitutes "good taste" has more to do with privilege and power than with what is most delicious. And quite often (though not always), the tastes of those in power end up shaping food for the rest of us. We find two examples of this in France and one in the Soviet Union.

In the early ninth century, King Charlemagne changed the face (and the color) of French winemaking by replanting white grapes instead of red at Corton-Charlemagne, one of the grand crus of Burgundy. To this day, more white wine is produced in the region than red, and Corton-Charlemagne is still considered the source of some of the world's best white wine.

In the fifteenth century, Pope Clement V didn't want to live in Rome, so he moved the papacy to Avignon, France, where it remained for 67 years. This brought development, prestige, and funds to the southern Rhône, particularly to the Châteauneuf-du-Pape region (whose name literally translates as "new house of the pope"). Pope John XXII succeeded Clement, and one of his greatest efforts was to improve the quality of the region's wines and to promote them nationally and internationally. Because of this, Châteauneuf-du-Pape is still considered one of the great wine regions of France.

In the Soviet Union in 1945, Joseph Stalin's efforts to collectivize agriculture and commerce extended to Soviet winemaking. This meant that only the government was allowed to produce wine, and the progress of wine-growing regions came to a screeching halt. The Hungarian region of Tokaj had been famous for its sweet wines, but its vineyards were commuted away from making good wine to making mass-produced wine. Only after the fall of the Soviet Union in 1989 did the region return to quality-minded wine production with great success; meanwhile, Bulgaria, Georgia, Romania, and the Czech Republic are still rebuilding their winemaking industries.

Finding Balance

Most foods have more than one flavor. Sauerkraut, for example, is both salty and sour, and its brine can be used to enhance a dish in both ways.

The Maillard reaction, which gives us the deep umami flavors of miso, also produces acidic flavor compounds as a byproduct. And our umami-filled shoyu and fish sauce are also time-honored ways to salt our dishes.

Finding balance in our food is part tradition, part imagination. As novelist Monique Truong says in *The Book of Salt*, "To be a good cook I had to first envision the possibilities. I had to close my eyes and see and taste what was not there. I had to dream and discern it all on my tongue." The focus of a flavor-balanced meal is to light up the whole tongue, and we must take care to balance the taste of the dish during cooking and during eating.

FLAVOR ACROSS CULTURES

The ways in which we describe flavors and the flavor experiences we prefer differ across cultures. Many Thai dishes, for example, emphasize a balance among flavors in a dish, whereas in American cuisine, one flavor often dominates (a steak dinner in the United States is all about that savory steak, even if it is served with side dishes). While there's variation within each culture's cuisine, the examples below give you a few different ways to think about how we describe flavor.

In Thai cuisine, the focus is on blending four basic tastes: sweet, sour, salty, and spicy. Thai cooking is informed by thousands of years of contact with other cultures and waves of new ingredients, but it also maintains a core identity that nourishes and excites the entire palate, and this is true across regional variations. In the landlocked north and northeast, for example, you'll find more fermented and pickled foods, but vinegar as a flavoring—as well as some pickles and ferments—is present throughout the country.

Filipino food is also characterized by four dominant flavors: sour, sweet, salty, and bitter. While spiciness is sometimes present as well, it is not emphasized as a central flavor. As food writer Maria "Ging" Gutierrez Steinberg notes in her writing on the Philippines, "There are many food pairings in Filipino cuisine that

Simple doesn't mean easy. I can describe simple cooking thus: Cooking that is stripped all the way down to those procedures and those ingredients indispensable in enunciating the sincere flavor intentions of a dish.

—ITALIAN COOKBOOK AUTHOR MARCELLA HAZAN

allow combinations of contrasting flavors to meld pleasingly on the native palate, such as sour green mangoes dipped in salty fermented fish or shrimp paste."

Sometimes a dish will emphasize one flavor while still striving for balance overall, resulting in combinations unique to a certain cuisine. In Sichuan cooking, for example, Sichuan peppers, chile peppers, sesame oil,

tiny bubbles

Flavor is central to the dining experience, but so is texture, and ferments around the world have as wide a range of textures as they do of flavors. One of my favorites is what food historian Rachel Laudan calls "tiny bubbles," which can occur in nonfermented things (for instance, fresh whipped cream) but also in carbonated alcoholic and nonalcoholic beverages and in leavened ferments such as bread, which rise in response to the output of CO_2 made by yeasts as they metabolize the starches in the dough.

In modern times, we can carbonate our beverages by using pressurized CO_2 and pumping it into a liquid to carbonate it instantly. But with fermentation, this process goes a bit more slowly, as the yeasts have to release CO_2 within a beverage enclosed in a tightly sealed container. The gases can't escape and, thus, reincorporate with the liquid, creating tiny bubbles.

Through much of history, fizziness was not an attribute people were used to in their fermented beverages. As Laudan says, "We forget that these are largely the result of forced carbonation and of bottles, caps, and cans, late inventions all." It wasn't until after about 1650, Laudan notes, that "cooks in northwest Europe and its colonies find all kinds of ways to introduce tiny bubbles into foods" by using fermentation for yeast bread and sparkling ciders and wines.

and doubanjiang (fermented broad bean paste) are used to create harmonies of flavor with names such as "strange flavor" (guai wei), "family flavor" (jiachang wei), and "hot-fragrant" flavor (xiangla wei).

The quest for balance informs how food is served, too. In Thailand, for example, an array of different dishes as well as tableside condiments (usually vinegar, sugar, hot pepper, maybe fish sauce) create a sense of overall balance. At home, families will share many dishes at dinner instead of focusing on one main dish. This ensures that the meal is healthy and the flavors are balanced; a fatty and spicy curry will be balanced by a milder, simpler dish, for example. In Korea, banchan (a variety of side dishes, including kimchi, served with the meal) adds balance and a diversity of flavors to the dining experience.

Sometimes it's up to the individual diner to balance the tastes in a dish. Lahpet (or laphet) thoke, a Burmese salad made of fermented green tea leaves (see the recipe on page 268), is a good example. To make the dish, green leaves are harvested and fermented anaerobically, traditionally in clay pots or in sacks weighed down with rocks, to produce pleasantly sour leaves with a hit of caffeine. The leaves are then often flavored with garlic, chile peppers, salt, fresh lemon juice, and peanut oil. It's a tasty pickled salad and a pick-me-up all in one. The dish is always served with a range of sides that contain different flavors and textures. The sides vary depending on who is serving it, but typical offerings include shredded fresh cabbage, deep-fried peanuts, crisp fried garlic, fried split peas or garbanzo beans, and toasted sesame seeds. The diner chooses what to add to the salad, with the ultimate goal of bringing balance. As author and fermenter Kirsten Shockey said in an interview with me about lahpet thoke, "The spicy, salty, bitter, crunchy, oily bits all go together magically and cannot be compared to anything in Western culture."

BALANCING FLAVORS IN FERMENTS

A balanced meal is not simply a nutritious one. It is also one where, as with lahpet thoke, all the flavors of sweet, salty, sour, bitter, and umami are present, singing in harmony. In order to balance flavors in our ferments, we need to think about how flavors interact, just as we would when mixing cocktails, and this can lead to some surprising revelations. Umami and bitterness are good complements, for example, so perhaps making miso paste with some chopped mugwort (a bitter herb) will lend extra-delicious results. Thinking of the flavors that different microbes impart helps us find balance, too. In Kirsten Shockey's sourdough bread miso, for instance, she notes that you want to keep the relationship between yeasts, lactobacillus, and koji in balance. If you end up with a really sour miso, you probably didn't have enough salt and lactic acid took over.

LAYERING FLAVOR WITH BRINES AND BREWS

Much of the flavor of our ferments comes from the ingredients themselves, of course, but we can also get a lot of flavor from the brine. When we use the brine, whey, and other liquids from our ferments to make other dishes, we're not only reducing food waste but also injecting a big flavor boost. Brines from lacto-fermented veggies can be used as a weak acid in cooking; food writers Ken Albala and Rosanna Nafziger Henderson compare it to "especially savory and aromatic diluted vinegar or lemon juice." The brine can be splashed into soup to brighten it before serving or added to marinades to enhance the acidity and flavor.

Whey-based cheeses, such as mysost, brunost, or gjetost, are another ingenious way to use up what we have to build flavor. Whey makes up the lion's share of excess liquid in cheesemaking, but rather than throw it away, we allow the toasty Maillard reaction to produce a delicious fudgy, caramelly cheese. And making pickling beds from sake lees is a time-honored tradition in Japan.

If you brew beer, mead, or wine, you may find that some batches aren't great for drinking but are still tasty enough to use in cooking. I love using these in marinades (mead is great for fish, pork, and root veggies) and as simple sauces. You can also let them turn into vinegar and use them in cocktails as shrubs (sweet and sour vinegars or liqueurs), giving your drink some extra depth and boozy flavor (pickle brines are a great cocktail addition, too).

Using brines and brews in our dishes offers another way to create balance as an interplay between the five tastes: sour, sweet, salty, bitter, and savory (umami). They're a reminder that ferments are, and have historically been, a critical part of the performance.

Sour

Sourness is the flavor associated with sauerkraut, yogurt, and other lacto-ferments. The sourness comes from acidity, and it is literally mouthwatering: When eating sour foods, our mouths produce extra saliva to protect our teeth from the acid.

Salt is said to enhance flavor, while acid balances flavor. This makes salty, sour ferments powerhouses of flavor, whether eaten alone, added to other dishes, or served as an accompaniment. Our ancestors certainly knew that sour foods can make eating more enjoyable. Lacto-ferments have been a part of traditional cuisines around the world for thousands of years, from the trays of pickles that have, for centuries, graced the daily table and sumptuous feasts in Baghdad to the dish of kimchi that has accompanied Korean meals for many generations.

Adding acidity to a dish brings it to life, whether it be vinegar in a dressing or marinade or a big spoonful of sour cream swirled into mashed potatoes. Meals benefit from having tangy, sour accompaniments such as pickles, as well as a bit of acid in the dishes themselves. The former allows people to customize the meal to their tastes, while the latter helps keep things in balance. As chef Samin Nosrat puts it, "Acid grants the palate relief, and makes food more appealing by offering contrast."

VINEGAR

Pastry chef Gina DePalma uses sourness to balance flavors in desserts; she adds light champagne vinegar to mango and raspberry sorbets for "a very intense experience of the fruit's flavor." The acid balances the sweetness of the fruit.

Vinegars are a critical component in many sauces, too. Examples include Catalonian romesco sauce (made of sherry vinegar, peppers, and toasted nuts) and mignonette for oysters (made with champagne vinegar, parsley, and shallot). Acid also breaks down the collagen in meats, which, as my dear friend Doc taught me, is why you should always add a splash of vinegar to your stock to make it particularly velvety and unctuous.

Across cultures, we see vinegar as a critical tableside condiment, part of a suite of flavorings meant to balance and customize the taste of a meal. Ruth L. Gaskins's 1968 cookbook A Good Heart and a Light Hand, which outlined the diversity of African-American cooking, notes that "eating without vinegar is like eating without salt." According to Gaskins, vinegar held the place of honor in the condiment tray, used for everything from preserving to presentation.

Given that vinegar is often fermented from wine, it is not surprising that the vinegars we find in a culture correlate to the popular alcohols of that culture: rice wine vinegar in Japan, where saki is popular; malt and cider vinegar in England, perhaps arising from beer and hard cider; and white wine vinegar and red wine vinegar in France. Just as our tastes are shaped by the ingredients we have on hand, the vinegars we could make helped give our cuisines their shape. Red wine vinegar would seem out of place on sticky rice, for example, just as rice wine vinegar might seem out of place in the French poulet au vinaigre (chicken cooked with vinegar).

Additional steps in aging or fermentation can significantly impact a vinegar's flavor. The Orleans method, for example, which dates from the Middle Ages, involves fermenting wine vinegar in wooden casks, laid horizontally and filled halfway to maximize the surface area exposed to air. Louis Pasteur noted that "the wine-vinegar of Orleans in part owes its fine qualities to the presence of aromatic substances" that are lacking in other methods not using wooden barrels. In another example from Japan, China, and elsewhere in Asia, black vinegar is made by fermenting cooked brown rice, brown rice koji, and spring water outside in stoneware pots and then aging it for extended periods.

SOUR MEAT

Fermented meat products are a hallmark of many global cuisines. The fermentation process adds depth, sourness, and texture to the meat, and it extends the shelf life of the meat.

Aspergillus oryzae is a fungus that is used to ferment sake, soy sauce, and miso. It can also grow on meat, tenderizing the meat as it ferments it. *Koji* is the Japanese name for this kind of mold fermentation, though mold fermentation processes exist in many cultures, including in China, Korea, Thailand, Nepal, India, and Malaysia. Each of these processes has its own name and distinct technique. Today, some modern Western recipes for cured meats such as salami sometimes include koji, which speeds up the fermentation process.

Fermented sausages are popular in a few countries in Southeast Asia (Thailand, Vietnam, and Laos) and in China. We know it was eaten in ancient China, and we also know it was eaten in Vietnam (where it is called nem chua), but we don't know if the two fermented sausage traditions developed independently or if they were shared across cultures.

The Thai term *naem* can refer to both fermented sausages (see the recipe on page 155) and to the fermentation style used to make the sausages (though a northern Thai dialect uses the name *jin som*, meaning sour meat, instead). The sausages are made of ground pork, boiled pork skin, glutinous rice, garlic, salt, and sometimes chiles. They are fermented for just a few days, during which time they take on their characteristic sour flavor, and then are often eaten uncooked (the fermentation process renders the meat safe to eat).

The Thai northern provinces are landlocked, and pork from the region's many farms is central to regional cuisine. So while fermented foods, for instance, fish sauces, are found around Thailand, fermented pork sausages are more commonly found in the north. Another regional specialty is naem maw, finely chopped pork that is cured with salt, sealed in a large pot or bowl, and left to ferment. In more recent times, it became common to ferment naem maw in logs or pyramidal shapes wrapped in banana leaves. Many modern vendors now wrap naem maw in plastic, so the buyer can see the color of the meat, but banana leaves are the traditional packaging, and for good reason: They help regulate the temperature of the meat so it doesn't get too warm as it ferments.

There are long traditions of fermenting fish in the region, too. Today, *nigiri-sushi* refers to fresh fish over seasoned rice, but some historians believe it was eaten differently in the past. Japanese food historian Naomichi Ishige says the first sushi was not from Japan but from the banks of the Mekong River in Southeast Asia, where the fish was enrobed in salted rice and fermented, and the rice was cleaned from the fish before eating (Ishige believes this practice made its way to Japan along with the technology of rice cultivation). This technique was initially used to preserve freshwater fish and was adapted to the saltwater fish in Japan. The technique can still be found near Lake Biwa, and related fish ferments can be found in Korea and southwestern China.

Other sources, including food historian Cherl-Ho Lee, Keith H. Steinkraus, and P. J. Alan Reilly, point to the Mekong River in southwestern China as sushi's point of origin, and specifically to narezushi, a process of fermenting fish or animal flesh with salt and cooked carbohydrates (usually boiled rice, though other grains such as millet are sometimes used). This technique then spread outward to Southeast Asia and then to Japan. As it spread, regional variations appeared, including the addition of garlic in Thailand (just like we see in naem, above), and once hot peppers were introduced, Korean versions began to include chili powder and malt.

Prior to the fifth century, says Ishige, the fish was fermented in rice to the point that the rice was so sour that it was inedible. But the move to short fermentation times in the fifth century CE meant the rice was sour but edible, and people began to eat the rice with the fish. Unfermented sushi appeared during the Edo period in Japan (1600–1867), and hand-rolled sushi is even more recent, appearing at the end of the eighteenth century.

SOUR MILK

Dairy ferments are another way for us to add sourness and balance flavor: We can top a salad with tangy cheese, spoon sour cream over potatoes, add buttermilk to biscuits or a chicken brine, and drizzle yogurt over kebabs.

Yogurt is an important part of cuisines throughout India and Central Asia. In India, cookbook author and food writer Nandita Godbole notes, yogurt has "a special place" and is a classic accompaniment for many meals. In Afghanistan, making yogurt is part of a widespread dairy fermentation practice. Researcher Helen Saberi found it is especially important in high mountain areas, where it fills a nutritional hole left by a lack of fresh vegetables and fruits.

The type of dairy being fermented impacts flavor; goat milk has an earthier flavor than cow's milk, for example. Throughout Central Asia, and in Kazakhstan in particular, horses are bred for riding and for food. Koumiss, or fermented mare's milk, is one of the products born from this tradition.

Dairy was very important to the ancient Celts, who hailed from many places in western Europe and whose diets varied between those places. This was especially true for the Celts within what is modern-day Ireland. The lush landscape meant lots of food for cattle, and dairy (and dairy fermentation) has been a staple on the island since pre-Christian times. And the Celts didn't just like drinking plain milk—*sour* milk was key. Food writer Sam Dean writes that in 1690, "one British visitor to Ireland noted that the natives ate and drank milk 'above twenty several sorts of ways and what is strangest for the most part love it best when sourest.'" Of particular note, the Celtic Irish drank what they called bainne clabair, milk that had been allowed to sit out just long enough to sour but not long enough to curdle. It is somewhat similar to yogurt. When Scots-Irish people immigrated to the southern Appalachian Mountains, they brought that tradition with them, calling it clabbered milk, or simply clabber.

SOUR PLANT FOODS

Lacto-fermented grains, fruits, and vegetables also add tang to global diets. In *Choctaw Food*, author and archaeologist Ian Thompson notes that sour fermented cornbread was more popular among the Choctaw people in the 1800s (and likely prior) than its nonsour counterpart. Its exquisite flavor is, as Thompson says, "exactly like a cross between unsweetened cornbread and sourdough." To make it, the unleavened dough would be prepared and then allowed to sit at room temperature for several days to ferment. Once it smelled sour, it would be baked. A fire would be built on moist clay, then the coals moved aside to make room for the bread, which baked under an inverted bowl on the warmed clay. The resulting bread was moist inside and had an outside that tasted like popcorn.

In Bangladesh, many people in rural areas eat panta bhat, a less-sour cousin to the fermented porridges of European countries, for breakfast. It consists of boiled rice that has slightly fermented overnight in water and then is mixed with salt and chile peppers. Fruits, vegetables, meats, and fish have been fermented here since ancient times, as there are limited ways to keep fresh food in the hot climate.

Nepal is one of the most ethnically diverse countries in the world (the 2001 census identified 92 languages belonging to four major linguistic groups—Indo-European, Dravidian, Sino-Tibetan, and Austro-Asiatic—and 103 distinct caste and ethnic groups), and the ferments in the region reflect this diversity.

Gundruk, a blend of greens that are fermented, then dried, then ground (see page 77 for more detail), is used in Nepal as a sour accompaniment to curries, soups, and other common dishes. It isn't the only sour accompaniment to the meal, though. Pickled vegetables are another essential component of Nepali meals, providing both flavor and preserved nutrition.

Kimchi is a sour staple in Korea. It rarely spoils, and if prepared correctly it can ripen for months or even years to become mukeunji, which is described on the *My Sweet Grandma* blog as deep and complex rather than puckeringly sour. It can be used to speak flavor into just about any vegetable and, as a finished product, to speak balance into a meal. We in the United States think of kimchi as a noun, but cooking writer Eric Kim says, "Kimchi is also a verb. . . . [It] is an umbrella term for a much larger world of dishes you can find on any given Korean table." Its versatility in historic and modern recipes is born by the fact that you can kimchi just about *anything*. Napa cabbage may be the most traditional ingredient, but even those ancestors building kimchi traditions centuries ago used other vegetables, such as radish and scallion.

The ubiquity of sour foods across global cuisines is summed up simply by Samin Nosrat: "Every culture has its pickles." We see this from Indian achar to Iranian torshi, Korean kimchi, Japanese tsukemono, German sauerkraut, and Appalachian chow chow. A few slices of steak can be transformed into very different flavors depending on which sour foods you have in your fridge: Add some kimchi and you've got a bowl of Korean bibimbap; add a few pickled carrots, some cilantro, and jalapeños and you have tacos; change up the sauce and the wrapping and you can make a banh mi–esque sandwich that's divine.

Sweet

Our bodies are hardwired to crave sweet things. Sweetness indicates the presence of carbohydrates, which offer quick fuel to our brains and bodies. As a result of our fascination with all things sweet, the flavor is interwoven into much of our food, and not simply for dessert. Our ancestors got their sugar fix from a variety of sources, including animal sources such as honey, plant sources such as sugarcane, and fermentations such as mead. In fact, the Sanskrit word for mead is *midhu*, which means "sweet," and the first mention of mead in English is in the Old English epic poem *Beowulf* (700–1000 CE).

Archaeobotanist Naomi F. Miller has found that the grape was initially cultivated not to make wine but for its sweetness, a precious commodity in a world without cane sugar. Winemaking quickly followed, though. Tartaric acid (which indicates the presence of wine) has been found in ceramic vats in southwest Asia dating to the middle of the sixth millennium BCE. This wine was likely produced using wild grapes, but it was an important forebear to viticulture in the area, which would not become prevalent until about three millennia later. In Iran, ceramics recovered from Godin Tepe dating from the fourth millennium BCE also show tartaric acid residue; this area of Iran is outside the range of wild grapes, suggesting the possibility of early grape cultivation. In Xinjiang, in northwest China, there is evidence of grape cultivation as far back as 390 to 210 BCE.

Spiced and otherwise flavored wines were considered a health tonic in western Europe for many years (see the hippocras recipe on page 216), and many were sweetened as well. We see the same flavor components—sugar, spices, and perhaps a bit of sour or bitter from citrus—layered together in winter holiday mulled wine and baked goods. French chef Auguste Escoffier had a recipe for hot wine, for example, that includes one bottle of red wine, 10 ounces of sugarloaf (refined sugar formed into a tall cone with a rounded top), orange zest, cinnamon, mace, and one clove. These are gently heated together, strained, and served warm, garnished with lemon.

Though sugar often provides the note of sweetness in fermentations, other fermented spices and herbs can add a sweet note as well. Vanilla, for example, lends our food sweetness and depth, despite not containing any sugar, and was used in Mesoamerica by precolonial Maya and Totonac people. Vanilla comes from an orchid native to the American tropics, and it is readily available today thanks to the work of Edmond Albius (1829–1880), an enslaved horticulturalist on the French plantations on Réunion Island, who, at the age of 12, developed an efficient method for pollinating the plants. Once pollinated, the orchids produce pods containing vanilla beans. When mature, the pods are harvested, sorted, graded, and then fermented. They are blanched in hot water to halt the fermentation process, then alternately dried in the sun during the day and sweated indoors during the night to develop their flavor.

Sometimes the smell of a ferment gives no indication of the sweetness it will produce. A prime example is Appalachian salt-rising bread (see page 45). Its starter has a distinctive smell (some people liken it to gym socks), but don't let that scare you: Salt-rising bread is sweet and toasts up beautifully. Fermentation itself can also bring out the sweet flavor of an ingredient. For example, amazake is a Japanese sweet drink and sweetener made by fermenting rice with koji, which produces enzymes that bring out the rice's sweetness.

Bitter

The bitter flavor has a lot to teach us about finding synergy among a meal's components. We rarely consume purely bitter ingredients all on their own. Instead, we use them for balance and contrast, a bit of a medicinal bite to counter cloying sweetness or to offer depth to savoriness. This interrelationship is a dance on the tongue, born of a cook's ability to consider a seemingly intimidating flavor within the larger constellation of a dish's taste and aroma to produce a delicious result. As culinary authors Karen Page and

Andrew Dornenburg remark, "Sourness tends to sharpen other flavors. In small doses, sour notes enhance bitterness, while in large doses, they suppress bitterness." In brewing, bitterness plays an important role, with bittering herbs used for flavor and for preservation. Today, we use hops for this purpose, but a bitter balance in beer is nothing new: Prior to hops, European brewers relied on gruit, a mixture of bitter brewing herbs besides hops (such as mugwort), to strike a flavor balance.

Bitter foods themselves often are not simply bitter alone but have complex flavors. This is part of the reason they work so well to add nuance to our dishes, fermented or otherwise. Cacao beans, for example, are unpalatable when fresh, but once fermented and dried they develop their characteristic cocoa flavor, which is the result of about 600 flavor compounds. All those aromatic compounds result in an incredibly complex and inimitable deep and rich taste and aroma.

Chocolate and coffee (both fermented) and tea (sometimes fermented) are three of our modern world's most common bitter foods. Originally from Mesoamerica, cacao (the pod, versus cocoa, the fermented product, and chocolate, the final consumer product) was key to the Aztec beverage chocolatl, which was consumed for medicinal and spiritual qualities as well as flavor; the emperor Montezuma is said to have loved it enough that he would drink little else.

Coffee originated around the Red Sea region, and coffee plants still grow wild in the area. The origins of its current form are uncertain. The Arabs were the first to use it as a drink in the thirteenth century, though it's unclear whether that was before or after the technique of roasting the beans to enhance flavor and aroma was developed. The first European colonizers to plant the shrubs were the Dutch in Java (Indonesia), and by the 1800s, the plant was cultivated across all the world's tropical areas. Coffee production was a big industry in Java, where entire forest ecosystems were replaced with coffee shrubs. Today, Indonesia is the fourth-largest coffee producer worldwide, after Brazil, Vietnam, and Colombia.

There are dozens of varieties of coffee beans, but much of what is produced in Indonesia is the

I used to love dishes that were rich on rich—but the older I get, the more I look forward to that bitterness, the cleansing bite that makes you want to go back for your next forkful of a dish.

—CHEF SHARON HAGE

robusta variety, which is said to have a stronger, harsher taste than arabica beans, which are sweeter and softer and have higher acidity. Arabica beans dominate global markets. Indonesia is also home to kopi luwak, a pricey coffee that undergoes a unique fermentation process: The beans are eaten by civet cats, pass through their digestive systems, and then are extracted from their excrement.

Born from tropical regions, chocolate, coffee, and tea were harnessed by indigenous communities who learned to ferment, dry, and prepare them. After these areas were colonized in the early modern period (1500–1800), Europeans were eager to commodify them, along with every resource possible. These bitter foods became curiosities, then luxuries, then staples, their production propelled by European markets demanding more and more as they proliferated throughout societies. As a result, tropical landscapes were razed and reshaped for tea and coffee plantations, forever altering the native communities, who were forced (or at the very least compelled) to work in dire conditions for little to no pay. Meanwhile in Europe, the story behind these foods became largely hidden, whitewashed under advertising and canisters with familiar brand names as each product became more affordable thanks to costs prepaid on the other side of the Earth by other peoples and lands.

In a presentation on turmeric, food historian Julia Fine gives us a new way to think about how food, including ferments, can be used to communicate cultural identity, even falsely, to people outside the culture. In the case of the British people, this results in "participation in the Empire through food." She found that British people in the early modern period would pickle melons in turmeric to emulate mangoes. "The coloring of turmeric allowed British eaters who may or may not have ever been to the subcontinent to emulate presumed Indian originals." As a result, "Turmeric . . . thus became a tool through which British people could participate in and translate the Imperial project to their own homes."

There are many examples, past and present, of people going out of their way to taste "exotic" foods, even if what they got was not the real deal (such as those pickled melons masquerading as mangoes). Tea, for example, was heavily adulterated in the early modern period; British people would regularly have "tea" that wasn't tea at all and might include anything from dried leaves taken from local trees to dung to lead. However, the growing interest in and demand for tea fueled the imperial expansion into tea growing, eventually resulting in an abundance of affordable tea. This allowed for participation in the imperial project in a new way: by consumption of the actual products grown in colonized areas rather than in the consumption of presumed originals. The same could be said of chocolate and coffee as well.

Salty

Salt is an important component for some fermentation processes, as we've seen, but as a flavor, salt offers what Samin Nosrat calls "a satisfying zing!" Our bodies can't store much salt, but we need it to perform basic functions, meaning we are hardwired to continuously crave it to ensure we get enough. This is one of the many reasons why a scoop of sauerkraut or a bowl of kimchi soup feels so satisfying to body and soul.

Salt enhances the flavor of ingredients and stimulates salivation. It also likes to be the star of the show, keeping its fellows from taking center stage. When you add salt to a dish, you diminish the effects of sour, sweet, and bitter components.

Numerous ferments contain salt, which supports the fermentation process. These ferments—including amino sauces and pastes as well as lacto-fermented veggies—can serve as a vehicle for adding a salty bite to a dish. Because a ferment also imparts other flavors, you can use less of it than you would salt alone to achieve the same flavor impact with less sodium. We'll talk more about the history of these savory and salty condiments later in this chapter, but suffice it to say that humans have been using fermentation in our quest for salty, satisfying flavor since ancient times.

Umami

In the West, we have always eaten savory foods, but we never really embraced or understood the concept of umami until very recently (and still not as fully as the other four tastes). However, umami has been a part of the Japanese flavor lexicon for more than a century. In 1909, Kikunae Ikeda, a chemistry professor at the Imperial University of Tokyo, sought to find out why it was that foods such as dashi (a savory stock used as the basis for many dishes) had a flavor distinct from the other four tastes. He discovered that glutamates (certain amino acids) were responsible, and he named the taste after the Japanese adjective for delicious, *umai*.

Glutamate appears naturally in many foods, and its presence is a flavor indicator to our bodies that a meal contains necessary proteins. Chefs and authors René Redzepi and David Zilber describe umami as "moreish"—that is, "when you taste it, you want more," or in other words, our bodies are built to find umami satisfying, meaning we crave it and actively seek it out. Glutamate appears naturally in a variety of foods, including seaweed and seafood, some vegetables (such as tomatoes), and mushrooms, but it also can be cultivated through fermentation. Some of the umami-enhancing microbes are *Corynebacterium glutamicum*, *Brevibacterium lactofermentum*, and *B. flavum*, though we do not yet understand how these microorganisms produce glutamate.

FISH SAUCE

Fish sauce is a rich, complex umami bomb with an incredible range of flavors that can vary based on fermentation time, type of fish, salinity, and other additions (for example, herbs). Sandor Katz calls it "the mother of all condiments." It is most prevalent in Eastern and Southeast Asian cuisines, though it has seen new popularity elsewhere in recent years. Fish sauce comes in various forms, from clear to cloudy and thin to thick, and you can even sometimes find it as a paste.

Fish sauce is made by salting ungutted fish and allowing it to liquefy through a process of autolysis (self-digestion) and hydrolysis (digestion into water). It is important that the fish viscera is intact, as it contains many of the enzymes responsible for breaking down the fish's cells.

GARUM. Although no longer the case today, there was a time when fish sauce had a foothold in European cuisines. In ancient Greece and Rome, the sauce, called garum or sometimes liquamen, was eaten "in surprisingly large quantities," according to food historians Sally Grainger and Andrew Dalby.

It was so critical, in fact, that there is evidence of large-scale fish sauce production in southern Spain and the Black Sea going back to the eighth and seventh centuries BCE—it was the only large-scale factory industry at that time. There was even a fish sauce production site in what is modern London. All such sites were typically located near the water, ensuring that the freshest fish were used.

The oldest known cookbook, Apicius, or De re coquinaria ("The Art of Cooking"), written by Apicius in the first century CE, offers us some clues as to garum's role in Roman cuisine. In it, we see fish sauce used in almost every dish. We also see that fish sauce was cooked into dishes, used in sauces, and served tableside as a condiment for nearly every dish (plain salt, on the other hand, was rarely used). In her book Cooking Apicius, Sally Grainger translates the ancient Roman recipes from Latin into recipes that could be prepared in the modern home kitchen. She includes a good amount of fish sauce throughout her book—for example, in oenogarum, a sauce made from wine, sweet wine, fish sauce, rue, and black pepper, which would be drizzled over lightly fried or grilled fish just before serving, as well as over cooked vegetables.

Just like fish sauce made elsewhere in the world, Greek and Roman garum was made with whole small, fatty fish (such as sardines) packed in salt and fermented for at least several months in the hot sun. The Greeks and Romans also included fresh herbs in their fish sauce ferments. If you don't feel like making your own garum but want to approximate the flavor of the Greek and Roman version, you can use a sauce of similar consistency, such as nuoc mam from Vietnam or nam pla from Thailand, and steep fresh oregano, rue, or other Mediterranean herbs into it.

The clear, first straining of the fish sauce was carefully extracted after the fish had been allowed to sit in the sun with salt. According to the Byzantine Geoponica, a tenth-century encyclopedia-like work, "a deep close-woven basket is inserted into the centre of the jar containing these fish, and the sauce seeps into the basket: so likouman [liquamen] is obtained, filtered through the basket. The solid residue makes alix." This clear sauce was highly prized and more expensive than the cloudier sauce obtained from subsequent pressings (we see this pattern across the history of fish sauce globally). Upon receiving a small jar of alix as a gift, the Roman poet Martial remarked, "Here is lordly garum, a costly gift, made from the first blood of a still-gasping mackerel."

The quality and desirability of garum would vary based on where it was produced as well, and Spanish fish sauce was considered the best in the Roman world. These fish sauces would be packed in amphorae, tall, narrow-necked vessels with two handles, and traded around the Mediterranean. However, the finest fish sauce was not from a certain place but from a certain fish: tuna, or, to be exact, its viscera, blood, juices, and gills.

Garum is an absolute delight to cook with. However, commercial garum making was a stinky process—so much so that its production was outlawed in some urban areas. If you make your own garum, I suggest putting it in a container with a sealed lid to keep out critters. While you might not expect it, I have never had an issue with smell when making small batches of garum at home.

FISH SAUCE IN ASIA. People across the Asian continent have been making fish sauces since ancient times as well, including nam pla in Thailand, nuoc mam in Vietnam, tuk trey in Cambodia, ngan-pya-ye in Myanmar, and padaek in Laos. They range in texture from thin liquids to thick pastes, and in flavor from relatively mild to sharp and pungent.

For centuries, fish sauce has been used both in food preparation and as a tableside seasoning. In Japan, *gyosho* is the generic term for fish sauce, and Nancy Singleton Hachisu, who lives on a Japanese farm and has authored multiple works on Japanese cooking, notes that "there are different names and ingredients depending where you go. *Shottsuru,* from Akita prefecture is fermented from sandfish, or sometimes from anchovies or sardines, for example. On the Noto peninsula, much of the surrounding water's bountiful sealife is used as the basis for fish sauce, and a barrel of *isihu/ishiri* (the name for this widely varied sauce) was a fixture in many fishing households until only about 20 years ago."

Fish sauce and paste have been consumed in Japan for more than a thousand years, though we don't have an exact date for when people started eating it. As historian and writer Naomichi Ishige says, "Since this food can easily be made with only salt, fish and a jar, surely it was eaten in Japan long before it was documented in writing, and from its close association with rice-field fishery, we may infer the possibility that fish paste

what's in a name?

Garum's name is derived from *garos*, the name of the fish used by the Greeks around the fifth century BCE to make a sauce of the same name. While I'm using the word *garum* here, there has been quite a bit of debate about the actual name of this stuff. Sally Grainger, who is the authority on classical fish sauces, notes that it was called *garos* in Greek, later transliterated into *garum* in Latin, and even later changed to *liquamen* (though there is debate about the latter's meaning), but we also see other terms such as *haimation* used to refer to different types of sauce (for example, those made with blood).

However, it took some creative digging for researchers to learn about the sauce's role in classical daily life, with Grainger noting that there was a "perceived absence of the term liquamen" in early Latin texts. Further digging revealed why this was the case, and it had to do with all those terms: "Fish sauce was originally a singular essential substance: a small-whole dissolved fish sauce and it is perfectly understandable that late Republican and even Augustan writers should transliterate *garos* into *garum* as they perceived this product in this way. The blood viscera sauce was invented some time at the end of the Republic but it was much later when this new *garum* became integrated into culinary use and recorded in culinary, medicinal and veterinary texts where it would be visible to us." Grainger notes that the whole-fish sauce was what most classical households would have used.

was eaten as early as the Yayoi period [300 BCE–200 CE]." Fish sauce was common locally in Akita, Ishikawa, and Shikoku prefectures for centuries, each of which has its own version. However, Hachisu says fish sauce was not a mainstay outside these regions until the 1990s, when "an increased interest in Southeast Asian cuisines brought fish sauce into more urban Japanese kitchens" alongside the shoyu that is commonly used.

In China, the historic record for fermented flavorings goes back even further. *Jiàng* is the general term used to describe these flavorings, including fish sauce and paste. Records from the court of the Zhou dynasty (roughly 1050–256 BCE) refer to various jiàng sauces used for different purposes, as well as professional brewers who served the court, showing that by this time the tradition of using fermented sauces (including fish sauce) was well established. During the Zhou period, the fermented paste was made with meat or fish with alcohol and koji mold mixed in. Later on, during the Han era (206 BCE–220 CE), it was also made with cooked grains or beans (particularly soybeans), giving us early versions of modern-day soy sauce and miso paste.

Mara King, a Hong Kong native who has studied Chinese fermentation history extensively, told me that the role of fish sauce in Chinese culture shifted over time:

> Fish sauces, meat sauces, and game sauces were used often in Chinese antiquity, much more often in the past than soy sauces are used today. Somewhere along the line, the Chinese moved away from these sauces and towards soy. The coastal regions, I think, kept their connection to abundant fish, and in Hong Kong there are traditions of using shrimp, and oysters in different preparations. I remember oyster cultivation in Hong Kong as a child, long beds of shells in shallow bays. These are long gone now. I would not be surprised if where the oysters once were, housing and development stand today. Fish, shrimp, and oysters are used often in the area where I am from in dim sum snacks and dumplings, as seasoning for noodle dishes. These applications are not really surprising or unexpected; they certainly didn't go into any desserts that I can remember. Fish and shrimp sauces were used

for broad applications for seasoning vegetable dishes, and oyster sauce was an extremely versatile seasoning that was used for all kinds of meats, mushrooms, and rice dishes.

People have been preserving their catch and eating fish sauces and pastes for millennia elsewhere in Asia as well. It is important to note that these sauces are not limited to coastal areas; many fish sauces, such as Cambodian prahok, were made with freshwater fish.

Most modern fish sauces are made with a higher percentage of salt than historic sauces. While ancient Roman recipes were probably about 15 percent salt, modern sauces comprise no less than 25 percent salt during the fermentation process, due to modern concerns about dangerous pathogens such as *C. botulinum*. However, research into foodborne pathogens has shown that 10 percent salt is enough to prevent the risk of botulism in fish sauce production. You can also make fish sauces with koji (*Koji Alchemy* by Rich Shih and Jeremy Umansky has some good ratios for doing so).

THE CREATION OF KETCHUP

In Europe, fish sauce fell out of popularity after the Roman period, but that doesn't mean the desire for umami went with it. Savory sauces of all sorts were employed in Europe from at least early Greek times and were common in the late Middle Ages and early Renaissance. We also see a good deal of "made sauces," which were essentially flavored vinegary mixtures found across the continent that offered some savoriness and sourness.

CHINESE CONDIMENTS LAY THE GROUNDWORK. Before and during the Elizabethan period (1558–1603), sauces were common condiments in England. In the 1600s, the English began to adapt savory condiments from China, such as fish sauce and soy sauce, to their cuisine. And therein lies the origin story of ketchup.

There are two possible versions of the story. The first, and the one most often pointed to, says that ketchup grew out of fermented fish sauce, called kê-tsiap in Hokkien Chinese, that traders from Vietnam are thought to have brought to southeastern China. Mushroom ketchup, the English precursor to tomato ketchup, was made to imitate the flavor of this sauce (a fact mentioned in Samuel Johnson's 1755 *Dictionary of the English Language*).

However, authors William Shurtleff and Akiko Aoyagi offer an intriguing alternate possibility, linking ketchup instead to soy sauce. Looking at a 1771 classified ad that mentions ketchup, they note: "The meaning of the word 'Ketchup' is unclear. Since the word meaning 'soy sauce' in Malay/ Indonesian is pronounced that way (but also spelled in various other ways, such as ketchap or kecap) it probably refers to soy sauce made in the Dutch East Indies (especially today's Indonesia). However it could possibly refer to a similar product from southern China or elsewhere in Southeast Asia. If this Ketchup was soy sauce made in the Dutch East Indies, was it the sweet, thick type (*kecap manis*) made only in Indonesia, or the salty type (*kecap asin*) made by Chinese throughout Asia?" They go on to note that when ketchup and soy sauce are mentioned in colonial and early republic American newspapers, the two were initially lumped together before later becoming more clearly differentiated.

It leads one to wonder (though we'll likely never know for sure) whether, because the English had access to both fish sauce and soy sauce and perhaps felt they had similar names, the term *ketchup* came to denote "thin amino sauces" in general. It certainly seems possible, given the proliferation of different ketchups we see during this period.

KETCHUP STARTS TO TAKE FORM. In the 1700s, three general types of ketchup could be found in England, none of which were made from tomatoes: mushroom ketchup, fish ketchup, and walnut ketchup. (The fish-based version confirms a direct link to the Chinese condiment.) At this time, the name *ketchup* didn't refer to a specific set of ingredients but rather to a class of thin, savory pickled or fermented sauces.

Of these three ketchup types, mushroom was most popular, and the earliest known recipe appeared in 1728. During this time, mushrooms were often eaten pickled with spices to make a savory seasoning. The pickling liquid became a valuable commodity: Once the liquid from the mushrooms mingled with the pickling vinegar or brine, it imparted a rich, dark color and deep flavor. Over time, this came to be regarded as a condiment in its own right, and in some cases the mushrooms, once the star of the show, would be removed prior to bottling the prized liquid.

This history suggests that while Chinese fish sauce and soy sauce laid the groundwork for savory sauces in Europe, mushroom ketchup itself may have come about for reasons not directly related to the original Chinese condiments. Perhaps people weren't actively trying to re-create fish or soy sauce; maybe they just tasted the pickling liquid from mushrooms and unexpectedly found a similar (though not nearly identical) flavor profile, which they liked.

By the mid-1700s, many cookery books and manuscripts include at least one ketchup recipe. Blending multiple ketchups was relatively common—it's how we got Worcestershire sauce, which was at the time a blend of walnut and mushroom ketchups, sometimes with "Canton soy" (Chinese soy sauce). All of these kinds of ketchups and sauces, including Worcestershire sauce, were layered together in dishes for the next century, including in J. H. Walsh's 1859 *English Cookery Book*.

TOMATOES COME ON THE SCENE. In 1804, James Mease's *Domestic Encyclopedia* noted that "love apples" (tomatoes) make "a fine catsup." Mease published the first known tomato ketchup recipe in 1812, consisting of unstrained tomato pulp with spices, making it much thicker than its liquidy forebears. Mease's recipe also uses brandy as its base, though most later recipes use vinegar.

Making mushroom ketchup involved a combination of cooking methods, including overnight fermentation with salt to pull the liquid from the mushrooms and allow them to develop their flavor, followed by simmering with aromatics for a deeper and more complex flavor. Tomato ketchup was simpler, typically skipping the overnight salting.

In 1876, Henry J. Heinz began making ketchup and sold it at the Philadelphia World's Fair. While he was not the first to bottle ketchup commercially, he was the first to make tomato ketchup a large-scale commercial enterprise. He was so successful that 97 percent of American homes today have a bottle of ketchup in the fridge.

The textures of early ketchups and modern tomato ketchups were different—mushroom ketchup is thin and liquidy, while tomato ketchup is thick and pasty—but the flavor principles at work are quite similar and are the same across all ketchups and amino sauces in general. Tomatoes are full of umami, giving you the same savory kick you would get from a fish sauce. Tomato ketchup is also sweet and sour, just like many of its precursors and its modern-day cousins. In the first-century Roman *Apicius*, many recipes use garum in tandem with vinegar and honey to season dishes, giving diners the savory/sweet/sour flavor profile we find with ketchup today. The same flavor profile was present in British mushroom ketchup, which used cloves and allspice to offer some sweetness to the sour and savory. Similarly, today's Vietnamese *nuoc cham*, a term used to describe dipping sauces containing ingredients such as fish sauce and citrus, is popular for its blend of umami and sour.

SOY SAUCE AND MISO

There are more than 50 names for the soybean and soy sauce across East Asia. The term *soy sauce* is said to derive from the Japanese word *shoyu*, though the Japanese term is thought to derive from the Chinese name for soybeans, *sou*. Wild soybeans originally grew in northeast China and Manchuria, and they have a long history of use, though the exact dates of cultivation are unknown. Thomas Sorosiak, who wrote about soybeans for *The Cambridge World History of Food*, says that around 2700 BCE, emperor Shennong ordered that plants be classified by their culinary and medicinal value, and soybeans were listed among the five principal and sacred crops. As Sorosiak notes, that date matches up with what we know of soybean cultivation, too, which appears to have taken place for more than 4,500 years. But he also cites other sources that give differing dates, some of which place the introduction of soybeans to China at only around 1000 BCE.

Whatever the date of their cultivation in China, the bean appears to have been spread around the Asian continent primarily by Buddhist priests, whose vegetarian diets spurred their interest in new foods and drinks that brought flavor and nutrition. In their monasteries, they made regular use of a variety of soy products, including flour, milk, curd, and soy sauce.

Many soy products, including soy sauce and miso, are fermented with species of Aspergillus fungi. Shoyu is typically made with A. *sojae*, and while some researchers suggest that Aspergillus fermentation moved across the Asian continent with soybeans, we do not have definitive evidence.

However, we do have evidence of soy sauce brewing in China going back 3,000 years. And in Japan, shoyu and sake breweries not only hold these microbes in their fermentation vessels but in the very bones of the structures themselves. Generations of A. sojae take up residence in the rafters and walls, helping generations of humans with their craft. Koji production, which in the case of shoyu making involves growing the spores on soybeans and often also wheat, is typically done in the cooler months (from the beginning of November to the end of February), when lower ambient temperatures support koji's slow growth and prevent other fermentation microbes from taking up residence and changing the final product's flavor.

In traditional koji fermentation, the microbial communities that live in fermentation vessels and are continuously stewarded through repeated batches of ferments lend their own flavor to those ferments. Kioke are wooden barrels that were used for all of Japan's fermented products, including soy sauce, miso, mirin, rice vinegar, sake, and pickles, up until the twentieth century. The wood itself hosts millions of beneficial microbes that aid in the fermentation process. After World War II, many farmers moved from the country to the city, and preservation practices once passed down through families were outsourced to large-scale manufacturers. Kioke were largely replaced by stainless steel tanks. However, there has been a recent resurgence both in small-scale brewing and in kioke use and manufacture. Cookbook author Nancy Singleton Hachisu calls these wooden barrels "the secret ingredient of soy sauce," and "the essential ingredient required to authentically ferment Japanese foods."

Traditional soy sauces are brewed over a long period from a combination of soybeans and wheat grains with salt and water. After it brews, the sauce is pressed from the bean mixture. Many soy sauces are still brewed this way today, though some larger manufacturers have resorted to less time-intensive processes.

Traditional miso pastes, made from soybeans, are allowed to ferment for months or even years, and there are many different types. Young miso pastes tend to be light in color and flavor: shiro (white) miso is lighter in color and body than its longer-fermented counterparts. It contains salt, koji inoculated on grains (such as rice or barley), and cooked, cooled soybeans. This is made into a paste that is rolled into balls and pressed or thrown into the fermentation vessel before being covered with weights to prevent exposure to air.

Miso is the Japanese name for this paste; elsewhere, fermented bean pastes are called *chang* in China, *jang* in Korea, and *tauco* in Indonesia. While miso is now strongly associated with Japanese cuisine, Hanamaruki Foods president Toshio Hanaoka argues that it was not originally developed there. He says there are two possibilities: It was introduced to Japan from Korea at least 1,300 years ago ("Misho [the original type of miso] was first cited in Taihouryou in 701 AD," he says), or it was introduced by Chinese Buddhists ("in the northeast district of China, it was called 'misun,' and in Korai [located in North Korea 935 to 1392 AD] 'misso' and in South Korea 'mijo'"). One thing is clear: The name itself is likely of Korean origin.

Like soy sauce, miso paste has a long fermentation time. It also has a long history of being used as a pickling bed: There are many examples, historic and modern, of burying fresh vegetables such as squash and beans in miso, as well as hard-boiled eggs, to preserve and flavor them. It has also been used for thousands of years as a seasoning or soup.

According to Nancy Singleton Hachisu, miso varieties are differentiated by flavor profile, color, and age, as well as ingredients:

- **SHIRO MISO** (white miso) is made with cooked soybeans, salt, and koji, and is fermented for 1 to 3 months.

- **INAKA MISO** (country miso) is made with seed miso (unpasteurized finished miso used to inoculate the new batch) along with a smaller proportion of koji to soybeans than shiro miso. It is the most versatile and most used miso in Japanese farm kitchens.

- **GENMAI MISO** is made with brown rice instead of white rice, which is the typical grain of choice.

- **MUGI MISO** is made with barley.

- **MAME MISO** (soybean miso) is made by adding koji-inoculated soybeans to the cooked soybeans, rather than adding koji-inoculated grains to cooked soybeans.

- **HATCHO MISO** is made by dusting cooked soybeans with crushed barley and koji spores. It takes 2 to 3 years to age fully.

Hatcho miso, in particular, has an interesting history. It is made primarily in Aichi Prefecture and has a history going back several centuries: The first commercial version dates back to 1645 and was the first brand-name soy product in Japan. After being steamed, the soybeans are left to oxidize overnight before being ground. The paste is then formed into large cross-like shapes (which increases the surface area), dusted with crushed barley, and inoculated with koji. After several days, the inoculated bean mixture is mixed with salt and a bit of water before being packed into massive cedar vats, where it sits under cloth and a weighted drop lid with 3 tons of stones that, according to Hachisu, are "piled on so carefully that the resulting pyramid is stable even during an earthquake." It then sits undisturbed for 2 to 3 years, resulting in a deep, mellow, and nuanced final product.

Beyond soy sauce and miso, we can stretch our understanding of amino pastes to include leftovers from other ferments, which can be reemployed to flavorful effect: Moromi, for example, is the mash left after soy sauce, sake, mirin, vinegar, or fish sauce is pressed and can be used as a pickling bed or a flavoring agent for a range of dishes. Other mashes have plenty of creative uses, too: Vinegar mash is used as a pickling bed, and brewing lees are used for pickling (like kasuzuke, pickles made using sake kasu—that is, sake lees).

I also enjoy making amino sauces using the method for making shoyu, but with ingredients from my immediate environment, as our ancestors would have. For example, green peanuts (eaten boiled here in Georgia), seasonal wild foods, and ingredients that evoke favorite food memories (for example, winter wheat for White Lily flour) allow me to play with amino sauces that speak to time and place. Traditional shoyu is ready after 1 to 3 years, but the aging times for these nontraditional shoyu-style sauces vary. I've let them go for a few months or a few years and have gotten some really interesting results in both cases, so it's worth experimenting!

Building Flavor

Hot peppers add a kick to ferments, while spices can add warmth, depth, brightness, or heat. Herbs and other fresh plant matter are often added for flavor, too, either during fermentation or after. Hops, for example, were added to beer during fermentation for flavor as well as preservation. After fermentation, beer might be flavored with fruit and spices, as in this recipe for "Very Rare Ale" from Lady Charlotte Bury's *The Lady's Own Cookery Book, and New Dinner-Table Directory,* published in 1844 (the first edition was published anonymously in 1840):

> When your ordinary good quality ale has been turned into a vessel that will hold eight or nine gallons and has done working and is ready to be stopped up, take a pound and a half of raisins of the best quality, stoned and cut into pieces, and two large oranges. Pulp and pare the oranges, then slice them thin. Add the rind of one lemon, a dozen cloves, and one ounce of coriander seeds well bruised.
>
> Put all these into a cloth bag and hang them in the vessel, then stop it up close.
>
> Fill the bottles but a little above the neck to leave room for the liquor to play. Put into every one a large lump of fine sugar. Stop the bottles close, and let the ale stand for a month before you drink it.

HEAT

The characteristic burn you get from eating hot peppers comes from the chemical compound capsaicin. Hot peppers appeared in Mexico and Peru as early as 5000 BCE and later spread across the continent and to the Caribbean. They didn't reach other parts of the world until after the Americas were colonized, so before then, people elsewhere got their kick from horseradish and various herbs and spices. In Nepal, for example, traditional spices included ginger, mustard seed (Nepal is the world's largest exporter), and timur, a berry similar to Sichuan pepper. This means that many dishes and cuisines that we today associate with hot peppers (such as Korean or Thai dishes) would have been very different centuries ago, as they would have relied on other sources for their heat.

Hot peppers can be the star of the fermentation show, as in the hot sauce recipe on page 212, or a supporting actor, as in the fire cider recipe on page 208 or in yuzukoshō, a fermented paste made from chile peppers, yuzu peel, and salt that's used as a condiment for several Japanese dishes such as sashimi.

HERBS AND SPICES

As a general rule, herbs differ from spices based on the part of the plant being used: *herbs* refers to the leaves and shoots, and *spices* to the roots, barks, and seeds. Both have been a critical component in all global cuisines. Humans have relied on aromatic plants for flavor and medicine since Neolithic times, and they were thoroughly entrenched in human cuisines worldwide when written records first appeared. Ancient Greeks and Romans drank spiced wines, for example, and Europeans in the Middle Ages drank hippocras, a spiced and often sweetened wine named after the famous physician Hippocrates.

Our preferences for herbs and spices fluctuate over time: Some endure in popularity through the millennia, such as ginger, while others fall out of common usage but are still available (such as long pepper), and still others are seemingly gone altogether, such as silphium, a mystery herb from ancient Greece and Rome that appears to have only grown wild and then was harvested to extinction. Some herbs and spices that are now regularly added to our ferments and considered central to their flavor profiles, such as caraway in sauerkraut and ginger in kimchi, were not traditional components in those ferments but late additions. This speaks to the ways in which our tastes, and our access to different flavorings, have changed over time. In nontropical areas (Europe in particular), spices used to be expensive, and wealthy folks would show off by packing them into every dish. But as colonization grew and spice production and trade moved spices more quickly, costs fell. No longer were spices pricey or coveted; instead, they were common and affordable enough to be added to even the most humble ferment.

> The production of mead does not require heat, and possibly it
> has been part of human life for even longer than controlled fire.
> Imagine the wonder and awe our ancestors must have felt as they
> first encountered fermenting honey-water in the hollow of a tree.
> Were they scared by the bubbling, or just curious? Once they
> tasted it, they must have liked it and drunk more.
>
> —SANDOR ELLIX KATZ, *WILD FERMENTATION*

Alcohol and Flavor

While our first experience with alcohol may have happened by accident
when our forebears discovered fermented honey water (an early mead), we
quickly learned to enjoy it and became eager to see what other enjoyable
flavors we could add to it. Some of the earliest alcohol found was a fruit
and rice wine from around 9,000 years ago in China; while the fruit was
probably the source of the wild yeasts that drove fermentation, it offered
flavor to the finished alcohol as well. The choice of which flavors to add
would have been informed by long-standing traditions of using food as
medicine. This tradition continues to influence some of our flavor profiles
to this day.

FLAVORFUL MEDICINE

In the Middle Ages, gin was medicine rather than a fun-time drink, used
to aid digestion, prevent some infections, and even fight heart disease.
Its usage began to shift in the early 1700s, when we see in printed recipes
from the time that the focus was on flavor balance, not medicinal qualities. Later, gin's flavor became of primary concern to English colonizers in
mosquito-heavy areas who began to consume quinine to combat malaria.
They added gin to their quinine drink primarily to help cut quinine's bitter
flavor (which is how we got the modern gin and tonic).

The African shrub gesho (*Rhamnus prinoides*, a member of the buckthorn
family) has historically been used for various medicinal purposes, including as a diuretic and to stimulate bile flow, and also to add bitter flavor. In
Ethiopia, twigs and leaves of gesho are added to tej (mead) and tella (beer),

both to add bitterness and to extend shelf life. The brewing of both tej and tella is an art form. The vintner or brewer must determine the exact timing to incorporate gesho for maximum flavor and health benefits. In Ethiopia (particularly the northern part of the country) as well as Eritrea, tej is typically made by mixing one part honey to three parts water and adding some stems and branches of gesho. The gesho is removed after 2 weeks, but the tej continues to ferment for another 3 to 4 weeks.

LAYERS OF FLAVOR

Brewers past and present have manipulated the use of microbes in the brewing process to produce different flavor results. English writer Pete Brown notes, "The history of the development of brewing is in large part the history of us learning more about yeast, how it behaves, what it doesn't like and what keeps it happy." Different yeasts have different behaviors and alcohol tolerances, which inform the flavor of the finished beverage. Wild yeasts tend to stop fermenting malt sugars at around 5 percent ABV, for example, while champagne yeasts have a much higher tolerance. However, yeasts working on their own are rarely able to produce a beverage above about 18 percent ABV. The most notable differences in yeasts are between those that work at the top of the ferment and those that work at the bottom. The former produce sweeter ales, while the latter produce lagers.

The first brewing yeasts were simply the wild yeasts already present in the environment. Over time, as people discovered what worked best or produced the best flavor, these yeasts would be saved and backslopped into future batches to inoculate them, creating starter cultures that eventually became their own specialty strains with their own unique properties.

Fermented beverages within a type (such as red wine) can vary significantly in flavor and alcohol, informed in part by the yeasts in addition to other factors, such as terroir and grape varietal. Wines even from the same varietals can vary in bitterness and sweetness, for example, not to mention their top notes and base notes and sometimes even mouthfeel. Vintners and brewers must balance factors within the ferment for the drinker's palate, while also considering them against a larger expectation of the characteristics of a given style of wine or beer. The flavor, and thus microbial makeup of a brew, is contextual. As Ken Albala notes, "Apart from bacterial colonization (which is a serious problem), contamination is really just a matter of not getting exactly what you aimed at. For instance, *Brettanomyces*, a yeast that is considered a contaminant in English ales, is celebrated in certain Belgian brews."

As we'll see in Chapter 4, our relationship with wine in the past was somewhat different than it is today. While people today tend to think that adding anything to wine constitutes adulteration, our ancestors used to add water and flavorings (with exceptions: The ancient Celts drank their wine unstrained and at full strength, which appalled the ancient Romans, who were accustomed to watering down their wine). Our ancestors would regularly add spices and herbs—in Germany, for example, they would add woodruff to wine to produce May wine. As Ken Albala says, "Drinks like vermouth are the only remaining members of a once huge tribe of medicinal fortified wines."

The Flavor of Place

In 2016, a study was published that reshaped how we consider the tree of life, the map of known species on Earth and their connections to each other. Historically the map has heavily emphasized eukaryotes (which make up multicellular organisms, though some also classify yeasts here, too), leaving many single-celled organisms in the lurch. The new tree of life, though, includes them, and we learn that roughly two-thirds of our planet's biodiversity is in bacteria.

Today, many of us are concerned about supporting biodiversity, particularly at a time when human behavior has resulted in so much loss of plant and animal life as well as shifts in landscapes. What if we extended our consideration to include microbial biodiversity, recognizing microbes as a critical part of our living world?

One way to do this is by using flavor as a guide to make wild ferments that speak to place, just as humans have done for

There are more microbial species on Earth than stars in the sky.

—BIOLOGISTS JAY T. LENNON AND KENNETH J. LOCEY

to boil or not to boil

Through the millennia, attempts to brew the best beer have resulted in endless rounds of experimentation, and not everyone agrees on the results. We see one example of this passionate discussion in a series of letters written in 1651 between Edward Conway, the second Viscount Conway and second Viscount Killultagh, and his nephew, Colonel Edward Harley, about a peculiar ale shared by Harley.

Harley's recipe called for boiling the water "by itself" for 3 hours before pouring it over the malt (8 bushels of malt per hogshead of water) and continuing to boil until the water had "taken the strength" of the malt. Once cooled, yeast was stirred in and the mixture was allowed to sit for a month.

Conway was skeptical of the recipe and pressed for details and explanations about the amount of malt used and the odd choice to boil the water alone (particularly for several hours) before adding malt. Harley insisted it improved the quality of the water, but Conway (as well as a local brewer consulted on the matter) said that it did no such thing, though the brewer suggested that perhaps the recipe had meant to boil the *wort* rather than the *water* for 3 hours, which would make more sense.

The letters meander through a series of philosophical and scientific pathways, as both uncle and nephew are intent on their perspectives: Harley's insistence that boiling water alone makes better beer, and Conway's insistence that it does not. Eventually, the younger of the two relented, saying he would make ale as his uncle did, with water that was "but little boyled." Though Conway later asked if Harley had successfully made the ale recipe, that was the end of their written back-and-forth on the subject.

millennia. I find this principle to be a great way to distinguish between the tastes of different places, and it's exciting: By making our fermentation practice about discovering new flavors, we encourage microbial diversity and explore different micro-spaces as a matter of play.

TERROIR

The term *terroir* (defined as "the taste of place") in winemaking refers to the exact growing conditions of grapes in a certain place (such as the soil composition, altitude, climate, and geography), recognizing that these each impact the taste of the final product. French winemakers take this concept quite seriously: The place-based influence on wine's flavor has resulted in classifications and industry changes that emphasize the importance of appellation. The key argument behind why it is important is that the terroir of a certain place produces characteristics in a wine that are irreplicable elsewhere.

The study of pedology (soil science) emerged in Russia in the late nineteenth century and was introduced to France several decades later, and some posit that it served as the foundation for the concept of terroir. Winemaker Thomas Parker, however, among other voices, argues that terroir can be seen centuries prior, back during the Renaissance, as a form of cultural mythology expressed through literature, language, and, of course, horticulture. All of these told a common story: That place matters to taste, and a place's value to our food and lives is inherent and central, not an aside. By the early twentieth century, wine had become one of the central objects of efforts to protect French agricultural products, which culminated in the creation of the Institut National des Appellations d'Origine in the 1930s.

While the term *terroir* often evokes the concept of physical environment, it is not limited to that. Terroir can refer to unseen forces, too: In wine, the microbes naturally present on the grapes' skin, if allowed to work their magic, produce a wild-fermented product unique to that time and place. And even if we are not master winemakers, we are able to play with terroir in our own fermentation experiments. Each place where we ferment food (and the food itself) will have its own microbial fingerprint, and that is reflected in our food.

NAEM

Naem is a delicious, flavorful sour sausage from northern Thailand. I've tried making it with standard supermarket ground pork and with ground pork from a local butcher or farmer, and not surprisingly, the latter makes for a much more toothsome, flavorful product.

I get the best flavor and texture when I ferment naem in the fridge for a couple of days, then let it finish up and develop its sour flavor at room temperature. This helps it dry out a touch, giving it a chance to develop a more cohesive texture than it otherwise might. However, don't let it dry out too much; you'll need some moisture to get your naem to sour quickly and develop the proper flavor.

Naem is traditionally eaten uncooked and sliced, served with sliced ginger, chopped bird's-eye chile, sliced shallot, scallions, and peanuts. However, it's also served all kinds of other ways, including in fried rice, fried with eggs, mixed into salads, stir-fried with chanterelles, or simply grilled (it's often cooked still wrapped in the banana leaves over coals). Feel free to experiment!

MAKES ABOUT 20 SMALL OR 12 LARGER SAUSAGES

1/2–3/4	pound pork skin
2	pounds ground pork
4–6	bird's-eye chiles, very finely minced
20	cloves garlic, minced or pressed
1¼	cups cooked glutinous rice, cooled
¼	cup plus 1 tablespoon sea salt
	Banana leaves, plastic wrap, or parchment paper
	Twine

1 Boil the pork skin in a large pot until cooked through, 15 to 20 minutes. Drain, then let cool.

2 Finely dice the pork skin with a very sharp knife. This stuff is slippery, so I've found it easiest to set it skin side (what would be the outside of the pig) down and slowly, carefully dice. It may help to partially freeze it first.

3 Place the pork skin, ground pork, chiles, garlic, rice, and salt in a large bowl. Press and mix together with your hands until thoroughly combined.

Recipe continues on next page. >

4   Lay the banana leaves out flat. If you got whole leaves (rather than pre-cut), you may want to cut them down to a size you can easily roll up.

5   Hand-roll your pork mixture into cigar shapes, several inches long. Place each sausage on a banana leaf and roll it up into a little packet, making sure to tuck the edges under so the leaf entirely surrounds the pork (see the instructions below). Make sure your banana leaf is tightly wrapped around the meat mixture and the air is pressed out!

6   Secure each packet with twine.

7   Place a wire rack in the bottom of a shallow dish to keep the bottom of your naem from getting soggy while fermenting (or do what I do and line the bottom of the dish with a layer of chopsticks, parallel to each other). Place your naem in a single layer on top of the rack and allow to sour in the fridge for 2 days. Then let them sit at room temperature until fragrant and slightly sour, about 3 days. Store in the fridge and use within 2 weeks.

HOW TO FOLD BANANA LEAVES

Folding banana leaves is a process with a bit of a learning curve. If folded wrong, the leaves can split, leaving you with a mess (and too much air getting to your sausage). Typically, they split across the leaf veins, so you'll have better luck wrapping with banana leaves if you work with the veins, rather than against them. Here's what works for me:

1   Lay down a large rectangle of banana leaf, with the veins perpendicular to the edge of your work surface.

2   Lay down a second, thinner strip (two to three times the width of your sausage) on top of the first leaf, but *parallel* to your work surface.

3   Lay your sausage down lengthwise on the smaller strip, then fold the ends of that strip over the ends of your sausage.

4   Roll up the whole thing in the larger leaf, gently and evenly pressing as you go to get it as tight as possible.

5   Tear off the loose edges of the outer leaf—just enough that they aren't flapping around so you can more easily fit the naem in a pan to ferment.

CARROT NAEM

This salty, garlicky carrot ferment is a fun example of using a technique developed for a particular dish with different ingredients. I find fermentation to be an inherently playful form of cooking, and carrot naem is one of the most joyous and exploratory ferments I've made recently.

Carrot naem came about soon after I worked on the traditional naem recipe on page 155. I had extra carrots lying about, and I had just stumbled across a banana flower. With naem on my mind, I decided to give these new ingredients a try. This vegetarian version of naem has some of the sweet and floral notes of the banana flower, with a bold hit of garlic and spice. It's also fun to watch ferment, as the banana petal oxidizes and gives you a technicolor show of purples, pinks, and yellows.

Carrot naem is divine crumbled over a salad or soup. It's also wonderful over rice with some veggies and herbs, or in banh mi. Of course, it doesn't taste like traditional naem, but that's half the fun.

MAKES
ABOUT
6 SMALL
VEGETARIAN
SAUSAGES

2	pounds whole carrots
4–6	bird's-eye chiles, very finely minced
15	cloves garlic, peeled
¼	cup sea salt
1	tablespoon sugar
1	banana flower
	Twine

1   Roughly chop the carrots and place in a food processor. Process just until roughly minced. Add the chiles, garlic, salt, and sugar, and process just until minced and combined. (Alternatively, roughly mince the carrots, chiles, and garlic by hand, then combine with the salt and sugar in a large bowl.)

2   Using your hands, shape the carrot mixture into little cigars (you'll want to keep them on the smaller side to accommodate the size of the flower petals) and place on a parchment-lined tray.

3   Peel off the outer few layers of petals from the banana flower and discard (preferably in your compost).

Recipe continues on next page. >

4   Begin peeling petals from the flower. Place a roll of carrot mixture in the center of each petal and roll it up, folding all sides in around the naem. Secure each packet with twine.

5   Set the packets back on the tray and leave out at room temperature until you get the flavor you like best, 2 to 3 days. You can start taste-testing after 24 hours.

6   Once the packets have the flavor you like, store the naem in an airtight container in the fridge and use within a month or so.

TEPACHE

Tepache, a fermented pineapple drink originally from Mexico, is one of my absolute favorite beverages. It is often made with pineapple scraps (core and rind), though I sometimes will use the whole pineapple for extra pineapple flavor. Tepache is popular in many Caribbean and Latin American countries, and it can have a lot of regional variation (for instance, my Dominican friend doesn't drink it with spices, but my friend from Acapulco, Mexico, does).

Though pineapple is the traditional base, the tepache method can be applied to whatever fresh fruit you desire. In *Mesquite: An Arboreal Love Affair*, ethnobotanist Gary Paul Nabhan, for example, gives a recipe using ripe yellow barrel cactus fruits and mesquite syrup.

For this recipe, you'll need a 1- to 2-gallon food-safe, nonreactive crock or container. I call for the whole pineapple, but you can use just the core and peels if that's what you have.

MAKES 1
GALLON

1   **pineapple, skin on, crown discarded, cut into wedges**

2   **cups sugar** (turbinado, white, or brown)

1   **tablespoon whole allspice berries**

3   **whole cloves**

1   **stick cinnamon**

     About 1 gallon water

1   Combine the pineapple, sugar, and spices in a crock or other food-safe container.

2   Add enough water to cover the pineapple, then stir to dissolve
     the sugar.

3   Cover with a lid or a tea towel to keep out bugs. For nonalcoholic
     or very lightly alcoholic tepache, let sit for 2 to 3 days. For alcoholic
     tepache, let sit for 5 to 7 days. Stir your ferment several times a day.

4   Strain, then store in the fridge, using within several weeks.

ANCIENT ROMAN GARUM

The dominant flavors in ancient Greek and Roman cuisine were honey, vinegar, garum, and what Andrew Dalby and Sally Grainger call a "vast array of fresh and dried herbs and spices." Garum, a fish sauce, is no longer easy to find, but thankfully it's easy to make. The basic method is similar to that for other fish sauces, giving you a good jumping-off point for exploring other versions.

Generally speaking, all you have to do is pack whole fish in salt (*whole* is key here; the guts provide the enzymes needed to break down the fish), then wait until you get a clear sauce oozing out of them (that's the garum). The only known historical recipe to provide a ratio for salt to fish is the one found in the *Geoponica*, a 20-book Byzantine collection from the tenth century, which suggests a 1:8 ratio. This means that for each 1 pound of salt, you would use 8 pounds of fish, though I typically use more salt (closer to a 1:4 ratio) to meet my personal tastes.

You'll want to use small fish (such as mackerel, sardines, and smelt). I find that I have the best luck cutting them into a few pieces if they run large.

Herbs were sometimes packed in with the fish. If you want your garum to be closer to the traditional ancient Roman flavor, make sure to use herbs that were available at the time (such as oregano and parsley, native to the Mediterranean region). I usually use thyme, oregano, and parsley, plus either lavender leaf or dill.

You'll want to make the garum in a glass jar or other food-safe vessel with a lid. It's best to avoid plastic here as your fish sauce will be sitting in it for months, and the plastic can leach into the ferment.

Recipe continues on next page. >

Begin with a layer of salt in your fermentation vessel, followed by a layer of fish and herbs, and another layer of salt (like making a lasagna). Make sure the last layer you put on is a thick layer of salt to protect your ferment from the elements. Then put a weight on it to keep everything in place and top it with a lid. I often use glass or ceramic weights; whatever you decide on, make sure your weights are nonreactive and food-safe.

Let the fish ferment for at least 6 months (a year, or more, is best). Set it in the sun, if possible; the warmth helps accelerate the enzymatic action. However, it will still ferment just fine on a shelf in your home; it will just take longer. You'll notice your fish sauce is ready when it has a layer of transparent liquid on top (typically the color and clarity, though not the texture, of maple syrup).

When it's time to pour off your garum, do so slowly and carefully, so that you don't upset the remaining solids in your jar. This will give you a thin, transparent, flavor-packed liquid. Once you have poured off as much liquid as you can, transfer it to a jar. Historically, this liquid was kept at room temperature out of direct sunlight, but if you prefer you can store it in the fridge, where it will last indefinitely.

Next (if you're up for it), transfer the fish concoction left in your fermentation vessel into a cheesecloth-lined mesh sieve set over a bowl. Press the remaining liquid into the bowl. This is alix, a cloudy but still delicious fish sauce. Like garum, it will store in the fridge indefinitely.

If you want to get really wild, you can also dehydrate the remaining solids for a delicious, umami-packed seasoning salt. Use a dehydrator set to 135°F/57°C or an oven on the lowest setting; the process will take a day or two. However, unless you live alone or have very understanding housemates, I recommend setting the dehydrator outside because drying the solids will make your house smell like fish for a few days.

MUSHROOM KETCHUP

The predecessor to today's sweet and savory tomato ketchup was a fermented mushroom sauce. Inspired by fish sauce, it is made by setting out salted mushrooms overnight, then cooking them (and their juices) with spices, then straining out the mushrooms. The resulting umami-filled sauce is thin, more akin to a fish sauce than a modern ketchup. However, if you want a thicker version, you can skip the straining and put your mushroom ketchup in a blender, blending it until smooth. The recipe below is based on recipes from the 1700s. If you prefer, you can swap shallot for the onion and add mace and/or nutmeg.

I encourage you to play around with using different mushrooms, as each offers its own distinct flavor profile. Shiitakes and portobellos both work great here. I especially enjoy using sustainably foraged mushrooms (make sure you properly identify them, of course), which in my area include lion's mane, oyster, and chanterelle. Doing so gives the final ketchup the flavor of a particular time and place. I also like adding seasonal herbs (rosemary is *fantastic* in this) to further help my sauce speak to locale and season.

MAKES
ABOUT
½ PINT

16	ounces mushrooms, rinsed and finely diced
¼	cup finely ground sea salt
¼	cup good-quality apple cider vinegar
1	small yellow onion, chopped
1	tablespoon prepared horseradish (just the grated stuff, not the creamy stuff; see note)
½	teaspoon whole allspice berries
¼	teaspoon whole cloves
1	bay leaf
	Pinch of ground cayenne pepper (or a splash of fermented cayenne hot sauce, my usual go-to)

NOTE I'll often use homemade pickled horseradish, which I make by fermenting sliced horseradish root in brine until soft, then chopping in a food processor until smooth.

Recipe continues on next page. >

1   Combine the mushrooms and salt in a nonreactive bowl. Using your hands, toss the mushrooms until they're evenly coated with the salt and then massage the salt into them slightly. You'll be able to feel the liquid start to come out of them.

2   Cover the bowl and let sit at room temperature. Check the mushrooms after 20 minutes or so to make sure that they are releasing liquid. If they aren't, add a bit more salt and massage again. Allow to sit out for around 24 hours.

3   Pour the mushrooms and their liquid into a saucepan (you'll be amazed how much liquid they produce!). Add the vinegar, onion, horseradish, allspice, cloves, bay leaf, and cayenne. Simmer for 15 to 20 minutes, then remove from the heat and let cool.

4   Line a strainer with muslin or cheesecloth and set it in a mixing bowl. Pour the mushroom ketchup into the strainer. Wrap the cloth up around the mushroom mixture and give it a good squeeze to release the rest of its juice. (When you're done, don't throw out those spent mushrooms! They're infused with a lot of tasty spices and can be dried and ground into a fantastic umami-rich seasoning blend.)

5   Transfer the mushroom ketchup to a jar or bottle and store in the fridge, where it will last for several months.

FERMENTED TOMATO KETCHUP

This ketchup is leaps and bounds better than the store-bought stuff. A short bout of fermentation renders a bit of sourness, funk, and depth of flavor, rounding out some of the salt and sweet in the tomato paste.

Though it is fantastic as is, this ketchup is even better with spices (some of my favorite combinations are listed below). Toasting them yields extra flavor and depth. If you're feeling really wild, you can replace the Worcestershire sauce or shoyu with your very own homemade mushroom ketchup (page 161).

MAKES
½ PINT

1   **cup tomato paste**

1   **tablespoon Worcestershire sauce or shoyu**

Splash of fish sauce (I like nam pla, a Thai fish sauce)

Whole spices, to taste (I go for about 1 tablespoon after grinding; see my favorites below)

1   Stir together the tomato paste, Worcestershire sauce or shoyu, and fish sauce.

2   Lightly toast the spices, then grind them to a powder (I use a coffee grinder dedicated to spices). Stir the ground spices into the tomato mixture.

3   Scoop the mixture into a jar, pressing to remove as many air bubbles as possible. Let ferment at room temperature, stirring daily, until it has a flavor you enjoy, at least 2 to 3 days.

4   Stick it in the fridge, where it should keep for at least a month.

MY FAVORITE SPICE COMBINATIONS FOR TOMATO KETCHUP

This recipe is a great place to use foraged spices such as mustard and juniper, as well as store-bought ones.

- juniper berry and lemon peel
- cinnamon, coriander, and mustard seed
- black peppercorn, clove, and juniper berry

AMINO SAUCES

Amino sauces are simply a flavorful mixture of legumes, koji, flavorings, and salt. Unlike shoyu (soy sauce), in which the legumes are inoculated with koji before being made into sauce, these amino sauces use koji grains directly in the sauce itself and are fermented for a shorter period.

The best thing about amino sauces is that you can make a whole range of interesting flavor combinations. For example, I make one sauce with pine nut, pear, and cinnamon bark, and I make another with green peanuts and all the seasonings I normally put in boiled peanuts. You can even add fruit, but keep in mind that fruit (and any other flavorings with natural sugars) can invite other microbes to the party, so keep an eye on how the flavors develop as the sauce ages. One of my favorite experiments with fruit included basmati rice and scuppernongs (white grapes native to the South).

Amino sauces require more salt than lacto-ferments because they will (potentially) be fermenting for a longer period. You'll want your salt to comprise around 10 percent of the solution.

Amino sauces are incredibly versatile and can be used just about anywhere you'd like to add a savory kick. I stir them in marinades, dressings, sauces, soups, and even baked goods. If you don't want the chunks of koji in your final dish, simply strain them out before using.

MAKES
1 PINT

1½–2	**cups nuts or cooked, cooled beans**
3–3½	**tablespoons unrefined salt**
1½	**tablespoons dried koji**
	Flavorings, as desired

1   Combine the nuts or beans, salt, koji, and flavorings in a pint jar and add enough water to fill it. Tighten the lid and shake to dissolve the salt.

2   Allow the mixture to ferment at room temperature, shaking daily. Check regularly for kahm yeast (a white film that won't hurt you or your ferment) and scrape off any that you see.

3   When the ferment achieves a taste and smell that you like, use it! How long you ferment is up to you. I'll sometimes let an amino sauce age on the counter for 1 month and then age it in the fridge for many more months. Other times, I let it ferment entirely at room temperature,

provided that it continues to taste and smell good. Amino sauces such as shoyu are historically stored at room temperature, but I tend to store these experimental sauces in the fridge once they have the flavor I want. They will keep in the fridge for years.

SHIO KOJI

Shio koji is just salt, koji, and water. It has a savory complexity that belies its simple nature, and it is absolutely transcendent as a marinade for meat and roasting vegetables. If you want to play with the flavor, there are endless other ingredients you can add, from citrus peels to fresh herbs to spices to hot peppers; one of the best ones I've ever made had pine needle and lemon.

If you're using koji blocks, make sure to break them apart with your hands before using. You want a 12-percent salt solution. Feel free to scale this recipe up or down as needed.

MAKES
1 PINT

2 **cups koji**

4 **tablespoons unrefined salt**

2 **cups water**

Other flavorings, as desired (optional)

Combine the koji, salt, and water in a pint jar. If you're adding other flavorings, these can make up 10 to 20 percent of the final product. Let ferment at room temperature for 1 to 2 weeks, stirring or shaking daily. Store in the fridge, where it will keep for months.

4

HEALTH

Fermented foods are tools for positive change in our bodies and our minds. Transforming raw foodstuffs into new iterations of themselves, ferments also ask our bodies to engage in partnership between micro and macro— between the tiniest bacteria and the complex human organism.

Ferments, and their associated microorganisms, have a long and storied history in connection to our health. Both praised and derided, they are sometimes the source of fear and controversy while also being upheld as a magical cure-all. While our relationship to specific microbes and the ferments they inspire has changed over time, one thing is certain: We have always depended on them, and that complex relationship has echoed throughout the human experience.

The Microbiome

Perhaps the best place to start a chapter on ferments and health is to discuss how the microbes themselves impact our bodies. Our understanding of the specifics of this relationship has evolved, and continues to do so, informed by scientific research, healing modalities, religions, and more.

ANCIENT UNDERSTANDING

The depth of our understanding of the microbiome and the processes at work appears to be unique to our modern world. However, we have long been aware of the connection between fermentation and health. In early modern Europe, for example, digestion was thought of as a fermentative act. And even in ancient times, our ancestors had a nascent understanding that microbes might be at play in our health, for good or ill. This can be seen in the writings of Taliesin, a Welsh bard from the sixth century CE, who wrote of a deadly pestilence, called the Yellow Plague of Rhos, that devastated the population of Wales. He described the illness as an embodied yet unseen force—a precursor to our modern understanding of microbes. His description, many centuries before we began to peer into the microscopic world, is a good reminder that we can draw sophisticated and nuanced conclusions about our world simply through observation, even if the science hasn't caught up yet. Was Taliesin "ahead of his time"? Sure. But he also approached his world with curiosity and a desire to learn, which will get you pretty far.

Each patient carries his own doctor inside him.

—NORMAN COUSINS,
ANATOMY OF AN ILLNESS AS PERCEIVED BY THE PATIENT

Here is an excerpt of one of his poems:

> Discover thou what is,
> The strong creature from before the flood,
> Without flesh, without bone,
> Without vein, without blood,
> Without head, without feet;
> It will neither be older nor younger
> Than at the beginning;
> For fear of a denial.
> There are no rude wants
> With creatures.
> [. . .]
> It is concealed
> Because sight cannot perceive it;
> It is noxious, it is beneficial;
> It is yonder, it is here;
> It will decompose,
> But it will not repair the injury;
> It will not suffer for its doings,
> Seeing it is blameless.
> It is wet, it is dry,
> It frequently comes,
> Proceeding from the heat of the sun
> And the coldness of the moon.
> The moon is less beneficial,
> Inasmuch as her heat is less,
> One Being has prepared it,
> Out of all creatures,
> By a tremendous blast,
> To wreak vengeance
> On Maelgwn Gwynedd.

What I find most interesting about this particular poem is that it shows that people centuries ago had a more nuanced understanding of how

germ theory

Louis Pasteur developed germ theory, the idea that illness is caused by microorganisms invading and multiplying within the body, but never got a chance to test it. In 1864, surgeon Joseph Lister began applying the theory to his practice by administering carbolic acid as a topical treatment to surgical wounds. The acid, which he called an antiseptic, killed microbes on contact and prevented wound infections.

Microscopy, and the human awareness of microbes, had been around since the 1660s, when Antonie van Leeuwenhoek invented the microscope and Robert Hooke published *Micrographia*, the first important work on microscopy. But at the time of Lister's experiments, we had not yet made the link between particular microbes and the specific diseases they cause. In 1877, however, German researcher Robert Koch used a microscope to examine blood samples from cattle that had died of anthrax, and he noticed rod-shaped bacteria in all the samples. When he infected mice with blood from those cattle, he discovered that they contracted anthrax and had the same bacteria in their blood. These specific forms of bacteria, Koch realized, were responsible for causing anthrax.

Though initially focused solely on the relationship between pathogen and host, our modern understanding of microbial diseases has evolved to include contextualizing factors (such as the environment and personal behaviors) as well as the complex microbiome and its impact on our state of health.

microbes move through the world than we tend to give our forebears credit for: invisible, able to be both noxious and beneficial, older than time, and all around us. We see this view reflected in various healing modalities as well, both in people's prescriptions based upon the effects of fermented foods upon the body and their perspectives about fermentation and digestion.

THE MICROBIOME TODAY

Microbes, both beneficial and not, are our oldest teachers, and as our planet's earliest life-forms, they are our ancestors as well. Eventually, the earliest microbes began living inside other microbes, functioning as organelles for them and creating the framework for multicellular life. We see, then, how the very shape and function of our bodies was in part determined by the relationships of microorganisms to each other. As our bodies continued to develop specialized organs and cells, we developed another relationship with all the microorganisms that live within and on our bodies: what we today call the microbiome. The number of microorganisms that make up our microbiome is vast, far outnumbering our own cells by a ratio of 10 to 1. The majority of them live in our gastrointestinal (GI) tract, and in total these microbes contain 100 times as many genes as our genome.

Our modern bodies are the way they are in part because of the microbes with whom we share our world. In some cases, our bodies, populations, and societies have been profoundly shaped by the impact of pathogenic microbes, and not always in a positive way (for example, the loss of life from the COVID-19 pandemic). But in others, beneficial microorganisms have taught our bodies about the delicate art of immunity, forming an ancient symbiotic relationship in which we serve as host and they serve as a critical part of our immune system. Today, our microbiome helps keep us healthy in the face of unwanted microbial intruders, and we're just now learning about some of its other benefits to our physical and mental health, such as better digestion, changes in mood and reduction of depression and anxiety, decreased inflammation, and more.

Each time I think of how central these tiny beings are to the web of life, I think of something my mom used to tell me as a child: Magic (or faith) and science do not have to be opposite ends of a spectrum. For her, as for me, the more I learn about the evolution of microbes and the intersection of microbes and our physical bodies, the more I believe in the existence of magic in the world.

Ferments for Flavor and Nutrition

Taste is one of the most important ways in which our body communicates to us the nutritive value of our food. Our senses of taste and smell actually developed to guide us toward foods that are beneficial to our bodies. We are born with aversions to certain tastes and smells (for example, the smell of rotting meat) because it was evolutionarily advantageous for us to avoid those objects, just as we are drawn toward flavors that indicate the presence of nutrition (for instance, the sweetness of calorie-rich ripe fruit). Fermentation has a role in that dynamic. Through fermentation, for example, the starches in grains are broken down from long chains of linked glucose molecules into simple sugars, and the proteins in soybeans and meat are transformed into free amino acids. In the process, the flavors we associate with nutrient-dense food (umami in protein-rich foods, for example) develop. This is an excellent example of how the concepts we cover in this book have overlapped throughout our history: We often make fermented foods for flavor, but the flavors we choose and enjoy, and the ingredients we pick, are based on a long evolutionary history of valuing what was most nutritious.

As human communities transitioned toward agriculture and away from hunter-gatherer lifestyles, we started to grow the nourishing foods that we found in the wild. And fermentation played a big role in allowing us to grow more and keep it longer so we could continue to nourish ourselves throughout the year. Milk, for example, could be turned into more shelf-stable cheeses, and vegetables turned into any manner of pickles. Both could be combined with grains and legumes to make tarhana, the Turkish dried soup mix from Chapter 1 (see page 54). Fermentation, in tandem with a variety of plant and animal crops, thus became a cornerstone of human nutrition, helping to keep people fed and healthy.

THE NUTRITION OF EARLY FERMENTS

Fermentation was an important part of keeping our ancestors healthy on diets that were limited both geographically and seasonally.

MILK AND DAIRY PRODUCTS, for example, are rich sources of calcium, protein, carbohydrates, and other nutrients, but these benefits cannot be accessed by anyone who is lactose intolerant. Lactose intolerance is common throughout many global populations, though it seems to be least common among those with northern European heritage for numerous reasons, including the development of mixed farming (crops and livestock) with dairy production. If the people in a community could not consume fresh milk but it was one of their available food sources, their health would depend on making that food digestible. Fermentation was often the answer. When milk is fermented, lactose is converted into lactic acid, which the body can tolerate.

BEANS AND SEEDS were relatively simple to grow and are among our earliest crops, present in all the great agricultural societies. As Ken Albala says, "Beans are perhaps the one food common and indispensable to us all." Beans are filling and nutritious, and even more so with fermentation. Fermentation "predigests" legumes, breaking down nutrient-blocking compounds (such as rigid cellulose compounds) and making proteins more digestible to our bodies. Raw soybeans, for example, contain slight toxins that are eliminated when the beans are cooked or fermented. When fermented, the B vitamins (except for thiamine) are increased, and the protein is hydrolyzed to amino acids, making it more bioavailable. When legumes are fermented together with grains, as in Indian idli and dosa, they become a complete protein, containing all the amino acids our bodies need to thrive.

GRAINS have been and are a critical part of human diets, but because of their thick outer bran, these nutritional powerhouses also take a lot of work to process into food. They must be broken down, for example, by being ground and/or boiled for long periods, both of which required our ancestors to use a lot of precious energy. Fermentation predigests the grains, making the nutrition contained within more accessible to our bodies, and it does so without using up a lot of fuel or our own physical energy. And just as with legumes, the fermentation process results in an increase in B vitamins.

Humans had all kinds of tools at their fingertips around 20,000 years ago—including tools for pounding, boiling over a fire, fermenting, and grinding—when they started to tackle grains as a food source. The existence of these tools suggests that porridges (fermented or not) were likely the predecessor to bread and beer. Both beer brewing and breadmaking are fairly tricky operations, and only worthwhile for feeding a group if they can be done regularly. Otherwise, it's a lot of work for a pleasant one-time meal, not a source of continuous nutrition.

Fermented porridges such as sowens are a good example of how our ancestors obtained calories by cultivating and processing whatever grains were available. Millet, for example, has been cultivated in Africa for thousands of years, and millet porridge has been a part of numerous African culinary traditions for at least this long. In the Balkans, likely one of the first European regions to plant the crop, broomcorn millet has been grown for almost two millennia and is used in a porridgy beverage called boza,

food as medicine

For millennia, ancient peoples around the globe recognized food as medicine—a concept we modern humans are among the first to ignore. According to Scottish folk writer Scott Richardson-Read: "In the lexis of Gaelic, any plant with a use was termed '*Lus*.' Even vegetables. People didn't differentiate between a plant to eat and herbs used medicinally as we do today. They were both called *Lus*. Intriguingly the Gaelic for drinking, *lusadh*, is derived from the *Lus*, a herb or plant. Boece [a Scottish philosopher and historian also called Boethius] says the old Scots were moderate drinkers using chiefly infusions of thyme, mint and anise. Famously, the Celtiberian tribe had a drink with a composition of apparently over 100 different plants."

which is also consumed in Turkey. In Scotland, not long after the introduction of oats, local communities were making sowens, or fermented oat porridges (see page 84). Whatever the grain, through the process of fermentation and cooking, the hard outer hull and bran of the grain were softened, thus making the nutrition inside the grain more available.

BEER AND BREAD appeared at about the same time as agriculture and sedentary (rather than migratory) communities. People now had stationary cooking areas in which they could make these more complicated, time-intensive foods. Early breads—often flatbreads—were made from fermented grains. The fermentation process broke down indigestible compounds and increased the bioavailability of nutrients. The grains that our ancestors found best to ferment into bread and beer influenced which grains we grew and how we used these grains over time to nourish our bodies. While wheat breads were common sustenance in the Fertile Crescent, barley was preferred in prehistoric Europe. However, Roman imperial expansion in the first millennium BCE shifted European diets toward wheat breads, and barley shifted toward being used as a brewing ingredient instead. While each grain has a slightly different nutritional profile, all provide our bodies with carbohydrates and some protein. And whether made into bread or beer, all grains are made more nutritious through fermentation.

Modern humans think of beer as an intoxicating drink, but some authors have argued that our ancestors didn't see it that way. There were other ways they could get a high (for example, through intoxicating or psychotropic plants), so our ancestors didn't need to go to the effort of brewing only for that purpose. Instead, it seems likely that beer served multiple functions: While an intoxicant in some cases, it was largely a nutrition source. Beers, such as English "small beers," had lower alcohol levels than modern-day beers but still offered the carbohydrates and nutrients made accessible by the fermentative brewing process.

Alcohol and Health

Perhaps no ferment has faced more controversy over the years than alcohol. And yet, it's possible we would not be here without it. Because our hominid ancestors were able to metabolize alcohol millions of years ago, they had access to the nutrition in fermented fruits that they otherwise would not have been able to eat.

MEDICINE

Our relationship with alcohol is not purely based on its use as a foodstuff. From ancient times to the present day, alcohol has played a role as a medicine. The Sumerians, who brewed at least 19 different kinds of beer, used it in some of their medicines. The ancient Greeks and Romans, as well as medieval Europeans, drank herb- and spice-infused wines for their healing qualities, and rice wines infused or brewed with medicinal plants were popular in Southeast Asia. In Korea, rice wines and other wines made at home incorporated a range of roots, barks, and leaves to support family health.

Alcohol has been used across many global cultures as a preventive or a curative at the onset of acute illness (such as a cold or the flu). The Irish hot whiskey and the English hot toddy are ubiquitous and used for preventing or reducing cold symptoms, and medical research has found that these folk remedies can in fact shorten the duration and intensity of a common cold.

Anecdotally, I first noticed this phenomenon perhaps 15 or 20 years ago, when a friend took a shot of whiskey after complaining of a cold, claiming that the antimicrobial substance would "knock a cold right out of you." It worked. I have heard the same said of various health tonics, such as fire cider (see page 208) and elderberry tincture. Since then, I've seen numerous examples of ferments and distillates made from those ferments (for example, whiskey) being used to shorten the severity and duration of colds. And indeed, the selective environment this ferment creates is not hospitable to many harmful microbes.

My own experiences with whiskey as a cold preventive are echoed in the historical record. We see examples of hot whiskies being consumed to help with winter colds and flus going back at least 200 years. In 1837, for example, the *Burlington Free Press* in Vermont published an article describing how to properly administer hot whiskey to sick children.

Alcohol's role in health care extended from community traditions and individual health practices into social programs. In England, records from the early nineteenth century give us a glimpse of how alcohol was administered through social relief programs. These records were kept between the sixteenth and eighteenth centuries by "overseers of the poor," administrators who would distribute relief, such as clothes, money, and food, to paupers (the term used at the time to describe impoverished folks) under what is sometimes called the "Old Poor Law." In *A Social History of Medicine*, historian Joan Lane notes, "Sugar, at 9d a pound in 1817, was a relative luxury and rarely provided by the parish, but malt, to brew beer, was regularly bought for the sick poor." This tells us the importance of brewing on a home scale and the importance of beer in English culture as food and as medicine across socioeconomic strata.

Beer, however, was not the only alcoholic beverage given to impoverished folks in nineteenth-century England: Ale, brandy, gin, rum, and wine were also present in account books. Ale was most often given to nursing mothers to improve lactation, while brandy and gin were reserved for the terminally ill and those close to death.

HERBAL ALCOHOL

Since prehistoric times, humans have used plant medicine to heal illness and injury and to promote and maintain wellness. One of the most common ways in which herbs are used for health is by adding medicinal plants to alcohol, either during or after fermentation or distillation. For 99.8 percent of our time on this planet, we have relied on wild foods, and so those medicinal plants would have been foraged. Our ancestors had a vast knowledge of wild plants—something that may be hard for us to fathom. As the English writer Colin Spencer notes, "There are over 3,000 species of plants that can be eaten for food, but only 150 of these have ever been cultivated, and today the peoples of the world sustain themselves on just 20 main crops. We underestimate the harvest from the wild that humankind gathered and the detailed knowledge, passed on from generation to generation, about which plants were toxic, which were healing, and which were sharp, bitter, sweet, and sour; such knowledge must have been encyclopedic."

Plants cultivated for food are also sometimes an important part of medical practice, and we see them used for both purposes in tandem in many cases. In Russia, for example, horseradish is commonly grown and used in both food and medicine. Herbalist and author Alma R. Hutchens documents an indigenous North American tradition of boiling horseradish in beer with juniper berries to prevent dropsy, with the precaution that "the beer should be from the old-time, naturally aged process, not artificial, fast-cured beer."

WINE FOR HEALTH

Wine, and wines infused with medicinal herbs and spices, were both central to Western medicine up until fairly recently. In ancient Greek and Roman humoral medicine (centered around the idea that four bodily fluids cause illness; we'll talk more about this on page 193), wine was considered warming, and when combined with other substances, it was used as a general curative as well as for specific ailments. Wine was also considered an excellent vehicle for herbal drugs because it dissolved more of the active parts of the herbs than plain water did.

EARLY EUROPEAN HERBAL WINES. Herb-infused wines predate the medieval period and even ancient Greece. According to medical researchers and doctors M. Ozen and E. C. Dinleyici, they go back at least to the reign of Scorpion I in Egypt (around 3150 BCE). The ancient Romans also made infused wines and added all kinds of ingredients for health and flavor, from salt water to honey to botanicals such as myrtle, juniper, rose petals, and wormwood.

Wine was central to the tool kit of classical physicians, and thanks to the variety of wines on the ancient Greek market (domestic and imported from Egypt and elsewhere), they had a virtual cornucopia from which to choose. The Greeks differentiated wine based on grape varieties, geography, and style, as we do today, but also by its physical effects. For example, the ancient Greek orator Athenaeus described one wine produced near Alexandria as "excellent, white, pleasant, fragrant, thin, not likely to go to the head, and diuretic."

In the West, our concept of medicinal herbal wines stems from hippocras (or hipocras, ipocras, or ypocras). This spiced wine was named after the ancient Greek physician Hippocrates (though it got its name in the Middle Ages, long after he died) not only because of its health benefits but because the spices were strained using a cloth bag called a *manicum hippocraticum* ("sleeve of Hippocrates"); according to legend, Hippocrates strained the herbs and spices from his preparations through his voluminous sleeves. Hippocras was a powerful medicinal tonic.

There are many, many iterations of hippocras out there in the world. Some contain a variety of medicinal local plants (including herbs such as rosemary), some contain cream and a hearty helping of sugar (which was also considered medicinal in the Middle Ages), and some included imported spices such as cinnamon, cloves, and grains of paradise. When it was made with milk, the milk would curdle on contact with the acidity of the wine and clarify it by capturing sediment and particles from the spices in that curdling process. In some versions, hippocras was syrupy and sweet (often sweetened with expensive imported sugar, but sometimes with honey). Robert May's *The Accomplisht Cook* (1660) appeared around the end of the time of hippocras's widespread popularity and offers a couple of options for making the drink (one with cream and mace, one without cream and with rosemary instead of mace). It, along with other hippocras recipes I've come across over the years, informed the recipe at the end of this chapter (page 216).

Hippocras was traditionally served as an after-dinner digestif with wafers, and it was gradually replaced by stronger spirits that served as the precursors of modern-day liqueurs. By the eighteenth century, it was considered old-fashioned, and while the occasional die-hard enthusiast is still interested in it, hippocras has yet to see a widespread resurgence in popularity.

In medieval times, because hippocras was often made with imported spices, it would have been largely a beverage of the upper classes. Spices were expensive, and when middle-class families were able to purchase them, they used them sparingly and would have been unlikely to add them to their daily beverage. That said, middle-class households sometimes had spiced wine, particularly because the spices helped impart flavor and sweetness to dry wines or those that were beginning to get a bit vinegary. I've seen varying accounts from modern researchers regarding how often spiced wines were drunk, with claims ranging from people of all classes drinking spiced wine regularly to only the wealthy being able to enjoy them. The truth is almost certainly somewhere in between.

Sweetened, spiced wine was certainly not the only infused wine being consumed. The use of other infusions in folk medicine traditions points to some gaps in our historical records on infused wines. It is not uncommon, for example, for Western herbalists to make infused wines using culinary herbs such as rosemary or medicinal herbs such as mugwort, and it seems likely that grabbing a handful of herbs from the wild or a garden and tossing it into wine would be an easy, accessible way to craft home remedies, which so often go unrecorded.

SOUTHEAST ASIAN HERBAL RICE WINES. Rice wine is believed to be more ancient than rice liquor, likely coming from the Yellow River Basin around 3,000 to 4,000 years ago, though the exact dates and the routes by which the fermentation starters spread in Southeast Asia are unknown. Whatever the history, similar fermentation methods are seen in rice wine production in Thailand, Laos, northern India, and other regions. A fresh starter (known by the names *marcha* or *murcha* in northern India and Nepal, *men* in Vietnam, and *thiat* in India, among many others) is made with each batch (as opposed to the process of making rice liquor, which uses existing starter). The starters vary considerably by locale or even batch or individual maker. While these are used in similar ways to other rice-based beverage starters (such as koji in Japan, nuruk in Korea, and chiu/chu in China), modern researchers found that the actual microbial makeup of some rice wine starters was not *Aspergillus oryzae* (koji), but a mix of different molds, including *A. penicillioides*, and yeasts.

Across Southeast Asia, knowledge of starter cultivation and winemaking is traditionally held secret and passed from parents to children. Women did, and still do, most of the work in preparing these rice wines, working quietly by themselves or with only a couple of others, following practices passed down through generations to create a healthy and palatable final product. The brewing processes vary and can involve pounding the rice, adding powdered starters or blowing rice liquor onto the rice, fermentation, blending in plant matter, and drying. Often these brews include various botanicals, usually a balance of spices, herbs, and sweet ingredients, from mimosa to tobacco, banana leaves, hot peppers, and dozens of others. These herbal additions bring flavor and a whole host of medicinal benefits, but they also bring microbes to the party, and they help jump-start fermentation. The microbes have a sufficient diet of starch (from the rice and typically sugar or sugar-rich plants) to ferment the beverages quickly.

HERBAL BEER AND SPIRITS

Herbal wines aren't the only fermented medicinal tipples out there. For thousands of years, we've brewed plants into our beers and distillations to take advantage of their medicinal properties.

BEER. Plants have long been used in brewing for flavor and medicine. The term *gruit* refers to beers brewed with botanicals (not just hops) rather than to a particular style of beer. Anything from a pale lager to a hearty stout can be called gruit, provided it's made with a mixture of botanicals. Gruit was a popular beverage across western Europe up until the seventeenth century, so much so that landowners would charge peasants a "gruit tax" to forage on their land for wild herbs for brewing. Some sources point to three main botanicals used in gruit: bog myrtle, yarrow, and wild rosemary. However, gruit could also include other herbs, such as mugwort.

These brewing botanicals offered a range of health benefits, aiding with everything from sleep to immunity to menstrual discomfort. But some authors believe that herbs such as bog myrtle and yarrow, when combined in a brew and consumed in sufficient quantity, also had psychotropic effects. Food historian Jeffrey Pilcher cites the use of henbane, an herb that is psychotropic in minute doses but deadly if you consume even just a little too much, in European brewing history. And German anthropologist Christian Rätsch says there is no known psychoactive plant that humans *haven't* added to beer at some point or other, including ancient Egyptian mandrake beer, Incan chica (corn beer), and Siberian toadstool beer. Henbane itself was associated with witchcraft during the Middle Ages, perhaps because brewing was at this time a domestic pursuit largely done by women (for more about women and brewing, see page 260).

The move away from gruit and toward hops was multifaceted, but it was in part due to the fact that brewing changed from being something women did on a domestic scale to something that men did on an industrial scale. Hops have some medicinal properties, but their primary function in beer is purely practical: They are preservative, meaning they make beer last longer and better able to withstand shipping, thus making brewing more profitable. The choice was based on pure profit rather than on nutritional or health considerations. Beer shifted from being a home-brewed source of nutrition and a remedy (and intoxicant) to being a commodity and an industry. Hops replaced gruit and other herbs, a change that was codified by brewing guilds and local ordinances, such as the 1516 Reinheitsegebot, a decree from the Bavarian city of Ingolstadt that beer could be brewed only with barley, malt, water, and hops.

Herbal beers, and the medicinal benefits herbs offered, were nearly wiped out as more brewers turned to hops as their sole source of flavoring. However, recent craft brewers have been returning to their roots and founded International Gruit Day, celebrated each year on February 1. And while the alewives who brewed and sold beer may have been barred from their craft, homebrewing did not disappear altogether, and herbal beers—either brewed with herbs or infused—continue to be made by herbalists and home cooks.

SPIRITS. Spirits, too, have been infused with medicinal plants for centuries, and many of our modern botanical spirits have their basis in plant medicine. Gin, as we mentioned earlier, was infused with juniper to provide a range of health benefits. The French liqueur Chartreuse was first distilled by monks in 1605 and is said to be based on an ancient recipe for an "Elixir of Long Life." Aquavit, the Nordic caraway-scented spirit, dates back to at least the 1530s and was believed to cure any known illness. And Sichuan paojiu is made by soaking medicinal and flavorful botanicals such as sour plums and ginger in baijiu, a sorghum-based spirit.

Over time, in many places, the medicinal properties of spirits were separated from the drinks themselves. Now many Western botanical spirits are consumed purely for flavor rather than health and are layered into cocktails based upon taste or texture rather than the combined health effects of the ingredients.

BEER FOR NUTRITION

Across England, beer in particular was an important source of nutrients. Often brewed by women, beer was made in England and around the ancient world for thousands of years, both for home consumption and in some cases to sell to neighbors. Even as commercial breweries overtook the broader market, homebrewing of beer and mead remained common enough into the nineteenth century that English newspapers mention the practice.

Beer was both drunk and brewed on ships as a safer, more shelf-stable beverage than just water, and it also provided nutrients. Prior to the ready availability of citrus in Britain, scurvy (caused by a deficiency in vitamin C) was warded off with specially formulated beers (including one called "scurvy ale"). The value of fermented beverages against scurvy was born out by contemporary scientists: James Lind's book *A Treatise on Scurvy* (1753) outlined his findings from testing various dietary supplements to treat sailors with scurvy, and while oranges and lemons had the most noticeable effects, another fermented drink—hard cider—was the runner-up. Seventeenth-century naval administrator Samuel Pepys (who is perhaps best known for burying his beloved wine and cheese stores to protect them from the 1666 Great Fire of London) observed that the French military gave their sailors rations of brandy and garlic to prevent scurvy and keep them warm, a practice he adopted for the British navy as well. The eighteenth-century author Sir John Pringle, a founder of modern Western military medicine, noted that Russian sailors would bake malt and rye bread, then grind the loaves and turn them into a beer called quas, drinking it for nutritional purposes.

INTOXICATION AND HEALTH

Across global cultures, the advice around drinking is typically to consume *moderate* amounts of alcohol for health. Humans have an enduring understanding that alcohol consumed in excess can cause not only drunkenness but also, when a regular habit, other health concerns. In a surviving fragment of a lost play, the Greek poet Eubulus (from the fourth century BCE) discusses the proper number of kraters (large vessels of water mixed with wine, served at parties) to serve: "For sensible men I prepare only three kraters: one for health, which they drink first, the second for love and pleasure, and the third for sleep. After the third one is drained, wise men go home . . . the eighth is for breaking furnitures, the ninth is for depression; the tenth is for madness and unconsciousness."

The ancient Greeks and Romans were not known for their restraint in the realms of food and drink (at least in the upper classes), but even so, they did have a respect for the benefits and harms they could reap from drinking wine. In their worship of Dionysus, the author Michael Pollan argues, the ancient Greeks explored "the full knowledge of alcohol's paradoxical nature, how the same drug could make angels of us or beasts, confer blessings or bring down a curse."

At various points in human history, intoxication has been framed as a personal or moral failing, with drinkers being characterized as bumbling, violent, irresponsible, and numerous other things. But various remedies were also offered to bring the heavy drinker back to sobriety. John Ovington, chaplain to William of Orange of England, encouraged tea in lieu of alcohol. Ovington's affinity for tea as an alcohol substitute was picked up in the nineteenth century as the Temperance movements in the United States and England pushed to reduce alcohol consumption and ban its sale.

The ill health resulting from alcohol intoxication has been used at different points as an excuse to censor and control. Throughout Mesoamerica, indigenous diets came under fire during colonial reign. Medical reasons were often cited as part of the concern, but under the veil of care for the health of colonized people was a clear effort to distance indigenous communities from their culture. For example, pulque, a mildly alcoholic drink fermented from maguey (agave) sap, was a traditional indigenous drink that predated colonialism. It became especially popular immediately after the conquest in the sixteenth century, and it was still widely consumed into the twentieth. However, it was regularly blamed for causing widespread alcohol abuse among indigenous and mixed-race communities in Mexico. Though other alcoholic beverages (for example, sugarcane-based drinks) were available and consumed, these were made from ingredients brought and profited upon by colonists, and only pulque was regularly dismissed by colonists on health grounds.

Nonalcoholic Beverages and Health

Beer and other alcoholic beverages are not the only fermented beverages our ancestors consumed for nutrition; nonalcoholic drinks played a role as well.

KVASS

Kvass is a staple nourishing tonic that has been made in eastern Europe possibly since the Middle Ages. There are many variations, but one of the more traditional versions is simply made with bread and beets. Kvass was a great way to use up what you had (bread heels, for example) to fuel your body rather than let the food go to waste. A good source of vitamins and calories, it was often promoted to aid digestion and improve gut health. As author Pascal Baudar notes, "Like those ancient beers, kvass was mostly a 'people's' drink, similar to the weak Belgian *saison* beers that were meant to quench the thirst of the working classes while adding some valuable nutrition to their diet."

AMAZAKE

Also called "sweet sake," amazake is a Japanese beverage consumed both for flavor and for health benefits. Amanotamuznake, an early version of amazake, appears in the *Nihon Shoki* (Chronicles of Japan), a history of Japan compiled in 720 CE. It is possible, however, that amazake's history goes back even farther. Some modern articles, including one by journalist Dave Afshar, formerly based in Japan, say the earliest known production of sake took place around 500 BCE, though it was made by chewing grains rather than the modern brewing method. This method, he says, was abandoned upon the discovery of koji fermentation. The first known mention of amazake (and sake) in European writings was in 1603, from a Japanese-Portuguese dictionary compiled by Jesuit missionaries in Nagasaki. The dictionary includes koji as well as amazake and sake; however, these (and other koji-fermented products) were not popular until the late 1970s in

Europe, and even later in the United States, where the first commercially made amazake didn't appear until 1985.

Amazake and sake both begin with the same process: fermenting a sweet, thin rice porridge with koji. Once the porridge is ready, it can be consumed as a healthy nonalcoholic beverage (amazake) or fermented a second time to make an alcoholic beverage that is sometimes filtered (sake). Both can be served cold or hot. Amazake is different from sikhye (Korean sweet rice punch), which is made with malted barley and sugar rather than with koji. Amazake has several health benefits, including making nutrients in the rice more bioavailable, and modern studies show that it helps with hypertension and perhaps even mood and memory.

Japanese food writer Makikoh Itoh notes that in the Edo period (1603–1868) amazake was used to combat warm-weather fatigue, not as a cold-weather drink as it is often consumed today. During this time, amazake was considered to be an essential energy source by the government and thus was price controlled, with a serving costing only a few yen. Interestingly, making amazake was one of the ways in which ronin (unemployed samurai) were able to discreetly make a living. Amazake's popularity and importance as a foodstuff continued for a millennia and beyond: We see amazake mentioned in at least two cookbooks from the 1600s, though a modern source notes that it reached its peak popularity during the Tempo period (1830–1844) in both Tokyo and Kyoto.

HERBAL VINEGAR

Hippocras is not the only herb-infused ferment used as medicine: Four thieves vinegar sits at the nexus of flavor, health, and magic. Its name supposedly comes from the tale of the four thieves who plundered around Marseille during the time of the Black Plague and used the concoction to ward off the disease. There are many variations—most including rosemary, thyme, and mint, and sometimes garlic—but the goal is to steep whatever aromatic herbs as well as spices you have on hand in apple cider or wine vinegar. Importantly, this medieval concoction was made with affordable herbs rather than expensive imported spices, meaning it was medicine accessible to the masses.

Four thieves vinegar, like hippocras, was part of a larger medicinal tradition. As authors Bettina Malle and Helge Schmickl note, "Herbal vinegars were important health remedies in Middle Ages: Hildegard von Bingen and Nostradamus both researched the effects of different medicinal plants that had been extracted into vinegar."

Four thieves vinegar is thought to have been the precursor to another beloved herbal remedy: fire cider. Fire cider traces its roots to herbal vinegars made by early colonizers in New England. While the original four thieves vinegar was probably made with wine vinegar, fire cider utilizes what was available on this new continent: apple cider vinegar. Hard cider was the drink of choice for colonial Americans, who grew small, hard cider apples in droves simply for that purpose. Lots of apple cider meant the likelihood of lots of apple cider vinegar (which is made from hard cider), and when people went to make their botanical vinegars, they relied on what they had around.

The flavor profile of fire cider shifted, too, and modern fire cider, unlike four thieves vinegar, is not simply an aromatic herbal infusion; it also includes hot peppers (the "fire" of fire cider), aromatic roots such as onion and garlic, and whole spices. The historical record is silent on when and why these shifts occurred, and while we might posit that hot peppers were added because they are native to this continent and spices may have been added later when their cost dropped, the aromatic roots remain a mystery. Perhaps it was connected to the garlic, which was sometimes added to four thieves vinegar, or perhaps it was simply an effort by our ancestors to pack every bit of medicine they could into each jar.

Ferments for Mental Health

When we step back and take a holistic view of health, we see that fermentation offers us more than physical health; it can offer mental and emotional well-being as well. A regular fermentation practice is grounding. It gives us space to bring a gentle awareness to the present moment. It can become a sort of meditation that results in epiphanies (as with many of the ideas in Sandor Katz's *Fermentation as Metaphor*) or simply put us in a more relaxed mental state.

For millennia, people have used simple, repetitive actions as a means to become more present. When built into a daily practice, these actions embody both the sacredness and the ordinariness of ritual: a special practice you create space for, but also a part of routine. During my time studying at the University of Iowa Center for the Book, I took several classes on medieval history with Kathleen Kamerick, who became one of my most beloved teachers. She told us about the cultural importance of labyrinths in medieval churches. Worshippers would intentionally walk these mazes, which were mapped onto the floor of a church or the grounds outside, from edge to center, which would allow them to, as Kamerick says, "prepare to encounter the divine." This idea that meditative action puts us in the headspace to encounter divinity appears across various traditions in several different ways, but the goal seems to be as much about the journey of becoming more present as it is about the final destination (which might be enlightenment or holy atonement, depending on the tradition).

Similarly, fermentation can form the foundation of a meditative practice through repetition, as well as through tactile and creative engagement with our world: regular checking and stirring, smelling, and tasting. Over time, this allows us to drop into a meditative headspace more easily; the act of cultivating awareness and presence becomes almost second nature. We can imagine, for example, the people caring for the taru (cypress or cedar barrels traditionally used for fermentation in Japanese culture) dropping into this meditative headspace. As cookbook author Nancy Singleton Hachisu explains, "Their care implies a regular fermentation practice as well as a present and intentional one: They must be used, or at least filled with water, periodically, or the integrity of the structure will weaken, and must be stored upside down, lest the wood shrinks and causes the bamboo rings holding the bucket together to slide down."

FERMENTS AND CRAFT

The art of fermentation is a whole-body experience. Taste and smell play a role, but so do all the other senses: We use our muscles and sense of touch to massage salt into cabbage or sense when a pan of grains is warm and toasted just enough; we use our sight to watch as our food is transformed by our microbial friends (to echo Sandor Katz's definition); and we listen eagerly for the fizzing, popping, and hissing that occurs as the microbes multiply and burst to life. Most fermentation guidance not only asks but demands that we mash or press with our hands or feet, that we knead dough or toss it in the air, that we smell and taste and listen, and that when we do stir our food we peer closely at it, examining it for bubbles, for growth, for signs of life. By preparing our own ferments by hand, we can engage in what art history professor Howard Risatti calls the "sensation of bodily position, presence, or movement." By making ferments, as with other handcrafts, we are able to live a more embodied life and more fully feel the world around us.

In one particularly poignant example, early medieval English king Alfred the Great (849–899) used the term *craeft* (craft) to translate the Latin term *virtus* (virtue), indicating that to him, working with our hands allows us to elevate our heads and hearts as well. It involves an incredible amount of intelligence—not only intellect, but also a physical intelligence and way of knowing that comes only from doing a task with both repetition and care. As archaeologist and historian Alexander Langlands says, "For Alfred, the labour and work associated with making and doing was comparable to the spiritual striving of philosophy."

FERMENTS AND PLAY

Fermentation as mindful practice guides us beyond the modern consumption-based concept of "mindfulness." It also reminds us that our practice is our own to shape. Michael Pollan, when describing Sandor Katz's approach to fermentation, notes that he has both a practical and a philosophical stance: "There is no 'right' way to ferment anything, no hard and fast rules. And, given how little we understand about the microbial world, one where bacteria can trade genes and their exact identities are often up for grabs, it would be hubris to pretend certainty."

Creative exploration is powerful, and play (with our food and beyond) is a form of mindfulness as well as a stand against cultural norms that would have us labor away nonstop. This is part of why I so strongly encourage people to use my recipes as guides, not as strict instructions: As you discover how you want to make something, you not only learn about your own tastes but you cultivate presence and awareness as well.

Fermenter and educator Nickawanna Shaw uses exploration as her guide as she cultivates a mindful fermentation practice. She says:

> I enjoy experimentation a lot. I have a "dumpcake" session every few to 6 months where I collect what's left in the fridge all the way in the back and taste/combine it into a new jar. It's an on-the-fly layering of different cultures (food and microbes), flavors, textures that benefit from 7 months of one item mixing with 10 months of something else. I've had more successes (I wanna eat it) than failures. It's exciting to think you could create using ingredients you created months prior not knowing they'd be used this way. It's like kintsugi or found object art. You don't know how a thing is beautiful until you take it apart and put it back together. Some of my next great adventures will be around challenging my own ideas around what an item should taste like or its appearance.

Fermentation as mindfulness is an invitation to partner with what Ken Albala calls "ambient yeasts" to make sourdough (which can be different species from commercial varieties), to learn whether dill seed or caraway will taste better in that sauerkraut, and to see if you like your mead better aged 2 weeks or 4 weeks. It's an invitation to dance into the kitchen (metaphorically or actually) and reclaim your own expertise, as the person best aware of your culinary needs and desires. Here we're becoming more present through messy experiments, trying new ingredients, or finding comfort in familiar ones. Fermentation mindfulness is the mindfulness of play.

The Parameters That Define "Good Health"

Our understanding of what is happening inside our bodies (and how to keep our bodies healthy) is heavily influenced by forces outside of them. While there are commonly agreed-upon metrics for what constitutes "health" across different places, times, and modalities, our understanding of health is also a social construct. Different healing modalities, both conventional and traditional or folk medicine, have offered us different lenses through which to understand the role of ferments in our health, and to understand the microbiome itself. Our understanding is also informed by religious beliefs and cultural norms, as well as government programs, health-related advertising, medical services, and the modalities they operate within.

FERMENTS, RELIGION, AND SPIRITUALITY

Religion was a major influence on how much and which types of ferments, including alcohol, were consumed throughout history. Alcohol has been the focus of religious ritual and restriction for millennia. As we'll see in Chapter 5, alcohol was central to Viking, Celtic, and other pre-Christian rituals as well as Christian ones, and it was restricted in other religions. One study by researcher Paul Fieldhouse notes that several religions (including Islam, Baha'i, Mormonism, Seventh-day Adventistism, and Rastafarianism) forbid or discourage alcohol use based on its ill health effects as well as its effects on judgment and self-control.

Religious views on alcohol have changed over time. Religious communities operating in the United States today, for example, may include alcohol in religious ceremonies, such as part of communion, but discourage its use otherwise. At certain times in history and in certain places, things were very different. Beer and cider were woven into the fabric of English society in the seventeenth century, and they provided necessary nutrition, and so it would not have made sense to call them into question on religious grounds.

You may think of a Puritan as being someone who would eschew alcohol. But in seventeenth-century England, Puritans were members of a society where alcohol played an important role, and they imbibed, too. When Puritans colonized America, they brought their brewing knowledge with them. They often brewed without hops, due to a lack of supply, and they also brewed beer using corn. By the late seventeenth century, "ordinaries" began appearing in New England. These were informal shops, run out of people's homes, that would sell beer and hard cider.

Elsewhere, fermented foods did face religious scrutiny. For example, the Catholic Church in Europe recognized the role of locally or regionally produced ferments (such as wine or beer) in the lives of congregations, but it was wary to some extent, and Protestant churches to a greater extent, of imported foodstuffs. Many fermented stimulants and depressants were the subject of religious scrutiny over the centuries, including tea, coffee, chocolate, and rum, and the use of each increased significantly from the seventeenth to the twentieth centuries.

In Korea, religion influenced the types of ferments made there. Mahayana monks, for example, developed a temple cuisine that was strictly vegetarian, which impacted the larger culinary culture of Korea. Monks used the vegetables and herbs they harvested in the mountains, which probably influenced the way that many Koreans made kimchi—out of any vegetable they could. The main seasonings of temple kimchi were salt, soy sauce, red chile powder, ginger, and sesame seeds—and some of these ingredients are still seen in kimchis today.

In Japan, ferments also became an important part of religious diets. Tamari was first used as a seasoning in Buddhist monasteries, for example, as it provided a flavorful substitute for fish sauce that was amenable to a vegetarian diet.

Ferments have been a part of ancient spiritual practices since well before colonialism and the global spread of Christianity. In South America, the ritual beverage ayahuasca is derived from the leaves of the *Psychotria viridis* shrub and the stalks of the *Banisteriopsis caapi* vine. The plant matter is sometimes fermented prior to being cooked, or simply soaked (and thus fermented) without being cooked, to make a strong tea. The beverage is used ritually both to purge the system and to promote euphoria and a sense of unity.

In modern-day Western magickal and pagan practices, infused wines are used both as medicine and as spiritual tonic. One such example is May wine infused with woodruff, which is used to celebrate the return of spring. Woodruff was also brought into Christian practices, hung around places of worship as a protective charm; it sat at the intersection of magical practice, health, and celebration. Spiritual beliefs often intersect with medicinal practices, as is the case with humoral medicine, traditional Chinese medicine, and Ayurveda. And all of them have clear dictates about the role of fermented foods in health.

FERMENTS IN TRADITIONAL MEDICINE SYSTEMS

Traditional or folk medicine systems exist outside the institution of Western allopathic medicine, and the terms often refer to long-standing established practices as well as emerging ones. While Ayurveda, traditional Chinese medicine, and humoral medicine all were passed along in written form, many equally ancient and commonly practiced traditions were passed on orally—for example, healing practices in indigenous communities of North America, Australia, and Africa. These oral traditions have been around for thousands of years. They developed in isolated pockets, independent of the influences of classical Greek, Ayurvedic, or traditional Chinese medicine, based on the needs of the local people. While there are countless other medicine systems to explore, comparing just a few of the more widespread systems can help us learn a good deal about our historic relationship between ferments and health.

BALANCE IS KEY

In Chinese medicine, humoral medicine, and Ayurveda, we see an emphasis on balancing the body, and diet is a big part of this. While each of these complex systems has varying practices based on geography, historical period, and individual interpretation, they share common larger principles rooted in balance of internal systems, interrelationship between human and environment, and the individuality of medicine. While historians have been unable to trace a common thread intertwining these three systems, it is possible that these ideas moved between communities along with trade and migration. Here is a (very simplified) summary of each.

HUMORAL MEDICINE (also called Galen's humoral theory or Galenic theory) focuses on the balance of four bodily humors, represented by different fluids (blood, black bile, yellow bile, and phlegm), each of which corresponds to its own temperament. Humoral medicine was first proposed in the fifth century BCE by the Greek physician Hippocrates. Galen, an ancient Roman physician from the first century CE, picked up the proverbial mantle from Hippocrates, formalizing humoral medicine into the system that would be used for more than a millennium and a half after his death. It was in use in Europe all the way to the nineteenth century, though its popularity had started to wane several centuries earlier. In humoral medicine, foods are balanced against a person's individual humoral makeup but also against each other (hot and dry with cold and moist, for example), so that each dish promotes balance within the body. See more on page 195.

TRADITIONAL CHINESE MEDICINE (TCM) is the modern version of Chinese medicine. This medical system itself goes back to the Shang dynasty (fifteenth to eleventh centuries BCE). Tsao-Lin Moy, an alternative and Chinese medical practitioner and founder of New York City's Integrative Healing Arts, notes that classical Chinese medicine once contained many schools of thought based on master practitioners and apprenticeship, before being standardized in the 1950s and 1960s under Chairman Mao. According to Moy, "The beauty of practicing Chinese medicine is that it is one of collaboration and cultivation of health that touches all aspects of life." In a study by integrative medical researcher Bhushan Patwardhan and colleagues, they note that TCM "considers the human at the center of the universe as an antenna between celestial and earthly elements."

Five elements (water, earth, metal, wood, and fire) make up the material world, which gives rise to two antithetical elements: yin and yang. These two forces are "opposites," but not with a negative connotation: Each is necessary, but they are considered antithetical because as one increases, the other decreases. The key to balancing them is in the four bodily humors (qi, blood, moisture, and essence) as well as the internal organ systems (zang fu). Health is achieved when the energies of yin and yang stay in balance and can properly circulate in the body; illness develops in part because of blockage and stagnation.

Moy notes that this balance extends to what we eat: "A well-balanced diet will have all five flavors." Moy also notes that balance does not just mean presence, but absence: "There is also a 6th flavor: bland or neutral. The 5 flavors need to be compared to a state of non-flavor." Zoey Gong, a traditional Chinese medicine chef and nutritionist from Shanghai and owner of Five Seasons TCM, notes that the individuality of treatments is part of what makes this medical system special: TCM "teaches us how to eat for our own body, to adjust imbalances rather than achieving a number. It aims to put our body in tune with the environment and our mind. Rather than being restrictive and demanding like many other systems, TCM allows flexibility and self-awareness." TCM is still widely practiced today, in China and elsewhere.

IN AYURVEDIC MEDICINE, the earth is made up of five elements: akasha (ether), vayu (air), teja/agni (fire), apas (water), and prithvi (earth). These elements exist in all parts of our world—in organic and inorganic materials, including ourselves. In biological systems (such as our own), these elements are coded into three forces to create the tridosha system, which regulates every psychological and physiological process. These three doshas (forces) are composed of one or two elements: vata (ether and air), pitta (fire), and kapha (water and earth).

Suresh Pillai, owner of Atina Foods in Catskill, New York, also notes that the body itself contains five layers: "The outermost is the physical body, the second layer is breath or prana, the third layer is the mind, the fourth is wisdom, and the innermost is happiness—to be one." How these elements manifest in an individual determines their physical and mental constitution, and balance includes happiness, which is "an inherent asset in all living things," according to Pillai. We must seek out imbalances, then, in our physical health and also examine our inner and outer worlds to see how they may be impacting our well-being.

As is the case in TCM and humoral medicine, in Ayurveda, harmony equals health, while imbalance—either excess or deficiency—can manifest as disease. And eating the right foods is an important part of finding balance. Pillai says, "According to Ayurveda, the physical body is an extension of earth—what we eat is what we are. If I exist, then the spirit exists, and I can only exist when I eat, drink, and breathe. So Ayurveda is a material science. It treats the whole universe as a divine creation that has a divine balance." Because Ayurveda considers all these moving parts, it requires continuous learning and curiosity: It is "an ever-changing science, one that rejects stagnation and embraces new knowledge," says Pillai. Ayurveda, like TCM, is still widely practiced today.

Across these systems, balance is based on the individual body; prescriptions are determined by an individual's overall constitution and are not based on treating a specific symptom or disease. Those symptoms are thought to be manifestations of underlying imbalances and thus best treated by addressing the issue systematically. As such, fermented foods aren't eaten in the same amount across the board; how much you might need would depend on what is best for your unique body.

EXAMINING SOUR FOODS

So how do fermented foods fit in? To find out, we can look at how each system considers sour food's role in overall health. And remember: The key to health in each system is balance. In humoral systems, the temperature and moisture of food must be balanced; in TCM, it's the five tastes; and in Ayurveda, it's the six tastes.

IN HUMORAL SYSTEMS, acidic foods are typically considered to be warming and drying, so they would balance cool and moist foods. Wine is warming, too (to varying extents, depending on the type), but beer is considered cooling, so in this system we would have to consider individual foods rather than simply classifying all ferments under one umbrella.

Ken Albala notes that a food's classification in the humoral system was based largely on flavor, and pleasant-tasting foods were often seen as more nourishing, and unpleasant foods less so. However, humoral makeup went beyond simply what the ingredient was; it also had to do with where and how it was raised or grown, adding a place-based and stewardship-focused element to the health system. Albala says, "Cattle fed cold and dry oats become cold and dry; sheep fed grass become cold and moist. Simply, the organism becomes what it eats. The predominant humor is passed from fodder to feeder down the food chain until it ends up on our table."

Interestingly, in humoral medicine, many fermented and salted foods were encouraged only in extreme moderation; they were considered, as Albala says, "too crass or too likely to stir up sour melancholic humors." This remained the prevailing wisdom in Europe until Thomas Willis, a seventeenth-century doctor who believed that fermentation was the basis of all life, described fermented foods as better tasting and more nourishing than their peers. This was possibly the first time in Western medicine that fermented foods were characterized as better than their nonfermented counterparts.

IN TCM, balance is seasonal, and sour foods are especially recommended in spring to support the liver and the flow of qi. As with Ayurveda and humoral medicine, sour foods are used to balance physical systems.

According to Moy, "The Liver energy is responsible for the smooth flow of Qi [life force] and emotions. When Liver energy is out of balance, it will affect the whole person." In seeking balance for an individual, then, sour foods are placed in concert with other tastes, and sour foods aid in saliva production, which in turn aids in digestion. Moy notes that our bodies and our brains tend to crave flavors (such as sour) that have the nutrients we need to find balance, and that "Understanding the role that the five flavors and Yin and Yang balance in Chinese medicine philosophy can help guide us to make informed choices about the foods we eat and on a deeper level the energetics that promote life force Qi."

Ferments can be found across all five tastes in TCM—for example, in pungent pepper pastes, sweet pickles, sour vinegar, bitter wine, and salty fish or soy sauce. Zoey Gong says it is important to consider the ingredients, not just the fermentation process, when thinking about how ferments fit in: "TCM food therapy does not really address fermented foods as a category much. The TCM classics never mentioned, as far as I know, that 'each meal should contain a fermented ingredient' or 'fermented foods are great for XYZ.' While they are not discussed as a whole, many single ingredients used in food therapy are fermented, such as vinegar, soy sauce, fermented soy beans, and so on. Each of them has different functions and properties, which are not really related to fermentation." These individual fermented ingredients are an important part of this medical system. Gong notes that "TCM appreciates wine a lot. The traditional Chinese character of 'doctor' contains 'wine' as part of it. A lot of tincture and medicinal wines are used in TCM food therapy and wine-making has thousands of years of history. The wines are usually made from grains like rice and sorghum."

IN AYURVEDA, the sour (amla) taste is an important part of the diet in moderation. It is one of the six tastes, along with sweet (madhura), salty (lavana), pungent (katu), bitter (tikta), and astringent (kashaya), all of which must be balanced in order to promote health. Ayurveda practitioner Luciana Ferraz says the sour taste helps restore blood flow, reduce excess kapha, increase appetite, and aid in digestion. It is particularly beneficial in the winter months for vata and kapha. The flavors used in a ferment can shift how it impacts the body, too: For example, a lot of spicy heat can aggravate pitta, so in such cases it may be helpful to counterbalance with cooling spices such as fennel or coriander seed.

Suresh Pillai notes that ferments aid health, but the preservative action of the fermentation process has an added benefit in that it helps keep our health-promoting ingredients fresh and edible for longer. This asks us to consider process as well as flavor (sour or otherwise), but there is an environmental component as well, just as with humoral theory. Pillai says that this preservative effect ties into the Ayurvedic principle that "each habitat has its own food and medicine," and part of the practitioner's work is to locate those foods/medicines where they are and, where necessary, find natural ways to preserve them.

*   *   *

All three modalities focus on promoting the overall health of the patient rather than simply treating symptoms of a disease, and food (as well as plant-based medicine) features heavily. Balance is sought not only for the body but for the plate, and this is reflected in how each system dresses food in addition to which main ingredients are used. Condiments, seasonings, and accompaniments are chosen in part based upon their ability to counteract and balance the primary temperament of the main dish. In humoral theory, sour food, for example, was often related to heat and dryness and so was to be avoided with hot and dry main dishes. But if you had

health tonics

Humoral medicine also gave us health tonics—drinks that combine what modern minds might see as seemingly disparate ingredients meant to cure a seemingly random list of diseases. However, the tonics—and the conditions they treated—were anything but random: All were caused by, or meant to address the imbalance of, a specific humor.

Lisa Smith, a historian of gender and medicine, gives the example of Dr. Stevens' Water, a tonic kept in well-to-do homes in the seventeenth century and used for palsy, dropsy, bladder stones, barrenness, weak sinews, gout, worms, toothache, and a handful of other conditions. As Smith says, "In a humoral body, with its properties of cold, hot, wet and dry, many seemingly different problems might have the same underlying cause," and in this case each of these diseases was in fact a symptom associated with cold and wet humors. In a world where food was often used in medicine, tonics made with medicinal plants (either made at home or purchased, like Dr. Stevens' Water) would be employed to balance the system. Dr. Stevens' Water, for example, included dry and warming foods such as nutmeg, cloves, mace, aniseed, lavender, and rosemary.

We continue to see general health tonics available today. Though our overarching medical theories have shifted, there is still wisdom in supporting overall health and well-being. Some general health tonics, such as the fire cider recipe on page 208, are believed to boost immunity and reduce the severity of illness. They are based, in both process and theory, on the medicinal infused wines and vinegars humans have been consuming for thousands of years. In folk medicine practices, these tonics would have varied considerably from place to place, adapted to what was available and needed in each locale.

something cool and moist, hot and dry accompaniments would balance it out. We still see some of these culinary combinations today, including mustard with pork and lemon or vinegar with fish.

Each system is also concerned with seasonality as a part of balance. Our bodies feel and behave differently at different times of the year, in part because of changes in heat, moisture, and sunlight. As a result, dietary recommendations change as well: Food that cools you down is welcome in summer, for example, but would be unbalancing in winter, something we see in commonplace advice about eating today.

Not only is our perception of health contextual, but also our determination of which foods taste "good" or healthy is contextual. By putting balanced food in our bodies, we increase the likelihood that our bodies will stay in balance, too. Thus, as culinary historian Cynthia Bertelsen says, "a good physician must be a good cook."

MODERN USES

Nickawanna Shaw, a fermenter and a college professor focusing on health and wellness, describes how some of these principles inform how she makes kombucha, a fermented tea. She says that she brews kombucha in the warmer months and jun in colder months because the microbial communities of each prefer those temperatures, and the drinks give her less gastric distress when she does that. Ayurveda would explain this by saying that the two drinks have different tastes, and their effects are amplified when consumed at certain times of the year and in higher volumes.

For food writer Tienlon Ho, pregnancy became a chance to reconnect with the principles of TCM as well as with family tradition. There are long and complex traditions around childbirth in Chinese culture, which are connected to larger understandings of medicine, gender, and family structure. Using food to balance the body's energies, using the guidance of TCM, is a critical component of this.

After childbirth, women undergo a monthlong period of rest, with restrictions on diet and activities that vary depending on who's caring for you and your own connection to tradition. In Ho's case, the use of food as medicine, with her father as her guide, became a central part of the experience. When she was about 6 months pregnant, she and her father brewed a concoction of ginger and black vinegar, which was used to cure pigs feet and eggs. Ho notes that "In the caustic brine, the cartilaginous feet and eggs would melt into a slurry of digestible calcium, minerals, and protein." The concoction sat for about 2 months, then was eaten beginning 3 days after the baby was born, to bring the body back into balance after the stress of childbirth.

medical texts are important source materials

For much of human history, people used food as medicine and performed minor medical procedures in the home. As such, people probably were more intimately aware of how their bodies felt and functioned because they needed to be. This wisdom was initially passed on through oral tradition, then it became codified in print as the printing industry expanded. Most people at the time did not consult a physician when they had an ailment. Instead, starting in the seventeenth century, they turned to medical books and especially to household manuals, which typically included recipes, guidance for home care, and recipes for medical treatments and sometimes even for minor surgical procedures (Gervase Markham's 1615 book *The English Housewife* is a good example). These books were particularly popular at the end of the eighteenth century, and they are still published today. As medical historian and physician Thomas Benedek says, "Until the middle third of the twentieth century, far more people were likely to have been influenced by the recommendations in these popular books than by any personal contact with physicians." Through these works and others, we're able to see how our understanding of fermentation and health has shifted over time.

THE SHIFT AWAY FROM HUMORAL MEDICINE

In humoral medicine, fermented foods were viewed within the context of the (im)balance they brought to bodily systems. However, as Western medicine moved away from humoral theory, eventually fermentation was placed at the center of medical theories on health and bodily functions. In the modern day, our view of fermentation and the body continues to evolve, informed by and building upon these older theories. We recognize fermentative action happening within our bodies as a critical component to health (as in the gut microbiome), and one that interacts with other physical systems to maintain balance.

Across traditional Chinese medicine, Ayurveda, and humoral theory is a belief in the power of good digestion. For centuries, we've understood that fermentation plays a positive role in the digestive process, even if its microbial basis was not fully understood. Aristotle considered fermentation a central part of the generation of life, as "all life arose out of the confluence of heat and moisture." Ken Albala explains, "Corruption, whereby living material is broken down, and fermentation, whereby matter bubbles and comes alive, as it were, Aristotle thought of as simply two sides of the same process. We now, of course, understand this as the action of bacteria, yeast, and mold on organic matter."

In Ayurveda and in traditional Chinese medicine, we see a continued emphasis on balancing our bodies and our digestive tracts with the right blend of foods. But in Western medicine, the decline of humoral theory also meant a shift away from thinking about balancing the humors and toward treating a specific disease. As a result, our conception of digestion and the role of food changed over time.

Centuries ago Europeans had a broader perspective about what digestion is. From their point of view, it was not only what was going on in the stomach but also the entire process of transforming living matter into blood, muscles, and ultimately "spirits" that circulate through our brain as our emotions and thoughts.

In the sixteenth century, the prevailing wisdom around digestion was that it was actually a form of cooking, an extension of the cooking metaphor being extended to all life-sustaining systems. Seeds were cooked into plants, and the heat of the sun then cooked those plants into ripe fruits and grains, for example. Humans could gather these and cook them into food, after which the body would cook the digestible portions into blood and dispel whatever was not digestible as feces. Those would join decaying flora and fauna to become dirt that cooks seeds, and the cycle would begin anew.

But by the middle of the seventeenth century, this all was changing: Physicians began to shift their perspectives thanks in part to Paracelsus, an abrasive and fanatically religious itinerant Swiss doctor who openly mocked the existing medical establishment, garnering himself a terrible reputation. Despite this, he did have some appealing ideas, and they ended up sticking and spreading. He argued that the idea of life cycles based on cooking and the Aristotelian elements needed revising.

Distillation became a critical part of this shift, which moved scientists away from the idea of cooking and toward digestion as a chemical process. Since the late Middle Ages, chemists had experimented with distilling various edible substances, noting across the board that each batch resulted in a volatile "spirituous" fluid, an oily substance, and a solid residue. The chemists proposed a shift from the four Aristotelian elements (fire, earth, air, water, corresponding to the four humors) to three elements: mercury (the essence of the spirituous liquid), sulfur (the essence of the oil), and salt (the essence of the solids). Paracelsus argued that, in relation to food, salt dictated taste and consistency, mercury produced aroma, and sulfur carried the properties of moistness and sweetness and bound the other two elements together.

One of Paracelsus's followers, Jan Baptista van Helmont, associated this specifically with chemical reactions in the body and developed the idea that our stomach breaks down food into nutrients our bodies can access. The dissolution of food via stomach acid became the focus of digestion-related theories. Scientists moved away from the idea that the stomach "cooks" the food and toward the idea that the stomach ferments it. As Rachel Laudan says:

> Because fermentation included gentle heat and the production of vapors, it seemed to resemble (or was possibly the same as)

putrefaction, distillation, and the interaction of acids and salts . . . Gastric juices, considered acid and sharp, acted on foods to turn them into a white, milky fluid, which then mixed with alkaline bile in the digestive tract. The mixture fermented and bubbled, producing a salty substance that the body could transform into blood and other fluids.

This move away from the four elements marked the beginning of the end for humoral theory: When we stopped seeing the body as containing the four elements, there was little need to use the principles of humoral theory to balance them.

The body as a fermentation vessel is an idea that persists today, as our knowledge about the microbiome's role in digestion and health continues to deepen. Just like our forebears, who saw digestion as pivotal to the body writ large, we now understand that nourishing our microbiome impacts not just the absorption of nutrients but everything from our moods to our immune systems.

THE CHANGING VIEW OF COOKING IN EUROPE

As Western ideas of digestion shifted, they also changed cooking patterns for chefs, who now were no longer cooking for humoral balance but were incorporating foods that could ferment readily in the body and thus did not require complex preparation. Popular cooking and dietary advice in Europe in the 1700s still was not simple, though. It mixed humoral, chemical, and mechanical theories (mechanical theories held that the body ground food down, hence its grumbling).

In *Traité des aliments* (1702), French botanist and chemist Louis Lemery said that cucumbers, though refreshing, were also viscous and phlegmatic, rendering them difficult to digest and thus requiring that they be mixed with onion, salt, and pepper. And while vinegar-soaked cucumbers were also hard to digest, fully pickled cucumbers were actually more digestible. Cheese was considered healthy in moderation, not only because of its nutritional profile but specifically *because* it was fermented, aiding in digestion by adding its own ferment to our body's existing fermentation processes—an early example of human understanding of probiotics.

Fresh fruits and vegetables, shunned in the past for being too cold and moist (especially melons and mushrooms!), were now welcomed at the table, and horticulture boomed as a result. Sauces rich in fats, used to bind the salt and mercury elements, became popular, as did fresh green salads with oil-based dressings. Alcoholic spirits and other distilled essences were considered useful medicine—including extracts made from nutritive foods—and hot spiced hippocras gave way to cool wines and sparkling champagne.

During the late seventeenth and early eighteenth centuries, travelers to other countries brought back stories of fermentation traditions that had continued unabated for centuries: a thickened sour milk drink from Turkey that English writer Ephraim Chambers's 1728 *Universal Dictionary* calls igur, or the leben mentioned in the records of a 1691 merchant voyage to Aleppo. As a result, the western European diet began to incorporate more living foods, and perspectives on dining and health continued to shift.

Rather than balance, the goal of cooking in the eighteenth century was what Francois Marin's gastronomy and cookery book *Les dons de Comus* (1739) calls "a kind of chemistry. The cook's science consists today of analyzing, digesting [fermenting or cooking], and extracting the quintessence of foods, drawing out the light and nourishing juices, mingling and blending them together." Interestingly the cuisine born from this period outlasted the theory that inspired it: By the end of the eighteenth century, chemists and physicians were conducting research that would eventually lead to the modern understanding of calories, macronutrients, and micronutrients. Though it had faded into the background, humoral theory continued to be used to a varying extent until the rise of germ theory in the final decades of the nineteenth century.

* * *

Though our relationship with, and understanding of, health and microbes has shifted and grown over time, much of our perspective on microbes is still rooted in fear. As Ken Albala notes, early modern scientists

coffee, tea, and chocolate defy classification

In the early modern period in Europe (from roughly 1400 to 1800), other theories, such as one based in chemistry, began to supplant humoral theory. As Europeans began to colonize the rest of the world, they began to encounter new foods that needed to fit into the humoral framework. New World beans were similar to the beans that Europeans already had, and turkey seemed similar to peacock, so they tended to just map existing traits on to those items. But three foods in particular threw a wrench in this system: coffee, tea, and chocolate.

All three foodstuffs were types of food that had not been encountered before. As Ken Albala says, "Some people say [chocolate] is fatty, therefore it's hot and moist, but other physicians say, if you don't add sugar, it's bitter and astringent, so it's dry and good for phlegmatic disorders. How can something be both dry and moist or hot and cold?"

While coffeehouses sprang up around Europe in the 1600s, serving tea and chocolate (at that time consumed as a drink) as well as coffee, physicians debated the healthfulness of all three. Some viewed coffee as having a heating effect, but others claimed it was cooling because it dried up certain fluids (an early acknowledgment of its diuretic properties), and all three were astringent unless mixed with sugar. This led to an additional question: Were they medicinal in every form, or only in some (and if the latter, which ones)? These foods were a paradox, seemingly presenting every curative property and none, all at once. This, along with the rise in mechanical- and chemical-driven theories, moved physicians in other nonhumoral directions.

began their exploration with microbes centuries earlier "without the fear of contagion that grips us and leads us to outright war against germs—what I would call a variety of speciesism. Nor did scientists of the past share our bizarre ambivalence as we wipe out legions of microbes with antibacterial soaps and antibiotics and then reintroduce some of these same species in yogurt, probiotic foods and dietary supplements." This puts modern folks at the intersection of germophobia (an intense fear of microbes) and what

the physiology of taste

The writing of renowned French gastronome Jean Anthelme Brillat-Savarin (1755–1826) shows us how scientific theories of digestion and fermentation intersect with physical sensation, but not in a purely scientific way. In his writing, Brillat-Savarin uses scientific knowledge as the basis for curious meditations on the nature of hunger. Are his musings entirely scientifically sound? No. But they are thought provoking and, most important for us, part of the history of fermentation and our understanding of it.

Brillat-Savarin was neither a scientist nor a scholar (he was a lawyer and a politician), but he combined the work of both in some curious ways. In the case of digestion, he basically argues that everyone is right (except for the folks who believe in a mechanical model of actual stones or gears grinding food in the stomach—he does not mention them). He writes, "There has for a long time been argument over the manner in which digestion takes place: whether it be by the action of heat, of ripening, of fermentation, of gastric or chemical or vital dissolution, etc. It has a little of each of these things in it; and the only trouble with the whole thing biologist Jonathan Eisen calls microbiomania (obsession with probiotics for health). While it's good to be microbe-aware, our symbiotic microbes are incredibly safe to cook with: Fred Breidt, the USDA's fermentation specialist, notes that there is neither historical nor current evidence of food poisoning from properly fermented vegetables (there are cases with cheeses and meats, however, hence the necessity to be microbe-aware but not microbe-afraid).

has been that a single one was blamed in each case for the result of many necessarily united causes."

He goes on to root our digestion and physical sensations of hunger within thirst. In his Meditation 8: On Thirst, he describes thirst as "the inner consciousness of the need to drink" and says, "It is my belief that the seat of thirst is found in the whole digestive system." In his view, all animals feel what he calls latent or habitual thirst: that feeling of being parched and requiring hydration. But he ascribes to humans, and humans alone, what he calls artificial thirst, which "comes from an inborn instinct which we possess to want in our drink a strength which nature has not put there, and which is made only by fermentation." The irony of this thirst, he points out, is that the liquids we use to quench it worsen our latent thirst, leaving us to drink more than needed and make a habit out of it. In this view, alcoholism has a physiological component, which we've confirmed with modern research, though no one has yet agreed that thirst is the basis of the digestive system writ large.

FIRE CIDER

Fire cider relies on unpasteurized vinegar and is typically made with apple cider vinegar. It also commonly emphasizes hot peppers and alliums (onion and garlic). Aside from that, the ingredients are extremely flexible and vary from person to person and even batch to batch. This is a great way to use up little bits of vegetable matter (such as onion tops) or herb stems from other cooking projects! The goal is to get as much goodness packed into the jar as possible.

I classify my ingredients into three main groups—roots, shoots and fruits, and spice—and mix and match between them.

Fire cider can be enjoyed as a daily tonic by the shot glass or spoonful, or it can be incorporated into recipes, dressings, and marinades in place of apple cider vinegar. You can also use it to culture butter, as in the recipe on page 6.

MAKES
1 PINT

ROOTS

Onion, garlic, turmeric, ginger, horseradish, carrot, etc.

SHOOTS AND FRUITS

Citrus peel, thyme, rosemary, parsley, wild greens, dried cherries or elderberries, etc.

SPICE

Hot peppers (any variety)**, cinnamon sticks, star anise, cloves, etc.**

CIDER

Unpasteurized apple cider vinegar

Honey (optional)

1   Slice, cube, or coarsely chop the roots, and cut the hot peppers in halves or quarters.

2   Pack all of the roots, shoots and fruits, and spices tightly into a pint jar, and fill all the way to the neck with the vinegar, making sure everything is submerged. Cover with a tightly fitting lid.

3   Let steep at room temperature for at least 1 month. If bits of herbs and spices float to the top, gently shake the jar each day to redistribute them.

4   Once it's ready, strain the aromatics from it. If you want to add honey, stir it in now. Bottle the finished fire cider and store at room temperature; it will keep indefinitely.

APPLE SCRAP VINEGAR

This is vinegar making at its absolute most basic: using up peels and cores from other projects to make a bright, appley vinegar that is fantastic on its own or made into fire cider (see the recipe on the facing page). It is different from apple cider vinegar because it is made from scraps and sugar rather than juice, giving it a lighter flavor.

As in the banana vinegar recipe on page 115, this vinegar requires a two-step process. Basically, make alcohol, then turn the alcohol into vinegar. Because it's easy to make a lot more apple scrap vinegar than it is to make banana vinegar, I've included some tips for storing your vinegar on page 210.

MAKES
ABOUT
1 PINT

2   cups apple scraps (cores and peels; remove any seeds) **or whole apples cut into large cubes**

1   cup sugar

Unpasteurized vinegar or vinegar mother (optional)

STEP ONE: MAKE ALCOHOL

1   Combine the apple scraps and sugar with 1 quart water in a blender and blend to a pulp. Add more water, ¼ cup at a time, as needed until the mixture is a slurry (with a porridgelike consistency). Pour the apple slurry into a fermentation vessel. Cover your vessel with a lid or a cloth, securing it with a piece of twine if necessary.

2   Let the mixture ferment at room temperature, shaking or stirring it twice a day, until you have a boozy brew and any bubbling has calmed down, about 2 weeks.

STEP TWO: TURN YOUR BOOZE INTO VINEGAR

3   Line a mesh strainer with a piece of cheesecloth and set it over a bowl. Pour in the contents of the fermentation vessel. Press the apple chunks

Recipe continues on next page. >

to remove any remaining liquid. Pour the liquid into a widemouthed container.

4   If you like, add a splash of the vinegar or a piece of vinegar mother to jump-start the process. If you have neither, don't worry; the liquid will still turn into vinegar on its own.

5   Cover your container with a cloth or tea towel and let it sit at room temperature out of direct sunlight. Don't stir it or mess with it, just let it be! Eventually within a couple of weeks, you'll see a rubbery mat form on the surface, which is the vinegar mother, though in some cases you may just get little pieces of mother throughout (for example, if you happen to stir the vinegar midferment and the forming mother was broken into smaller pieces). If your vinegar tastes like vinegar and smells like vinegar, it's vinegar. There's no hard-and-fast rule for how long it needs to ferment. Once it tastes good to you, it's ready! Store your vinegar in an airtight, narrow-necked vessel (for example, a swing-top or screw-top bottle) to minimize exposure to air, or store it in the fridge.

TIPS FOR STORING YOUR VINEGAR

Vinegar isn't hard to make, but it is a bit finicky about being stored long term. Acetobacters, the same microscopic buddies who helped us make our vinegar, can be detrimental to our vinegar once it's finished. If they continue to metabolize, they will eventually convert the acetic acid in the vinegar into water and carbon dioxide, and once the acidity of your vinegar falls below about 2 percent, other microbes can set up shop.

You can prevent this by storing your vinegar in sealed containers, preferably bottles with narrow necks to reduce the amount of liquid exposed to air. You can also refrigerate it, which slows the action of the acetobacters. Or you can pasteurize your vinegar by heating it to between 140° and 150°F (60° and 65°C) and keeping it there for 15 seconds. Don't heat your vinegar above 160°F (70°C) or you'll evaporate off your acetic acid. Of course, if you want raw vinegar, don't do this step!

In *The Art of Fermentation*, Sandor Katz offers another option: aged vinegar. After being put in sealed bottles, vinegar makers will often wax-seal those bottles and allow them to age for at least 6 months. As with wine, aging creates deeper, rounder flavors.

THREE-ROOT PASTE

This simple seasoning paste is an easy way to use up any extra knobs of aromatic roots you have lying around, and it offers a lot of flavor payoff without a lot of work. I prefer to pack the jar very tightly with my sliced roots, both because they are more likely to stay under the brine and because I get a thicker end product. Of course, your paste can be as thick or as thin as you want; when you blend it up, you may find you don't need to add any of the brine at all.

Three-Root Paste is also the basis of one of my favorite winter meals: Three-Root Soup (see page 212), which is basically an amalgam of whatever needs to be used in the fridge and changes drastically with each reimagining. The paste is also wonderful in marinades, salad dressings, or just about anything else you could imagine. I haven't yet used it in a dessert, but I suspect if you switch out some carrot for that garlic, it might work quite well.

The sky is the limit for adaptations here. I've added carrot, horseradish, hot peppers, lemongrass, and plenty of nonrooty things, too. I've also added onion, though I find that onion can develop some undesirable flavors if it ferments for too long. You can even add foraged roots such as burdock or dandelion—these may make for a bitter, medicinal paste, but it will still have some wonderful culinary applications when used sparingly.

Rather than blend the fermented roots to a paste, you could dehydrate and grind them to make a dried seasoning blend (more guidance on that is in the recipe for Pickle Powder and fermented seasoning blends, page 315).

MAKES
1 PINT

1	head garlic
3	pieces fresh organic turmeric root, sliced
1	large piece fresh organic ginger, sliced
1/2	tablespoon sea salt or other unrefined salt

NOTE When using ginger as the basis for a wild-fermented food, always use organic ginger (and other organic roots, to the extent possible). Nonorganic ginger is often imported and irradiated, which kills the microbes that you want present to kick-start your ferment.

Recipe continues on next page. >

1   Fill a pint jar one-third of the way full with a layer of unpeeled garlic cloves, followed by a layer of sliced turmeric, and finally a layer of sliced ginger. The skins on all of these will soften as they ferment, so there's no need to peel!

2   Add the salt and fill with enough water to cover. Seal tightly and shake until the salt is dissolved. Make sure the brine is still completely covering the roots (if it isn't, push the roots back under the brine).

3   Ferment at room temperature until the mixture reaches a flavor you enjoy, 7 to 10 days.

4   Pour the contents of the jar into a food processor or blender and blend to your desired consistency. For the best flavor, store in the refrigerator, where it will keep for at least a month.

THREE-ROOT SOUP

Pour a splash of light-bodied olive oil (or ghee, coconut oil, or whatever fat you prefer) in a large pot over medium heat. Add a heaping spoonful of Three-Root Paste and gently simmer until the heat releases the paste's aroma and the garlic just begins to brown, 1 or 2 minutes.

From here, what you add is up to you. I'll usually pour in a quart of homemade stock right away to keep the paste from burning, and then, as it simmers, I'll toss in whatever I feel like. Sliced sausage left over from dinner last night? Perfect. Kale that's starting to go limp? Fantastic! Chopped or grated veggies, canned beans, and noodles, quinoa, or rice? Sure!

HOT SAUCE

Like Three-Root Paste (see page 211), this recipe is simply a matter of packing a jar, pouring in some salt and water, and letting it sit until it's ready to enjoy. Also like Three-Root Paste, it's fertile ground for experimentation. These basic lacto-ferments are easy to make, but the real gift in their simplicity is how adaptable they can be to our pantries and taste buds.

I will sometimes pack my hot sauces with medicinal plants or with the same ingredients I use to make fire cider, then blend it up into a thick, complex sauce. Or I'll brighten up things with fruit (pineapple is a great choice, as are strawberry tops), add some vegetal notes with carrot, deepen the flavor with spices or cocoa nibs, or keep it simple with just peppers, garlic, and salt.

MAKES
1 PINT

2–3   **cloves garlic, unpeeled**

Whole hot peppers, hot pepper tops, and any other add-ins you want

½   **tablespoon sea salt**

1   Arrange the garlic cloves at the bottom of a pint jar. Tightly pack in the hot peppers and any other add-ins to fill the jar.

2   Add the salt and fill with enough water to cover. Seal tightly and shake until the salt is dissolved. Make sure the brine is still completely covering the botanicals (if it isn't, push them back under the brine).

3   Ferment at room temperature until the mixture reaches a flavor you enjoy, about 21 days.

4   Pour the contents of the jar into a food processor or blender and blend to your desired consistency. Store in the fridge, where it will keep for months.

BEET KVASS

Here in the United States, when we think of fermented health tonics we're likely to think of kombucha. But another simple health tonic that doesn't require a SCOBY (symbiotic culture of bacteria and yeast) is kvass. Kvass, or kvas, is not always made with beets, but it does traditionally include bread or flour. Kristina Razueva, a food history enthusiast from Saint Petersburg, says a version made with rye malt, rye flour, and sugar was a popular summer drink during her childhood. This Russian and Eastern European beverage, simply brewed with beets, yields two wonderful products: a delicious, refreshing drink and lightly pickled beets to add to salads (or to eat straight).

You can also use beet kvass to pickle eggs, a trick I learned from my friend Jillian Ross. Just hard-boil and peel the eggs, then drop them (gently) in the kvass and refrigerate. After several days, you'll have beautifully beet-colored and delicious pickled eggs!

Recipe continues on next page. >

Many people brew kvass with a piece of bread, and if you happen to have a small heel of stale bread sitting around (rye bread tastes particularly delicious), this is a good use for it. Toss in large chunks or slices of bread to keep it from dissolving entirely as it ferments. If you don't eat gluten, you can omit the bread; without it, the kvass will ferment a bit more slowly, so add an extra day or two to the ferment time. Feel free to experiment by adding other veggies, too. I sometimes add carrots.

MAKES
ABOUT 1½
QUARTS

3	**beets**
½	**cup cubed yeasted bread, or the equivalent size heel of bread**
2	**teaspoons sea salt**
1½	**quarts water**

1 Cut the beets into large cubes and place them in your fermentation vessel. Add the bread.

2 Dissolve the salt in the water and pour the brine over the beets. Cover the jar with a towel or cheesecloth, secured with twine if needed.

3 Allow the kvass to ferment, gently stirring twice daily, until it is slightly tangy and sour and a deep purple-red hue, 1 to 2 days.

4 Strain and store in the fridge. Use within 2 weeks.

FERMENTED SQUASH AND APPLE CHUTNEY

This is a delicious, warming winter ferment made to serve as a side for holiday meals or a cozy spiced snack when the weather is cool. Fermented squash has a firm texture and fresh flavor that goes nicely with the apples. If you'd like it to be a bit softer, ferment the squash alone in the brine for several days, then add the apples to ferment for another day or two (or however long you'd like) before storing the chutney in the fridge.

1	**medium butternut squash, peeled and cut into 1-inch cubes**
4	**apples, cubed** (use any variety and no need to peel)
3/4	**cup toasted pecans**
2	**sticks cinnamon**
1	**(2-inch) piece fresh organic ginger, cut into slices**
1	**star anise pod**
1	**teaspoon black peppercorns**
1/2	**teaspoon whole cloves**
	Other add-ins (nuts, cubed beets, dried or fresh cranberries, citrus peel, and so on; optional)
2 1/2	**tablespoons unrefined salt**
2	**quarts water**
	Sugar or honey (optional)

MAKES ABOUT 3 QUARTS

1   Place the squash and apples in your fermentation vessel. Add the pecans, cinnamon sticks, ginger, star anise, peppercorns, cloves, and any add-ins. For easier removal later, put your spices in a bundle of cheese-cloth and secure with food-safe twine.

2   Dissolve the salt in the water and pour the brine over the mixture, making sure the materials are completely submerged.

3   Place a weight on your ferment to keep everything under the brine. Let the mixture ferment at room temperature for 4 to 7 days, checking it every couple of days. When it has developed a flavor you like, it's finished! If you want a sweet chutney, add a bit of sugar or honey to taste after fermenting.

4   Remove the whole spices and store the chutney in the fridge, where it will keep for several weeks. A storage note: Pint jars will fit in the fridge more easily than quarts, and they will be easier to gift to friends and family.

HIPPOCRAS

Hippocras, an infused wine, is the medicinal predecessor to today's mulled wines and other infused wines. This recipe is based on the recipe in Robert May's *The Accomplisht Cook* (1660), but feel free to substitute whatever spices and other flavors you prefer. For a historically authentic version, use cinnamon, cardamom pods, grains of paradise, and long pepper as your spices, and use claret as your wine base.

Hippocras was typically served sweet, though spiced wine is also lovely without any sugar.

MAKES ONE 750 ML BOTTLE OF WINE

2	**cinnamon sticks**
1	**sprig fresh rosemary**
1	**teaspoon whole cloves**
1	**teaspoon black peppercorns**
1	**(1-inch) piece fresh ginger, peeled** (see note)
1	**nutmeg nut, scored a few times with a Microplane to help release its flavor**
1	**750 ml bottle red wine**
3/4	**cup granulated sugar or 1/2 cup honey** (optional)

NOTE It's easiest to peel ginger if you use the edge of a spoon to scrape the peel from the root.

1   Place the cinnamon sticks, rosemary, cloves, and peppercorns in a mortar and gently bruise them with a pestle.

2   Cut a square of cheesecloth and lay it flat. Place the cinnamon sticks, rosemary, cloves, peppercorns, ginger, and nutmeg in the middle of the cloth and tie it up into a secure bundle. Place the bundle in the bottom of a food-safe container. Pour in the wine.

3   Let the mixture infuse for 24 hours, or longer if desired.

4   Add the sugar or honey, if using, and stir to dissolve. Remove the spices, give the wine a quick stir (and a strain, if needed), and serve. Consume any unused portion within several days.

5

COMMUNITY

Throughout our history, fermentation has been central to human community. Ferments appear on our tables but also in our rituals and in the fabric and objects we use to adorn ourselves and our homes. Ferments of many sorts—from wine to indigo dye to bread— have knit communities closer together and torn them apart.

> As my exploration of fermentation unfolds, I keep coming back to the profound significance of the fact that we use the same word—culture—to describe the community of bacteria that transform milk into yogurt, as well as the practice of subsistence itself, language, music, art, literature, science, spiritual practices, belief systems, and all that human beings seek to perpetuate in our varied and overlapping collective existences.
>
> —SANDOR ELLIX KATZ, *THE ART OF FERMENTATION*

Ferments serve as a touch point of our personal and community identities and as a way to connect to our ancestral heritage. In a very real sense, their microscopic communities have been a vital force in shaping our own.

What Is a Community?

To answer this question, we must look at what defines a microbial community and what defines a human community: the micro and the macro. Their commonalities may surprise you.

MICRO-COMMUNITIES

A community could perhaps be defined, in part, as a group of organisms that occupy a given space, together, over a period of time. Like human communities, microbial ones tend to form in environments with the features they want: factors and resources that will make them feel safe and comfortable and able to thrive. As it does for us, this includes access to nutrition, a comfortable temperature, and somewhat static environmental conditions (we don't want to live in a place that's constantly in the throes of upheaval, and neither do microbes).

Like human communities, microbial communities also change over time: The community present in your sauerkraut, for example, is going to be a bit different by day 10 than it was at day 2. Shifting environmental conditions, access to food resources, and population density as well as population makeup (among other things) all play a role. The makeup of the community itself changes, too: Your sauerkraut contains not only

Lactobacillus plantarum and *L. brevis* but also other microbes, including other bacteria and yeasts as well.

Microbial communities work together toward common goals. The goal depends on the microbe in question, and their success in achieving it depends on environmental conditions (including access to resources). The shared vision of one community might be to populate a host organism, or to process elements in seawater, or to break down the starches in food. Their demographics and numbers shift, but they shift within the context of their larger microbial world, protecting themselves and their partners (in the case of fermentation microbes, this includes protecting us), and exchanging information with individuals and communities that cross their paths. In our quest to move in partnership with our world, we create protective environments for them as well: brine for lactic acid bacteria, sugary liquid for yeast, a bed of warm substrate for koji.

But there is another element of protection involved, too, and that is passing on the knowledge of how to care for our microbial friends. Just as there are many different types of microbes, so too are there many different ways in which human cultures have cared for them over millennia. If we don't identify these fermentation traditions and make sure we have access to them, we may lose this knowledge. As Sandor Katz notes, their micro-communities have sustained us for millions of years, and so we owe it to them and to ourselves to pass on the stories of the foods they help us prepare. We'll talk more about this in Chapter 6.

MACRO-COMMUNITIES

There are many different ways we've defined our human communities over the years: a tribe or clan, a friend group, a village, a neighborhood, a city, a family. Both the beauty and the downfall of this term is its flexibility. It implies connection, but what connections and to whom (and how they are performed) are not always clear.

There are many different definitions of the term *community*. A 2001 public health study by public health researcher Kathleen MacQueen and her colleagues calls it "a group of people with diverse characteristics who are linked by social ties, share common perspectives, and engage in joint action in geographical locations or settings." Researcher John van Willigen says it is simply "any social group in which members want to enact some change." Our definitions of community may change across time and place, but at its core the term refers to people together in some way, for some reason. In our human communities, the fermented food made by microbial communities has played a pivotal role for millennia.

THE INDIVIDUAL IN COMMUNITY

Food sits at the intersection of the self and the other. What we create and share is consumed and absorbed by the individual body, but it took many, many sets of hands to get it there: those that planted and raised the seed, those that brought the food to market, and those that prepared it (among many others).

When someone shares food with you, they are engaging in intimacy. What they make for you becomes quite literally a part of you, nourishing your body and soul and facilitating your continued existence on this planet. The food you feed yourself is an act of individual intimacy. Even the most simple meal is a commitment to nourishment and to continued existence in this time and place. In Chapter 3, we encountered the idea of *son-mat*, the Korean term that refers to the special flavor a person imparts to their food, a concept that in the West might be understood (in part) by the idea of "food made with love." We recognize when we are given food made with love and care, just as we recognize the particular fingerprint of a familiar cook (say, a beloved grandparent) upon a dish or a meal. That is son-mat.

Your first relationship as a human being is about food. The first social experience we have is being put to the breast or bottle. The social act of eating, is part of how we become human, as much as speaking and taking care of ourselves. Learning to eat is learning to become human.

—ANTHROPOLOGIST
RICHARD WILK

Ferments sit at this intersection as well, wherein the personal and individual meets the communal. Our fermented foods are, of course, filled with their own communities, teeming with bacteria, yeast, and fungi that intersect with our senses and our own microbiomes. But they connect us to macro-communities as well: As one of our most ancient preservation methods, and one that fundamentally has not changed over time, fermentation gives us direct access to a lineage of food shared by humans all over the world for thousands of years. Our foods offer a map of the abundance and shortage they faced, as well as what stories were passed down through history versus what history has been lost or buried. We pass on those stories and foods through heritage starters, family recipes, and the myths and legends that weave their way through each family line. Ferments are a direct tether between our ancestors and ourselves.

Food Culture

The way food is savored, how it is eaten and with whom, is central to our understanding of food culture, both with fermented foods and beyond, no matter where and when we look. Shanghai-based food writer Crystyl Mo says that in Chinese cuisine, food is eaten for taste but also for texture (jellyfish and sliced pig ear, for instance, both have little taste but they do have a desirable texture). Temperature matters, too, she says: "Foods must either be scalding hot or very cold; if it's warm, there's something wrong with the dish." And at traditional Chinese banquets, Mo says, "the most expensive things are served first, such as scallops or steamed fish, then meats, then nice vegetables, and finally soup, and if you're still hungry, then rice or noodles or buns."

Food culture in France is about emotion as well as flavor. Chef Mark Singer notes, "Food in France is still primarily about pleasure. . . . Cooking and eating are both pasttime and pleasure." Culinary culture, has, however, changed in the last 20 years: While food for birthdays and holidays is still very often traditionally prepared, this is not necessarily the case with everyday meals. Nutrition and food studies scholar Jennifer Berg notes that perception, from both within and without, does not always align with these changes. She says, "I led a course in Paris this summer on myth-making and myth-busting and the performance of Frenchness. The students want to believe that France is this pastoral nation where people are spending 5 hours a day going to 12 different markets to get their food. The reality is most croissants are factory made, and most people are buying convenience food, except for the very elite. But part of our identity relies on believing that mythology."

In Italy, as in France, eating take-out food is relatively rare. Italian food expert Marco Bolasco notes, "Eating fast is not at all part of our culture. . . . Our meals are relaxed, even during lunch break." This is true whether you're eating alone or with others.

The dining pace of Italians and French people contrasts sharply with that of Americans, who have an "eat and run" ethic of shoveling food into mouths between meetings, while running errands, or while driving. We then top this off with social experiences such as happy hours that are part work function and part space to unwind (rather than, say, a leisurely glass of wine with a friend or a couple of colleagues). In America, a slow and relaxed meal feels almost luxurious: Time taken to drink a bit of wine, slowly savor food, and relax in the company of loved ones is a necessary act we give ourselves precious little time for.

In the process of learning about other cultures' eating habits, I hope we can also examine our own. We have so much more to learn than just what ferments others are eating. Perhaps just as important, we may learn *how* others are eating them.

How Ferments Forge Community

Countless fermented foods are central to global cuisines and community meals, and many individuals prepare them in their own homes. In some cases (for instance, that of gundruk, Nepalese fermented greens), these ferments have largely stayed in their geographic area or within the diasporic community from a particular region. In other cases (such as that of sauerkraut), ferments have spread between multiple cultures, and in still others (such as that of sowens, Scottish fermented oats), the food has fallen out of favor within its original community—though, of course, it may then be adopted by another culture.

Ferments can be dietary staples that connect individuals to a shared food identity. In eastern Europe, for example, the ferments a family makes are an important part of their heritage, and because these practices tend to be highly localized, the dish connects them to a very specific identity (say, a village or region). In the Baltic states, beer, gherkin, and sauerkraut recipes vary depending on where you are, and gherkins in particular vary by location. Flavorings for gherkins include wild and cultivated plants, from horseradish and garlic to sour cherry, black currant, and oak leaves. Sauerkraut could include apples, carrots, caraway, or cranberry (among other things), and rose hips are a feature in all kinds of ferments, from drinks to vinegars and beyond. Such local and regional differences in staple ferments, and in their role in community and identity, can be found across the globe. By using sauerkraut and kimchi as case studies, we can explore how a ferment (recognizing that there are many subtypes of each) can forge community connections within a culture.

SAUERKRAUT

In eastern Europe, where it is most prevalent, sauerkraut was made by and for individual families, or perhaps by a community member who sold it to others within the town or village, or by families who pooled together harvests (and labor) to make it together. Sauerkraut in Germany reaches back to at least the Middle Ages, though sauerkraut itself has existed in some capacity since the Bronze Age. In German towns in the eighteenth and nineteenth centuries, women sold numerous foodstuffs at local markets, including sauerkraut, even though their legal rights as businesspeople were much more limited than men's rights. Selling sauerkraut and bread was considered an extension of their normal duties, and thus allowed in most markets.

As German and eastern Europeans migrated to other countries in the 1900s, sauerkraut preservation became part of life in their new communities. Recalling her family's harvest rituals in Iowa between the two World Wars, writer and historian Lenore Salvaneschi wrote, "The harvesting of cabbage was always done in the heat of the summer, probably on a scorching July or August day. Early in the morning Father cut all the best heads of cabbage in the garden, trimmed off the outer leaves, then brought the white, still sweet-smelling heads to the shade of the grape arbor behind the house. There the sharpened butcher knives were used to cut the cabbages in fourths." After that, they would be shredded on a sauerkraut

wildcrafted ferments

For all our ancestors, at one point or another, wildcrafting (harvesting and working with wild, rather than cultivated, plants) was a way of life that was necessary for survival. Plants were often gathered and processed in groups, where knowledge could be passed down from generation to generation and from community to community.

Even with the advent of agriculture, wildcrafting and wildcrafted ferments maintained an important role in many communities, either in an ongoing sense (such as the harvest of wild plants for medicine in parts of the Himalayan mountains) or an acute one (for example, increased wild plant consumption during famine or wartime, as we saw in the turbulent early Middle Ages).

We still know about and prepare some of the wildcrafted foods our ancestors made, but many others, as well as the knowledge of the plants used, have been lost due to various factors—from colonization and genocide to changing landscapes and the emergence of convenience foods. In Spain, for example, wild cereal grains used to be collected regularly to feed humans (added to breads and other dishes) and animals, but with the modern introduction of herbicides and deep plowing (rather than hand-weeding), many wild grain populations that were foraged by community members have been eliminated. In Poland, a fermented cornflower beverage that was documented in the mid-twentieth century has now disappeared from the culinary landscape due to the use of herbicides that drastically reduced cornflower populations.

cutter, layered with salt in a large crock, and left to ferment, weighted by a plate and large rock.

Households and towns would often make sauerkraut together. In some rural areas, family- or community-level sauerkraut production was frequently performed by stomping on the cabbage to extract the salt and to evenly pack it into vessels, and even today, fermenter and author Kirsten Shockey says that "bare feet stomping on shreds of cabbage in barrels hits a decidedly European collective nostalgia," which we can see in modern-day festivals where sauerkraut stomping is a celebrated activity. Sauerkraut forms a basis (or in some cases, *the* basis) of many fall festivals, including German food festivals, small-town community festivals and fairs in the Midwest, and specific festivals such as Lisbon Sauerkraut Days in Iowa.

In New York City, the first delicatessens were run by Christian and Jewish Germans, then mostly by Jewish immigrants from around eastern Europe. The most iconic ferments at these delis are the pickles (full sours and half sours), but these delis also sell sauerkraut, either on sandwiches or alone. In my experience, it is made with just cabbage and salt or perhaps with caraway seeds. The Jewish deli, a benchmark of New York food identity (sadly many have closed in recent decades), is one of many, many examples of cultural identity being shaped by how and what (and where) a community eats when they dine in public.

In the twentieth century, sauerkraut making (and eating) declined in popularity in Germany, though it was still eaten on holidays, including the traditional New Year's dish of sauerkraut and pork. Many Germans had turned to purchasing commercially made sauerkraut, and in many cases family sauerkraut traditions, or even basic fermentation practices in general, were not passed on. But as the twenty-first century began, Germans have embraced it again, in part for health reasons. Professional fermentation teachers teach fermentation classes to eager learners, and books and recipes abound.

KIMCHI

The importance of kimchi in Korea cannot be overestimated. The United Nations says that kimchi transcends "class and regional differences" in

Korea, and it serves as the backbone of Korean cuisine. Served as a condiment or stirred into dishes such as kimchi jigae (kimchi soup), it has a place at the table for every meal.

Kimjang (or gimjang) is a yearly kimchi-making gathering that takes place as the weather cools, though preparation for it spans the seasons. Korean-American food writer Dakota Kim notes, "Kimjang celebrates seasonality, community harmony and ecological balance in a way that is utterly vital to recognize in times of extreme global warming. It is a collaborative process in every sense of the word. Not only do a village's neighbor women come together, but many ingredients come together from many sources, and a family following the rhythms of the earth collects the ingredients for kimjang all throughout the year." These include seafood gathered in spring, salt in summer, and vegetables during the harvest season.

Kimjang dates back to the Three Kingdoms period in Korea (57 BCE–668 CE). It began as a way for the village to preserve food. All the households would pool their resources to ensure that everyone had enough to eat to last them through winter. While the main ingredients have changed (for example, the introduction of hot chile peppers in the fifteenth century resulted in the spicy, chile-laced baechu-kimchi, or napa cabbage kimchi, which is what most Americans are familiar with) and there is now a wider number of flavor variations, the core community spirit of the gathering has remained consistent, even when it is no longer a matter of survival.

Multiple generations would be involved in kimjang. This was important for a couple of reasons: Putting up hundreds of cabbages on the family farm required many hands, and it provided a time to pass along critical family knowledge. Dakota Kim recalls:

> Another reason to do kimjang? You can up your kimchi game, since you add different tricks from your mother, mother-in-law, grandmother, sisters, aunties and cousins. My mother always stops me from putting too much of the wet chile pepper filling between the leaves of the cabbage, but makes sure every leaf is completely covered with the filling—no leaf should be white and green by kimjang's end. I often laugh at her admonitions, but no matter how much I try to make my kimchi taste just like hers,

her decades of experiences seem to always create a much better end product. I hope that through our annual kimjang process, I can someday gain *sohn-mat* (a delicious taste that comes from the unique skills of particularly talented hands getting personal with the food) as good as hers.

Kimjang connects not only members of one family or community but generations of people who have been following the tradition for centuries. The practice of kimjang is declining in Korea in general, in part due to cramped urban living quarters and also to the year-round availability of cabbage, which makes it unnecessary for communities to preserve large amounts of cabbage all at once. But just because kimjang is no longer necessary doesn't mean it is without value (UNESCO agrees, having added the gatherings to its Intangible Cultural Heritage list). As Kim notes, "With the advent of urbanization in Korea, kimjang seems to be fading and changing, and the deep essence of what kimchi means is also changing. Just like so many other intangible things, the true value in kimjang lies not in the practical process, but in the emotional byproducts." Kimchi, and the accompanying kimjang, both speak to the power of ferments for community: They nourish community members not only physically but in their souls as well.

How Drinking Forms Community

Making and drinking alcohol is a big part of many communities worldwide, both past and present. From its presence in religious rituals to its use as a social lubricant and the centerpiece of celebrations, alcohol has been a staple in the lives of humans for millennia.

COMMUNITY ALCOHOL PRODUCTION

Winemaking, and alcohol production in general, is as old as civilization. Wine presses, drinking cups, and amphorae (special pottery vessels for holding wine and other liquids) tell of wine's presence in the Bronze Age Minoan civilization (roughly 3000–1100 BCE) and Mycenaean civilization (roughly 1700–1100 BCE) in Greece, and by the time we get to classical Greece (about 510–323 BCE), wine was considered an important part of the economy. Unlike in nearby Egypt and Anatolia (and even in Bronze Age Greece), where wine was reserved for elites, in classical Greece it was a basic food, and it was served mixed with water rather than consumed straight.

In Tuscany, Italy, the grape harvest (la vendemmia) has long been an anticipated and celebrated event. The history of grape stomping (or grape treading), where wine grapes are mashed with the feet before fermentation, goes back at least to ancient Greece and Rome. During these gatherings, community members come together and, after pouring the grape harvest into large barrels, proceed to climb in with bare feet and stomp to break down the grapes and release their juices.

Multiple Roman artworks and other artifacts, such as the depiction of satyrs stomping the grapes at the Musée Ingres that dates from between the first century BCE and the first century CE, show us that this activity was already central enough to community life to be included in harvest scenes. Wine grapes are native to the Mediterranean region, though, so it is possible that this practice is much older. As my friend Ellen Ireland, a bioanthropologist and medical college faculty member, wisely says, "It's safe to assume that anything with sugar in it has been fermented into alcohol at some point by ancient people."

Some modern winemakers still prefer grape stomping over mechanical crushers, and it is possible to sometimes find grape-stomping events in Italy and other wine-growing regions (there are many tourist packages that cater to those who want to get their feet grapey). Most farmers these days, however, take their grapes to a nearby crusher, just as they might take grains to a miller.

ALCOHOL MAKING AT HOME

Alcohol was traditionally, and continues to be, made at home for home consumption as well as for several community-connected ends, including sharing with neighbors or family, preserving foodstuffs, or generating extra income. Just as with food production, the kind of alcohol produced historically depended on which ingredients were available. In the southern Appalachian Mountains, for example, wines are made from various local fruits, including wild grapes. In western Africa, sorghum is used to brew sour beer. In Peru, families ferment corn into chicha, a traditional drink that has been consumed since before colonial times. In Uganda, a weak beer is sometimes brewed from banana juice, and this is almost entirely made and consumed at home.

Shui communities of southwest China have an extensive history of using wild plants as starters (xiaoqu) to prepare fermented beverages. While that practice was once prevalent throughout China (the earliest known record of wild-plant starters is from 533 CE), this is no longer the case. The starter quality is traditionally considered to be the most important factor in making good liquor, and the starter itself (which includes mold and wild bacteria) is made with a wide diversity of plants, ranging across 88 genera and 57 families. In one study of Chinese home producers who still made liquor this way, most of the respondents noted that using more plants in the starter meant you'd get a better liquor as a result, with the average producer using about 15 species for their starter (and some using more than 50). Starters include asters, roses, legumes, mulberries, myrtles, and more, chosen based in part on availability and on the environment they create for the microorganisms.

BREWING WITH HONEY

Perhaps the most famous alcohol brewed with honey is mead. Anthropologist Mikal Aasved argued that mead is so ancient that the term *medhu* (the linguistic root for mead) is the same across all Indo-European languages, suggesting that fermented honey was the oldest alcohol known to humans. And because of its centrality, it takes an important place in community gatherings.

In Ethiopia, tej, a local form of mead, is made from a simple list of ingredients: honey, water, and leaves (and/or twigs) from the gesho plant, fermented together to make a beautiful, sunny orange-colored beverage. It is traditionally consumed out of flasks with a rounded bottom and a narrow neck, called bereles.

Once the drink of nobles and military, now tej is consumed by everyone. It is served in bars called tej bets, which are run almost exclusively by women but frequented almost exclusively by men (it is considered gauche for women to drink in bars). But there is a sense of connection to history behind the brew. When an American journalist visited a tej bet in Addis Ababa, he asked a local painter named Wasyehune why he drank tej over other alcoholic beverages. Wasyehune answered, "To feel the real essence of the people. . . . It's not just about putting alcohol in your stomach. It's about socializing. It's what our fathers did. We are drinking history!"

In Europe, the most famous mead drinkers were probably the Vikings. Mead consumption was an important community practice, though mead brewing itself seemed not to be. As Charles Riseley noted in his 2014 master's thesis on Viking history, "The ceremonial consumption of alcohol played an important role in the social landscape of Viking Age Scandinavia, where it framed some of the most important gatherings and rituals. One need only take a glance at the Norse myths to see the prominent place that alcohol held in the Early Medieval mindset."

In Viking cultures, the consumption of mead was highly ritualized. It played a large role in both social and religious rituals and was used, among other things, as a binding agent between people, lending weight and significance to vows and pledges.

SOCIAL LUBRICANT

Alcohol has been the centerpiece of many community gatherings, formal and informal, helping to ease nerves and facilitate conversation (and in some cases, perhaps a fight, too). Drinking is part of many festivals and holiday celebrations the world over—in public spaces during an outdoor festival, in private homes over a holiday meal, or in a bar with new and old friends.

Private dinners have relied on alcohol as a social lubricant for millennia. In ancient Greece, the symposium, an after-dinner gathering of men who would drink wine from shallow, two-handled cups, was a space for conversation, entertainment, and drinking games (women, unless entertainers, prostitutes, servants, or enslaved, were not permitted).

New Year's is a good example of alcohol used in celebration: Whether you go to a bar or a private party in the Western world, you're likely to pop a bottle at midnight in a toast to tradition and the future. While New Year's celebrations in Europe and the Middle East go back about 4,000 years, they used to take place in March at the vernal equinox, when the days began to lengthen and plants would begin to emerge from their winter slumber. (When Julius Caesar introduced the Julian calendar, he added several months to it and insisted that January 1 be the start of the year, in part to honor the god Janus, who can see both forward and back. Though there were some changes during the Middle Ages, we eventually returned to January 1 as the start of the new year with the Gregorian calendar.)

Champagne got an invitation to the party due in part to marketing and social climbing. The journalist Wayne Curtis calls champagne "one of civilization's great examples of a flaw evolving into a feature." Champagne actually stems from England, not France, originating in the 1600s. When wine was not allowed to ferment fully before being bottled, it would carbonate, which was considered a mark of poor-quality wine—that is, until some fiddling with the process produced a consistently palatable product. On December 17, 1662, after some experimentation, English scientist Christopher Merrett reported to the Royal Society of London that adding sugar to wine "promoted effervescence." With the ability to control the bubbling in a more refined way, French winemakers began experimenting, and by the 1720s, the sparkling beverage was well established in England and in the French court.

Champagne was a status symbol. For example, in *L'accord fraternel*, a print published at the outset of the French Revolution, we see three men sharing a toast: a nobleman drinking champagne, a farmer drinking beer, and a priest drinking wine. After the revolution, champagne became a secular symbol of celebration. You could, for example, "christen" a ship without a priest present by smashing a bottle of champagne on its side.

Champagne's popularity quickly grew, and in the early 1880s, when it became a popular drink for holiday gatherings, champagne producers jumped at the opportunity. Marketing it as a drink to celebrate special occasions with loved ones proved to be a boon,

> From man's sweat and God's love, beer came into the world.
>
> —SAINT ARNOLDUS

and it intersected nicely with the growing middle class emerging from the industrial revolution. Sales of sparkling wine skyrocketed from 6 million bottles in 1850 to 28 million by 1900.

The marketing efforts continued, further connected to New Year's by the likes of Martin's restaurant in New York City—one of the city's finest French restaurants and the first place to go "champagne only" after nine o'clock on New Year's Eve. While it took a blow during Prohibition, champagne slowly returned to the New Year's table in the United States, and it has been a constant guest ever since.

Plenty of public drinking happens outside formal celebrations, too: Bars, nightclubs, chicharias, pubs, beer gardens, and various other venues worldwide offer drinks without the need for a special occasion. In the United States (and increasingly elsewhere), happy hour is our version of teatime: a bit of time to unwind and converse over a beverage and perhaps a light snack.

While happy hour is a relatively recent phenomenon, pubs and bars are a long-standing tradition in the United States. New York City, for example, has been a mash-up of cultures since soon after its colonization, and early colonists (wherever they hailed from) were big fans of drinking, and drinking a lot. The area was originally colonized by the Dutch, and the West India Company built a brewery on Staten Island almost immediately after arriving, in addition to importing wine and brandy. Soon after, a letter back to the Netherlands noted that nearly one-quarter of New Amsterdam's buildings were shops selling alcohol and perhaps also tobacco. When the English arrived in 1664, local taverns became the city's social centers, though unlike under Dutch rule (where all social classes would mingle over the same bar), the English taverns began catering to different social classes of clientele. Later, New York food writer Arthur Schwartz tells us, German immigrants "introduced light, low-alcohol lager beer to a nation weaned on the heavy and strong English style of beer. They opened breweries and beer gardens and eventually made New York City the beer capital of the country."

UNDER THE TABLE

Alcohol has been the subject of a good deal of scrutiny (and legislation) over the centuries, leading many entrepreneurial producers around the world to craft and market their wares outside the law. In the southern Appalachian Mountains near my home, moonshine (traditionally a home-made, unaged, clear whiskey with a high alcohol content) is perhaps the most famous example, steeped in legend and mystery as well as actual history. Liquor has been distilled extralegally in many parts of the United States in different time periods (and it is currently illegal for an individual to distill liquor at home, even for personal use), but the term *moonshine* is heavily associated with this region, where it has been a source of income and pride for many generations. Even before moonshining was illegal, moonshiners didn't pay taxes on their product, causing long-standing tensions with government officials who felt they should.

Moonshine, so called because it was often prepared only by the light of the moon and the small fire that heated the alcohol, is made with whatever sugar source is available: corn syrup, for example, or cane sugar or perhaps molasses. In my region, many of the people who make moonshine are descended from the Scottish and Irish, who brought traditions of home-brewing whiskey with them from their home countries.

Many parts of the Appalachians are geographically isolated, at certain times cut off from resources such as government assistance, services, and amenities, and often looked down on by much of the rest of the country. For these reasons, people here tend to be distrustful of outsiders and of the government. Why, after all, should you pay taxes on the whiskey you sell for income when you rarely see any benefit from the government having your money? The tensions between moonshiners and authorities came to a head during the Whiskey Rebellion in western Pennsylvania in 1794, near the Allegheny mountains (which are part of the Appalachian mountain range). The cash-strapped government was desperate to raise funds to cover debts from the Revolutionary War and to keep the infant country afloat. In an attempt to raise funds, they began taxing homemade whiskey.

Decades later, during the Civil War, several Confederate states passed laws prohibiting the use of grains for anything besides food (including prohibitions on brewing and distillation), but these proved hard to enforce.

It wasn't until the 1870s that federal taxation on home distilleries was enforced, causing confusion, as many of those arrested early on had not realized that home distilling was illegal, nor did they understand why it was.

When Prohibition went into effect in 1920 (lasting until 1933), people were no longer able to drink as openly as before, but people still drank a good deal (even in public venues). Alcohol could still be had in private clubs and homes (in some cases, you had to BYOB to clubs while staff turned a blind eye), but as food writer Sophie Egan says in her book *Devoured*, "The stuff that could be had was less reliable in terms of flavor and quality. Mixing the hooch with another liquid helped mask these circumstances." (In this way, while Prohibition did not mark the invention of the cocktail, it did help ensure its survival in the United States as drinkers became accustomed to adding flavorful mixers to their tipple.)

Ultimately, government efforts to get folks to lay off the booze backfired. As Arthur Schwartz says in *New York City Food*, "Prohibition was very good for drinking. What Prohibition killed was fine dining in public. . . . Given how disastrous Prohibition was for one large segment of the restaurant business, it's astounding how many new restaurants opened in the 1920s, and how many of them remained important well after the repeal of Prohibition in 1933: The Colony, Sardi's, '21' Club, and Leon & Eddie's all opened during the dry period, and only Sardi's didn't serve alcohol, although Vincent Sardi did allow regular customers to bring their own booze as long as they drank it from coffee cups."

Illegal alcohol production was big business during Prohibition, as well as during the Great Depression, and though production has slowed down considerably, you can still find it if you know where to look. Chef and cookbook author Vivian Howard from eastern North Carolina calls apple pie moonshine "our version of a classic cocktail," explaining, "When bootleggers had to hide their shine, they'd mix it with apple cider and store it in the cider jug. The juice-colored camouflage quelled suspicion and made white lightning easier to drink. Eventually apple pie moonshine, also called applejack, became a concoction moonshiners hung their hat on. My dad still gets several mason jars of the stuff every Christmas."

FOLLOWING TRENDS

Our social behavior is informed in part by what is popular at a given moment. In the past, it was also informed by our gender. Women were not able to go into tea shops or coffee shops in England until 50 to 100 years after they first opened in 1652, for example, and thereafter they were often seated in gender-segregated areas.

Sophie Egan argues that food trends move in many ways through society. One example is the top-down approach, where something becomes fashionable among the wealthy and "avant-garde," is widely adopted by people seeking to emulate the food trend, and then is dropped by the original adopters as it becomes mainstream.

There's also what anthropologist Richard Wilk calls a "style sandwich," where people at the top and at the bottom of the socioeconomic ladder are consuming a particular food or beverage, but not the people in the middle. In the 1950s, for example, very rich Americans drank wine to emulate the French, and immigrants drank it because they or their families had been accustomed to doing so in the old country, but for middle-class Americans, it was not a common beverage.

The cocktail started out as a beverage for the more well-to-do. In New York City, the heyday of the cocktail ran from the post–Civil War period—the Gilded Age—through the end of the nineteenth century, when men's cafés or bars opened in elegant hotels. Cocktails were the focus of these venues, and they were the culmination of decades of mixed drink experimentation. These upscale venues also served cocktails as a counterpoint to the beer and straight whiskey offered in saloons and beer halls, and inventive bartenders served the city's elite a variety of mixed beverages.

By the late 1920s, day drinking became popular among the upper classes, and mixed drinks and cocktails became a brunch fixture (Egan refers to brunch as "secular church"). Egan notes, "These AM drinks usually combined vodka or champagne with something gentle and citrusy, pulling in the Parisian innovations of mimosas and Bloody Marys, but also Bellinis and Greyhounds (the wisdom about the hair of the dog that bit you as the best way to cure a hangover was already well established). That said, middle-class women were warned about how it might look to be hitting the bottle before noon. As opposed to, say, tequila on the rocks during the wee hours, mixed drinks cleared the path for day drinking as a socially acceptable activity for all tiers of society. And so, since at least the 1970s, moms nationwide have been getting tipsy on Mother's Day bubbly."

When it comes to long-standing trends, Americans are a drinking culture: In the 1800s, they outdrank almost everyone globally, save for the French, Scots, and Swedes. Today we've calmed down a bit, but we still rank 48th globally for alcohol consumption, behind various eastern European countries at the top, a few other European countries, and Australia and South Korea.

France and Uruguay are top for whiskey consumption, Europe (especially eastern Europe) and Venezuela drink the most beer, and America is number one for tequila consumption (Mexico is second). For wine consumption, the Vatican is by far the highest ranking, and even the United Kingdom drinks twice as much wine per person as Americans do.

Sharing Fermented Meals

Fermented food and drinks are a critical component of shared meals worldwide. The sourness of lacto-ferments and vinegars balances the flavors of a range of dishes, which is often encouraged for health reasons as well as gustatory ones. Fermented beverages are used to wash down many meals, with the added advantage of serving as social lubricants. Yogurt and cheese add creaminess and tang to spreads, and yeasted bread offers a medium for other meal components—whether as host to a spread or as a vehicle to sop up a meal's juices. Some ferments—such as kimchi and certain pickles in Korean banchan—appear in everyday meals as well as ones for a special occasion, while other dishes—such as fine wines and specialty spirits—are often reserved for celebrations.

THE EVERYDAY IS SPECIAL

In many global communities, you don't need to wait for a special occasion to enjoy ferments. They're often staples, forming the basis of a meal, as we saw with breakfasts of fermented porridge in Chapter 1, or regularly served as side dishes.

In many cultures, a particular fermented ingredient—such as labneh in Syrian cuisine or kimchi in Korean cuisine—is ubiquitous, serving as both an ingredient and a stand-alone side or condiment. As foods (and people) move through migrations and those ingredients become more widely available, it is critical to honor the cultures and meals they originated from by understanding their context.

JORDAN AND SYRIA: LABNEH

Labneh (or labna, labaneh, lebnah, labne, or labni) is a cheese made from strained yogurt that is common across many Middle Eastern cuisines, including those of Syria and Jordan. It can be made from the milk of cows, sheep, goats, or camels, and it can be eaten plain or mixed with herbs. It is a breakfast staple in many places. It can also be dried into jameed, balls of dehydrated yogurt cheese that store well and can be used to flavor and thicken soups and other foods.

Both jameed and labneh have historically been useful ways to lengthen milk's shelf life. Fermenting milk into yogurt helps it last longer, and pulling out moisture increases its longevity even further. Dairy farming in Jordan and Anatolia goes back 9,000 to 10,000 years, and yogurt is believed to have first been made and consumed in this region. Jordanian cheesemaker Nisreen Haram says the prevalence of yogurt in many Middle Eastern cuisines has to do with climate: "Naturally, if you leave fresh goat or sheep milk with all of its native cultures out in the hot climate of the desert, it turns into yoghurt," Haram says.

In both Jordan and Syria, labneh is a critical component of mansaf, lamb cooked in a labneh-based sauce and served with rice pilaf and flatbread. It is served on a large platter, and while it's Jordan's national dish, it's a popular food in both countries, especially at celebrations. In 2014, Oxfam Italia interviewed Syrian refugees who fled to nearby Jordan. One of these refugees was Abu Mustaffa, whose family kept the traditions of eating labneh and mansaf alive, serving the lamb dish at his brother's wedding to a woman from a neighboring tented settlement.

Culinary traditions move not only between places but often pass between generations in the family's new home. In an interview with Jehan Nizar, second-generation Syrian cook and food photographer Omayah Atassi notes:

> I've always really loved food but growing up, Syrian food was something I took for granted. A big part of Syrian cuisine is the communal table and coming together and there's also the other fact of our cuisine being quite diverse. A lot of people think of Levantine cuisine as just falafels and shawarma but really there's a lot of care to the ingredients. Syrian cuisine is very seasonal and regional and so the ingredients and specificities and how they're taken care of to create a dish are really important. Of late, I've begun to really notice how much people use things like za'atar and sumac and labneh in dishes. Like if you look at the *Bon Appetit* feed on Instagram, it's labneh crazy. A lot of the time, many are using these ingredients and have no clue about their background or the history of its people. This is why I think it's so important to be telling these stories so that it's not just something on a plate because this food actually means something to a big population.

KOREA: KIMCHI AND BANCHAN

Kimchi is a critical part of banchan: the colorful array of side dishes laid out with a meal in Korean cuisine. The small side dishes are considered to be just as important as the main dish, offering a variety of flavor, nutrition, texture, and color. The banchan service epitomizes the family-style nature of a traditional Korean meal. Writer and hospitality professional Andrea Sung says, "It's not heaps of food like a medieval buffet; rather, a communal gathering and sharing of entrees and sides, serving elders first, and refilling small plates and empty glasses with a sense of innate hospitality. It is a universal commonality that all ethnic cultures express history, tradition and celebration through food."

The banchan service allows a cook to extend hospitality to everyone at the table by offering a spread that feels abundant and diverse, and it offers everyone the chance to customize their meal into something that feels most enjoyable for them. The sides are often brought out prior to the rest of the food and are meant to be enjoyed through the entire meal (rather than as an appetizer or strictly as a side dish). Banchan are often prepared in advance, so they are ready to go when it is time to eat.

There is an infinite number of banchan dishes out there, including ones that are fermented, steamed, and stir-fried, as well as a variety of savory pancakes, and a whole host of seasonings and sauce preparations. Korean food, of course, has regional variations, with fish and seaweed being more common in coastal areas, but across the Korean diet both jung (fermented soy products, such as soy sauce or shoyu) and medicinal plants (for example, hot peppers, garlic, onion, ginger) have been used for centuries to enhance flavor and health benefits. In all cases, ferments, along with other preparations that emphasize what is local and seasonal, make an appearance. Even the simplest banchan service has three main ingredients: kimchi, namul muchim (a really broad category that refers to seasoned vegetables), and jorim (side dishes simmered in sauce).

FERMENTS FOR FEASTS

As sustainable food activist Ellen Gustafson notes, "The celebratory nature of food is universal. Every season, every harvest, and every holiday has its own food. . . . It helps define us." The experience of eating a meal with others involves far more than just the act of eating itself. Anticipating the meal, discussing what is being prepared and how, and even waiting in line at a restaurant are all a part of the experience and shape how we experience our food as a result. When it is a meal for a special occasion, these peripheral experiences seem to increase in importance, perhaps because there are more of them—more guests, more dishes, or a more elaborate dining ritual (for example, dining out at a fine restaurant or pulling out the fine china for a meal at home).

In some cases, everyday foods are served alongside those reserved for celebration. In Senegal, for example, sour porridge (called lakh) made from sorghum or millet is a common breakfast, as it is in many other parts of Africa. However, add a few more ingredients, such as yogurt,

peanut butter, or baobab, and it transcends the everyday to become something worthy of a feast. According to Senegalese artist Abdala Faye, the
lakh served at celebrations is thicker than everyday porridge, made to be
molded into a freestanding shape to be served as part of wedding meals
and other feasts.

LAHPET

Lahpet is a flavorful, delicious Burmese green tea salad whose ingredients
show the connection between Burmese cuisine and those of surrounding
countries, including Thailand. While pickled tea itself is uncommon outside of Myanmar (northern Thailand is one of the few places you can find
it), there are similarities between lahpet's flavor profile and the flavor profile of neighboring cuisines.

According to Burmese food writer MiMi Aye, there are two main styles
of lahpet: ahlu lahpet (whose name means "almsgiving or donation ceremony lahpet"), also known as Mandalay lahpet, and lahpet thoke, also
called Yangon lahpet. (See the recipe for lahpet thoke on page 268.) These
are often served in a lahpet ohk, a divided lacquerware dish with a lid. For
ahlu lahpet, the tea leaves are dressed with groundnut or sesame oil and
placed in the center. A wide range of garnishes—including fried garlic and
hyacinth beans, toasted sesame seeds, roasted chana dal, fried red-skinned
peanuts, dried shrimp, shredded pickled ginger, and sometimes fried
shredded coconut—are served in separate piles so that guests can choose
their own flavor combination. To eat it, you pick up a little bit of the pickled
tea leaves with your fingertips or a spoon, mixing them with different garnishes each time, so no two mouthfuls are the same.

Another version of lahpet thoke is made by mixing the ingredients from
ahlu lahpet with sliced tomatoes, fresh garlic, and green chiles (as well
as green cabbage, though Aye notes this is usually used as a filler), then
dressing it with groundnut or sesame oil and a generous squeeze of lime.
This version is a common snack at home and is ordered at restaurants and
tea shops as a stand-alone dish (unlike ahlu lahpet, which is presented at
the end of the meal). The tea leaves offer astringency, and the accompaniments balance them with other flavors (sour, bitter, salty, sweet, and spicy).
As with most things, the ingredients vary depending whom you ask, and

some versions include lettuce or cabbage, herbs such as cilantro, peanut oil, or other flavorings.

MiMi Aye notes: "*Lahpet* has huge cultural, religious and political significance in Burma. It was an ancient symbolic peace offering between opposing kingdoms: it was literally used to end wars. In pre-colonial and colonial times, *lahpet* would be served after a judge made a verdict, and if the arbitrators ate it, this conveyed their formal acceptance."

Ahlu lahpet is an important part of community gatherings, including wedding meals, and at soon-kyway, a ceremonial offering of food to Buddhist monks. Aye says, "It's even left as offerings to nats, the guardian spirits of forests, mountains, rivers and fields, who we revered long before the Buddha came onto the scene." However, it is not limited to special occasions. Every household has a lahpet ohk, which is kept at the ready for visitors and served with a pot of green tea, just as Westerners might offer biscuits or cake with tea or coffee. Lahpet is so critical to Burmese culture that the best of the tea harvest is set aside, traditionally in bamboo vats, to ferment for it.

POI

Poi is a Hawaiian fermented porridge made from taro root that is eaten both for everyday meals and on special occasions. This is a very ancient food: There is evidence of humans eating it 28,000 years ago in the Kilu Cave on the Solomon Islands, and there is later evidence of taro domestication in multiple areas of India and Southeast Asia. From there it spread out both west and east: east to China, Japan, and Polynesia (and eventually to Hawaii), and later west with the slave trade to Africa, the Caribbean, and Latin America.

In early Hawaiian communities, only men were allowed to work with taro. Taro was an important source of nutrition, but it had to be processed quickly through pounding and either cooking or fermentation. To make poi, the taro corm is peeled, boiled, and pounded (or, these days, perhaps blended up in a food processor) before being fermented to the desired degree of sourness. Poi became a staple in the Hawaiian diet, and though it's typically made with taro, it doesn't necessarily have to be. Food historian Rachel Laudan notes that it can be made with sweet potato or breadfruit, for example. During World War II, when taro supplies were limited, it was sometimes made by pouring boiling water over flour or potato starch, then stirring in taro poi and letting the mixture sour. Laudan notes that poi "was served in wooden calabashes, often gorgeous hand-carved wooden bowls, some of them huge. After Western contact, earthenware crocks began to take their place, crocks called kelemania (Germany), presumably from their place of origin. According to the Hawaiian ethnobotanist Isabella Abbott, it was not unusual in the old days for a man to consume 5 pounds of poi at one sitting."

Poi was an important part of everyday meals and luaus for indigenous Hawaiians for millennia, where its subtle flavor and smooth texture were a welcome accompaniment to the salty bite of kalua pig and lomi lomi salmon. And by the end of the nineteenth century, it was also adopted by the colonists who settled in the area, whose luxurious suppers came to include a mixture of European dishes and traditional Hawaiian ones.

The taro plant plays an important role in Hawaiian myth and legend. Hawaiian studies professor Kanalu G. Terry Young noted, "The spiritual significance of the taro plant goes all the way back to at least one story of human origins. . . . The aboriginal Hawaiians had a belief that plants were the natural forms of certain deities. In one tradition, it's one of the four great Polynesian gods, Kane, the god of sunshine and fresh water." In another myth, the taro stem is depicted as the first offspring of the sky father and his daughter the stars, while the secondborn was the first human. Poi is a food that is best eaten with friends, and it is always accompanied by other dishes on the table. While it will never be the sole focal point of a meal, meals still would not be the same without it.

MEAD HALLS

Mead halls appeared in Viking-age Scandinavia and early medieval English cultures and were the center for great feasts: large, one-room buildings erected by nobles to entertain their guests. While we call them mead halls, they would have served other alcohols as well, though mead certainly would have been a popular choice. Food historian Ann Hagen says, "A wide range of drinks, some of which approximated to those we know today, was available in Early Medieval England. The most important, judging by the number of references, were the fermented drinks: *win, meodu, beor* and *ealu.*" This etymology gets a bit confusing because while win, meodu, and beor seem straightforward enough, the word *ealu* apparently means "ale," but the difference between beor and ealu was not as straightforward as the modern difference between, say, ale and lager. Jereme Zimmerman, author of *Make Mead Like a Viking*, notes that "when we see ale, mead, or beer referenced in the literature of the time, the word chosen to represent strong drink is more likely a literary decision than an accurate representation." Alcohol was a central part of the festivities, of course, but it fueled socialization, political deals, and game play. Games such as kubb (sometimes called Viking lawn chess) are rumored to have their origins in this time period and are still played today in Scandinavia.

FERMENTS FOR GRIEF

Sometimes being in a community means we must mourn the loss of community members, and ferments show up surprisingly often during periods of grief—both as comfort food for those grieving a loss and as ritual foods for funerals and other ceremonies. By consuming ferments—often bread, wine, and pickles—we are partnering with microbial life to honor death and the deceased.

For author Kristen Iskandrian, the sour flavor of pickles became not only a flavorful pleasure but also a force for grounding and connection. In her story *Grief Pickles*, she says, "There are foods we enjoy because they taste good; they ingratiate themselves with immediacy to the pleasure-centers of our palate, whether for their sweetness or their saltiness or their inarguable succulence. These foods offer a straightforward sensory experience almost like a call-and-response. . . . The pickle may be one of those foods for some people—it certainly is for me—but I think, more interestingly, there are also categories of foods that we love for more nebulous or romantic or even genetic reasons. Foods of our forebears, foods that we see ourselves in." In those moments when we feel unmoored—whether from grief or stress or any of the other challenges that life throws at us—having connection to the foods that reflect ourselves and our culinary comforts can be a powerful balm.

A SOOTHING ACT

It is not only the act of eating ferments that soothes us but the act of making them as well. Working with our hands when we feel unmoored can be grounding and calming, and with fermentation, that effect can be even more profound as we watch something come to life, growing thanks to the effort we put in. Iskandrian recalls that, during a particularly grief-filled moment, she opened her "crisper drawer full of languishing vegetables, reminders of meals I was supposed to have made, and the sight of them made me feel even more like a failure." In that moment, she turned to pickling, peeling and chopping without a specific plan of what exactly she wanted to make. The next day, her cathartic pickle-making endeavor paid off, when she and a grieving friend popped open some champagne and the "Grief Pickles," as she named them: "We ate the alone-food together and felt, I think, less alone. Sometimes you have to celebrate sadness, too."

When I create ferments during times of grief, it feels like I am adding life back into the world—both breathing life into the spaces that feel unlively in myself, and, in a real way, carrying on the memory of the deceased by fermenting a food that was connected to them. For example, I fermented the tops of the last carrots my friend Justin grew before he died, and I fermented the apple peels from the last meal I made my grandma before she passed. And when my friend Darcy left me a honeycomb from the last gift she had received from a deceased friend, I turned it into mead, honoring both their memories at once.

When Iskandrian transformed a drawer full of wilting vegetables into pickles, she was tapping into an age-old tradition of making and sharing sour treats during grief. In North America, particularly in rural areas, pickles appear as a part of postfuneral spreads. They are a regular part of funeral meals in Manitoba's Mennonite country, as shown in this excerpt from the Mennonite satirical news site *The Daily Bonnet*: "Springtime funeral-goers in Mennonite country expect a crisp and tart pickle to accompany their grief. . . . The intense pucker really contributes to an atmosphere of appropriate bereavement." Pickles are a part of funeral spreads elsewhere, too, including here in the American South.

FOODS AT FUNERALS THROUGH HISTORY

Funeral food traditions go back many, many thousands of years. Culinary historian Sarah Lohman cites evidence of cannibalism on remains from Paleolithic Europe as an early example of consumption culture around death. The early ritual practice would honor a loved one by absorbing (and thus preserving) their physical essence or, as she says, "to emphasize that a body is just meat—a physical vessel for a human life."

Around 5,000 to 10,000 years ago, those early peoples stopped consuming the human body and started leaving offerings of spiritual nourishment for the deceased. At least 4,000 years ago in ancient Egypt, bread and beer would be left in tombs to nourish the deceased, and paintings of birds and cattle on the walls would offer additional nourishment once the foods of this realm ran out.

In the eighth century, we see a shift away from nourishing the dead to also nourishing the living: At King Midas's funeral in Anatolia (modern-day Turkey), a feast of goat stew and fermented beverages was presented to his tomb for his spiritual nourishment, but then it was consumed by funeral attendees, some of whom had traveled long distances to pay their respects and needed sustenance. Afterward, the table, dinnerware, and leftover food and drink were sealed in the tomb with the king's body. As we see throughout the history of mourning, how we engage with food (and ferments in particular) shows a connective thread between the living and dead, not only in memory but in the very act of consumption and spiritual nourishment itself.

During the Middle Ages in Germany and rural Sweden (where in some places this custom survives to the present day), funeral cakes or corpse cakes were an important part of the funerary meal. Leavened dough was prepared and allowed to rise on the corpse's chest before being shared with funeral goers—what researcher and author Victoria Williams says was a way of symbolically "eating the deceased" (you can see here a continuation of the Paleolithic tradition of literally eating the dead).

Funeral cakes are not limited to Germany and Sweden but exist in many places around Europe, including the Victorian English practice of baking cakes and tying them with a black ribbon to distribute as invitations to an upcoming funeral. Most modern European funeral cakes resemble shortbread, forgoing the leavening (and the resting period on the deceased), though sometimes a seedcake, made with caraway, may also be served. Typically, modern funeral cakes are consumed with a glass of spiced beer or Madeira, a fortified wine from the Madeira Islands on the Portuguese archipelago.

Sometimes our grief practices extend to offering food to the creatures that help us make our ferments (and other foods as well). In Derbyshire, in central England, for example, Williams says that typically "when the keeper of a beehive dies, funeral biscuits that have been soaked in wine are left in front of the beehive so that the bees can toast their keeper." This is part of a larger tradition of telling the bees of someone's passing, and in some cases sitting with the bees in mourning or adorning their hives in funerary gear (for example, black cloth), for after all, bees provide us with the honey for our mead and sweets and the wax for candles and salves, among several other useful gifts. Telling the bees was considered an extension of telling the family, and it was done both from a love of the bees themselves and from a concern that by excluding them from the mourning process they would feel slighted and might abandon their hives for more appreciative pastures.

Honey appears in many funeral rituals past and present: The dead from China to Africa were once buried with pots of honey, and the ancient Greeks buried their dead with a honey cake the deceased could use to bribe Cerberus at the gates of Hades. Halvah, a honey-sweetened confection first created in the fifth century, is still served at contemporary Muslim funerals. And, of course, telling the bees was an important ritual up until fairly recently (and likely still is in some places), all of which shows the importance of honey—fermented or otherwise—in our lives and deaths.

Ferments and the Divine

Ferments have played a role in connecting humans to the divine for millennia. Perhaps it's because they alchemically transform one substance into another, or perhaps it's their hypnotic bubbling, or their intoxicating properties. In some cases, ferments play a role in formal religious rituals and celebrations (such as the Catholic Eucharist, ancient Greek rituals for Dionysus, or the Muslim iftar meal that breaks the Ramadan fast), and in other cases, they simply enhance an individual's spiritual connection. The use of ferments in religious traditions is especially interesting because it combines many of the elements of community discussed in this chapter: the gathering of the community itself, the performance of ritual, and often the centrality of a place or food within a celebration or observation.

FERMENTS IN RITUALS

Religious and spiritual communities alike have both produced and consumed ferments as the basis of metaphor as well as ritual. Wine is a part of many European pagan rituals, for example. And sacred or mind-altering plants are added to ferments, too, for medicinal and culinary reasons, but also because in some cases (as with yarrow) the fermentation process can increase their ability to alter human consciousness.

Inebriating herbs—those that can alter consciousness—are often a part of sacred brews. These can range from psychotropic plants to others, such as yarrow, that are innocuous or only mildly stimulating on their own, but their effects are dramatically increased with fermentation. In Europe, we see examples of this in heather mead, brewed in Scotland for at least 4,000 years, and gruit, an ale typically prepared with sweet gale or bog myrtle, yarrow, and wild rosemary, which has been consumed for at least the last thousand years in Norway, Sweden, and beyond.

Ferments of varying kinds have been an important component of many traditional spiritual practices worldwide, but as with other important religious symbols and tools, they are sometimes repressed. In the Andes, for example, chicha de jora (a beverage typically brewed with fermented maize) has been repressed and deemed degenerate since colonization. Some archaeologists think that the drink, originally called a-qa in Quechua or k'usa in Aymara, dates back to the Chavin culture, which got its start around 900 BCE.

> The preparation, cooking, and eating of food is a sacrament. Treating it as such has the potential to elevate the quality of our daily lives like nothing else.
>
> —KAREN PAGE AND ANDREW DORNENBURG, *THE FLAVOR BIBLE*

humans as fermentation vessels

Hildegard von Bingen, a twelfth-century German abbess and writer, shared many mystic visions during her life. In one that she writes about, humans are not the consumers or producers of ferments but are fermentation vessels themselves, highlighting the importance of fermentation as a concept and practice that was both personal and spiritual. In von Bingen's world, humans contained aspects of both the earthly and divine, but those earthly elements meant the possibility of corruption by vice and sin—in particular, pride. Von Bingen's vision connected this corruption of the spirit to the transformation of milk into cheese. In her vision, people carried milk in earthen vessels, and the cheeses that resulted showed the corruption (or lack thereof) of the maker's spirit; in other words, making their very souls a part of the fermentation process. Several different cheeses came from these vessels: One had thick milk and a resulting strong cheese, another held thin milk from which weak cheeses were curdled, and another was corrupted (perhaps rotten), which resulted in a bitter cheese.

As the scholar Zachary Jordan Young says, "The body, as represented by the earthen vessel, is filled with the soul, the milk. Hildegard spoke of the diversity of semen in reference to the milk, but the argument is still the same, as she declares that strong cheese is equivalent to those who 'flourish in prudence, discretion,' while those made of weak cheese are 'foolish, languid' and are 'not actively seeking God.' The bitter, she declares, are based in 'weakness and confusion.'"

Archaeologist and cultural heritage professional Justin Mugits notes, "In pre-colonial societies, *chicha* served as a ceremonial beverage; it maintained societal bonds, toasted ancestors and invoked the supernatural. In the Inka empire an order of chosen virgin women known as *Acllas* were charged with ritual duties that included tending to terraces of sacred maize and the brewing of *chicha* for imperial use." Though its production and consumption was later restricted by the Spanish colonial authorities and the Catholic Church, some people have continued to prepare the beverage, share it with others through chicharias, and use it as an in-kind payment for communal work, despite church and government's long-standing efforts to stop them. These people provide a critical link to the past—not just to how the beverage was made, but also to the rituals that surrounded its production and consumption.

Fermented foodstuffs, wine in particular, play an important role in Judaism, Christianity, and Islam, too. The Eucharist, for example, is representative of Jesus's physical sacrifice to save his followers, and it is an important part of many Christian church services. Some denominations believe that when a spiritual leader (such as a priest) blesses the Eucharist, it transforms into the body and blood of Christ; others believe the connection is purely symbolic.

Ferments also play a role within religious texts. Texts from Abrahamic traditions include tales of hunger and plenty, alongside instructions for using food as a vehicle of worship through certain restrictions or preparations. Turning water into wine is one striking example, rich with metaphor. Orthodox Christians and Byzantine Catholics bake a holy bread called prosphora (Greek for "offering"). The bread is used as a host in Easter Mass, but unlike in western Catholicism, it is leavened and made of two slabs of dough, meant to simultaneously represent Jesus's two sides as human and divine.

FOOD OF THE GODS

The importance of fermentation can be seen in the linkages between certain ferments and the deities that were a part of each culture's landscape. In some cases, as with Dionysus and Bacchus in ancient Greece and Rome, a god was connected to one particular foodstuff (in this case wine). But in others, the god is connected to an agricultural product related to fermentation (such as Demeter's connection with agriculture and with wheat in particular) or to the fermented products related to a particular crop (such as Isis's connection to bread and beer, made from grains). Zulu goddess Mbaba Mwana Waresa takes a holistic view, covering the environmental conditions needed to grow crops (rain and rainbows), agriculture and crop harvesting, and the product of those crops (beer).

Dieties were not the only figureheads to be honored in religious and cultural lore for their connection to fermentation. In the Middle Ages in Europe, we see a continuation of fermentation worship in the Catholic Church, both through the sacrament itself and through the sainthood of individuals such as Brigid (who lived in the fifth century CE), the Irish patron saint of beer. In China, Li Bai, a revered poet from the seventh century CE, is sometimes dubbed "the god of wine" (this delineation seems to point to the immortality of his work, from the sources I've read). Li Bai was an incredibly prolific and gifted writer and a lover of wine; historian and poet Guo Moruo (1892–1978) noted that 16 percent of Li Bai's poems are about wine. In both these cases, their lived experiences around ferments became a part of their legacies and became engrained within the culture they came from: Brigid, for example, is a popular Celtic saint for Irish Catholics as well as a popular deity for Celtic pagans and Druids.

Some ferments are said to exist to feed both humans and gods. Lahpet thoke is one such food, used as a temple offering. Wine was a temple offering in classical antiquity, and in Senegal, lakh is sometimes brought as an offering to the gods. These foods have an air of importance about them, and perhaps because they are fermented, their very nature asks us to move at the slower speed of the divine rather than our fast-paced day-to-day modern lives.

FERMENTS IN RELIGIOUS COMMUNITIES

Ferments are not only consumed within spiritual communities but also produced within them. In Japan, sake production was a government monopoly until the tenth century, when shrines and temples began to brew their own, becoming the primary producers of sake for centuries. Food was produced as well: Toshio Hanaoka, president of Hanamaruki Foods in Japan, notes that miso was originally made in Buddhist monasteries for their own use and to share within aristocratic circles.

In European monasteries, ferments (wine, beer, and bread) formed the backbone of monastic diets and became the objects of experimentation and improvements in fermentation processes. For example, like many places during the fourteenth century, the Evesham Abbey in England had to worry about water safety. This was mitigated, as it was in many places, with fermentation, and as a result you see beer and wine being used as beverages in place of water. At the abbey, brothers each received half a pint of wine each day, at least on special days, with more allowed during the summer heat or periods of labor-intensive work. Ale was the most common beverage in England, however, and the brothers each received 8 pints a day, although less on days when they also had wine. Because alcohol was a daily beverage, the monks had to brew it in large quantities, and they did a good deal to contribute to the brewing traditions we have today.

While the monks drank ale and unflavored wine, they also drank spiced wines. Wine and honey would be boiled together gently before being steeped with spices such as white pepper and cinnamon, then bottled and allowed to age for a year. They also drank hippocras, which was often aged.

Ferments as Aphrodisiacs

For thousands of years, people have turned to ferments to get in the mood and improve sexual performance. Alcohol, and in particular wine, appears to be the most common ferment listed as an aphrodisiac, though author and master herbalist Stephen Harrod Buhner also points to beers brewed with medicinal plants that contain aphrodisiac properties. The sixteenth-century German physician Jacobus Theodorus promoted "beer brewed from wheat, above all as a beverage, but also when used in food: on soups, sauces, and porridge, increases the natural seed, straightens the drooping phallus up again, and helps feeble men who are incapable of conjugal acts back into the saddle."

Wine has been touted as a cure for erectile dysfunction since at least the Middle Ages, with Maimonides noting it was "even more effective than all medicines and foods" in this regard. A good deal of the guidance from this period deals with male arousal and orgasm; perhaps not surprisingly, women's sexual pleasure took a back seat. But Chaucer, in *Canterbury Tales*, makes one of the few inferences we see from that time that wine may impact women similarly. The most famous literary example of wine in this context comes from *Macbeth*, in which Shakespeare notes that it is only useful as a sexual stimulant up to a point: "Lechery, sir, it provokes and unprovokes; it provokes the desire, but it takes away the performance. Therefore, much drink may be said to be an equivocator with lechery."

In southern China, snake wine (wine packed in a jar with a snake) is sometimes used as an aphrodisiac, among other things (it is said to be good for virility, boosting sex drive, and reducing hair loss). While you can buy it with the snake still intact in the bottle, some versions involve adding the snake to the wine and burying it deep underground. After a year, the snake will have dissolved and the formerly clear kaoliang wine will have turned a deep yellow.

The types of plants that are added, as well as the quantity and their growing conditions, all impact the drinker's amorous potential. In the Middle Ages, the first printed book on wine in Europe (printed in 1478) by Arnaldus de Villanova argues that specific varieties of wines have specific medicinal effects, and that "wine made from fennel seeds stimulates sexual urge, consumes dropsy and leprosy. . . . It increases milk and the natural sperm."

Lazing around with a lover and a glass (or bottle, or two) of wine may sound like the ideal aphrodisiac, but it's not the only ferment used as one. Modern pop science and health materials abound espousing the use of apple cider vinegar to cure erectile dysfunction, though I have yet to see any research studies on the matter.

Fermentation and Folklore

A critical part of building community is communication, and since we began to communicate with writing and symbols (whether through letters, images, or other recorded information such as Andean quipu knot records), we have communicated about food. Cuneiform tablets recorded grain harvests, household receipt books documented families' treasured recipes, and eventually printed books could distribute a cook's culinary knowledge more broadly. But ferments appear in more than how-to books: They are woven into the fabric of many tales, both ancient and modern.

In ancient folklore around the world, fermentation has played a central role. In many cases, a fermented beverage has ritual importance, believed to impart certain powers to its consumer. But these drinks go well beyond just quenching thirst: Ferments in these stories embody beliefs, skills, and even deities. The Scottish anthropologist Robert Gayre notes that mead is "the ancient liquor of gods and men, the giver of knowledge and poetry, the healer of wounds, and the bestower of immortality." Ninkasi, ancient Sumerian goddess of beer, inspired the "Hymn to Ninkasi," penned around 1800 BCE, which not only praises the importance of brewing and brewers in ancient Sumeria but also gives us our oldest known beer recipe. Ninkasi herself oversaw not only brewing but the women who brewed it, strengthening the association between women and the production and distribution of beer. Historian Paul Kriwaczek notes that the hymn probably expresses techniques passed down orally for a thousand years, finally committed to a clay tablet because of its popularity. By the time the "Hymn to Ninkasi" was pressed into clay, brewing had been going on in Mesopotamia for more than a thousand years and had resulted in a good deal of beer varieties and brewing techniques. Ninkasi's story embodies the high value of beer as well as the importance of encoding and passing on brewing knowledge within Sumerian culture.

CERRIDWEN

The Celtic goddess Cerridwen sits at the intersection of fermentation and magic. One of her roles is as the goddess of barley, but she is also a brewer, overseeing her bubbling Cauldron of Inspiration, within which she would create life-altering brews to share with humanity (or other gods). Within her cauldron she would ferment the Brew of Inspiration of Knowledge, using the same grain (barley) that formed the basis of Celtic beer.

In the most famous story about her, Cerridwen prepares a potion for her son that must be boiled for 1 year and 1 day, giving the task of tending the fire beneath the cauldron to a blind elder and the task of stirring the mixture to a young boy named Gwion Bach. While the presence of a fire suggests boiling by heat, I've always wondered whether this particular story, with its long "cooking" period, refers to fermentation just as other stories about her do, with the fire being used to keep the brew's temperature steady throughout the changing (and sometimes chilly) seasons in northern Wales.

MEAD OF INSPIRATION AND POETRY

Similar to Cerridwen's brews from the Cauldron of Inspiration, the Mead of Inspiration and Poetry was a gift from the Viking gods, albeit an accidental one. According to legend, mead was first made from the saliva of the gods, melded together into one vessel and embodied within the physical form of Kvaser (or Kvasir), one so wise that there was no question he could not answer. Kvaser long walked the heavens as a symbol of godly unity, but on one such wander he was taken captive by dwarves, who killed him and mixed his blood with honey, creating mead.

The mead was powerful, divine, and mind altering, being a medley of the essence of the whole pantheon of deities, and it was highly sought after. The dwarves jealously guarded it until it was stolen by a giant, and later by the god Odin, who flew back to the realm of the gods as quickly as he could. But in their haste to pour the stolen mead into vessels, three drops fell to earth, which were collected by humans who, upon tasting them, were able to channel the divine through poetry and other artistic pursuits. In this case, mead exists in two worlds, being both of the earthly and divine, embodying (in a literal sense) the gods who shared the gift with us, having touched many different worlds within ours on its journey to us. And it is created by honey from bees, the messengers long thought to pass between the heavens and the earth.

FERMENTATION AS A SACRED ACT

In many traditions, knowledge of fermentation, and particularly how to ferment alcohol, was given sacred status. This makes sense, as alcohol was central to ritual and celebration and, as we saw in Chapter 1, to daily life. The idea of fermentation as a sacred act features prominently in many myths around the world.

In the ancient poem from Mesopotamia called the Epic of Gilgamesh, for example, Siduri (who is referred to as the "bartender at the end of the world") is accustomed to solving crises and helping folks have a good time, in her line of work. She runs a tavern overlooking the sea at the end of the world, and when Gilgamesh, the mortal hero-king of the tale, hopes to find immortality (but can't because the gods "kept it for themselves"), the woman who dispenses ferments also dispenses knowledge:

> Now you, Gilgamesh, let your stomach be full.
> Day and night keep on being festive.
> Daily make a festival.
> Day and night dance and play.

The connections between ferments and literature, knowledge, and the sacred exist elsewhere in the world as well, echoed in the stories of the Mead of Inspiration. And in the Rig Veda, a collection of Vedic Sanskrit hymns, Vishnu and Indra are called Madhava, or honey-born ones. They speak to the long-standing connection between sacredness, human wisdom, and the consumption of honey or mead. As the ancient Roman poet Horace (65–8 BCE) wrote, "No poems can please long or live that are written by water drinkers."

Some of the fermentation tales we have discovered are recorded versions of much older tales that had been passed down orally through the generations. But just like today, simply recording a story does not make it infallible to destruction and change or to editing based on changing social norms. Our stories of fermented foods thus may be somewhat (or even very) different from their original tellings.

Later versions of the story of Cerridwen, for example, frame her as a jealous and murderous sorceress, though it seems likely now that her early incarnations were more positive: someone brewing and sharing knowledge—and inspiration, just like the mead in Viking myth. I have always been curious about what these stories could tell us about our relationship to ferments, and to food in general, if we had access to them in their original form. I hope some day to write a follow-up book to this one on how fermentation shows up in our myths as well as our real-life magical practices.

Trading Ferments across Cultures

No ferment, or any other food for that matter, exists within a vacuum. As we've seen throughout this book, the intersection of cultures—whether through trade, geographic proximity and intermarriage, chosen or forced migration of peoples, or colonialism—often leaves a mark on both cultures, and while some aspects of a culture's diet remain consistent, others change in response to these shifting forces.

The advent of human-directed fermentation, discussed in Chapter 1, was one such big change for many cultures, offering new avenues for preservation as well as new food products to enjoy. As our food storage, shipping, and production technologies became more sophisticated, these foods began to make their way between communities through trade, political negotiations, war, and immigration. This has been the case for many thousands of years, and examples abound of prepared ferments being traded, such as the wine traded along Silk Road routes, or fermentation techniques being brought to a new place (such as African akara, brought to Brazil by enslaved Africans and sold as acarajé). These cultural connections, unlike positive and consensual cultural exchange, often leave us with complex and sometimes dark histories to engage with.

WAR AND FERMENTS

Boundaries and conflicts over them have impacted our foodways since time immemorial, barring access to trade, for example, or levying taxes or other fees on imports or exports. When the needs and desires of one ruling body bump up against another, agriculture and trade are often impacted.

During the Hundred Years' War between England and France, which lasted from 1337 to 1453, the wine trade in Gascony, France, which was deeply tied to England, felt the effects of the ongoing battles. Gascony was at the heart of the conflict because it was the last remnant of the vast swath of land the English monarchy had once ruled in France. The English felt that it was crucial to maintain control of Gascony both because the duchy was the primary source of French wine and because Gascony was one of the most important overseas markets for English goods and ships. Thus, Gascony became a flash point for English-French relations.

The resulting war, lasting several generations as each claimed anew its right to the disputed territory, caused incredible disruptions in the shipping of wine from the region, which had ripple effects in the wine trade throughout the country and, more important, left heavy tolls upon the French citizenry. Eventually the war ended without a treaty. England lost all its holdings in France, save for the port city of Calais (and its control over a portion of the French wine trade, too).

There are many, many other examples of fermented products being at the center of clashes, sometimes because those making the products sought a better life and fairer working conditions. One such example is indigo. Indigo dye, which is made by fermenting the indigo plant, is one of the most beautiful and coveted natural dyes. When textiles are dipped in this fermented liquid and exposed to air, they transform from a simple yellowish brown to a stunning blue right before your eyes. Indigo is also more colorfast than other similar blues (such as woad) and thus was in high demand prior to the production of the synthetic blue dyes that we use today. Indigo thrives best in very warm climates, and so as Europeans colonized warm-weather areas, they were quick to plant the cash crop. But this did not just have an impact on ecology: It had a profound impact on humans, too. Indigo plantations appeared relatively early on in European colonization, planted by the French in the West Indies and the English in Jamaica, and many others as well.

In 1740s South Carolina, indigo saw a huge surge in popularity as plantation owners rushed to cash in on the popular crop, and their hunger for indigo resulted in more and more enslaved Africans being brought to the colony to grow and process it. With the start of the Revolutionary War, the market for indigo from the American colonies waned, then fizzled out with American independence. Plantation owners focused their attention on other crops, but the human cost to enslaved people remained. One hundred years later, indigo was still grown by English colonizers elsewhere in the world, and workers continued to be exploited.

The Indigo Revolt in Bengal took place in 1859, when growers rose up against the brutal living and labor conditions enforced by English colonizers. The wealthy plantation owners, as well as the East India Company that oversaw the indigo industry, quickly and ruthlessly ended the revolt, hanging revolt leaders and slaughtering several growers. The colonial government formed The Indigo Commission the following year, which was supposed to improve the conditions for growers planting indigo on their own or on plantation land. Soon, however, synthetic blue dyes would replace indigo and production would drop off: In 1896, indigo dye exports from India weighed in at more than 9,366 tons, but quickly fell to only 846 tons by 1911.

Ferments and Social Power

Social status has always had an incredible impact on what people eat and how. The history of fermentation is thus in part also the history of social power. While the process of fermentation has been practiced across all social groups, in some cases specific ingredients and techniques were employed primarily by certain classes. To draw from an example earlier in the chapter, wine has long been a valuable commodity in many places, but high-quality wine was out of reach to all but the very wealthy or well connected in the ancient world—in China, ancient Celtic regions, and elsewhere.

After the outbreak of bubonic plague in 1348, the drastic decrease in population meant that those who remained had access to greater resources. Spices, formerly a foodstuff reserved for the wealthy, became accessible to the middle classes, and the very wealthy had to look for new ways to distinguish themselves. This meant finding rare and expensive ingredients out of reach to most people, ranging from the finest spices (such as saffron) to expensive meats (such as peacock), imported wines and cheeses, and a range of other goods. This growth in access to and interest in new ingredients aided in the proliferation of the cookbook, as the new recipes were recorded and used to train up-and-coming chefs. The most famous cookbook of the time, *Le Viandier*, was written by Guillaume Tirel, chef to King Charles V of France (though it included recipes from other, unnamed authors). The cookbook was very popular, and the recipes continued to be copied in other cookbooks for years to come.

In these early cookbooks, such as Robert May's *The Accomplisht Cook* (1660), we see the use of fine wines and vinegars in sauces for the wealthy. We also see instructions for fermenting food and drinks, and in English-language texts the focus is particularly on cheesemaking, winemaking, and brewing. Such instructions mostly appear in books geared toward the country gentry and middle classes (for example, Gervase Markham's 1615 volume *The English Housewife*), suggesting that while fermentation was valued across both wealthy and middle-class households, it was approached differently by each. Certainly fermentation was undertaken to some extent by cooks in both contexts (particularly in baking leavened breads), but it seems that wealthy households were more likely to buy some fermented ingredients, such as wine, rather than make and store them. This makes sense, as the wealthy had the means to buy expensive wines, and cooks for wealthy households had to contend with the expensive palates of their employers and employers' guests. These palates may have demanded higher-quality ingredients across the board—regardless of whether or not the use of an expensive fine wine or imported vinegar would significantly impact the outcome of the dish.

But money isn't the only power dynamic at play: Gender is also intimately connected to social position, and thus access to foodstuffs and to how a person's work is described and valued. The eighth-century Irish legal text known as the *Bretha Comaithchesa* includes a curious passage about "man's baking" being twice the size of women's baking. While this may read as innuendo to the modern mind, what these gendered descriptions suggest is that there were two different social contexts for baking. "Man's baking" here referred to the loaves made by monks, who were cooking for their monasteries and thus for many more people than a housewife cooking for her family. Author and archaeologist Morgan Smith, who writes about medieval Ireland, explains that "the terms may then be seen as referring first to the secular sphere, with women's loaves, as bread-making was predominantly a female task, pertaining to ordinary domestic needs; and men's loaves belonging to the more professional production consistent with the male monastic communities."

ALEWIVES IN EUROPE

Women around the world have been a central part of brewing culture since it first began, making beer for family and community and quietly guiding our brewing knowledge and the brews themselves in homes, inns, abbeys, and other spaces. Once considered a tedious homemaking task, the brewing of most beverages (except perhaps wine, depending on where you were) was for many years considered the purview of women, domestic servants (enslaved and free), and some folks who would sell their brews to others who couldn't or didn't want to make their own (as English alewives did).

Because regular homebrewing was considered unremarkable, it was barely recorded in literature. Instead, it showed up in other documents, such as medieval English court records, where women appeared as brewers more than in any other profession. Little was written in England about brewing until the 1600s, when suddenly what had been "women's work" became a subject of interest to male writers.

After the Black Death in the mid-fourteenth century, Europeans' incomes rose and more people began making and consuming beer, causing an increased interest in brewing. At this point, men decided that they wanted to take over brewing, and in Europe this meant "professionalizing" brewing into something codified with increasingly strict laws and guild regulations. Guilds were not open to women, and thus brewing as a professional act became inaccessible to them. As Claire Monk of Welbeck Abbey Brewery says, "Women were the first brewers, similar to the first bakers and cheesemakers. It wasn't until brewing, as with other food production, was industrialized that it became a man's job."

The impact was devastating: By 1725, only 7 brewers in Edinburgh were women (versus 230 in the sixteenth century), and in 1695, Aberdeen had only 10 women brewers (compared to 150 in the sixteenth century). Women's centrality to brewing and the relative economic freedom and control the profession provided were likely driving factors behind male brewers' desire to remove women from the field. When women were cut off from brewing, they couldn't pose a competitive threat to male businesses and they couldn't exert their own financial independence.

Women brewers were demonized, partly in the form of a smear campaign: Women standing over bubbling cauldrons of brews, accompanied by the cats they kept to deter rodents from their grains and often wearing large hats and shouting to advertise their wares on street corners, suddenly became witches. They were doing the same things they had always done, but now those things were considered *bad*. As food and drink writer Jeanette Hurt says, "Nothing sinks your livelihood faster than being accused of witchcraft." This was one iteration in a long, long history of churches, magistrates, and feudal lords persecuting women who seemed in some way counter to the patriarchy's goals (for example, by being outspoken). So while framing female brewers as witches was definitely a smear campaign by male brewers, and it does contribute heavily to our modern image of a witch, we can't divorce this ferment-specific history from a larger and complex history of women brewers, healers, and others being subjected to violence and death across Europe.

While these stereotypes of conniving women with cauldrons don't give brewers or witches a fair shake, they also run counter to the heart and soul of brewing. The story of brewing is the story of nourishing and caring for loved ones and community. Women, it turns out, had a critical role in this equation: They quietly fed their families and communities by finding ways to preserve food, ensure safe beverages to drink, and establish an income source by selling their products. By looking at their involvement, we come to far more compelling answers about the how and why of brewing than we would by simply considering it a commercial enterprise.

WOMEN IN SAKE BREWING

In Japan, women were central to sake production until the mid-1800s. For many centuries prior, the historical record shows women at the heart of sake production, brewing it as shrine attendants in the sixth century, for example, and for business in the eighth century.

Historian Paula R. Curtis notes that one of sake's origin stories connects the feminine and the divine: As a goddess chews rice, the intermingling of saliva and rice creates a ferment that brings her followers to ecstasy. Japanese historian Naomichi Ishige points out that there is historical evidence of people using this production method, possibly alongside koji fermentation:

> The oldest known such beverage, mentioned in eighth-century literature, utilized the starch saccharification potential of saliva. Raw or boiled rice was chewed and expectorated into a container where it mixed with saliva. This primitive technique survived until the beginning of the twentieth century in Okinawa. By tradition, virgins prepared this type of liquor for special religious ceremonies. Another practice—that of applying kōji fungus to rice as an initiator of fermentation (introduced from China)—has also been in general use since ancient times.

Women's role in sake production begins to shift in 1603 with the start of the Edo period, when taboos around women became more prevalent—particularly taboos about women being inherently polluted because of menstruation. By the time of the Meiji Restoration in 1868, Japan's economy had rapidly shifted away from small, village-based family enterprises and into more centralized and formalized businesses, which (as in Europe) were inaccessible to women. The combination of cultural taboos and widespread economic changes resulted in women being pushed out of, and in some cases banned from, sake breweries. Today, women are beginning to return to brewing but head only about 50 of Japan's 1,500 licensed sake breweries.

Across beverage production facilities worldwide, women brewers are becoming more numerous, but they continue to cite discrimination in

hiring, sexual harassment, and belittlement by male colleagues and customers who assume they aren't serious or knowledgeable because of
their gender.

WORLDWIDE DISCRIMINATIONS

A person's power and access to food are heavily impacted by racism, xeno-
phobia, and other forms of discrimination. These have resulted in harmful,
sometimes fatal impacts on communities worldwide, and the history of
these power dynamics appears in modern-day foods. Cuisines across West
Africa, for example, regularly incorporate ferments (such as porridges and
sorghum beers) alongside nonfermented foods. However, when Africans
were enslaved and removed from their homelands, they were barred from
continuing their cultural practices. As a result, their foodways shifted dramatically, causing the loss of many traditions and foods. Michael Twitty
notes that the loss of these nutrient-rich ferments is an example of how
losing cultural knowledge can profoundly impact a people's health. The
same is true for many other peoples around the world.

Brewing and distilling in the United States were heavily influenced by
enslaved Africans, though many of their contributions have been either
underplayed or erased completely from history. One of many examples is
Nathan "Nearest" Green, who, in the 1850s, created the Tennessee whiskey technique and taught Jack Daniel how to make whiskey. Thanks to the
work of historians and beverage professionals such as Tiffanie Barriere
and others, we're beginning to learn about more of their stories, though
racism in the beverage industry remains rampant at all levels of employ-
ment: At the time of this writing, less than 1 percent of US breweries are
Black-owned.

Thankfully, there are many chefs, writers, artists, and others working
to recover and rebuild stores of lost cooking and fermentation knowledge. Many of these stories are from historically excluded communities
and cultures whose traditions were swept aside or intentionally buried by
colonizing forces. Enslaved Africans, for example, were forcibly torn not
only from their homes but also from their cultural identities as they were
moved around the world. Today, historians, writers, and chefs such as Leni

Sorensen, Stephen Satterfield, Michael Twitty, Jessica B. Harris, and Toni Tipton Martin are uncovering and recovering narratives that had been buried by the Middle Passage. Reconnecting their descendants to those foodways, then, is an act of empowerment and reclamation—an example of how the "simple" act of sharing a recipe is anything but.

FERMENTS AS A STATUS SYMBOL

Food has often been used as a marker for social class, and certain foods are heavily interconnected with elitism. When you think of the fanciest ferments, you might be envisioning a pricey bottle of red wine or champagne, and you wouldn't be wrong: The most expensive and exclusive ferments in history are often not food but beverages.

The most famous story of a pricey drink is perhaps that of Cleopatra's pearl. According to Pliny the Elder's *Natural History* (77 CE), Cleopatra made a wager with her lover Marc Antony that she could spend 10 million sesterces (ancient Roman currency) on a single meal. The meal itself, and the accompanying entertainment, were sumptuous but "no better than his [Antony's] usual repast." Antony joked with her that the cost was well below what she had wagered, to which she responded by calling for the second course. When she did, her servants placed a single glass of vinegar in front of her. As Antony sat perplexed, she took off one of her pearl earrings and dropped it into the vinegar, dissolving and drinking it.

Classicist Prudence Jones found that when she put a roughly 1-gram pearl in standard grocery-store white distilled vinegar with 5 percent acetic acid, it would dissolve in a little more than a day. White vinegar was, as Jones says, the most common kind found in ancient Greece and Rome, so perhaps the legend is true after all.

Our obsession with drinks and status is not limited to the past, though: In his 1979 *Distinction: A Social Critique of the Judgement of Taste*, French sociologist Pierre Bourdieu examined elites who enjoyed fine food and wine for the sake of pleasure rather than their monetary value (and who had the money to enjoy them). The finer things moved beyond food, of course, into home decor and art and beyond, but food was central to this experience. And here, too, ferments make an appearance.

FINE WINE

Ferments, particularly wine, have often been an important status symbol. Historian Frank Trentmann says that when displaying these symbols, humans "used taste to justify and maintain social hierarchies." As Elizabeth Jaeger of Freemark Abbey winery said in 1981, "For $28,000 one can buy a Jaguar X6, 306 shares of McDonnell Douglas stock, a one-tenth interest in an Oklahoma gas well, 4½ years of undergraduate life at Stanford, or one bottle of Château Lafite, vintage 1806. That's $1,166.67 an ounce. At this moment gold is worth only $275 an ounce, and you can't smell or drink it. Nine years ago, $70 could persuade a Paris restaurant to part with this same bottle of liquid gold. . . . All this goes to show that wine, the right wine, in the last 10 years has provided the prudently daring investor with a spectacular return."

Château Lafite, which still today is one of the world's most expensive wines, has been commanding the attention of status-hungry drinkers for generations. The most expensive bottle ever sold, a Bordeaux, went at auction for $156,000. The wine, bottled in 1787, was surrounded by an air of mystery: Supposedly owned by Thomas Jefferson, it was said to have lived a good deal of its life underground, from a Paris cellar to a Nazi bunker to a con artist's basement, each story adding to the intrigue (and ultimately, the price). In the end, the buyer's quest for status ended up being their undoing. Eager to display the bottle and show off their wealth, the buyer placed it under a hot light, causing the cork to fall in and ruin the wine before anyone ever had a chance to taste it.

For one of Bourdieu's research subjects, "drinking fine wine was a 'liturgy,' to be celebrated 'only with certain people, who are capable of enjoying it in the same way.'" Here we see an implication that wine, or at least "good" wine, is the purview of an exclusive few: those who can afford it but who also *understand* it, implying the drinker's worthiness of the beverage in multiple contexts and that wealth alone is not enough. This view is certainly not limited to the twentieth century; I imagine nineteenth-century French gastronome Jean Anthelme Brillat-Savarin (author of *The Physiology of Taste*, 1825), for example, would heartily agree with the sentiment.

RARE FOODS

Rarity plays a role in food as a status symbol, as we see with the spices added to Renaissance-era agliata, an Italian vinegar and garlic sauce with a range of spices that could include saffron, black peppercorns, coriander, and ginger, and certainly with vintage wines. Modern drinkers might seek out a bottle Château Lafite, but also (for much less money) the coveted limited-release Pappy Van Winkle bourbon, produced by Buffalo Trace Distillery. Beer seems to be a bit different, rarely commanding the sorts of high prices you might find with a fine whiskey or wine. However, beer has its own devotees, particularly with the somewhat recent growth of the craft beer industry, and beer serves as a status symbol within these spaces—both through the ownership and the consumption of coveted bottles. Hunahpu's Day at Cigar City Brewing, for example, a beer festival built around the one-day release of the brewery's specialty imperial stout, draws thousands of people looking to try rare brews from Cigar City (Tampa, Florida) and beyond. But cost is not the only metric connected to status: Social perception is critical, too. After all, the high cost of these status-raising ferments is driven by demand.

Connecting with Our Ancestors through Ferments

An unexpected result of my fermentation practice has been finding a deeper and fuller connection with my own family tree. When testing the Scottish sowens recipe for this book, I was amazed by how deeply I was moved. I had not originally planned to make sowens (and if I'm being honest, I was not even entirely sure what they were), and then suddenly I got a nudge that seemed to say "Hey, this might be something worth exploring." The process felt incredibly intuitive, as though my hands were performing a dance they had learned long ago but never entirely forgotten. And through the process, I cried.

My family never cultivated a deep connection with our ancestral home of Scotland, though we knew who our ancestors were and where they lived, which in and of itself is a great privilege. As I harvested and processed the oats, and later drank and ate the swats and sowens I'd fermented from the hulls, I began to understand the dish and its place in my ancestors' world more fully. I understood it as a food used for both subsistence and celebration, taking the "waste" from a harvest that we today would overlook and turning it into something so special and celebrated that it has its own holiday. I firmly believe that the best way to learn, and learn deeply, is through slowing down and creating, tasting, and thinking. It was as though in that moment, I felt my ancestors speaking to me through the food: "Look here, this is a gift we passed down but it has been forgotten. It has sustained us for millennia, and now it can sustain you, too."

I've had many conversations during the years with home cooks, chefs, and other food enthusiasts who attest to feeling a connection with their ancestors through cooking. A friend who sings and hums as he cooks, not knowing where the songs came from, or perhaps even what the words mean. A friend who started blending together spices on a whim, only to later discover that the medley she created was very similar to the blends her ancestors made in northern India. And a friend who started making akara after learning of his West African lineage.

Even if you do not know your ancestors' exact story (as is the case for many people), you may be able to make foods from a region you believe your ancestors came from and discover which ones speak to you. Wherever you or your ancestors are from in the world, and however you came to be where you are, learning about the foods of those spaces is a powerful way to connect with the people whose stories are written in your very cells and bones.

Oftentimes, particularly for groups that have been marginalized or had their stories erased, the common perception of what people in a particular community ate differs from reality. Learning about the history of ferments and of food in general can help bridge these gaps. For example, Michael Twitty, author of *The Cooking Gene*, notes that we think of soul food as being heavy on fried food and light on vegetables, but that is not necessarily true (the African American diet is also not a monolith). Many people grew (and grow) gardens and have vegetable-heavy meals and a variety of meats, starches, and sides.

> Follow closely to your ancestors.
>
> —GAELIC PROVERB

LAHPET THOKE

The Burmese term *lahpet thoke* literally translates to "green tea salad." It is a flavorful, delicious salad that has existed since ancient times and speaks to the many culinary influences that have made their mark on Burmese food, including north Indian, Thai, and Chinese. The flavors of the salad are similar to those in som tam, or Thai green papaya salad (see the recipe for Som Tam Sauerkraut on page 313).

Lahpet thoke traditionally includes lahpet (fermented green tea leaves) and garnishes of beans, sesame seeds, fried garlic, peanuts, dried prawns, sliced fresh chiles, fresh garlic, and green and red tomato. Customarily, the salad is served in the middle of a tray or plate, surrounded by piles of garnishes, so that guests can choose their own flavor combinations. The salad is a wonderful combination of sweet, sour, and spicy, with a whole range of textures to accompany the range of flavors.

As with most things, the ingredients vary depending whom you ask. Some versions include lettuce or cabbage, herbs such as cilantro, peanut oil, and other flavorings. These are the basic components, as I understand them. However, as with all foods, variations abound, as dictated by necessity, the availability of ingredients, and the natural evolution of cuisine over time.

SERVES
4 AS A
SNACK

FERMENTED TEA LEAVES

- 3/4 **cup dried green tea leaves, loosely packed** (high-quality organic ones work best here)
- 1 **cup finely shredded cabbage** (I like napa, but green cabbage works, too) **or kale**
- 1/2 **cup finely chopped scallions**
- 1/3 **cup finely chopped fresh cilantro**
- 3 **cloves garlic, minced**
- 1–2 **green bird's-eye chiles, finely chopped**
- 2–3 **tablespoons grated fresh ginger**
- 1 **teaspoon unrefined salt**
  Juice of 1 lime

GARNISHES

2 **tablespoons sesame seeds**

½ **head garlic**

2 **tablespoons peanut oil**

Sliced tomato, roasted peanuts, shredded greens or cabbage
(optional)

TO MAKE THE FERMENTED TEA LEAVES

1   Place the tea leaves in a heatproof bowl or dish and pour 3 to 4 cups
of hot water over them; you want enough water for the leaves to freely
swirl around. Let them soak until they're cool enough to handle.

2   Strain out the leaves, squeezing out any excess water, and rinse them
with cool water. (Save the water that you strain out. You can use it for
watering your garden, for making tea brines for meat, or as a beverage—
though it will be strong!)

3   Repeat with another soak in hot water, then rinse the tea leaves again.

4   Pour enough room-temperature water over the leaves to cover them.
Let them sit out for at least 2 hours and up to overnight to leach out
some of the bitterness.

5   Pack the ingredients into a jar, crock, or other fermentation vessel and
seal with a lid. Allow to sit out at room temperature and ferment until
the salad has the flavor you'd like, 2 to 4 days. (I tend to like the flavor
best around the beginning of day 3.)

6   Combine the cabbage, scallions, cilantro, garlic, chiles, ginger, salt, and
lime juice in a bowl. Add the tea leaves and massage them into the other
ingredients. Alternatively, you can keep the cabbage, scallions, cilantro,
and chilies separate if desired, and set them in piles on the plate with
the other garnishes.

TO MAKE THE GARNISHES

7   Toast the sesame seeds in a dry skillet until golden. Remove from the
heat and transfer to a separate dish to cool.

Recipe continues on next page. >

8　Peel and thinly slice the garlic cloves. Warm the peanut oil in a skillet over medium-low heat, then add the garlic slices and gently fry until just golden. Remove from the oil and set on a paper towel–lined plate. Save the garlicky oil.

TO ASSEMBLE THE DISH

9　Taste your pickled tea leaves to see if they need any flavor adjustments. You might want to add another squeeze of lime juice, a splash of fish sauce, or even that garlic oil you just made (if you end up having some oil left over, it makes a great addition to future meals!). I often add all three, as well as salt if needed.

10　Place the leaves in a bowl to form them into a mound, then turn it upside down on the middle of a large plate or a tray.

11　Arrange the toasted sesame seeds, fried garlic, and, if using, sliced tomato, roasted peanuts, and shredded greens in piles around the salad and serve.

KIMCHI

This is my regular small-batch recipe, which I use when I've got one head of cabbage and just a few things to mix in. There is an endless variety of kimchis out there. Use this recipe as a template, substituting whatever veggies suit your fancy. As with sauerkraut, you can add all kinds of scraps (such as grated apple), depending on what you need to use up.

Just as there is a variety of kimchi ingredients, there is also a variety of methods for making kimchi. This is the way I was taught to make kimchi, but feel free to experiment with other techniques. For example, a good number of my friends make kimchi with whole cabbages, rubbed with pepper and stuffed with other ingredients before being fermented whole in a large vessel.

MAKES
6 TO 8
PINTS

1　**large head napa cabbage**

2　**tablespoons unrefined salt**

2　**quarts water**

1	**carrot, grated**
1	**daikon radish, grated**
1	**bunch garlic scapes, finely chopped**
1	**(4-inch) piece fresh ginger, grated**
½–1	**cup gochujang** (Korean fermented chili paste), **dried pepper flakes, or ground chiles**
3–4	**tablespoons Korean fish sauce** (or some shredded seaweed for a vegan version)

1   Remove 6 to 8 outer leaves from your cabbage and set them aside. Quarter and core the cabbage, then chop it into bite-size pieces. Place the chopped cabbage in a large nonreactive bowl.

2   Stir the salt into the water, which will give you a 2- to 3-percent brine. Pour the brine over the cabbage and let soak overnight.

3   Drain the liquid from the bowl, reserving it to use later.

4   Add the carrot, daikon, garlic scapes, ginger, and gochujang to the bowl of cabbage. Put on a pair of latex gloves. Massage the pepper paste into the mixture to evenly coat.

5   Add the fish sauce to taste and toss until evenly coated. Massage the mixture to begin breaking down the cell walls of the cabbage leaves, allowing them to soften somewhat.

6   You have a couple of options for aging this. As with sauerkraut, you can pack the kimchi into individual jars, filling them about three-quarters full and topping with a folded cabbage leaf to hold the mixture under the brine. Alternatively, you can pack the mixture into one large container and place the leaves on top, topped with a weight and a tea towel or other cloth secured with twine, or topped with a lid.

7   Pour the reserved brine over the top of each jar or container, as needed, until the mixture is covered, then put on the lids loosely. Set aside to ferment at room temperature, away from direct sunlight or heat. The speed of fermentation varies dramatically depending on all sorts of environmental factors, so check the kimchi every day—open the jars or container, smell the kimchi, and pluck a piece out to taste. If it's not done, you'll know (really—it'll taste like fresh cabbage rather than pickled). Once it gets to a level of softness and fermenty flavor that you like, go ahead and put it in the fridge.

AMISH FRIENDSHIP BREAD

I created this recipe by bringing together two friendship bread recipes I found among my mother's collection. While the specifics of each are a tad different, the overall process is the same.

    This recipe assumes you've been given a friendship bread starter. If you haven't, you can substitute regular sourdough starter, but the resulting bread will taste different.

FEEDING AND DIVIDING YOUR STARTER

MAKES
1 LOAF, PLUS
STARTER TO
SHARE

You've been given a bubbly little starter, and it's time to propagate it. If you have been given more than 1 cup of starter, give the extra away or keep feeding it if you'd like a larger starter batch. Making friendship bread is an act of sharing as well as baking, which means that after you mix in the final flour, sugar, and milk to the starter, you'll divide it into four portions. Three of these will go to friends, and one is used to bake your bread. If you would like to continue cultivating the starter, keep one of the remaining three starters and feed it using the instructions below.

Day 1: Pour 1 cup of the starter into a medium bowl and cover with a tea towel or cloth. Let sit at room temperature.

Days 2–4: Stir each day.

Day 5: Add 1 cup flour, 1 cup sugar, and 1 cup milk and stir well.

Days 6–9: Stir each day.

Day 10: Add 1 cup flour, 1 cup sugar, and 1 cup milk to the starter and stir well. Scoop out 3 cups of the starter, 1 cup at a time, and put each cup in a separate container. Give to three friends with a set of feeding and baking instructions. Make bread with the remaining starter.

BAKING BREAD

1	cup **Amish friendship bread starter**
2/3	cup **oil**
3	**eggs**

2	cups all-purpose flour
1	cup sugar
2	teaspoons pure vanilla extract
1½	teaspoons baking soda
1½	teaspoons ground cinnamon
1	teaspoon ground nutmeg (optional)
½	teaspoon salt
1	cup chopped dried fruit, chopped nuts, or chocolate chips (optional)

1   Preheat the oven to 350°F/180°C. Oil an 8½-inch loaf pan.

2   Place the starter in a large bowl. Add the oil, eggs, flour, sugar, vanilla, baking soda, cinnamon, nutmeg (if using), and salt. Stir well using a spoon (do not use an electric mixer). Add the dried fruit, nuts, or chocolate chips, if using, and stir to incorporate.

3   Bake for 45 to 55 minutes, or until the bread springs back when lightly pressed in the center. Let cool slightly, then turn out onto a serving plate and allow to cool completely before enjoying.

JAMAICAN-STYLE GINGER BEER

This beverage crosses two continents. English colonists brought ginger, which was native to the Caribbean, back to England, where it was brewed into a gingery drink. The recipe then traveled back to Jamaica, where it became wildly popular.

Feel free to adjust the amount of ginger or the soak time to make the beer more or less spicy. Or adjust the amount of lime juice or sugar for a less sour or sweet drink. You can add herbs and spices to the ginger as it soaks if you want to experiment (while it's decidedly not traditional, I like brewing ginger beer with tulsi). Just be sure to use organic ginger, as conventional ginger is sometimes irradiated when imported, removing many of the beneficial microbes that you need to initiate fermentation.

Ginger beer makes an excellent cocktail; just mix it with a bit of rum or whiskey and enjoy.

Recipe continues on next page. >

1 pound fresh organic ginger

1 gallon water

   Juice of 4–6 limes

1 cup turbinado sugar

1 Rinse and scrub the ginger to remove any dirt. Do not peel.

2 Grate the ginger by hand using a box grater, mince it with a food processor, or chop it roughly, then combine it with some of the water and blend in a blender.

3 Combine the ginger and the remaining water in a large bowl and stir to distribute the ginger. Cover the bowl with cheesecloth or a tea towel to keep out bugs and dust, and allow to sit at room temperature for at least 6 hours and up to overnight.

4 When the ginger is done soaking, strain it through a fine-mesh strainer into a nonreactive bowl. Squeeze your ginger pulp to release all the remaining gingery goodness.

5 Add the lime juice and sugar to the fermented liquid, whisking until the sugar dissolves.

6 Transfer the ginger beer into glass bottles or other narrow-necked, food-safe containers. For a still, nonalcoholic beverage, refrigerate immediately. For a fizzy or slightly alcoholic drink, let the mixture bottle-condition for a couple of days by leaving it out at room temperature to ferment a bit more.

BASIC PEACH COUNTRY WINE

Country wine is as simple as can be. It's the kind of wine our ancestors would have made with whatever fruits they had around. This is a wild ferment, meaning that we rely on the yeasts already present on the fruit instead of adding commercial yeast. This produces a pretty wide range of possible flavors (not all of them great), but using local fruits and their yeasts is a testament to time and place: a memory in a bottle.

This recipe is adapted from the grape wine recipe in the book *New Era Home Economics and Cookery*, published in 1903. I make it during the summer in Georgia, so I often use local peaches instead of grapes. Feel free to experiment with whatever ripe fruit you have on hand. Like many such recipes, this one allows you to take what is available and transform it into something extra amazing. Use this recipe as a template as you begin that journey, adding more or less sugar, bottle-conditioning it, and doing whatever you need to make it yours.

MAKES ABOUT 1 GALLON

6 **pounds ripe peaches, pitted and chopped**

5 **cups sugar, plus more for carbonation** (optional)

1 Place the peaches in a blender or food processor and blend to a chunky pulp. You can achieve the same result with a potato masher, too.

2 Pour the pulp into a large jar or crock. Cover with a cloth and secure with a rubber band or twine. Let sit at room temperature, stirring several times a day, until the mixture stops bubbling, 7 to 10 days.

3 Strain the mixture through a mesh bag or cheesecloth, squeezing out as much of the liquid as you can.

4 Transfer the juice back into your fermentation jar or crock. Add the sugar and stir until it is dissolved. Cover the jar or crock with a cloth. Let ferment again, stirring daily. The mixture will bubble vigorously the first few days, then start to slow down. Once the bubbling has mostly subsided and the brew tastes alcoholic, it's ready to serve. (You can also test the ABV with a hydrometer, if you prefer, and there are many instructions online for doing so. I tend to let my taste buds guide me.)

5 Pour the wine into bottles. At this point, you can carbonate your wine or enjoy it as is. To carbonate, add 2 tablespoons of sugar per gallon of

Recipe continues on next page. >

wine (caster sugar is easiest to work with here) and whisk to dissolve. Tightly cap your bottles (swing-top bottles work great for this) and allow to ferment at room temperature for several days until good and bubbly. The wine at this point will be quite sweet, as many country wines are. You can age it in the bottles in a cool place for 1 to 2 months to mellow out the sweetness a bit; just make sure your bottles are completely full and tightly capped to minimize the amount of oxygen coming into contact with the wine.

WINEMAKING JARGON

In the 1972 version of *The Foxfire Book*, which is devoted to the traditional skills of Appalachian folks, a recipe for muscadine (wild grape) wine involved mashing grapes by hand, then adding the mash with sugar into a churn, where you "let it work [ferment] for about a week, until it quits." This is a very common dictate in many fermentation recipes, and it is much more accurate than giving a specific time, due to the many environmental factors I talk about elsewhere. In practical terms, this means that you let it ferment until it gets active and then the activity dies down, which is a sign that the mixture has completed its initial bout of fermentation. The mixture is strained, put back in the churn with more sugar, and fermented "until it quits" again.

(ALMOST) MIMI'S PICKLED WATERMELON RINDS

Each year Mimi (my great-grandmother Helen) would make these pickles, and my father and aunt have fond memories of enjoying them when they went to Mimi's house. Now, in an act of building intergenerational community, I make her recipe each summer, can it, and share it with the family.

This recipe is part ferment and part quick pickle. I've seen other recipes that call for simply a vinegar pickle, but I prefer Mimi's approach: a simple overnight lacto-ferment, followed by just a little boiling. Of course, boiling kills the lactobacilli and their probiotic benefits, but they still impart their many benefits to the texture and taste of the pickles.

As with many recipes, you can easily adapt this one to other ingredients. This recipe is based on Mimi's guidance, taking a few liberties with spices (and spice measurements) to make it distinct. I promise, it's very much worth a try!

MAKES
ROUGHLY 3
QUARTS

½ **cup sea salt**

4 **quarts plus 1 cup water**

1 **medium watermelon, flesh removed and rind cut into ½- to 1-inch cubes**

4 **cups distilled white or apple cider vinegar**

3 **pounds white or light brown sugar**

3 **pieces candied ginger**

2 **sticks cinnamon**

½ **tablespoon whole allspice**

½ **tablespoon whole cloves**

1 Add the salt to the 4 quarts water and stir until dissolved. Place the cubed watermelon rinds in a bowl and pour the brine over them. The brine should completely cover the rinds. If it doesn't, you can make up more brine (1 tablespoon salt per quart of water). Cover the entire thing with a tea towel or cheesecloth and allow to sit at room temperature overnight.

2 In the morning, drain and rinse the rinds with cold water. Transfer them to a pot, cover with cold water, and boil until just tender. Drain and set aside.

3 Combine the remaining 1 cup water with the vinegar, sugar, ginger, cinnamon sticks, allspice, and cloves in a large pot and bring to a boil. Boil for 5 minutes.

4 Drop the rinds into the boiling syrup and boil until they are translucent and can be pierced easily with a knife. Once they reach this stage, they are done, and you can turn off the heat and let them cool. If you want to can them, follow the instructions for canning pickles from a reputable source such as *The All New Ball Book of Canning and Preserving*.

5 Store your pickles in an airtight container in the fridge.

 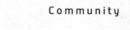

6

THE FUTURE

As we look to the history of fermentation, we see not merely what people did but also the dreams they had for transforming the world around them, feeding people when food wasn't otherwise to be had, adding new flavors, or altering their state of consciousness. Fermentation invites us to imagine a world of radical transformation, one based in possibility and potential.

We shaped the vessels we needed to create the foods we wanted to make, and similarly we have shaped the meaning around those foods within our lives and our communities. When we build what we need, we are able to reenvision food systems that work for all of us, recognizing what is needed (such as familiar comfort foods) and what isn't (for example, exploitative farm labor practices). What will the future we build look like?

Getting Creative

Fermentation has long been a source of creative inspiration, serving as a foundation for artistic and craft practices as well as for culinary adventures and beyond. There has been a recent interest in using SCOBY (symbiotic culture of bacteria and yeast) for making art, clothing, and various other objects such as wallets. And sometimes the practical overlaps with the creative. For example, according to Harry Rosenblum, author of *Vinegar Revival Cookbook,* vinegar is said to have been used to cool Louis XIII's cannons, to give samurai strength and focus, to disinfect battlefield wounds, and even to break boulders as Hannibal and his army did when they crossed the Alps.

FERMENTING NATURAL PIGMENTS

The act of intentional fermentation may have started with food, but it didn't end there. Over the years, we have fermented all sorts of plants and other natural substances such as mud to make our lives and homes more beautiful.

MUDCLOTH

Bogolan or mudcloth is a handmade cotton fabric made in several parts of West Africa (particularly Mali and Burkina Faso) that is colored using fermented mud. The mud oxidizes on contact with tannins added to the fabric, producing a rich black or dark brown hue. Bleach can then be used to paint or stencil designs onto the fabric.

Senegalese-born multimedia artist Abdala Faye uses both hand painting and stenciling to create designs on mudcloth as a part of his artistic practice. According to Faye, it is critical to use natural fibers (cotton in particular) rather than synthetic fabrics to ensure proper absorption of the color. He also notes that you aren't limited to just brown and white: By adding a variety of other botanicals and/or ashes to your mud, you open up an entire playground of color possibilities.

INDIGO DYE

One of our most stunning natural pigments, indigo dye was historically made from fermented *Indigofera tinctoria*, a member of the pea family (today, most indigo-hued fabric is colored with synthetic dye). Indigo dye has been around since at least the third millennium BCE and likely was discovered by the Bronze Age Harappan civilization in the Indus Valley, where archaeologists have recovered seeds from several *Indigofera* species. While it is unclear how indigo fermentation was discovered, we do know that indigo dye was being made into small cakes and sold by peasants in the northwest of India to the ancient Greeks and Romans.

To make the dye, the plant matter is fermented in a vat of alkaline liquid. Historically, a wide variety of substances—from madder root to lime to even human urine—have been used to balance the pH as it cures. The plant is fermented for anywhere from 4 days to 2 weeks, during which time the fermentation process breaks down the pigments and releases them into the liquid. When you first dip your textiles in the vat, they are dyed a yellow-green color, and then the pigment oxidizes before your eyes, turning into a luscious, rich blue when exposed to air.

Because it was so laborious to produce (and thus expensive), the pricey pigment was available only to nobles, royalty, and high-ranking clergy in Europe (for a while, it was rivaled only by a dye extracted from snail mucus called Tyrian purple). For those who could not afford indigo, woad, a member of the mustard family, was often used as a blue pigment, though it was less rich and colorfast than its expensive counterpart.

> You have to act as if it were possible to radically transform the world. And you have to do it all the time.
>
> —ANGELA DAVIS

According to Elliot McNally, who studies and teaches natural dyes in Atlanta, Europeans were eager to use the warmer growing conditions of many places they colonized to grow the cash crop, and so indigo cultivation became a driving force behind colonization and slavery. In the state of Georgia, for example, indigo was one of the colony's first cash crops, and slavery was actually banned there until they needed workers to ferment the indigo.

Indigo was grown by enslaved people on plantations everywhere from South Carolina to Jamaica to Guatemala to India. When it became clear that the best indigo came from Southeast Asia, many of the American and Caribbean indigo plantations shifted to other crops such as cotton or sugarcane (still with enslaved workers growing and processing the crops). After the development of synthetic indigo in the nineteenth century, the demand for farmed indigo dropped considerably, and with it also fell the use of enslaved and/or exploited labor to grow the crop. Today, indigo (either the dye or dyed fabrics) can sometimes be found in specialty and craft stores.

FERMENT YOUR WORDS

People have also used fermentation to create certain papers as well as inks. Cotton rag paper was an incredibly durable and high-quality paper made in Europe in the fifteenth century. It was made to replace vellum (treated and dried animal skins) after the advent of Gutenberg's movable-type printing press, as the rag paper was more plentiful and had a shorter turnaround time than vellum. It was a staple in bookmaking until the industrial revolution, when it was replaced by cheaper (and less durable) wood pulp paper, which is still in use today.

Rag paper was, as the name suggests, made from old rags. In a step of the papermaking process called retting, old rags would be fermented multiple times as part of a larger process of bleaching the fabric and breaking apart its fibers so it could be made into paper pulp.

Vinegar was also used during the fifteenth century (and before) as a preservative in writing inks. Oak gall ink, for example, was made using the wasp galls (larvae) left behind on oak trees, which have a high tannin content. The galls were fermented to extract the tannins and then combined with iron sulfate (for color), gum arabic (for consistency), and vinegar or wine to increase the ink's acidity and thus prolong its shelf life. While oak gall ink is a very striking purplish black when first used, the color does fade over time to a warm brown, and the acidity of the ink will often eat through paper or vellum, leaving ghostly traces of the letters behind.

FERMENTING FOODS IN SURPRISING WAYS

How can the process of crafting ferments, and the ferments themselves, help us reconsider and unlock our creative potential today? We're seeing more and more ferments appear in surprising ways on restaurant menus—from fine-dining establishments to delis to catered events and beyond. Perhaps the most well-known example is Noma restaurant in Copenhagen, which has its own fermentation lab. But Noma is far from the only one. Chefs Jeremy Umansky, Allie La Valle-Umansky, and Kenny Scott of Larder in Cleveland rely heavily on ferments, as does chef Sean Doherty of Scales restaurant in Maine. And at Atlanta's unique one-person, one-table outdoor restaurant called Ett (which closed in 2021), chef Jessamine Starr regularly folded vinegars, misos, and more into her creations. Of course, simple ferments such as sauerkraut and kimchi are staple workhorses on menus around the world, but chefs and home cooks alike are adopting a wider variety of ferments, as well as a broader application of fermentation processes.

There are plenty of ways for home cooks to creatively engage with fermentation, too. For example, I have an "adventure ferment" that joins me every time I travel (except when flying, thanks to those pesky 3.4-ounce containers). When I get to a new place, I add a new fruit or vegetable I find there. Then, back home, each time I top off the brine, I am reminded of every place I've been with that ferment, and the smells and tastes of each place.

When you consider the symbiotic nature of your relationship with the microbes in your ferments, you can engage with them in a new way. As Ken Albala describes it during an interview with me, it's "knowing you are caring for a living community of creatures that will sustain you. Like a herd of sheep or field of wheat, except on your countertop. And they have moods just like plants and animals. You have to care for them. It's why I always name my starters."

And historical data is providing inspiration as well. The Egtved Girl, who was buried outside Egtved, Denmark, in 1370 BCE and whose well-preserved remains were discovered in 1921, was interred with a honey-sweetened beer, infused with plants that spoke to the time and place around her. The plants used were identified by their pollen and included cowberries, wheat grains, bog myrtle, and lime pollen. Re-creating foods like this offers a window to the past beyond simply the novelty of enjoying "old food": Like a strand of mycelium, these foods build a connection between us and our ancestors. I know from my own experience that you can make amazing realizations when you re-create historical foods. And the personal feelings of comfort, joy, and revelation that emerge when you make food that speaks to your deep self are well worth the effort.

Today, culinary creatives of all stripes—from home cooks feeding their families to fine-dining chefs—are (re)discovering the power of allowing our immediate environment to feed us while returning to simple and time-honored preparations, such as ferments. Fonta Flora Brewery in North Carolina, for example, is already doing this, adding wild plants to its beers to delicious effect. Food historian Leni Sorensen both ferments and teaches about it, bringing together the joy of creating fermented food and the art of sharing in the truest sense. Her work, wherein she draws on old culinary traditions to make history come alive, is one example of the potential in this kind of work. And many fermentation enthusiasts are discovering connections between their fermentation practice and other areas of their identity, including Stephanie Maroney's queer fermentative praxis, found in Sandor Katz's work and elsewhere.

Buddhist nun Jeong Kwan, quoted at the beginning of Chapter 3, sees soy sauce, and the making of soy sauce, as a confluence of past, present, and future. To me, this is creativity in its truest sense: to see our food as a reflection of our culmination of experiences and hopes and dreams. With ferments, we are pushing those hopes and dreams out on a raft into the ocean of the future, to watch them evolve and grow in ways we may not have ever imagined. As Jeong Kwan reminds us, "If you free yourself from the comparing and jealous mind, your creativity opens up endlessly. Just as water springs from a fountain, creativity springs from every moment. . . . There is no way you can't open up your creativity."

Ferments for Mindfulness

When we make our own ferments, we are actually boosting our health in two ways: First, we support our mental health through the meditative, grounding action of making the ferments, and second, we gain physical nourishment through the nutritional benefits that come from eating them. The experience of making our own healthy food offers us a counternarrative to a culture that pushes "health" through consumption and spending.

Truly democratic, accessible, and inherently community oriented, fermentation offers us a window to other paradigms of eating and being. And these paradigms are not so foreign to us as we might believe. As we've seen throughout this book, they've been with us for thousands of years, only being subsumed and replaced in many areas after the industrial revolution. And we have been eagerly reconnecting with ferments in the last decade or two. Plenty of people never stopped making them, of course, but there is a blossoming interest among home cooks and chefs to dive more deeply into those foods that food blogger and fermenter Marie-Claire Frédéric calls "ni cru ni cuit" ("neither raw nor cooked").

Fermentation how-to articles, cookbooks, and classes abound, and Google Trends tracks steady high interest in fermentation through keyword searches on both the term *fermentation* and related terms or phrases (for example, *homemade sauerkraut*). The online tool AnswerThePublic, which also posts online search trends, shows a range of common search terms both related to understanding what fermentation is and practical advice on making ferments.

As we become more mindful of how we move through the world, we become more mindful of our impact upon our environment, too. Heavily processed foods not only take away the joy (and nourishment) of eating, but they have a huge environmental cost. For those who have other food options, how can ferments help us live in greater harmony with the world around us?

Nickawanna Shaw notes how her fermentation practice intersects with cultivating mindfulness while considering the health of her body and of the planet:

> Instead of thinking, "I like that, let's make it," I think, "What's seasonal? How can it be transformed to be more edible, storable, etc.?" I am thinking this way because it's when foods are in season they are cheapest. . . . Having access to locally grown foods is a luxury. At the same time, eating outside of the American diet . . . of 20 mass produced/farmed items is a stretch for many palates. Learning to eat seasonally also brings different microbes into the gut, naturally improving gut health and immune function.

Ferments for Justice and for Future Generations

Knowing the history of our food is incredibly powerful. It helps us appreciate how our ancestors shared and understood what they ate, which opens our understanding of their larger world. But to know this history, we must seek out not only the information we were given but also that which was hidden, and we must critically examine our sources.

REEXAMINING HISTORICAL RECORDS

We learn about the history of ferments through written records, archaeological dig sites, and our very bones themselves, which contain (for example) evidence of ancient microbiomes on the dental plaque of skeletons. However, the history of our food is not consistently well recorded. This is particularly true of fermentation, which is so widespread and has been baked into our daily diets for so long that perhaps it did not feel exceptional enough to merit much record. But its very ubiquity underscores the importance of recording this cultural memory. Without that piece of the puzzle, the picture of a culture's food is far from complete.

If we want a comprehensive and factual account of information, we must be willing to revisit what we already know and see what we've overlooked. Pete Brown, author of *Miracle Brew,* argues that part of why our record on brewing is incomplete is because "historically, it seems academics just don't like beer. As with so much in the history of brewing, the significance of barley farming and malting in broader British history has gone largely unrecorded. The possibility that ancient, smooth floors pitted with grain impressions might just have been evidence of prehistoric malting was mostly ignored by those who made the finds until others challenged them. While researching previous books, I was astonished to discover that brewing was second only to cotton in Victorian British industry, because this is scarcely mentioned in histories of the Industrial Revolution."

Connecting with historic records also helps us rediscover and explore once-popular dishes and techniques. As Mara King told me:

> One of the books I have referenced often in my research for my book on Chinese fermentation has been the *Qinmin Yaoshu.* An agricultural guide that was written around 544 AD, the book's title translates to *Essential Techniques for the Welfare of the People.* Its contents include guides for land and livestock maintenance; growing guides for fruits, crops, even aquaculture; and, interestingly, an amazing diverse collection of recipes for fermented foods, some of which have long fallen to obscurity and some of which are still ubiquitous in China and much of Southeast Asia today. I feel that a book like this is a very civilizing tool, giving people the ability to thrive and sustain themselves in an agricultural way. These techniques are more important today than ever, as we live in an industrialized space that is so very disconnected from the natural world. I feel strongly that more people need access to histories such as *Qinmin Yaoshu* to reconnect with our cultures and heritage.

We must also consider our fermentation cultural record within its larger context. Recorded history is not neutral. Far from it. What gets written down, and how, is heavily dependent on who is doing the recording.

Outsiders from a culture may miss significant clues hidden in cultural context (such as a certain tone or phrasing), but they also may misrepresent a culture entirely. As historian Karl F. Morrison says, "Always, thoughtful readers have to interrogate the texts before them, searching out negative values as well as positive ones. What do these authors tell us when their narratives plainly suppress information that was at hand or when, in their effort to preserve the memory of events, they committed significant actors (such as women) to the river of forgetfulness?"

DOCUMENTING ALL VOICES

It is critical not only to be sure our histories reflect the most powerful voices but also to persistently seek out the *least*-documented voices. We must encourage documentation within cultures and/or cross-cultural sharing of records to preserve not only fermentation processes but knowledge about the use and importance of ferments within a household, a village, or a country.

Because so many of our food traditions are passed orally between generations, there is a real risk of their being lost, particularly if family members are separated or if some choose not to carry on traditional culinary preparations. It is especially critical that we document food traditions of marginalized groups or those that are primarily practiced by elders. In the case of traditions mostly practiced by elders, it is important to document those practices quickly so that future generations have the opportunity to learn from them. Even something as simple as "my grandma puts a palmful rather than a handful of salt in her fermenting crock" can be incredibly useful later for those trying to re-create or understand traditional foods.

We know, for example, that while there are living traditions of brewing grain and fruit beverages in eastern Europe, there are no modern accounts of adding juniper to these beverages, but we know that was a tradition at one time. We know this because multiple informants told researchers that they recalled their parents or grandparents doing so (though it is unclear why later generations stopped). It is only because these home fermenters noticed and shared familial brewing practices that we have an understanding of those practices shifting.

In many cases, the very ubiquity of particular ferments, which were often prepared in the home (and many times, though not always, by women), has hastened their loss. Because they were so common, these traditions were seen as too mundane to record. As a result, fermentation knowledge has been lost, and it continues to be at risk of being lost if we do not record elders' fermentation practices with the same enthusiasm with which we record other history.

It is encouraging to see that more and more researchers are documenting the history and present-day accounts of fermentation, and some nonprofits and other organizations are as well. The Slow Food Ark of Taste, for example, captures and preserves information about various global food traditions in fermentation and beyond. The Micropia museum in Amsterdam uses exhibitions and public-facing educational programming to help the history of microbes reach a wider audience.

There is incredibly fruitful ground for collaboration here, such as between anthropologists well versed in ethnography and librarians and other cultural heritage professionals. Through collaboration, each can benefit from the strengths of the other's field and be presented with different perspectives, which hopefully reduces the likelihood of overlooking or misrepresenting information.

Recording our history literally shapes the future. At a moment when Western culture is finally coming to terms with the human costs of oppression and colonialism, recording the stories of those things (for instance, traditional foodways) that have historically been overlooked or seen as "not worth" documenting by those in power, is an act of resistance. If we want to fully heal the damage, that means providing space and resources for everyone to contribute their voice to the fermentation future.

PROVIDING ACCESS

Having access to traditional knowledge is incredibly empowering for those who have had so much of their culture ripped away from them. The key term here is *access*: It is not empowering to have the information recorded but located behind a paywall or uncataloged in an archive. If we provide resources not only to document stories but also to make them available, the impacts on dietary knowledge could be profound. Access is a social justice issue—one that is beginning to be addressed, hopefully on an ever-greater scale moving forward.

For millennia, communities have passed down knowledge about how and what to ferment. However, for the last handful of centuries, systems of colonization and other disrupting forces have stopped that transfer of knowledge. Centuries of colonialism have separated many people from the diets that traditionally nourished them. Culinary historian and writer Michael Twitty notes, for example, that while enslaved Africans did make some fermented foods, their diets shifted dramatically under slavery, and their disconnection from traditional fermented foods was a large part of this. Twitty says, "Slavery harmed Black folks in another way—it took away the processes by which they made a cuisine full of probiotics. There was simply very little time for everyday cooking that involved fermentation." Twitty and others are doing work to reconnect Black Americans with the African and African American foodways that have been erased or sub-sumed, and there are others (such as Sean Sherman, a.k.a. the Sioux Chef) doing the same for other oppressed communities.

Providing access to nutritious fermented food itself is important as well. Fermented foods have been shown to play an important role in our health, in our vitality, and in our memory. As Nickawanna Shaw, who teaches well-ness at a California community college, explains, "If we eat poorly, the sys-tem experiences distress which affects memory. If we are upset, the brain literally adaptively blocks the hippocampus, which in turn affects memory. If we experience distress, the ramped up nervous system competes, and wins, the fight for dominance with the parasympathetic nervous system, causing us to digest poorly and purge nutrients quickly. The loss of nutri-ents means we can't repair the body and we digest the lining of the organs including the brain. And again, memory suffers."

Those with reduced access to healthy foods could especially benefit from fermented foods, as well as from the practice of fermentation itself. As discussed in Chapter 4, preparing fermented foods is a meditative act that can lead to a greater sense of presence and even a reduction in stress. As Shaw explains, "If someone can't afford good food, they likely live under stressful conditions. Breathing and moving slowly and with focused intention calms the body. If someone can't move well, they likely have frustrations living in a world that limits their access. Learning to breathe can lower the stress on their bodies of that persistent feeling. When we feel maintained and present, we have the resiliency to repair our bodies and to make choices using all of our senses without pain or distraction."

BUILDING ACCESS THROUGH TEACHING

If we are to build an equitable future for fermentation, culinary instruction must be accessible to all. It does not serve the larger community if every fermentation class can be attended only by the well-to-do. Offering scholarships and other access points is a great start, but so, too, is shaping the instruction itself with access in mind.

Many fermentation instructors I know choose the simplest methods and equipment when teaching. Most classes I teach require little more than a jar and some salt, and many of us try to give people as much information about what to substitute and where to get cheap jars (recycling centers!) rather than teach about custom-made fermentation vessels and luxury ingredients. Those things are fun to play around with, but if you're just trying to teach (or learn), starting simple is best. Use equipment and knowledge within most people's reach.

Fermentation and justice also connect back to mindfulness. When we consider the social justice component of our food, it has an impact on how much and what we consume because we are concerned with the well-being of those who feed us. And it turns out that in most instances, when we buy foods that are more equitably produced (such as those from local growers), we are doing something beneficial for the environment as well.

CHANGE COMES STEP BY STEP

While it may be overwhelming to think of the changes that must happen to expand access to fermentation, we need to remember that the push toward food justice is not one heroic leap but rather a series of steps. And even if you don't have the ability to start a fermentation practice or the means to buy fermented foods, other small decisions can improve your health and support the environment. As writer Christina Ward says, "Each one of us is confronted daily with difficult choices about how we feed ourselves and our families. A multitude of outside stressors influence those decisions. Not everyone can acquire locally grown food. Not everyone has the capability or capacity to make a choice. . . . Change rarely comes in the form of a blinding light; it comes by making small adjustments to your regular routines." This might include buying more local produce, eschewing disposable flatware, or finding ways to repurpose food scraps. Fermentation is an important part of this, but it is also part of a larger picture that supports sustainable, healthy eating.

All around the country, we see people making changes large and small, bringing fermented foods to the people who need them. Erica Clahar, who runs Umi Feeds in Atlanta, for example, feeds the city's unhoused population balanced, nutritious, and delicious meals. Her goal is to give people a meal that tastes and feels like home—not just a loveless ration of food. She and I have talked a lot about the nourishment she puts into these meals, and she has repeatedly mentioned the importance of including ferments for their probiotic health benefits. Most foods accessible to the unhoused community lack probiotics, yet probiotics are especially important for this population because access to health care is also severely limited.

In Brooklyn, Contraband Ferments' underground fermentation CSA was, for years, a source of delicious and affordable fermented foods and an example of creatively feeding communities. In 2020, free fridges, which popped up all over the United States, offered a way for community members to share food with hungry neighbors. While these fridges contain all kinds of groceries, I'm pleasantly surprised by how often I see ferments on the shelves when I go to make a donation.

In Nagasaki Prefecture, in Japan, Yoshida Toshimichi uses fermentation to recycle food waste while bringing healthy ferments to schools and day-care centers. Through his guidance, dozens of day-care centers are now growing their own organic vegetables, and they are incorporating these vegetables along with fermented foods into the meals for their children. He uses fermentation to enrich his compost and, thus, his garden soil as well as meals, explaining, "*Lactobacilli* and other friendly microbes found in naturally fermented foods can help maintain a healthy environment in the gut, just as they do in the soil." After the vegetable gardens and fermented foods were introduced, student absences from illness dropped dramatically and parents noted that their children seemed more robustly healthy overall.

Ferments for the Whole Community

When we examine fermentation's role in our current global community, we see that our individual and professional fermentation practices are part of a constellation of supply chains, knowledge systems, and production systems that do not benefit everyone involved.

Miin Chan, a self-described "microbe wrangling MD PhD" who wrote about the whitewashing of fermentation, traces the Western world's current fermentation obsession to the agrarian movement of the 1960s and '70s. The back-to-the-land idealism of this movement resulted in many white members of the rising counterculture developing an obsession with ferments from "the Orient" and old Europe, and this later spread to include the ferments of many global communities.

The desire to grow and prepare natural foods coincided with the larger natural foods movement, which gave us things such as co-ops and health food stores. To varying degrees, these businesses have created a market for mass-produced fermented goods. As a result, ferments such as kombucha and tibico (water kefir) are now big business, but those businesses are largely run by white Westerners rather than by members of the communities of color who first created the ferments and who passed down the knowledge for generations. Chan points out that in many cases, these traditional ferments have become divorced from their histories, instead marketed for their health benefits to niche segments of white audiences. In addition, as fermentationist and owner of St. Pete Ferments Sarah Arrazola notes, the fermentation industry relies heavily on underpaid laborers to harvest the tea, sugar, produce, and the like that are used in mass-produced ferments. By not acknowledging that, we are overlooking another way in which our fermentation practices may be cultivating harm.

In an interview with Chan, Mara King noted, "People are not even aware of the subtle ways they embody racism." She says it is critical to recognize the delicate balance needed when trying to represent someone else's culture, namely by not saying "my way is the only way" but also by "always being open to learning and being submissive to somebody else's understanding."

PLACING FERMENTS IN CONTEXT

Here in America, home fermentation exists across socioeconomic spectra in various forms as a hobby, a status symbol, a survival mechanism, a health tool, and more. There is absolutely space for all the different ways we experience ferments, from limited-run craft beers and high-end spirits to homemade wine brewed in a bucket and small-batch vegetable ferments. But it is critical, especially for producers selling their ferments, that we put those foods within their context, understanding their history and engaging in cultural exchange rather than appropriation. Emily Chen, Edric Huang, and chef Jenny Dorsey of Studio ATAO define cultural appropriation as "the adoption of elements of one culture by another, especially in cases where a dominant culture exploits aspects of a minority culture outside of its cultural context and/or at the expense of the original culture for personal gain." For example, if you're selling starter cultures, one question you may ask yourself is: Do you know where the starters come from, and are you educating consumers about their history?

Fermenting for the whole community also means recognizing how our businesses might impact our immediate geographic communities. If you are a brewer, for example, you can question whether your brewery is contributing to gentrification if it is moving into an area slated for "revitalization": Are you interacting with longtime residents? Do they feel comfortable in your space?

Reshaping Our Identities with Ferments

Choosing what to eat each day may seem like a small thing, but it can actually be a powerful act of creation. When we choose to ferment something ourselves instead of buying a packaged food, we are choosing to shape our identity. As Sandor Katz says in *Wild Fermentation*:

> What to eat is a choice that we make several times a day, if we are lucky. The cumulative choices we make about food have profound implications. Food offers us many opportunities to resist the culture of mass marketing and commodification. Though consumer action can take many creative and powerful forms, we do not have to be reduced to the role of consumers selecting from seductive convenience items. We can merge appetite with activism and choose to involve ourselves in food as cocreators.

When we honor the history of a ferment by sharing its story and by acknowledging legacies of appropriation or theft and their impact, the act of preserving our food takes on a much deeper meaning: that of collectively stewarding our culture toward a hopefully more equitable future.

When we pour love into something such as food, so long considered "just" domestic labor, we acknowledge the value of the labor and identities so long devalued. Within the larger realms of craft and cooking, there is a good deal of writing about how elevating "women's work" (and, while not as commonly mentioned in these contexts, also the work of enslaved people) elevates the history of those whose cooking and care supported everyone else's work. Writer Christina Ward describes her own experience of reevaluating "women's work": "As a teenager discovering punk rock and feminism, my eyes opened to the value of so-called 'women's work.' The making of things. Food preservation became more than a jar of pickles; it became a direct link to our matriarchal history." To elevate fermentation is to say that the stories of those who built our fermentation traditions have a place in the modern day.

While fermented products are closely linked to cultural identity, social status, and numerous other identities, we are at a unique moment where the *process* itself is considered within the context of identity. Stephanie Maroney describes "the possibilities of a queer fermentative praxis" when doing a close reading of Sandor Katz's *Wild Fermentation*. Part of this praxis is not simply fermentation as an act of transforming food, but an act of using that transformative mindset to impact our world and to express and understand our identities. Fermentation is inherently multilayered, with multiple microbial communities coexisting with a range of substrates to produce a range of outcomes. It is hard to see the world in terms of binaries or purity when you have such intermixed communities bubbling away on your counter. Similarly, it creates space for nuance in our understanding of ourselves and our own identities: Queerness does not have to mean purely one thing to all members of the queer community. Another example is the wonderful organization known as food feminism fermentation (fff), which encourages us to consider how ferments intersect with our lives and identities writ large.

This moment feels new but has ties to the past. Our ancestors understood and were shaped by both process and product, so in a way we are returning to that worldview. But unlike our ancestors, we are now equipped to discuss nuances of identities and experiences (such as queerness). Exploring our identities through what we ferment opens a whole world of inquiry and discovery that's brimming with possibility.

Fermentation is also a space for exploration. How does it feel to create a food that our ancestors used to make? Or that someone from our own past used to make? How does the act shape us? And how are we shaped by learning how to make a fermented food from another culture? Organizer and educator Noel Didla and writer and herbalist Sumi Dutta note in their work through the Matti Collective, which they referred to as their South Asian sister circle, that food creates collective memory and allows us not only to perpetuate traditions but to craft new memories and futures together. And Nickawanna Shaw's work as an educator engages in pedagogy in context and in the concept of food as a creative and healing space, drawing together the threads of mindfulness, environment, documenting process, and fostering creative play.

Ferments for the Planet

When we consider the future of fermentation, we must look beyond our food and drink and consider the environment, too. The microbes we rely on live in the soil, and when we nourish it, we nourish the microbes and ourselves as well. Ecologist Nance Klehm describes soil as "the dark cosmos," a place with incredible complexity and a diversity of life and entire interconnected systems. Fungi, bacteria, and other microorganisms are critical to these systems. If we view our soil, oceans, and other natural spaces as cosmos, we are asked to recognize the agency and aliveness of the beings, visible and otherwise, with whom we share our world. As Ken Albala has said, "That we can even think of ecology as preserving flora and fauna, while we obliterate bacteria without blinking an eye—in the soil, in the kitchen, on our hands, seems the most remarkable example of speciesism."

After all, a life without microbes would be plantless, full of waste, and probably short and uncomfortable. As researchers Jack Gilbert and Josh Neufeld wrote in their paper "Life in a World without Microbes," "In short, we argue that humans could get by without microbes just fine, for a few days. Although the quality of life on this planet would become incomprehensibly bad, life as an entity would endure." (But, they note, "if we do include mitochondria and chloroplasts as Bacteria, as we should, then the impact would be immediate—most eukaryotes would be dead in a minute.")

REDUCING WASTE

If we shift our perspective toward working *with* beneficial microbes rather than against them, wonderful things can emerge. They can, for example, revolutionize our relationship with waste, both through transforming our food scraps into something delicious and by transforming nonedible materials into ones that are inert or even beneficial to the environment. Some fungal strains, for example, are useful for bioremediation of petroleum-polluted soil, as are some marine bacteria.

In restaurants, fermentation can be employed to reuse scraps as much as possible, as fermentation and food science consultant Johnny Drain does in helping restaurants design low-waste, fermentation-focused menus, sometimes reenvisioning traditional foods or applying old methods in new ways. In some cases, this involves revisiting and sharing a traditional food rather than reinventing the wheel. Akoko, a West African restaurant in London, aims to expose new palates to the magic of West African food. Ferments such as ogiri egusi (fermented melon seeds) play into this, and this dish helps those new palates find new possibilities for ingredients they might not normally work with.

And in home kitchens around the world, people continue to employ the waste-reducing practices that we have for millennia. Chef Dan Barber notes that the global cuisines humans have developed are just as much about restraint as they are about progress. "One of the great things about cuisine is that it is the best way to hold back our worst kind of hedonism," says Barber. "There is no landscape in the world that sustainably allows us to eat how we think we want to." In another sense, says Barber, food is the physical manifestation of our relationship with the natural world. It is where culture and ecology intersect, with the potential to be of even greater importance than language or geography to a culture.

Our waste-reducing and food-preserving habits have, as we've seen, given us the ability to live within the confines of our environment while ascribing deep social and personal significance to those foods that help us do so. For fermenter and author Kirsten Shockey, for example, making foods to fully utilize the output of her homestead guided her toward her fermentation journey. An abundance of milk became cheese, and a sizable apple harvest became cider, all of which resulted in usable products but also moved her family toward abundance and away from waste. She and her husband, Christopher, initially sold these products at markets, but people didn't want to just buy the ferments, they wanted to *understand* them, leading her to become a teacher of fermentation (in my opinion, one of the best). For food historian and farmsteader Leni Sorensen, raising food heavily informs what she eats and preserves, though she notes that it's all about "taste first"; each thing she preserves is made with the goal of a delicious final product. Taste is critical, because, as Kirsten Shockey notes, "if it doesn't taste good it doesn't get pulled out of the fridge and eaten."

FORAGING MINDFULLY

Many people today are interested in eating wild foods. Foraging has been a critical part of the human experience for millennia, but it is a skill many of us have forgotten, or perhaps never learned in the first place. Learning to gather wild food sustainably and thoughtfully links us to the past; it is a way of reconnecting with the world as our ancestors once saw it.

Particularly in this moment, foraging can help us feel empowered to feed ourselves and to feel more connected to our environment. However, it also requires us to consider our role within our ecological community. In an online class we taught together in 2020, Mallory O'Donnell of the blog *How to Cook a Weed* said, "It's not 'Can I eat that?' It's 'Should I eat that?'" Ripping up ramps by their roots, harvesting half of the berries off a bush, or stomping over stands of other plants to get to what you want is blatantly irresponsible. Instead, it's critical that we take a long view when considering our impact on the environment.

The making of jiuqianjiu (in Chinese) or kaojiuqian (in Shui) by the Shui people in southwestern China is an example of indigenous knowledge being developed to promote environmental harmony. Jiuqianjiu is a fermented alcoholic beverage made using water, rice, and a starter derived from wild plants. Through a process of social negotiation, everyone works together to prevent overharvesting of the wild plants used for the starter, and new starters are created only occasionally (every 3 years or so) to prevent overharvesting and allow wild plants to grow back between harvests.

* * *

Learning to ferment not only offers useful skills but is a way to reconsider our food systems themselves: what we eat and where it comes from, and how to produce our own food or support local and sustainable ecosystems through our purchasing choices and waste reduction. As Kirsten Shockey says, "Touching and controlling some aspect of food is so important in grounding people and fermentation plays a huge role in that."

Ultimately, fermentation is one of the key ways that we can improve our own health (mind and body) and the health of the planet, and those teaching and sharing knowledge play a critical part in this endeavor.

Ferments for a Sustainable Craft

Each time we create a ferment in our home or restaurant, we're challenging the narratives around use and waste that are so central to modern Western thinking. These narratives externalize the labor required to make our food (and grow it as well) and to outsource the cost of its convenience onto laborers and the planet through low wages and harsh conditions, overuse of pesticides and herbicides, unsustainable shipping and packaging practices, and the staggering waste of edible products.

When we draw upon millennia of knowledge around the *craft* of fermentation, we can situate it within the trajectory of craft production proposed by British historian and archaeologist Alexander Langlands (or at least begin to move in that direction):

> tended landscape / sustainable production of raw materials / intelligently processed / beautifully made / fit for purpose / fondly used / ingeniously reused / considerately discarded / given back to the earth

How do these relate to fermentation? Here's my perspective:

TENDED LANDSCAPE AND SUSTAINABLE PRODUCTION OF RAW MATERIALS. Sourcing from local, small-scale growers is a great way to allow your fermentation practice to support community economics and environmental sustainability. The "production of raw materials" can also include other creative ways of gathering food, such as (sustainable) wildcrafting or food rescue.

INTELLIGENTLY PROCESSED AND BEAUTIFULLY MADE. You may already be aware of the way we gain intelligence through crafting handmade works, but with ferments we have an additional layer: the bacteria, yeast, and fungi we're working with. These living collaborators bring with them their own intelligence, wrought from millions of years of evolution, that tells them how to multiply, what conditions they thrive in, and how to communicate with others—all of which informs our ferment. Beauty in this context is far beyond something being physically attractive— which not all ferments are! Instead it is the beauty of beginning a process and watching it unfold to its final form, appreciating it as it progresses along the way. Even if your ferment doesn't turn out, the process itself contains a lot of beauty, and the learning you take from it is beautiful, too.

FIT FOR PURPOSE. When we make a ferment, sometimes we have a particular outcome in mind (such as wanting a sour beer with 7 percent ABV), but other times we are just creating for the sake of creating. Both are equally valid purposes, and both have just as much to teach about the fermentation process.

FONDLY USED AND INGENIOUSLY REUSED. Of course, here is where we enjoy our ferment, adding a scoop of kimchi to our bowl of rice, stirring some vinegar into a sauce, or sipping on a glass of homemade wine with friends. Ferments, adaptable as they are, have many reuses that we've covered elsewhere in greater detail, including baking with spent grain, using scraps to make vinegar or seasonings, or using brine to add flavor to dishes.

CONSIDERATELY DISCARDED AND GIVEN BACK TO THE EARTH. For those ferments that are more of a learning experience than a gustatory delight, compost heaps and chicken feed are two welcome ways to mindfully recycle the ferment without adding it to the landfill. The same holds true for any other scraps from our ferments (for example, the layers of leaves on top of a crock of sauerkraut). The microbes we work with are in the soil, and when we give those microbes back to the soil through composting, we are nourishing the earth and our future selves.

Langlands applies his trajectory to various tangible handcrafts—from baskets to scythes—noting that our understanding of a product should be rooted in the skill and process, just as it has been historically: "Herein lies the true *craeft*—the power, the knowledge and the skill—in the rural crafts of old." As fermenters, this perspective allows us to move away from the concept that what we make is a stand-alone object (or in this case, foodstuff), instead returning to the knowledge that it is a part of our human ecosystem of knowledge, as well as the ecosystem writ large. Humans have long engaged with making things using their hands—whether tools or food—in this way. When we connect to the larger implications and history of our craft itself, and by extension are in closer community with the planet and each other, we can return to that way of being. As Langlands says of trying to separate toolmaking from the act of agriculture and harvest, "It's clever to make a scythe, it's even cleverer to use it effectively."

On a larger scale, our individual acts of fermentation are tied to our systems of agriculture and production, and our planetary history itself. Langlands also notes the "deep time signatures" of many crafts, and I apply this to fermentation as well. "If we ever find ourselves running short on ceramic crockery and kitchenware because of some apocalyptic collapse in the global network of exchange, I know that, like our ancestors in early medieval Britain, I need to use a chaff temper when I'm mixing the short clay sourced from the bottom of the garden. These deep time signatures also serve as a tacit reminder of the human condition: that we are makers, and that we have always lived in a world of making," writes Langlands.

In the case of fermentation, we are considering the deep time signatures associated not just with our fermentation vessels (for example, the ceramics mentioned above) but with fermentation itself. Our ferments, in both ingredients and process, were adapted over time based on where and when we were making them: using a salt brine rather than rice wine to pickle cabbage, for example, or using kegs to store beer rather than amphorae. As we've seen throughout this book, fermentation has been with us since before we were fully human, but when we started to *make* ferments mindfully and *in community* with microbes rather than simply interacting with the results, it changed our trajectory and, over the course of millennia, changed the world itself.

Ferments and the Future of Science

Theory and practice are two sides of the same coin within any field, and in a perfect world they inform each other: Theory offers the undergirding structure to guide practice, and its implementation and adjustment within practical spaces informs theory. What if we applied this to our work with fermentation, both as researchers and as practitioners? When I prepare a historic dish, for example, I have my own theories about how something will look or taste when I prepare it, but I won't know for sure whether those theories will hold true unless I get in the kitchen and try them. Similarly, if we watch microbes only in one particular environment (say, in one fermented food in a lab setting), we may not know what other microbes they interact with or understand how they do so in a natural environment.

BIOARCHAEOLOGY

Even as scientists are learning from research on living microbes in the present day, they are also learning new things from research on microbes from the past. As this book was being written, scientists were recovering 100-million-year-old bacteria from the deep sea floor that are dormant but still alive, proof that our understanding of the microbial world—edible and otherwise—is always evolving.

Research in bioarchaeology (the study of human skeletal remains from archaeological sites) has begun to explore the significance of microbes in shaping human history, and no doubt this will continue to be a fruitful avenue for research. Typically when we think of research into how microbes have impacted a community, we think of how pathogenic microbes have shaped populations through the spread of disease. However, more researchers are beginning to see that this is a small and incomplete part of the microbial story.

Bioarchaeologists face challenges because most of the microbiome decomposes after death, save for a few instances, for example, dental tartar and preserved feces. But observations of these remains have proven promising. As researchers Irina M. Velsko and Christina Warinner note, "Because the gut and oral microbiomes are home to the two most intensely studied and best understood human microbiota, there is great potential to compare ancient and modern microbiomes in order to observe changes through time, to infer the impact of specific activities and behaviors on the microbiome, and to correlate these with other evidence of health and disease determined through archaeological and osteological assessments." So far, exciting food-related findings have been revealed, such as the consumption of cooked plants by Neanderthals, and surely others are on the horizon. Velsko and Warinner note, "Knowledge about past foods and medicines gained from metabolites could be used to trace the introduction of specialized products into historic and prehistoric food supplies, or to confirm that only certain groups of people were consuming a given substance at a particular time and location." And this is only one of many potential avenues for exploration.

BIOSCIENCE AND MEDICAL RESEARCH

The possibilities are endless for bioscience and medical research, too. For example, we know that epigenetics (the study of heritable changes in our gene expression) has a nutritional component, and that fermentation boosts the bioavailability of nutrients that are critical to epigenetic processes (such as folate, an important nutrient for preventing birth defects). Numerous studies have looked at the effects of epigenetics across generations to see what information is passed along and what is not (this is where we get studies about the genetic component of intergenerational trauma). I have not seen any studies yet, however, that explicitly cover the impact of fermented foods on epigenetics or intergenerational epigenetics, but I do hope someone researches it, particularly as it may offer very useful findings to individual and family health.

Bioanthropologist and medical college faculty member Ellen Ireland talked me through a bit of the science behind epigenetics and nutrition, and how our nutrition can impact our genetic expression, and in some cases cause changes to our DNA itself. As she notes, while our understanding of intergenerational epigenetic changes is limited, we do know that there are long-lasting epigenetic changes within a single individual during their lifetime. As such, the study of ferments and genetics could have a real and powerful impact on medicine.

Research, for example, shows that for people deficient in vitamin B_{12}, iron, and folate (such as some elderly people and vegetarians), fermented foods might supply these nutrients in ways that are most usable for the body. As Ireland explains, "Some of these nutrients can be produced by microbes (most famously yeasts) and some can be made more bioavailable due to microbial action." Research is beginning to emerge that the impact of these nutrients is profound and long lasting: This pathway is an important part of mitochondrial DNA methylation (a mechanism that controls how our bodies express our genetic code), and research with rats shows that changes in vitamin B_{12} and folate intake in a rat can result in changes in the DNA expression in their offspring. This has potential implications for nutrition and genetics studies, but also for research on intergenerational trauma, healing, and environmental stressors, which current research suggests can alter DNA methylation (and thus gene expression and health) and thus have physical effects on future generations.

MICROBIOLOGY AND BOTANY

While there are many exciting areas to begin exploring, researchers are already regularly forging new paths in microbiology, helping us more clearly understand our longtime relationship with our microbial friends. A 2020 study by neuroscientists Katherine Bryant, Christi Hansen, and Erin Hecht (still under review at the time of this writing) points to the exciting possibility that fermented foods had an impact on the evolution of our brains, not just our gut microbiome. The researchers argue that the consumption of fermented foods triggered the evolutionary expansion of our brains. In other words, eating fermented foods literally made our ancestors' brains larger. They write, "Here, we propose that the initial metabolic trigger of hominid brain expansion may have been the consumption of externally fermented foods. We define 'external fermentation' as occurring outside the body, as opposed to the internal fermentation that occurs through the gut microbiome. This practice could have begun accidentally and with limited understanding, but over time, fermentation technologies may have become increasingly intentional, socially-transmitted, and culturally-reinforced."

Botanists are also making microbial connections to plants through a greater understanding of mycorrhizal networks in soil—vast underground networks of mycelial fungi that are in a symbiotic relationship with plant roots. For example, evolutionary ecologist Monica Gagliano's research has shown the importance not only of recognizing interconnectivity but also of using it to guide responsible action. As Gagliano says, 'Responsibility is that which you are moving toward,' the plants have told me. 'It is not a moral obligation, but rather the actual movement that supports the expression of care.'"

When we consider a single thread of fungus alone, its ability to nourish the plants around it is inherently limited. But when we consider it in a network, it becomes a powerful part of something bigger. And it becomes nourished in turn as it nourishes others: While the fungus brings needed nutrients and water to trees, it also receives sugars from them, which the fungus cannot produce by itself. In order for that network to be successful, nourishment must flow in both directions, and all actors participate in nourishing and being nourished in turn. This means thinking of the long-term health of the community and supporting all its members.

BIOTECHNOLOGY AND COMMUNITY INVOLVEMENT

We have learned a lot through the scientific study of fermentation and the business of creating microbes in a lab, but we are only beginning to scratch the surface. Undoubtedly we'll continue to see studies that further outline how our eternal relationship with microbial collaborators has changed our bodies and minds. But what if we look beyond the microbial actions themselves to the impact of their results? Studies show that fermented foods have higher levels of certain nutrients, as we saw in Chapter 4, but what else can we learn from them?

Sudeep Agarwala is a program director at Ginkgo Bioworks, a synthetic biology company in Boston focused on engineering more efficient microbial metabolisms (or the process by which bodies convert fuel into energy)—specifically, for different yeasts. When he discusses his work within microbiology with me, he approaches it with an air of excitement that's almost palpable:

> I love being able to think about genes inside microbes. With single-celled microbes—yeast and bacteria—because they're so small and because they grow so quickly, you have a collection of mutations that span every gene in their DNA in a small tube you hold in the palm of your hand. You can "understand" their genetics using different tests of their capability to grow, and you can be clever about understanding how they function. It's a unique opportunity to understand biology.

In early 2020, during coronavirus lockdowns, Agarwala wrote a Twitter thread about capturing and working with wild yeasts to bake bread, at a time when many people found themselves stuck at home without access to starter cultures (such as instant dry yeast). His thread went viral. Many people have come to microbiology through their cupboard, and hopefully this interest will lead to more conversations about what the world of microbiology can do because, as Agarwala notes, the research happening now in biotechnology will have big impacts into the future. Exciting things are afoot, and the time to learn and discuss is now. Agarwala says:

> Biotechnology is at such an exciting juncture right now. I think a lot of people are thinking about food right now, but there is so much more that can be done. How can we develop microbes to help with climate change? How will we use them for beauty products? For fashion? How can we make quality of life better? Can we use them for drugs? We've been exploring these topics for a very long time, but we're entering into an age where exploration stops and we start

developing solutions. And we need to be thinking about this as a society, too: How will we think of a world that has been changed by biotechnology? Is that something we want? And if not, what are we willing to change in order to not have this become a necessity? I hope people would start talking about these issues with scientists—we're so close to exciting (or terrifying) things.

The future of fermentation research is incredibly bright, and we are only now beginning to plumb the depths of understanding our history—and future—with the unseen beings of our world. Research into the health benefits and other ways that fermented foods impact humans continues to be published, but, of course, the study of fermentation goes well beyond its effects on humans.

Ferments and Interconnection

When you conduct research on any topic, microbes included, you must frame what you're studying within the larger context of the world in which it exists. For fermentation microbes, this means their physical environments (our world and our own bodies) as well as the impacts we and other forces have upon those environments. According to Janine Benyus, "What life does is create conditions conducive to life." Kenny Ausubel notes in *Dreaming the Future: Reimagining Civilization in the Age of Nature* that for millennia, indigenous communities worldwide lived alongside and within their natural surroundings, recognizing themselves as interconnected within the natural world rather than separate or "better." Over time, some European cultures and others shifted toward viewing nature as a commodity, asking "What will this give me?" rather than living in exchange, as mycorrhizal networks do.

As these cultures colonized other areas of the globe, they treated the natural world and the humans in those spaces as commodities rather than communities—"natural resources" to be used, transplanted, destroyed, or replaced to serve market needs. In fact, some authors and indigenous activists frame the idea of "wilderness" itself as a colonial

> Fermentation [also] provides us with a powerful metaphor with
> infinite regenerative power. Especially at this perilous precipice,
> we need the creative force of fermentation. We are desperate for
> agitation and excitement in every realm of our lives. Our multiple
> existential challenges demand broad movements for social change.
> Simultaneously, and inextricably linked, are growing psychosocial
> challenges, demanding transformation in more ethereal interior
> realms, such as mental health, sexuality, and spirituality.
>
> —SANDOR ELLIX KATZ, *FERMENTATION AS METAPHOR*

concept, as it creates a separation between us and the natural world, with parts of the world being considered "wild," while others (such as a suburban grass lawn) are removed from natural spaces. This othering makes it easier to continue encroaching upon wilderness: It's much easier to cut down a forest to build a development if humans are the only creatures you consider to be part of your community.

Thinking about how microbes operate in community—from mycorrhizal networks to our very own microbiome—moves "wilderness" and all its messy and beautiful interconnections away from being something that is at a distance and puts it within our homes and bodies. Like communities on a macro scale, micro-communities fight over resources and displace each other, and like our human communities, microbial communities (along with the flora and fauna those communities support) continuously work toward the goal of caring for the communities that are important to them, whether it's a community of yeasts feeding and multiplying upon fallen fruit in an orchard or a community of bacteria or fungi offering nourishment and protection to its host (like your microbiome does for you).

These networks exchange nutrients, but they do more as well. Forest mycorrhizal fungal networks are colloquially called the Wood Wide Web (a term coined by Suzanne Simard, the forest ecologist who first published about these networks), as these fungal networks carry messages between trees, allowing them to communicate with each other. Likewise, our own microbiome sends us messages, influencing the foods we crave and even our mood, showing that perhaps we depend upon our interconnection with microbes more than we realize.

Understanding microbes and ourselves in an interconnected world means personalizing that world—what author and environmentalist Kirkpatrick Sale calls "human scale." Sale argues that returning to interconnection requires decentralization: breaking apart and restructuring (or not) the institutions within our world that serve as barriers between ourselves and the environment around us. In doing so, Sale argues, these "human-scale" units of power will be local: local communities rooted in local environments, guided by local citizens.

To me, this means building up community power so that our neighborhoods and towns are more interconnected and less reliant on top-down systems that control, for example, what food is available and for how much. While some large-scale systems (such as the internet) serve us well, other large-scale systems may not. Our relationship with microbes can serve as a useful metaphor here: Though we are a host for and in close relationship with our microbiome, we can influence it but not control it entirely. Instead, we (larger entity) and microbiome (community of smaller entities) work together toward a common goal (the overall health and well-being of all members in this communal relationship).

As Sandor Katz notes in *Fermentation as Metaphor*, this is as much about adjusting our expectations of ourselves as it is adjusting our view of the environment:

> What we need is contraction: each of us leaving a much lighter footprint, with more equitable distribution of resources. We also need to shift from our focus on individualism to more cooperative, collaborative models for working together and mutual aid. I have no grand plan, and in our current corporate-dominated political system I've become skeptical of grand plans. But moving in this direction definitely involves getting more people plugged into the earth and life around us, the plants and animals and fungi and even the bacteria. This is what food production forces us to do— to be more tuned into our environment. Certainly this is true of fermentation.

What seems clear is that human knowledge of fermentation arose independently throughout human cultures, that each culture attributed its appearance to divine intervention, and that its use is intimately bound up with our development as a species. Frederich Nietzsche touches on this truth when he remarks that "Man is no longer an artist, he has become a work of art."

—STEPHEN HARROD BUHNER, *SACRED AND HERBAL HEALING BEERS*

A Bright Future

When I think of the future of fermentation, I don't think of a particular production method, flavor profile, or culinary trend (although there are plenty of each I'm excited about). Instead, I think about people: the community of humans interacting with communities of microbes for the many and various ends toward which we use fermentation. It is this human element—using food as a bridge between people and as a way to expand our minds and palates—that really gets me excited.

The fermentation community is, by and large, an incredibly rich, friendly, open, and connected space. The #kojibuildscommunity hashtag started by Rich Shih, for instance, is a powerful example of fermenters sharing knowledge within an evolving space (Instagram). When folks use the hashtag on posts showing what they've made, there is an implicit understanding that the posts are meant to be interactive. Commenters share ideas and ask questions, making that koji-loving community a particularly dynamic one.

We have many ways we can grow our connection to our microbial partners in our home kitchens and personal lives. One thing I've found in teaching fermentation is that many of us are eager to connect more fully to place and to people. With modern food systems so depersonalized, it can be hard to make these connections when we're using produce or prepared food from a grocery store. Doing a fermentation project, which adds heart and soul back into food, is a powerful way to connect with people and places (as is, of course, supporting your local growers or growing some of your own food). We have a desire to seek out alternatives to the homogenized foods that globalization has brought us—to seek out foods that are made by people, perhaps small business owners, using simpler methods and more care than can be accommodated when food is produced on a massive scale.

We also have a desire to return to homemade foods as a way to build and share identity and to taste ingredients and dishes that feel more meaningful than mass-produced products. After all, many of the staples we now buy from the store—bread, butter, cheese, pickles—were all once made at home. As Ken Albala and Rosanna Nafziger Henderson write, these recipes "can all be made in the smallest of kitchens without expensive equipment, capturing flavors that speak of place and reflect the labor that rewards only through the sweat of one's brow."

We begin to see a paradigm shift away from being externally focused and toward being internally focused when we ask ourselves: What am I able to make? What do I want to make? Who do I want and need to make food for, and how can I prepare that food while honoring my own internal compass to explore, with ferments and beyond? As Albala and Nafziger Henderson say, "It is time—not to literally turn back the clock, but to reclaim our food heritage. To proudly eat and drink food difficult to prepare because we now know it is worth it, to benefit our bodies, our souls, and the health of our planet and its inhabitants."

Ferments offer us so many ways to play and connect to ourselves as we work alongside our microbial friends. The ideas I've shared in this chapter just barely scratch the surface of possibilities for how our connections with ferments will grow in the future. And the ferments themselves will grow, too. If you look up synonyms for *ferment*, they include *uproar*, *agitation*, and *effervescence*. These words, like our ferments, seem exciting and, in many cases, tumultuous, but in all cases, they are infused with action: Whether tumultuous or calm, fermentation is never still.

PAWPAW "AMBA"

Amba is a pickled mango condiment that is popular in Iraq and Israel. Here I've taken a rough approximation of the amba process and applied it to wild foods indigenous to my area. As our climate continues to feel the impacts of our behavior, one of the ways we can lessen those impacts is through a return to the sustainable consumption of wild plants and locally grown foods.

Pawpaw is sweeter and more banana-y than a mango, so I find that adding some vinegar keeps the amba from becoming cloying. I also find that a short fermentation time works best: Because the pawpaw is so sweet, fermenting it for too long can add some funky, yeasty flavors. As always, experiment to see what you like!

MAKES
1 PINT

1	**cup pawpaw fruit pulp** (see facing page)
1	**tablespoon unrefined salt**
¼	**teaspoon whole coriander seeds**
¼	**teaspoon whole fennel seeds**
¼	**teaspoon whole fenugreek seeds**
¼	**teaspoon whole mustard seeds**
¼	**teaspoon whole peppercorns**
1 or 2	**dried cayenne peppers or a spoonful of ground Aleppo pepper**
1	**pinch ground cinnamon**
1	**pinch ground cloves**
1	**pinch ground mace**
1	**pinch ground sumac**
1	**head garlic, peeled and minced**
¼	**cup extra-virgin olive oil**
1	**tablespoon red wine vinegar**
1	**tablespoon distilled white vinegar**

1   Combine the pawpaw pulp and salt in a pint jar and mix until the salt dissolves. Seal with the lid and allow to ferment at room temperature for about 24 hours.

2   Toast the coriander, fennel, fenugreek, mustard, and peppercorn in a dry skillet over medium heat until fragrant, then grind them along with your whole cayenne pepper(s) or Aleppo pepper.

3   Add the toasted spice mixture and the cinnamon, cloves, mace, sumac, and garlic to the fermented pawpaw. Add the oil and red and white vinegars. Stir to evenly incorporate all the ingredients.

4   Store in an airtight container in the refrigerator. The amba will keep for several weeks.

GETTING PAWPAW PULP

If you live in the mid-Atlantic region or southern Appalachian Mountains of the United States, pawpaw is a native fruit worth getting to know. With a flavor reminiscent of banana and mango, it's equally at home in a vegan frozen custard or eaten raw. I like it in chutneys and pickles. You can use pawpaw as a substitute for mango or banana, but keep in mind that pawpaw fruit tends to be very soft, so this works best in recipes that use mango or banana sauce or pulp rather than firm cubes.

To separate the pawpaw fruit pulp from the seeds, I find it's most efficient to cut the fruit in half and press it through the holes of a colander that's been placed over a mixing bowl. This is far easier than trying to pull out each seed individually!

SOM TAM SAUERKRAUT

Som tam, or green papaya salad, is one of my favorite Thai dishes, and the complex, balanced flavor translates well to a fermented sauerkraut-like dish. The traditional salad is pounded together using a mortar and pestle, so to emulate that somewhat I pre-chop the aromatics, then massage them together with the cabbage and papaya. The recipe calls for long beans (sometimes called asparagus beans or Chinese long beans), a mild-flavored long, skinny legume. If you can't find them, you can substitute fresh green beans.

Recipe continues on next page. >

You can and should adjust the ratios of the ingredients to suit your palate. I taste and adjust throughout the preparation process, bearing in mind it will get more sour over time.

MAKES
ABOUT 1
QUART

2	**cloves garlic, minced**
2	**tablespoons nam pla** (Thai fish sauce)
1/2	**tablespoon small dried shrimp**
2	**teaspoons palm sugar**
1	**tablespoon tamarind juice**
	Juice of 1 lime
1/2	**green papaya, julienned**
1	**small head cabbage, shredded**
1	**small carrot, grated or julienned**
1/2	**pint cherry tomatoes, halved**
2	**red bird's-eye chiles, finely diced**
1	**long bean or 4 or 5 fresh green beans, cut into 1/2- to 1-inch pieces**
1	**tablespoon peanuts, toasted on the stove until just fragrant**

1   Combine the garlic, nam pla, shrimp, sugar, tamarind juice, and lime juice in a large bowl and whisk together.

2   Add the papaya, cabbage, and carrot, and massage or pound all the ingredients together until the cabbage begins to release its liquid. Taste and adjust the seasoning as needed. You're going for something that lights up every part of your palate: sweet, sour, salty, perhaps a touch bitter, and savory.

3   Add the tomatoes, chiles, beans, and peanuts, and toss to combine.

4   Transfer the mixture to a crock or other fermentation vessel and cover with a lid or a cloth secured with twine. Allow to ferment until it reaches the flavor and texture you want. I usually let this ferment for only 4 to 7 days, so the cabbage stays pretty crisp and the papaya pieces aren't overly soft.

5   Store in the fridge, where the kraut will keep for several months.

PICKLE POWDER

Fermenters are always reconnecting with old ways of doing things. This recipe for using up scraps is a way to reconnect to old food-saving traditions as well as a chance to experiment with new seasoning blends.

I first made dried fermented seasonings like these years ago, using ferments I had in excess (for instance, sauerkraut) as well as the scraps from vinegar projects and other ferments. Of course, the more I learned about the history of fermentation, the more I saw examples of our ancestors creatively using up food scraps or preserving excess food stores. What is old is new again.

1   Collect the fermented fruit or vegetable (or even fish or meat) scraps and pop them in a dehydrator set to around 130°F/54°C to preserve their probiotic properties. If you don't have a dehydrator, you can set them out on racks or sheet pans and place them in an oven on its lowest setting. Or if you have a safe place outdoors away from critters and bugs (such as a solar dehydrator), you can also sun-dry them. Dehydrate your scraps until they are bone-dry; any moisture could cause mold later on.

2   Once the scraps are dry, use a mortar and pestle, coffee grinder (dedicated to spices), food processor, or blender to grind them to the desired consistency.

3   Store in an airtight jar.

FAVORITE PICKLE POWDERS

I make pickle powders with just about anything I can get my hands on. Here are a few favorites:

- **LACTO-FERMENTS WITH GREAT FLAVOR BUT MUSHY TEXTURE.** If you let your full-sour cucumber pickles sit too long, this is a great way to repurpose them.

- **FRUIT SOLIDS FROM WINEMAKING AND FROM OTHER BEVERAGES.** The grape skins strained from my muscadine wine yield a subtly flavored but beautifully colorful seasoning to make my food pop visually. Ditto for the beets from beet kvass.

- **SCRAPS FROM MAKING FIRE CIDER.** After you strain fire cider, you're left with a heaping helping of aromatic scraps. Drying them gives you a flavor-packed seasoning that is fantastic on meats, roasted veggies, or anything grilled. Fire cider seasoning also makes a wonderful wintertime gift.

- **VINEGAR SUBSTRATES.** If, like me, you use vegetable scraps for making vinegar, this can yield some really fun results. I regularly make vinegar from jalapeño and strawberry tops, and both the vinegar and the resulting pickle powder are amazing! Another favorite uses scraps from peppers, onions, and garlic, or the peels and little end pieces from ginger along with bird's-eye chile and garlic.

- **FISH SAUCE.** After I strain the liquid from my garum (or any other fish sauce), I take the salt and fish solids (removing any large bones) and pulse them in a food processor to incorporate them with the salt, then I dry the whole thing. This is significantly easier than drying them first and trying to grind them later.

- **MEAT AMINO SAUCE.** As with the fish sauce pickle powder, I strain out the meat solids and salt, pulse them in a food processor, then dry the whole thing. I made a pickle powder with the dregs of a rabbit, peach, and muscadine amino sauce, and it made a great seasoning. Just make sure to remove the bones before processing.

CHERYL PASWATER'S ROASTED CORN MISO

Cheryl Paswater of Contraband Ferments is one of the many amazing fermenters out there doing creative things with koji. Here is one of her many creations: a tasty roasted corn miso that is ready in less than 2 weeks.

MAKES 1
QUART

2 **cups fresh corn kernels**

1 **cup koji**

3 **tablespoons unrefined salt**

Flavorings (jalapeños, garlic, thyme, or red chiles; optional)

1   Preheat the oven to 350°F/180°C.

2   Place 1½ cups of the corn kernels on a sheet pan and roast until golden and fragrant with slightly blackened bits here and there, about 15 minutes. Allow to cool.

3   Combine the roasted corn kernels with the remaining ½ cup raw corn kernels, the koji, and the salt in a quart jar. Add enough water to cover, then put on the lid. Shake the jar well. Place in a cool, dark place and ferment until the corn miso is foggy in color and shows signs of bubbling, 5 to 10 days.

4   Transfer the mixture to a blender and blend until it has the consistency of loose paste. Add flavorings, if desired, and blend again. Then ferment until its flavor is deeper and slightly savory, another 2 to 10 days. Once it has a flavor you enjoy, store in the fridge in an airtight container.

Appendix: Tricks and Tools

There are many how-to books out there that give a more in-depth review of basic fermentation equipment and techniques, and I encourage you to explore those. Some of my favorites are the books by Kirsten and Christopher Shockey, Sandor Katz's *Wild Fermentation*, and Alex Lewin's *Real Food Fermentation*.

This section offers you a brief overview of how I collect and use tools as a historian and generally curious cook, along with some basic tips and terminology.

SIMPLE TOOLS, USED WITH INTENTION

Most of the time, I don't use high-tech gadgets in my kitchen, and I insist on teaching without them. An exception is a thermometer, though when I use one in the classroom it's to teach students how a temperature feels so that eventually they may not need to use one.

Everything we use—unless it's a raw material—could and should be considered technology: fermentation crocks, refined sugar, and even a simple wooden spoon. The term *technology* is a combination of the Greek *techne* (an art, skill, or craft) and *logia* (the study of something). It is, very simply, the creation of tools and techniques to serve certain purposes in our lives. As food writer Bee Wilson says, a wooden spoon "looks like the opposite of 'technology.' . . . It does not switch on and off or make funny noises. . . . There is nothing futuristic or shiny or clever about it. But look closer at one of your wooden spoons. . . . Countless decisions—economic and social as well as those pertaining to design and applied engineering have gone into the making of this object. And these in turn will affect the way this device enables you to cook."

Everything from the length of a spoon's handle to its shape and depth to the type of wood that was used to craft it is a choice made by its maker, who was engaging in technological creation when making these decisions. Well before modern times, our hominid and early human predecessors relied on technologies they crafted for cooking and serving food as well as catching it. They also had the know-how to choose certain tools for certain situations (say, when to use stone or clay rather than wood). As demands changed and tools were no longer needed, tools were adapted or abandoned. As Wilson notes, "Scientific discovery does not depend on usage for its validity; technology does. When equipment falls out of use, it expires. However shrewdly designed it may be, an eggbeater does not fully achieve its purpose unless someone picks it up and beats eggs."

This is why some of the historic tools found at archaeological sites leave researchers scratching their heads. The tools worked for that time period but then were left behind as our ancestors' cooking needs and habits changed. This is also one of the reasons why I encourage you to start simple: By cultivating an understanding of what tools work for you and your practice (Do you prefer crocks and weights over jars? Are you making more beverages than food?), you can focus on *which* of those simple tools you want to invest in. Then you won't have to worry about the technologies you choose going obsolete in your kitchen. Of course, if you want to play with fancy airlocks and prefabricated incubation chambers to get more consistent results, that's great (and it can be a lot of fun!). But there's no harm in, and there are many benefits to, starting simply and building up.

The other reason I encourage minimal equipment is that it makes it easier to engage mindfully with our food. When we aren't hiding behind extensive gadgetry, we have more control (and responsibility) as well as more understanding of the processes taking place. We can discover what koji feels like when the warm grains begin to inoculate with soft, fragrant spores, or experience how a fresh cabbage releases liquid as it is massaged on its journey to becoming sauerkraut. Starting simply means engaging physically with a process and being present throughout, truly understanding what is happening so that we are better able to appreciate, troubleshoot, and enjoy.

Below are my go-to tools—the ones I always have on hand. I hope these simple technologies bring you years of fermentation joy, as they have for me.

CROCKS AND WEIGHTS

A good fermentation crock is worth its weight in gold to a fermentation enthusiast. You can buy new crocks and weights from larger companies such as Ohio Stoneware and from a whole host of individual artisans. Look around your local community to see who is slinging clay and who may already be making crocks or might be willing to custom-make one for you.

If you buy an antique crock, make sure that it has a lead-free, food-safe glaze and that it's watertight and free of cracks, or else it can make a mess on your counter and also harbor unwanted microbes. If you don't want to use crocks (or can't find one), there are other options. Korean markets, for example, often have affordable plastic kimchi makers, which are simply rectangular boxes with a snap-on lid.

There are weights designed to be set inside crocks to keep your substrate submerged in the brine. They are handy to have around because they fit inside the crock like a glove, leaving little room for errant bits of fruits and veggies to float to the surface. If you want to purchase weights, they are available in a range of sizes, from small glass weights that fit in a mason jar to huge stoneware disks for massive crocks. A simple search online will reveal a world of options, across many materials and price ranges.

If you don't have weights, you can use a bowl, plate, ceramic pie pan, or other food-safe and nonreactive dish to weigh down your substrate. Some folks use a plastic bag filled with water or dried beans, though the waste-averse among us may not appreciate that option. You can also use river stones, a personal favorite of mine. If you do, just make sure you boil them for at least 30 minutes before you use them to kill off any lingering microbes and to remove dirt that might be clinging in nooks and crannies.

TEA TOWELS OR CUT-UP SHEETS

If your fermentation vessel does not come with a lid, it's key that you have another covering on hand. Thrift-store sheets, thoroughly washed and cut up, make great coverings, but a simple tea towel is perfect, too. Cloth coverings are also useful when you're doing something where you *want* oxygen, as with vinegar making.

Whether you use a tea towel or a sheet, use a length of twine or a rubber band around the top of your container to secure the cloth in place. This keeps it from being accidentally pulled off by human or animal kitchen helpers, and it prevents fruit flies and other bugs from climbing under the towel and getting into your ferment.

PERMANENT MARKER AND MASKING TAPE

Labeling your ferments is critical, particularly as you start to make a lot of them. I simply use a roll of masking tape or blue painter's tape and a permanent marker, as in commercial kitchens, but you should use whatever method of labeling you prefer.

At the very least, put the name of the ferment and the date you made it on your label. I will often also list the ingredients that went into the ferment and in what amounts, and I will note the dates that I made any follow-up changes to the ferment (such as bottling a mead) as well as the date I put it in the fridge.

JARS OF ALL SIZES (PLUS LIDS)

If you have been a fermenter for some time, you know that jar hoarding is not only practical, it's a way of life. If you're new to fermentation, welcome to the fold: You'll want to start clearing out some shelf space now for all your future jars.

Like a lot of fermenters, I have an emotional attachment to some of my favorite jars, and I prefer certain jars for certain purposes. Short, wide, hinged jars are perfect for small batches of miso paste (one modern brand is Le Parfait, but you can also find them in thrift stores from time to time). And 1-gallon mason jars are perfect for making shrubs or for fermenting mead; they hold a good-size batch but I can still shake them rather than stirring, saving me from having to wash another spoon. I keep a variety of

canning

I do not recommend canning sauerkraut and other living foods because it kills the beneficial microbes, but if you do want to can your ferments, make sure to follow guidance from the *Ball Blue Book* or another trusted source.

jars, and I save ones that I particularly like from products I buy. And I've amassed a lovable hodgepodge of shapes, sizes, colors, and styles of lids.

For simplicity's sake, I enjoy jars with hinged tops because everything is in one place: I don't risk losing a specially sized lid within my unwieldy lid collection. But you will want to make sure you have lids for all the other jars (and a few extra to boot) for those ferments that need to be sealed. Reusable plastic lids for mason jars are the best for fermenting because they don't corrode. Metal lids for mason jars are fine for short ferments or to use when giving gifts, but the acid in many ferments can wear at the metal lids, leaving you with a corroded lid (that sometimes rusts itself to the jar!) as well as the potential to get rust from the lid into your food, which can affect the flavor and color.

CARBOYS, AIRLOCKS, FUNNELS, AND HOSES

You can buy these from a brewing supply store, and they're pretty cheap. Carboys are large jugs for fermenting alcohol, and airlocks are fitted to carboys to keep oxygen away from your ferment while it works its magic (you can also buy airlocks for other containers, such as mason jars, if you feel so inclined).

A funnel is useful for transferring alcohol or other liquids between containers with less mess, and a hose is useful for siphoning liquid between two containers to prevent oxygen from reaching it.

MIXING BOWLS OF ALL SIZES

I have about 30 mixing bowls in my kitchen. I live alone, and yes, this seems like far too many for just one person, but as with my jars, I use every single one of them regularly. I use small mixing bowls for quickly throwing together a small batch of veggies, gigantic bowls for when I want to get elbow-deep in a batch of kimchi, and everything in between. If you don't want to go as crazy as I do with bowls, just make sure you have a set of small, medium, and large bowls. I recommend two of each so you don't have to interrupt your flow while cooking in order to wash a dish.

MEASURING CUPS AND SPOONS

You'll need these for measuring ingredients, of course. Liquid measuring cups are also useful for pouring liquids between containers without dumping them all over the counter (or yourself).

A STRAINER AND CHEESECLOTH

A colander is helpful for straining out big chunks of stuff (such as pieces of fruit), and either a fine-mesh strainer or cheesecloth is good for catching smaller particulates. Cheesecloth is also useful for making cheese (of course) as well as for squeezing the liquid out of ingredients, for example, soybeans during shoyu making. I recommend having at least one or two fine-mesh strainers, plus a colander and a couple of packages of cheesecloth.

A SALTCELLAR

A saltcellar is simply a container of salt. It isn't a strictly necessary tool, but I like it for easy access, and for keeping my cabbage-covered hands from getting all over a bag or box of salt while I'm making sauerkraut. It's also much easier to dip fingers or a measuring spoon into a saltcellar and get just the right amount.

A saltcellar can be whatever kind of container you wish: a lidded bowl on the counter or a jar or something fun you found at a thrift store. My saltcellar is an old ceramic cheese crock from an Iowa creamery.

YOUR IMAGINATION

Our ancestors were incredibly imaginative, creative folks, just like us, and they used the tools they had available to them to build the world they wanted to live in. It is especially rewarding to connect to the natural world around you through your fermentation practice. For example, instead of layering cabbage leaves over that sauerkraut, why not use the (edible) leaves of a local foraged plant, such as invasive wild mustard? Or use a tender length of grapevine to secure a cloth over the top of a fermentation crock? You are limited only by your imagination, and the more you experiment, the wider and wilder your imagination will get!

A FEW TIPS

I offer specific tips in the recipes throughout this book, but here are more general tips that I share when I teach fermentation classes.

USE UNREFINED SALT (such as sea salt, Himalayan salt, or kosher salt). Make sure your salt contains just salt: no anticaking agents or other additives that can inhibit fermentation or alter flavor. Don't use iodized salt.

SET YOUR FERMENTING FOODS ON A TRAY or other container to catch overflow and prevent staining your countertops.

"BURP" YOUR FERMENTS ONCE A DAY IF THEY ARE IN A SEALED JAR (you can do this every couple of days if the temperature is cold). "Burping" releases built-up carbon dioxide, minimizing pressure in the jar and possibly preventing the jar from exploding. To do this, gently loosen the lid to allow excess gas that has built up during the fermentation process to escape. Top off with more brine if needed. If your container has an airlock, you don't need to worry about this step.

USE WEIGHTS TO KEEP WHATEVER YOU'RE FERMENTING UNDER THE BRINE! This inhibits the growth of mold, kahm yeast, and other unwanted critters.

quick pickles

kay, quick pickles aren't true ferments, but I often get asked about the difference between them and ferments. They are fruits, vegetables, or meats that have been preserved by being cooked or soaked in a solution of vinegar, salt (and/or sugar), and water. The vinegar creates an acidic environment that prevents microbial growth and allows for shelf stability (and delicious flavor). Quick pickles do not have the same probiotic qualities as fermented foods.

CHECK YOUR FERMENTS EVERY DAY. I have a daily practice of waking up and making coffee while I go through and check on my ferments—stirring who needs to be stirred, peeking to make sure no one has popped up out of the brine or overflowed on the shelf overnight. Regularly checking your ferments helps you catch potential issues, such as kahm yeast on top of a ferment, before it gets out of hand. And if you interact with your ferments regularly, you'll be able to better determine when to pull them.

USE FRESH, RAW VEGETABLES. Good bacteria are naturally present on fruits and veggies, and you will need this bacteria to proliferate in a wild ferment. In some cases, I've heard of people putting a bit of cooked vegetables, such as corn niblets, into a ferment, but if you do so make sure that you have far more fresh substrate than cooked.

PUT YOUR FERMENTS IN THE FRIDGE WHEN THEY HAVE THE FLAVOR YOU WANT. This slows the fermentation process to a near standstill and allows you to enjoy the ferments for a longer period of time.

SOME COMMON TYPES OF FERMENTATION

There is a good amount of overlap between different types of fermentation, so this is meant to be a quick reference and not an exhaustive list. For example, in wild fermentation, multiple types of microbes are likely to be in play, and the end result depends heavily upon the specific ways in which you set up the environment for the microbes (for example, lacto-fermenting in brine versus adding sugar to produce soda, alcohol, or vinegar).

ALCOHOL. The action of yeasts—either wild or cultured—convert sugars to ethanol. All alcohol comes from this fermentation process. Alcohol is consumed either in its postfermentation state (wine, beer, mead) or distilled (spirits).

LACTIC ACID (ALSO CALLED LACTO-FERMENTATION). The process by which *Lactobacillus* bacteria convert carbohydrates to lactic acid, which offers our bodies nutritional support while creating a more acidic environment that is inhospitable to harmful bacteria. Lacto-ferments include yogurt, cheese, kimchi, sauerkraut, and a wide variety of pickled vegetables.

MOLD. Mold starters are used to create tempeh and koji (which is grown on grains and used to make amazake, sake, and miso). Some cheeses are also mold-ripened.

SCOBY. This stands for "symbiotic culture of bacteria and yeast" and refers to a mother starter that is added to liquid to culture it. SCOBYs are used to make kombucha and kefir. Unlike other starters that are often in powder or liquid form, a SCOBY looks either like a slippery mat (for kombucha) or like translucent, soft granules (for kefir).

SOURDOUGH. A yeast starter cultivated from wild yeast, sourdough has a sour flavor from the longer action of the yeast on the carbohydrates in the grains (sourdough rises more slowly than commercially yeasted breads but also requires less kneading). Sourdough has a flavor unique to its place of origin (for example, San Francisco sourdough).

VINEGAR. Acetobacter are bacteria that produce acetic acid, the main component in vinegar, from alcohol and oxygen.

brine for sauerkraut

For sauerkraut, which is made by massaging salt into cabbage, I usually eyeball my measurements. But if you're just starting out, it can be helpful to measure.

I typically assume that half a head of cabbage will give me 1½ to 2 cups of brine (this also varies some, and that's okay). Using the measurements on the facing page, I would use roughly ½ tablespoon of salt. The science of this kind of fermentation is such that we have a little room to play with, so don't be afraid to explore a bit!

(VERY) BASIC BRINE

The measurements below are for a pour-over brine (which is used to ferment all kinds of fruits and veggies, such as carrot sticks, cucumbers, and more). When you're first learning, it can be helpful to go by weight in grams, rather than measuring by volume, because the actual measurement will vary based upon the size of the salt grains you're using. Vegetable fermentation can happen in brines between 1.5- and 5-percent salt, but a brine that is 2- to 3-percent salt yields the best flavor with most vegetables (this is a good area in which to experiment and see what you like!). Here are the measurements I teach students who are just starting out.

FOR 1 QUART (4 CUPS) OF WATER:
2% = 19 grams or about 1 tablespoon salt
3.5% = 33 grams or about 2 tablespoons salt
5% = 47 grams or about 3 tablespoons salt

FOR 1 LITER (1,000 GRAMS) OF WATER:
2% = 20 grams salt
3.5% = 35 grams salt
5% = 50 grams salt

Bibliography

ARTICLES, CHAPTERS, AND WEBSITES

Aaronson, Sheldon. "Fungi." In *The Cambridge World History of Food*, edited by Kenneth F. Kiple and Kriemhild Coneè Ornelas, 313–34. Cambridge: Cambridge University Press, 2000.

———. "Important Vegetable Supplements." In *The Cambridge World History of Food*, edited by Kenneth F. Kiple and Kriemhild Coneè Ornelas, 231–58. Cambridge: Cambridge University Press, 2000.

Abusch, Tzvi. "Mourning the Death of a Friend: Some Assyriological Notes." In *Gilgamesh: A Reader*, edited by John R. Maier, 109–21. Wauconda, IL: Bolchazy-Caducci Publishers, 1997.

Aesculapian. Volume 49: North Side Branch, Chicago Medical Society (1958).

Afshar, Dave. "A Brief History of Japanese Sake." Culture Trip, February 10, 2017. https://theculturetrip.com/asia/ japan/articles/a-brief-history-of-japanese-sake/.

Aino, Keiichi, et al. "Microbial Communities Associated with Indigo Fermentation That Thrive in Anaerobic Alkaline Environments." *Frontiers in Microbiology* 9 (2018): 2196. https://doi:10.3389/fmicb.2018.02196.

Albala, Ken. "The Origins of Probiotic Theory." *Table Matters*. https://tablematters.com/the-origins-of-probiotic-theory.

———. "Premodern Europe." In *Food in Time and Place*, edited by Paul Freedman, Joyce E. Chaplin, and Ken Albala, 21–40. Oakland: University of California Press, 2014.

———. "Superfood or Dangerous Drug? Coffee, Tea, and Chocolate in the Late 17th Century." *EuropeNow* (September 4, 2018). https://www.europenowjournal.org/2018/09/04/superfood-or-dangerous-drug-coffee-tea-and-chocolate-in-the-late-17th-century/.

Allen, Katherine. "Springtime in Recipe Books." *The Recipes Project*, March 17, 2016. https://recipes.hypotheses.org/7545.

Al Musari, Nada. "Stories of Syrian Refugees." *Oxfam Italia* (2014). https://www.oxfamitalia.org/wp-content/uploads/2014/03/Storie-di-profughi-siriani.pdf.

American College of Traditional Chinese Medicine. "Chinese Medicine." Accessed November 10, 2020. https://www.actcm.edu/chinese-medicine.

Anderson, E. N. "China." In *Food Cultures of the World Encyclopedia: Volume 3: Asia and Oceania*, edited by Ken Albala, 61–72. Santa Barbara, CA: Greenwood, 2011.

Anderson, Jarod K. "TheCryptoNaturalist." Twitter post, May 27, 2020, 3:50 p.m. https://twitter.com/CryptoNature/status/1265732003497984000.

Answer the Public. "Ferment." November 8, 2020. https://answerthepublic.com/reports/93e0bf75-af9a-44c6-aaec-ae7b80fca1e5.

Antique Book Collecting. "Paper: Cotton vs. Wood Pulp." March 30, 2013. https://bookcollecting.wordpress.com/2013/03/30/paper-cotton-vs-wood-pulp/.

Appadurai, Arjun. "Gastro-Politics in Hindu South Asia." *American Ethnologist* 8, no. 3 (1981): 494–511.

Arbor Teas. "Burmese Tea Leaf Salad or Laphet Thoke." Accessed November 11, 2020. https://www.arborteas.com/pages.php?pageid=355.

Arranz-Otaegui, Amaia, Lara Gonzalez Carretero, Monica N. Ramsey, Dorian Q. Fuller, and Tobias Richter. "Archaeobotanical Evidence Reveals the Origins of Bread 14,400 Years Ago in Northeastern Jordan." *Proceedings of the National Academy of Sciences* (July 2018): 7925–30. https://doi:10.1073/pnas.1801071115.

Ascione, Elisa, et al. "Cultivating Activism through *Terroir*: An Anthropology of Sustainable Winemakers in Umbria, Italy" *Food, Culture & Society* 23, no. 3 (April 2020): 277–95.

Asiaticus. "The Rise and Fall of the Indigo Industry in India." *The Economic Journal* 22, no. 86 (1912): 237–47.

Atassi, Omaya. "Ink on My Apron: A Second-Generation Syrian Story." Interview by Jehan Nizar. *Asiaville News*, May 15, 2019. https://www.asiavillenews.com/article/ink-on-my-apron-second-generation-syrian-story-5931.

Atina Foods. "Are Atina Pickles Ayurvedic?" Atina Foods (blog), November 23, 2020. https://www.atinafoods.com/blog/2020/11/17/why-atina-pickles-are-ayurvedic.

Awry, Wren. "Chef Mike Costello on the Power of Nuanced Food Narratives." *Bone and All*, 2019. https://www.boneandall.com/latest/nourishing-resistance/mike-costello.

———. "Spirits in the Food with Sumi Dutta." Bone and All, September 30, 2018. https://www.boneandall.com/latest/2018/9/30/spirits-in-the-food?rq=ferment.

Ayrton, Elizabeth. "True Oatmeal Flummery." 1975. Accessed November 2, 2020. https://app.ckbk.com/recipe/ cook61886c11s001ss002r007/true-oatmeal-flummery.

Bansal, R. K. "Maize." In *Plant Breeding in New Zealand*, edited by G. S. Wratt and H. C. Smith, 35–40. Wellington, NZ: Butterworths of New Zealand, 1983.

Barrett, Timothy. "European Papermaking Techniques 1300–1800." *Paper through Time: Nondestructive Analysis of 14th- through 19th-Century Papers* (August 2011). Accessed November 12, 2020. http://paper.lib.uiowa.edu/european.php.

Batsha, Nishant. "Curry before Columbus." *Contingent Magazine*, June 25, 2020. https://contingentmagazine.org/2020/06/25/curry-before-columbus/.

Battcock, Mike, and Sue Azam-Ali. *Fermented Fruits and Vegetables, a Global Perspective. FAO Agricultural Services Bulletin 134*. Rome: Food and Agriculture Organization of the United Nations, 1998. http://www.fao.org/docrep/x0560e/x0560e05.htm#Fer.

Behre, Robert. "Indigo is Long Gone as an SC Cash Crop, but Traces Linger in the Lowcountry Landscape." *Post and Courier*, July 24, 2019. https://www.postandcourier.com/news/indigo-is-long-gone-as-an-sc-cash-crop-but-traces-linger-on-the-lowcountry/article_395137ee-96af-11e9-ac0d-abac04e4e41e.html.

Beiler, Kevin J., Daniel M. Durall, Suzanne W. Simard, Sheri A. Maxwell, and Annette M. Kretzer. "Architecture of the Wood-Wide Web: *Rhizopogon* spp. genets Link Multiple Douglas-fir Cohorts." *New Phytologist* 185, no. 2 (October 2009): 543–53.

Benayoun, Mike. "Burma: Lahpet Thoke (Fermented Tea Leaf Salad)." 196 Flavors. Accessed November 11, 2020. https://www.196flavors.com/burma-lahpet-thoke-fermented-tea-leaf-salad.

Benedek, Thomas G. "Food as Aphrodisiacs and Anaphrodisiacs." In *The Cambridge World History of Food*, edited by Kenneth F. Kiple and Kriemhild Coneè Ornelas, 1523–33. Cambridge: Cambridge University Press, 2000.

Berinato, Scott. "The Restorative Power of Ritual." *Harvard Business Review*, April 2, 2020. https://hbr.org/2020/04/the-restorative-power-of-ritual.

Bhandari, Aparita. "Learning How to Eat Banchan." *The Star*, March 22, 2017. https://www.thestar.com/life/food_wine/2017/03/22/learning-how-to-eat-banchan.html.

Blakely, Julia. "Beer on Board in the Age of Sail." *Unbound: Smithsonian Libraries and Archives* (blog), August 2, 2017. https://blog.library.si.edu/blog/2017/ 08/02/beer-board-age-sail/#.X4SDi1l7nMU.

Boczkowska, Maja, Wiesław Podyma, and Bogusław Łapiński. "Oat." In *Genetic and Genomic Resources for Grain Cereals Improvement*, edited by Mohar Singh and Hari D. Upadhyaya, 159–225. Cambridge, MA: Academic Press, 2016.

Boissoneault, Lorraine. "How Coffee, Chocolate and Tea Overturned a 1,500-Year-Old Medical Mindset." *Smithsonian Magazine*, May 17, 2017. https://www.smithsonianmag.com/history/how-coffee-chocolate-and-tea-overturned-1500-year-old-medical-mindset-180963339/.

Bond, Sarah. "The Debate over Hops in Craft Beer is Positively Medieval." *Forbes*, June 22, 2016. https://www.forbes.com/sites/drsarahbond/2016/06/22/sorry-craft-beer-fanatics-but-ancient-brewers-did-not-brew-hoppy-beers/#20fa202451e7.

Bordo, Susan. "Anorexia Nervosa: Psychopathology as the Crystallization of Culture." In *Cooking, Eating, Thinking: Transformative Philosophies of Food*, edited by Deane W. Curtin and Lisa Maree Heldke, 28–55. Bloomington, IN: Indiana University Press, 1992.

Boss, Donna. "Fermented Foods Will Be No. 1 Superfood in 2018: Dieticians." *Supermarket News*, December 23, 2017. https://www.supermarketnews.com/consumer-trends/fermented-foods-will-be-no-1-superfood-2018-dietitians.

Brooke, Clarke. "Khat." In *The Cambridge World History of Food*, edited by Kenneth F. Kiple and Kriemhild Coneè Ornelas, 671–83. Cambridge: Cambridge University Press, 2000.

Bryant, Katherine, Christi Hansen, and Erin Hecht. "Fermentation Technology as a Driver of Human Brain Expansion." *Preprints* (2020): 2020100135. https://doi.org/10.20944/preprints202010.0135.v1.

Budhwar, Savita, Kashika Sethi, and Manali Chakraborty. "Efficacy of Germination and Probiotic Fermentation on Underutilized Cereal and Millet Grains." *Food Production, Processing and Nutrition* 2 (2020).

Burlington Free Press (Burlington, VT). February 3, 1837. *Chronicling America: Historic American Newspapers*, Library of Congress. Accessed November 10, 2020. https://chroniclingamerica.loc.gov/lccn/ sn84023127/1837-02-03/ed-1/seq-1/.

Bush, Austin. "Capturing Tej Bet: The Art of Drinking Ethiopia's Honey Wine." *LA Times*, November 7, 2019. https://www.latimes.com/food/story/2019-11-07/tej-bet-honey-wine-ethiopia.

Caldwell, Zelda. "The Surprisingly Sophisticated Diet of a Medieval Monk." Aleteia, September 19, 2018. https://aleteia.org/2018/09/19/the-surprisingly-sophisticated-diet-of-a-medieval-monk/.

Campana plaque (satyrs stomping the grapes), 100 BCE–100 CE, terra-cotta. In the collection of Musée Ingres, Montauban, FR.

Cemental, Ruby. "The Hotty Toddy: Grandpa's Cure for the Common Cold." *Caring Senior Service* (blog), 2021. https://www.caringseniorservice.com/blog/the-hotty-toddy-grandpas-cure-for-the-common-cold.

Chan, Miin. "Lost in the Brine." Eater, March 1, 2021. https://www.eater.com/2021/3/1/22214044/fermented-foods-industry-whiteness-kimchi-miso-kombucha.

Chang, Te-Tzu. "Rice." In *The Cambridge World History of Food*, edited by Kenneth F. Kiple and Kriemhild Coneè Ornelas, 132–48. Cambridge: Cambridge University Press, 2000.

Chartreuse. "History of the Chartreuse Liqueurs." https://www.chartreuse.fr/en/histoire/history-of-the-chartreuse-liqueurs/.

Charles, Michaela, Tasha Marks, and Susan Boyle. "A Sip of History: Ancient Egyptian Beer." The British Museum (blog), May 25, 2018. https://blog.britishmuseum.org/a-sip-of-history-ancient-egyptian-beer/.

Chen, Angus. "Were Carbs a Brain Food for Our Ancient Ancestors?" *The Salt*. NPR, August 17, 2015. https://www.npr.org/sections/thesalt/2015/08/17/432603591/were-carbs-a-brain-food-for-our-ancient-ancestors.

Chen, Emily, Edric Huang, and Jenny Dorsey. "Understanding Cultural Appropriation." Studio ATAO. https://www.studioatao.org/post/understanding-cultural-appropriation.

Choi, Amy S. "What Americans Can Learn from Other Food Cultures." Ideas.Ted.com, December 18, 2014. https://ideas.ted.com/what-americans-can-learn-from-other-food-cultures/.

Cigar City Brewing. "History of Hunahpu's Day." *Cigar City Brewing* (blog), March 15, 2020. https://www.cigarcitybrewing.com/blog/history-of-hunahpus-day/.

Cole, Brendan. "Pope Francis Praises Eating and Sex as Pleasures That 'Come from God.'" *Newsweek*, September 10, 2020. https://www.newsweek.com/pope-francis-vatican-sex-food-pleasure-divine-1530929.

Cooper-Bribiesca, Barbara, et al. "Lactic Acid Fermentation of Arabinoxylan From *Nejayote* by *Streptococcus infantarius* ssp. *infantarius* 25124 Isolated From Pozol." *Frontiers in Microbiology* 9 (2018): 3061. https://doi:10.3389/fmicb.2018.03061.

Costa, Dora L., Noelle Yetter, and Heather DeSomer. "Intergenerational Transmission of Paternal Trauma Among US Civil War ex-POWs." *Proceedings of the National Academy of Sciences* 115, no. 44 (October 2018): 11215–20.

Crane, Stephen. "In the Desert." Poetry Foundation. Accessed November 8, 2020. https://www.poetryfoundation.org/poems/46457/in-the-desert-56d2265793693.

Cryan, J. F., et al. "The Microbiota-Gut-Brain Axis." *Physiological Reviews* 99, no. 4 (2019): 19. https://doi:10.1152/physrev.00018.2018.

Curtis, Wayne. "Why We Drink Champagne on New Year's Eve." *Imbibe Magazine*, December 30, 2019. https://imbibemagazine.com/why-we-drink-champagne-on-new-years-eve/.

Daily Bonnet. "Local Woman Introduces New Extra Sour Funeral Pickles." April 30, 2017. https://dailybonnet.com/local-woman-introduces-new-extra-sour-funeral-pickles/.

Dash, Hirak R., et al. "Marine Bacteria: Potential Candidates for Enhanced Bioremediation." *Applied Microbiology and Biotechnology* 97 (2013): 561–71. https://link.springer.com/article/10.1007/s00253-012-4584-0.

Dashko, Sofia, et al. "Why, When, and How Did Yeast Evolve Alcoholic Fermentation?" *FEMS Yeast Research* 14, no. 6 (2014): 826–32. https://doi:10.1111/1567-1364.12161.

Day, Ivan. "More on Hippocras." *Historic Food*. Accessed November 2, 2020, https://www.historicfood.com/Hippocras%20Recipes.htm.

Dean, Sam. "What the Irish Ate Before Potatoes." *Bon Appétit*, March 11, 2013. https://www.bonappetit.com/trends/article/what-the-irish-ate-before-potatoes.

Delwen, Samuel. "Archaeology of Ancient Egyptian Beer." *Journal of the American Society of Brewing Chemists* 54, no. 1 (1996): 3–12.

de Wet, J. M. J. "Sorghum." In *The Cambridge World History of Food*, edited by Kenneth F. Kiple and Kriemhild Coneè Ornelas, 152–57. Cambridge: Cambridge University Press, 2000.

Dictionary of the Scots Language. "Sid." https://www.dsl.ac.uk/entry/snd/sid.

Dinakaran, Vaishali. "Why This German 'Rum Pot' Will Always Have a Place in My Kitchen." Food52, December 4, 2019. https://food52.com/blog/24813-what-is-rumtopf.

Dinerstein, Rebecca. "Ode to Norwegian Brown Cheese." *The New Yorker*, June 11, 2015. https://www.newyorker.com/culture/culture-desk/ode-to-norwegian-brown-cheese.

Dirar, Hamid. "Sudan's Fermented Food Heritage." In *Applications of Biotechnology to Traditional Fermented Foods*, 27–34. Washington, DC: National Academies Press, 1992.

Dorsey, Jenny. "A Sound Way to Organize Your Spices." *Diced* (blog), June 9, 2020. https://www.ice.edu/blog/best-way-to-organize-spices.

———. "Building Flavors with Pantry Staples." Preserving Abundance Virtual Festival, May 2, 2020. https://root-kitchens.com/events/may-2nd-preserving-abundance-virtual-festival/.

———. "Naem: The Art of Fermentation with Sticky Rice." *Life & Thyme*, January 29, 2019. https://lifeandthyme.com/recipes/naem-the-art-of-fermentation-with-sticky-rice/.

Downes, Lawrence. "Poi, the Root of All Hawaii." *New York Times*, July 16, 2003. https://www.nytimes.com/2003/07/16/dining/poi-the-root-of-all-hawaii.html.

Dunn, Frederick L. "Beriberi." In *The Cambridge World History of Food*, edited by Kenneth F. Kiple and Kriemhild Coneè Ornelas, 915–19. Cambridge: Cambridge University Press, 2000.

Dutta, Sumita. "Spirits in the Food: A Pedagogy for Cooking and Healing." Thesis, Georgia State University, 2016. https://scholarworks.gsu.edu/wsi_theses/57/.

Easterday, Nicole. "Cheesemaking: What to Do with All That Whey?" FARMcurious, April 1, 2020. https://www.farmcurious.com/blogs/farmcurious/17599408-cheesemaking-what-to-do-with-all-that-whey.

Emi, Doi. "The Fermentation Prescription: Building Immunity from the Ground Up." Nippon.com, May 11, 2020. https://www.nippon.com/en/japan-topics/c08001/.

Endo, A., T. Irisawa, L. Dicks, and S. Tanasupawat, "Fermentations of East and Southeast Asia." In *Encyclopedia of Food Microbiology, 2nd ed.*, vol. 1, edited by Carl A. Batt and Mary-Lou Tortorello, 846–51. London: Academic Press, 2014.

Europe Now. "Terroir, Wine Culture, and Globalization: What Does Terroir Do to Wine?" September 5, 2018. https://www.europenowjournal.org/2018/09/04/terroir-wine-culture-and-globalization-what-does-terroir-do-to-wine/.

Facaros, Dana, and Michael Pauls. "Formadi Frant." Italian Food Decoder. Accessed November 1, 2020. https://www.facarospauls.com/apps/italian-food-decoder/10757/formadi-frant.

Fantahun, Arefaynie. "Tej Bet: Ethiopia's Honey-Wine Houses." Explore Parts Unknown, July 18, 2018. https://explorepartsunknown.com/ethiopia/tej-bet-ethiopias-honey-wine-houses/.

Farag, M. A., M. M. Elmassry, M. Baba, et al. "Revealing the Constituents of Egypt's Oldest Beer Using Infrared and Mass Spectrometry." *Scientific Reports* 9 (2019): 16199.

Fermentation Association, The. "Functional Food & Beverage Sales Grew 7.5% to $68 Billion in Sales." May 23, 2019. https://fermentationassociation.org/functional-food-beverage-sales-grew-7-5-to-68-billion-in-sales/.

Fermentation Culture. "Fermented Southern Chow Chow Relish." May 24, 2017. http://www.fermentationculture.com/southern-chow-chow-relish/.

Ferraz, Luciana. "The Ayurvedic Perspective on Fermented Foods." Banyan Botanicals, May 25, 2021. https://www.banyanbotanicals.com/info/blog-the-banyan-insight/details/ayurveda-on-fermented-foods/.

Ferry, David. "Does Your Gut Hold the Secret to Performance?" *Outside*, January 15, 2018. https://www.outsideonline.com/2274441/no-gut-no-glory.

Field, Robert C. "Cruciferous and Green Leafy Vegetables." In *The Cambridge World History of Food*, edited by Kenneth F. Kiple and Kriemhild Coneè Ornelas, 288–98. Cambridge: Cambridge University Press, 2000.

Fine, Julia. "'Half-Coloured with Turmeric': The Visual Function of Spices in Early Modern Britain." The Oxford Symposium on Food and Cookery, July 10–August 2, 2020.

Fleischmann's Yeast. "History of Fleischmann's Yeast." https://www.fleischmannsyeast.com/our-history/.

Flowers, FreeDom. "Herbal Beer: An Ancient Drink for Modern Times." The Herbal Academy, October 5, 2018. https://theherbalacademy.com/herbal-beer-recipe/.

Fontaine, Laurence. "Makeshift, Women and Capability in Preindustrial European Towns." In *Female Agency in the Urban Economy*, edited by Deborah Simonton and Anne Montenach, 56–72. New York: Routledge, 2013.

Food Feminism Fermentation. Accessed November 9, 2020. http://www.foodfeminismfermentation.com/.

Food Journal. "Sowans." November 1, 1871, 478.

Forster, Francoise Sabban Elborg. "China." In *The Cambridge World History of Food*, edited by Kenneth F. Kiple and Kriemhild Coneè Ornelas, 1165–74. Cambridge: Cambridge University Press, 2000.

Frédéric, Marie-Claire. *Ni Cru Ni Cuit* (blog). http://nicrunicuit.com.

Fuhrman, Jed A. "Microbial Community Structure and Its Functional Implications." *Nature* 459 (2009): 193–99. https://doi:10.1038/nature08058

Fullas, Fekadu. "Gesho (Rhamnus prinoides L 'Hér): A Flavorant and Medicinal Plant." *Satenaw News*, December 5, 2017. https://www.satenaw.com/gesho-rhamnus-prinoides-l-flavorant-medicinal-plant/.

Gänzle, M. G. "Sourdough Bread." In *Encyclopedia of Food Microbiology, 2nd ed.*, vol. 1, edited by Carl A. Batt and Mary-Lou Tortorello, 309–15. London: Academic Press, 2014.

Galloway, J. H. "Sugar." In *The Cambridge World History of Food*, edited by Kenneth F. Kiple and Kriemhild Coneè Ornelas, 437–49. Cambridge: Cambridge University Press, 2000.

Gattuso, Reina. "The Return of Japan's Female Sake Brewers." Gastro Obscura, December 10, 2019. https://www.atlasobscura.com/articles/women-sake-brewers-in-japan.

George Washington's Mount Vernon. "Cherry Bounce." Accessed November 2, 2020. https://www.mountvernon.org/inn/recipes/article/cherry-bounce/.

Gibson, Rosalind S., Leah Ancheta Perlas, and Christine Hotz. "Improving the Bioavailability of Nutrients in Plant Foods at the Household Level." *Proceedings of the Nutrition Society* 65, no. 2 (2006): 160–68.

Gilbert, Jack A., and Josh D. Neufeld. "Life in a World without Microbes." *PLOS Biology* 12, no. 12 (December 2014): e1002020. https://doi:10.1371/journal.pbio.1002020.

Goody, Maria. "Trust Your Gut: A Beginner's Guide to Intuitive Eating." NPR, November 5, 2019. https://www.npr.org/2019/05/23/726236988/trust-your-gut-a-beginners-guide-to-intuitive-eating.

Google Trends. "Ferment" search term interest over time. Accessed November 10, 2020. https://trends.google.com/trends/explore?q=ferment&geo=US.

Gorvett, Zaria. "The Mystery of the Lost Roman Herb." BBC, September 7, 2017. https://www.bbc.com/future/article/20170907-the-mystery-of-the-lost-roman-herb.

Goto, Keiko. "Indonesia." In *Food Cultures of the World Encyclopedia: Volume 3: Asia and Oceania*, edited by Ken Albala, 103–12. Santa Barbara, CA: Greenwood, 2011.

Grainger, Sally. "Garum, Liquamen and Muria: A New Approach to the Problem of Definition." In *Fish & ships: production et commerce des "salsamenta" durant l'Antiquité, Bibliothèque d'archéologie méditerranéenne et africaine* 17, edited by Emmanuel Botte and Victoria Leitch, 37–45. Arles, FR: Errance, 2014.

———. "*Garum and Liquamen,* What's in a Name?" *Journal of Maritime Archaeology* 13 (2018): 247–61. https://doi:10.1007/s11457-018-9211-5.

Gramene. "Avena Introduction." 2021. https://archive.gramene.org/species/avena/oat_intro.html.

Gray, Michael W. "Lynn Margulis and the Endosymbiont Hypothesis: 50 Years Later." *Molecular Biology of the Cell* 28, no. 10 (2017): 1285–87.

Gregory, Catrina. "A Brief History of Cheese in the Middle East." *Culture Trip,* June 12, 2018. https://theculturetrip.com/middle-east/jordan/articles/a-brief-history-of-cheese-in-the-middle-east/.

Grovier, Kelly. "Tyrian Purple: The Disgusting Origins of the Colour Purple." BBC, August 1, 2018. https://www.bbc.com/culture/article/20180801-tyrian-purple-the-regal-colour-taken-from-mollusc-mucus.

Grout, James. "Garum." *Encyclopaedia Romana.* Updated September 12, 2020. https://penelope.uchicago.edu/~grout/encyclopaedia_romana/wine/garum.html.

Gupta, Raj Kishor, Shivraj Singh Gangoliya, and Nand Kumar Singh. "Reduction of Phytic Acid and Enhancement of Bioavailable Micronutrients in Food Grains." *Journal of Food Science and Technology* 52, no. 2 (2015): 676–84. https://doi:10.1007/s13197-013-0978-y.

Hachisu, Nancy Singleton. "'Kioke': The Secret Ingredient of Soy Sauce." *Japan Times,* July 29, 2016. https://www.japantimes.co.jp/life/2016/07/29/food/kioke-secret-ingredient-soy-sauce/.

Hamiltona, Alan C., Deborah Karamurab, and Esezah Kakudidic. "History and Conservation of Wild and Cultivated Plant Diversity in Uganda: Forest Species and Banana Varieties as Case Studies." *Plant Diversity* 38, no. 1 (2016): 23–44.

Han, Thazin, and Kyaw Nyein Aye. "The Legend of *Laphet*: A Myanmar Fermented Tea Leaf." *Journal of Ethnic Foods* 2, no. 4 (2015): 173–78. https://doi:10.1016/j.jef.2015.11.003.

Hanaoka, Toshio. "Miso Preparation and New Uses." In *Proceedings of the World Congress on Vegetable Protein Utilization in Human Foods and Animal Feedstuffs,* edited by Thomas H. Applewhite, 369–74. Champaign, IL: American Oil Chemists' Society, 1989.

Harkiolakis, Tatiana. "Snake Wine." *Gastro Obscura.* Accessed November 12, 2020. https://www.atlasobscura.com/foods/snake-wine-china-vietnam.

Heard, Edith, and Robert A Martienssen. "Transgenerational Epigenetic Inheritance: Myths and Mechanisms." *Cell* 157, no. 1 (2014): 95–109. https://doi:10.1016/j.cell.2014.02.045.

Heidt, Amanda. "Scientists Awaken Deep Sea Bacteria After 100 Million Years." *The Scientist,* July 29, 2020. https://www.the-scientist.com/news-opinion/scientists-awaken-deep-sea-bacteria-after-100-million-years-67778.

Historical Italian Cooking. "Renaissance Pork Tenderloin with Garlic Sauce." https://historicalitaliancooking.home.blog/english/recipes/renaissance-pork-tenderloin-with-garlic-sauce/.

Ho, Tienlon. "The Months of Magical Eating." In *Women on Food,* edited by Charlotte Druckman, 80–92. New York: Abrams, 2019.

Holzapfel, Wilhelm, Ulrich Schillinger, and Herbert Buckenhüskes, "Sauerkraut." In *Handbook of Fermented Functional Foods,* 2nd ed., edited by Edward R. Farnworth, 395–412. New York: CRC Press, 2008.

Hong, Liya, et al. "Ethnobotany of Wild Plants Used for Starting Fermented Beverages in Shui Communities of Southwest China." *Journal of Ethnobiology and Ethnomedicine* 11, no. 42 (2015). https://doi:10.1186/s13002-015-0028-0.

Horsthemke, Bernard. "A Critical View on Transgenerational Epigenetic Inheritance in Humans." *Nature Communications* 9 (2018): 2973. https://doi:10.1038/s41467-018-05445-5.

Hubell, Diana. "A Brief History of Hallucogenic Beers." *October Magazine,* July 8, 2020.

Huch, M., and C. M. A. P. Franz. "Coffee: Fermentation and Microbiota." In *Advances in Fermented Foods and Beverages,* edited by Wilhelm Holzapfel, 501–13. Cambridge, UK: Woodhead Publishing, 2015.

Hug, Laura A., et al. "A New View of the Tree of Life." *Nature Microbiology* 1 (2016): 16048. https://doi:10.1038/nmicrobiol.2016.48.

Hunger and Health. "What is Food Insecurity?" 2019. https://hungerandhealth.feedingamerica.org/understand-food-insecurity/.

Imperial War Museums. Royal Navy Amenity Ship MV Menestheus—The Floating Brewery (1946 film). Accessed November 10, 2020. https://www.iwm.org.uk/collections/item/object/1060009499.

Ishige, Naomichi. "Japan." In *The Cambridge World History of Food*, edited by Kenneth F. Kiple and Kriemhild Coneè Ornelas, 1175–83. Cambridge: Cambridge University Press, 2000.

Iskandrian, Kristen. "Grief Pickles." In *Eat Joy*, edited by Natalie Eve Garrett. New York: Black Balloon, 2019.

Itoh, Makiko. "'Amazake': The Wintertime Sake That Isn't What It Seems." *Japan Times*, February 19, 2016. https://www .japantimes.co.jp/ life/2016/02/19/food/ amazake-wintertime-sake-isnt-seems/.

Jaffe, Kelila. "Māori." In *Food Cultures of the World Encyclopedia: Volume 3: Asia and Oceania*, edited by Ken Albala, 169–72. Santa Barbara, CA: Greenwood, 2011.

Jaeger, Elizabeth. "To Save or Savor: The Rate of Return to Storing Wine." *Journal of Political Economy* 89, no. 3 (June 1981): 584–92.

Jeong-yeo, Lim. "What Flavor Is Your Hand?" *Korea Magazine*, April 2016, 50.

Jones, Josh. "Discover the Oldest Beer Recipe in History from Ancient Sumeria, 1800 B.C." *Open Culture*, March 3, 2015. https://www .openculture.com/2015/03/the-oldest-beer -recipe-in-history.html.

Jones, Prudence. "Cleopatra's Cocktail Challenge." *Analytical and Bioanalytical Chemistry* 398, no. 5 (November 2010): 1841–43.

———. "Solution to Cleopatra's Cocktail Challenge." *Analytical and Bioanalytical Chemistry* 399, no. 7 (March 2011): 2307.

Jurafksy, Dan. "Ketchup." *The Language of Food* (blog), September 2, 2009. http:// languageoffood.blogspot.com/2009/09/ ketchup.html.

Kamozakowa, Aki, and H. Alexander Talbot. "Making Vinegar at Home." *Popular Science*, December 8, 2008. https://www.popsci.com/ diy/article/2008-12/making-vinegar-home/.

Karki, Tika, Pravin Ojha, and Om Prakash Panta. "Ethnic Fermented Foods of Nepal." In *Ethnic Fermented Foods and Alcoholic Beverages of Asia*, edited by Jyoti Prakash Tamang, 91–118. New Delhi: Springer India, 2016.

Katz, Sandor. "Dosas and Idlis: Turn Beans to Bread." *Fermentation*, winter 2019. https://www.myfermentation.com/grains/ dosas-and-idlis-zm0z19wzwoo.

Katz, Solomon H., and Mary M. Voigt. "Bread and Beer." *Expedition* 28, no. 2 (January 1, 1986): 23–34.

Kennedy, Alicia. "On Booze and the Pursuit of Sustainability in Spirits." *From the Desk of Alicia Kennedy*, September 21, 2020. https:// aliciakennedy.substack.com/p/on-booze.

Ketchum, Alex. "Labna from Jordan." *The Historical Cooking Project*, November 20, 2014. http://www.historicalcookingproject .com/2014/11/labna-from-jordan.html.

Kim, Chi-Hoon. "Kimchi Nation: Constructing Kimjang as an Intangible Korean Heritage." In *Urban Foodways and Communication: Ethnographic Studies in Intangible Cultural Food Heritages Around the World*, edited by Casey Man Kong Lum and Marc de Ferrière le Vayer, 39–54. Lanham, MD: Rowman & Littlefield, 2016.

Kim, Dakota. "Let's Continue the Intangible Tradition of Kimjang." *Comestible* 6 (2020). https://www.comestiblejournal.com/blog/ kimjang-kimchi-tradition.

Kim, Eric. "Think of Kimchi as a Verb." *New York Times*, July 2, 2020. https://www.nytimes .com/2020/07/02/dining/quick-kimchi-recipes .html.

Kim, Nikki. "Kimjang: The Making and Sharing of Kimchi." December 23, 2019. https://storymaps.arcgis.com/stories/ 46f45e3867684b3898da50edc87075ea.

Kim, Soon Hee, et al. "Korean Diet: Characteristics and Historical Background." *Journal of Ethnic Foods* 3, no. 1 (2016): 26–31. https://www.sciencedirect.com/science/ article/pii/S2352618116300099.

Kimbell, Vanessa. "The History of Sourdough Bread." The Sourdough School, March 21, 2015. https://www.sourdough.co.uk/ the-history-of-sourdough-bread/.

Kioke Project. "Company Profile: Kioke Project." https://kinbue.jp/en_profile.

Kiple, Kenneth F., and Kriemhild Coneè Ornelas. "The History and Culture of Food and Drink in Asia." In *The Cambridge World History of Food*, edited by Kenneth F. Kiple and Kriemhild Coneè Ornelas. Cambridge: Cambridge University Press, 2000.

Kockmann, Norbert. "History of Distillation." In *Distillation: Fundamentals and Principles*, edited by Andrzej Górak and Eva Sorensen, 1–44. London: Academic Press, 2014.

Kuijt, Ian. "What Do We Really Know about Food Storage, Surplus, and Feasting in Preagricultural Communities?" *Current Anthropology* 50, no. 5 (2009): 641–44.

Kukovics, Sándor, ed. *Goat Science.* United Kingdom: IntechOpen, 2018.

Lane, Marta. "The Sweet Legacy of Sour Poi." TASTE, April 20, 2018. https://www.tastecooking.com/sweet-legacy-sour-poi/.

Laudan, Rachel. "Birth of the Modern Diet." *Scientific American*, December 1, 2006. https://www.scientificamerican.com/article/birth-of-the-modern-diet-2006-12/.

———. "Bread First or Beer First? A Bad Question." *Rachel Laudan* (blog), November 21, 2009. https://www.rachellaudan.com/2009/11/an-aside-on-the-bread-first-beer-first-controversy.html.

———. "In March, of All Months, Americans Went Food Shopping to Shelter in Place." *Rachel Laudan* (blog), April 5, 2020. https://www.rachellaudan.com/2020/04/in-march-of-all-months-americans-went-food-shopping-to-shelter-in-place.html.

———. "Tiny Bubbles: Where Food Met Science, Medicine, and Religion." *Rachel Laudan* (blog), December 27, 2014. https://www.rachellaudan.com/2014/12/tiny-bubbles.html.

Lee, Jennifer 8. "The Hunt for General Tso." TED, July 2008. Accessed November 12, 2020. http://www.ted.com/talks/jennifer_8_lee_looks_for_general_tso?language=en.

Lee, Mooha. "Uniqueness of Ethiopian Traditional Alcoholic Beverage of Plant Origin, *Tella*." *Journal of Ethnic Foods* 2, no. 3 (2015): 110–14. https://doi:10.1016/j.jef.2015.08.002.

Lee, Patty. "Things You're Doing Wrong When Eating Thai Food." Thrillist, November 2, 2016. https://www.thrillist.com/eat/nation/eating-thai-food.

Lennon, Jay T., and Kenneth J. Locey. "There Are More Microbial Species on Earth Than Stars in the Galaxy" Aeon, September 10, 2018. https://aeon.co/ideas/there-are-more-microbial-species-on-earth-than-stars-in-the-sky.

Lessafre Yeast Corporation. "About Us." Accessed 2020. https://lesaffreyeast.com/about-us-2/.

Levi, Jane. "Kazakhstan." In *Food Cultures of the World Encyclopedia: Volume 3: Asia and Oceania*, edited by Ken Albala, 127–34. Santa Barbara, CA: Greenwood, 2011.

Lewis, Nancy Davis. "The Pacific Islands." In *The Cambridge World History of Food*, edited by Kenneth F. Kiple and Kriemhild Coneè Ornelas, 1358–59. Cambridge: Cambridge University Press, 2000.

Lin, M. Paramita. "Explore the Curious (and Sometimes Creepy) Traditions of Funeral Foods." The Takeout, December 7, 2016. https://thetakeout.com/explore-the-curious-and-sometimes-creepy-traditions-o-1798255240.

Linares, Olga F. "African rice (*Oryza glaberrima*): History and Future Potential." *Proceedings of the National Academy of Sciences* 99, no. 25 (December 2002): 16360–65.

Lindemann, Bernd, Yoko Ogiwara, and Yuzo Ninomiya. "The Discovery of Umami." *Chemical Senses* 27, no. 9 (November 2002): 843–844. https://doi:10.1093/chemse/27.9.843.

Liokatis, Akis. "Sourdough Drink." Greek Chemist in the Kitchen, 2021. https://www.greekchemistinthekitchen.com/post/_boza.

Loha-unchit, Kasma. "Don't Miss Naem Sour Sausage When Visiting Northern Thailand." *Thai Food & Travel* (blog), March 1, 2013. http://www.thaifoodandtravel.com/blog/naem-sausage-northern-thailand/#1.

Lohman, Sarah. "Eating Our Emotions: A Brief History of Funeral Food." Wine History Project, October 4, 2018. https://winehistoryproject.org/eating-our-emotions-a-brief-history-of-funeral-food/.

Londero, A., et al. "Inhibitory Activity of Cheese Whey Fermented with Kefir Grains." *Journal of Food Protection* 74, no 1 (2011): 94–100.

Lopata, Rob. "Tepache: Refreshing Memories of Mexico." *Chicago Tribune*, August 16, 2012. https://www.chicagotribune.com/dining/ct-xpm-2012-08-16-ct-dining-0816-tepache-20120816-story.html.

Lorenzi, Rossella. "Cleopatra Pearl Cocktail Proven Possible." *NBC News*, August 3, 2010. http://www.nbcnews.com/id/38536846/ns/technology_and_science-science/t/cleopatra-pearl-cocktail-proven-possible/#.X4b46117mV4.

Lu, Z., F. Breidt, V. Plengvidhya, and H. P. Fleming. "Bacteriophage Ecology in Commercial Sauerkraut Fermentation." *Applied and Environmental Microbiology* 69, no. 6 (June 2003): 3192–202.

Mack, Glenn R. In *Food Cultures of the World Encyclopedia: Volume 3: Asia and Oceania*, edited by Ken Albala, 49–60. Santa Barbara, CA: Greenwood, 2011.

MacQueen, Kathleen M., et al. "What Is Community? An Evidence-Based Definition for Participatory Public Health." *American Journal of Public Health* 91, no. 12 (December 1, 2001): 1929–38.

Magner, Lois N. "Korea." In *The Cambridge World History of Food*, edited by Kenneth F. Kiple and Kriemhild Coneè Ornelas. Cambridge: Cambridge University Press, 2000.

Mahajan, Aatish, Divika Sapehia, Shilpa Thakur, Palani Selvam Mohanraj, Rashmi Bagga, and Jyotdeep Kaur. "Effect of Imbalance in Folate and Vitamin B12 in Maternal/Parental Diet on Global Methylation and Regulatory miRNAs." *Scientific Reports* 9 (2019): 17602.

Mandia, Scott A. "The Little Ice Age in Europe." Last modified February 3, 2018. https://www .sunysuffolk.edu/explore-academics/faculty -and-staff/faculty-websites/scott-mandia/lia/ little_ice_age.html.

Mann, Charles C. "America, Found & Lost." *National Geographic Magazine*, May 2007, 32–55.

Mark, Joshua L. "The Hymn to Ninkasi, Goddess of Beer." World History Encyclopedia, March 2011. https:// www.worldhistory.org/article/222/ the-hymn-to-ninkasi-goddess-of-beer/.

Marks, Tasha. "Pleasant Vices: Beer." AVM Curiosities, May 31, 2018. https://www .avmcuriosities.com/blog/2018/31/month/ pleasant-vices-beer.

———. "A Sip of History: Ancient Egyptian Beer." The British Museum (blog), May 25, 2018. https://blog.britishmuseum.org /a-sip-of-history-ancient-egyptian-beer/.

Maroney, Stephanie. "Sandor Katz and the Possibilities of a Queer Fermentive Praxis." *Cuizine: The Journal of Canadian Food Cultures* 9, no. 2 (2018). https://doi:10.7202/1055217ar.

Maskevich, Adam. "We Didn't Build This City on Rock 'N' Roll. It Was Yogurt." *The Salt*. NPR, July 16, 2015. https://www.npr.org/sections/ thesalt/2015/07/16/422684872/we-didnt-build -this-city-on-rock-n-roll-it-was-yogurt.

Mather, Robin. "Artisan Bakers Bringing Back Salt Rising Bread." *Chicago Tribune*, September 26, 2016.

Mattson, Anne. "Indigo in the Early Modern World." University of Minnesota Libraries. Accessed November 12, 2020. https://www.lib .umn.edu/bell/tradeproducts/indigo.

Maynard, David, and Donald S. Maynard. "Cucumbers, Melons, and Watermelons." In *The Cambridge World History of Food*, edited by Kenneth F. Kiple and Kriemhild Coneè Ornelas, 298–312. Cambridge: Cambridge University Press, 2000.

Mayo, Baltasar, Mohammed Salim Ammor, Susana Delgado, and Ángel Alegría. "Fermented Milk Products." In *Fermented Foods and Beverages of the World*, edited by Jyoti Prakash Tamang and Kasipathy Kailasapathy, 263–88. Boca Raton, FL: CRC Press, 2010.

McCorriston, Joy. "Barley." In *The Cambridge World History of Food*, edited by Kenneth F. Kiple and Kriemhild Coneè Ornelas, 81–89. Cambridge: Cambridge University Press, 2000.

Macfarlane, Robert. "The Secrets of the Wood Wide Web." *New Yorker*. https://www .newyorker.com/tech/annals-of-technology/ the-secrets-of-the-wood-wide-web.

McFarling, Usha Lee. "Making Ink from Oak Galls." *Verso*. The Huntington Library, May 1, 2019. https://www.huntington.org/ verso/2019/05/making-ink-oak-galls.

McGovern, Patrick E. *Biomolecuar Archaeology Project*. University of Pennsylvania Museum. https://www.penn.museum/sites/ biomoleculararchaeology/.

McGovern, Patrick, et. al. "Early Neolithic Wine of Georgia." *Proceedings of the National Academy of Sciences* 114, no. 48 (November 2017): E10309-18.

———. "Fermented Beverages of Pre- and Proto-Historic China." *Proceedings of the National Academy of Sciences* 101, no. 51 (2004): 17593–98. https://doi:10.1073/pnas.0407921102.

McKenna, Dennis J. "Ayahuasca: An Ethnopharmacologic History." In *Sacred Vine of the Spirits: Ayahuasca*, edited by Ralph Metzner, 40–62. Rochester, VT: Park Street Press, 1996.

McLendon, Russell. "Almost 2/3 of Earth's Biodiversity Is Bacteria." Treehugger. Updated April 26, 2018. https://www.mnn.com/ earth-matters/wilderness-resources/blogs/ two-thirds-earths-biodiversity-bacteria.

Meng, Grace. "The Taste of Your Hands." *One Fork, One Spoon* (blog), April 24, 2009. https:// oneforkonespoon.wordpress.com/2009/04/24/ the-taste-of-your-hands.

Messer, Ellen. "Maize." In *The Cambridge World History of Food*, edited by Kenneth F. Kiple and Kriemhild Coneè Ornelas, 97–111. Cambridge: Cambridge University Press, 2000.

Micropia. "Museum of Microbes." Accessed November 10, 2020. https://www.micropia.nl/ en/visit/what-is-micropia/museum-microbes/.

Miller, Naomi F. "Sweeter than Wine? The Use of the Grape in Early Western Asia." *Antiquity* 82, no. 318 (2008): 937–46.

Miller, Olivia Ray. "The Fermentation King and All His Wisdom." *Only Good Simple* (blog), October 30, 2020. https://www.onlygoodsimple.com/blog/the-fermentation-king-and-all-his-wisdom.

Mintz, Sidney. "The Absent Third: The Place of Fermentation in a Thinkable World Food System." In *Cured, Fermented, and Smoked Foods: Proceedings of the Oxford Symposium on Food and Cookery 2010*, edited by Helen Saberi, 13–29. Totnes, Devon, UK: Prospect Books, 2011.

Mohsenzadeh, Fariba, Abdolkarim Chehregani Rad, and Mehrangiz Akbari. "Evaluation of Oil Removal Efficiency and Enzymatic Activity in Some Fungal Strains for Bioremediation of Petroleum-Polluted Soils." *Iranian Journal of Environmental Health Science & Engineering* 9, no. 1 (2012): 26. https://www.ncbi.nlm.nih.gov/pmc/articles/PMC3561093/.

Molan, P., and T. Rhodes. "Honey: A Biologic Wound Dressing." *Wounds* 27, no. 6 (2015): 141–51. https://www.ncbi.nlm.nih.gov/pubmed/26061489.

Molina, Jeanmaire, Martin Sikora, Nandita Garud, Jonathan M. Flowers, Samara Rubinstein, Andy Reynolds, Pu Huang, Scott Jackson, Barbara A. Schaal, Carlos D. Bustamante, Adam R. Boyko, and Michael D. Purugganan. "Molecular Evidence for a Singular Evolutionary Origin of Domesticated Rice." *Proceedings of the National Academy of Sciences* (2011). https://doi:10.1073/pnas.1104686108.

Melina, Remy. "Why Do We Celebrate with Champagne?" Live Science, December 28, 2010. https://www.livescience.com/32829-why-celebrate-with-champagne.html.

Monaco, Farrell. "Baking Bread with the Romans: Part II—Panis Quadratus." *Tavola Mediterranea* (blog), September 5, 2017. https://tavolamediterranea.com/2017/09/05/baking-bread-romans-part-ii-panis-quadratus/.

———. "Baking with the Greeks: A Recipe for Prosphora." *Tavola Mediterranea* (blog), May 4, 2019. https://tavolamediterranea.com/2019/05/04/baking-with-the-greeks-prosphoro/.

Moncorgé, Marie Josèphe. "Hippocras." Translated by Leah Hunt. Old Cook. https://www.oldcook.com/en/medieval-hippocras.

Moodie, T. Dunbar. "The Moral Economy of the Black Miners' Strike of 1946." *Journal of Southern African Studies* 13, no. 1 (1986): 1–35.

Morabito, Greg. "'Chef's Table' Recap: Jeong Kwan." Eater, February 18, 2017. https://www.eater.com/2017/2/18/14653382/jeong-kwan-buddhist-nun-chefs-table.

Morrell, Robert. "The Disintegration of the Gold and Maize Alliance in South Africa in the 1920s." *International Journal of African Historical Studies* 21, no. 4 (1988): 619–35.

Mugits, Justin. "The Persistence of Chicha." *American Indian* 19, no. 2 (Summer 2018). https://www.americanindianmagazine.org/story/persistence-chicha.

My Sweet Grandma. "The Art of Mukeunji." https://www.msg.kitchen/thoughts/the-art-of-mukeunji.

Nash, Colin E. "Aquatic Animals." In *The Cambridge World History of Food*, edited by Kenneth F. Kiple and Kriemhild Coneè Ornelas, 456–66. Cambridge: Cambridge University Press, 2000.

National Center for Complementary and Integrative Health. "Lavender." https://nccih.nih.gov/health/lavender/ataglance.htm.

National Museum of Denmark. "The Egtved Girl's Beer." Accessed November 10, 2020. https://en.natmus.dk/historical-knowledge/denmark/ prehistoric-period-until-1050-ad/the-bronze-age/the-egtved-girl/the-egtved-girls-beer/.

National Museum of Natural History. "Early Life on Earth—Animal Origins." Accessed November 10, 2020. https://naturalhistory.si.edu/education/teaching-resources/life-science/early-life-earth-animal-origins.

Neela, Satheesh, and Solomon Workneh Fanta. "Injera (An Ethnic, Traditional Staple Food of Ethiopia): A Review on Traditional Practice to Scientific Developments." *Journal of Ethnic Foods* 7, no. 32 (2020). https://doi:10.1186/s42779-020-00069-x.

Negi, K. S., et al. "Cultural Significance of *Brassica nigra* in Central Himalayan Region." *Asian Agri-History* 17, no 3 (2013): 275–79.

Neimark, Jill. "Porridge, the Food That Builds Empires, Stages a Savory Comeback." *The Salt.* NPR, October 27, 2016. https://www.npr.org/sections/thesalt/2016/10/27/499358436/porridge-the-food-that-built-empires-stages-a-savory-comeback.

Nicosia, Marissa. "Hippocras, or Spiced Wine." *Cooking in the Archives*, December 10, 2018. https://rarecooking.com/2018/12/10/hippocras-or-spiced-wine/.

Nielson-Stowell, Amelia. "Harnessing Fermentation for Sustainability, Part 2 of Our Conversation with Johnny Drain." The Fermentation Association, September 15, 2020. https://fermentationassociation.org/harnessing-fermentation-for-sustainability-part-2-of-our-conversation-with-johnny-drain/.

Nkhata, Smith G., Emmanuel Ayua, Elijah H. Kamau, and Jean-Bosco Shingiro. "Fermentation and Germination Improve Nutritional Value of Cereals and Legumes through Activation of Endogenous Enzymes." Food Science & Nutrition 6, no. 8 (2018): 2446–58. https://doi:10.1002/fsn3.846.

Nordic Spirits. "The History of Aquavit." https://www.nordicspirits.com/en/article/history-aquavit.

Nuraida, L., M. C. Wacher, and J. D. Owens, "Microbiology of Pozol, a Mexican Fermented Maize Dough." World Journal of Microbiology & Biotechnology 11, no. 5 (1995): 567–71.

Nyffenegger, Remo Bryan. "Microencapsulation of Probiotics and Prebiotics (Inulin) by Using Extrusion Method and Its Application in Thai Traditional Pork Sausage (Naem)." Thesis, Assumption University of Thailand. https://repository.au.edu/handle/6623004553/21415.

O'Driscoll, Bill. "African-American Craft Beer Brewers Unite to Host a Festival of Their Own." The Salt. NPR, August 10, 2018. https://www.npr.org/sections/thesalt/2018/08/10/637285637/african-american-craft-beer-brewers-unite-to-host-a-festival-of-their-own.

Odunfa, S. A., and S. Adeyele. "Microbial Changes during the Traditional Production of Ogi-Baba, a West African Fermented Sorghum Gruel." Journal of Cereal Science 3, vol. 2 (1985): 173–80.

Okagbue, Richard Nnamdi. "Food Technology in Africa." In Encyclopedia of the History of Science, Technology, and Medicine in Non-Western Cultures, edited by Helaine Selin, 940–44. Dordrecht, NL: Kluwer Academic Publishers, 1997.

O'Neill, Molly. "A 19th-Century Ghost Awakens to Redefine 'Soul.'" New York Times, November 21, 2007.

Osawa, Yoshimi. "Glutamate Perception, Soup Stock, and the Concept of Umami: The Ethnography, Food Ecology, and History of Dashi in Japan." Ecology of Food and Nutrition 51 no. 4 (2012): 329–45.

Oura, Shin, Sachiko Suzuki, Yoji Hata, Yoji, Akitsugu Kawato, and Yasuhisa Abe. "Evaluation of Physiological Functionalities of Amazake in Mice." Journal of the Brewing Society of Japan 102, no. 10 (2007): 781–88. https://doi.10.6013/jbrewsocjapan1988.102.781.

Overton, Mark. "Agricultural Revolution in England 1500–1850." BBC. http://www.bbc.co.uk/history/british/empire_seapower/agricultural_revolution_01.shtml.

Ozdemir, S., D. Gocmen, and A. Yildirim Kumral. "A Traditional Turkish Fermented Cereal Food: Tarhana." Food Reviews International 23, no. 2 (2007): 107–21.

Ozen, M., and E. C. Dinleyici. "The History of Probiotics: The Untold Story." Beneficial Microbes 6 no. 2 (2015): 160. https://doi:10.3920/BM2014.0103.

Panara, Kalpesh B., and Rabinarayan Acharya. "Consequences of Excessive Use of Amlarasa (Sour Taste): A Case-Control Study." Ayu 35, no. 2 (2014): 124–28. https://www.ncbi.nlm.nih.gov/pmc/articles/PMC4279316.

Park, Kun-Young, and Hong-Sik Cheigh. "Kimchi." In Handbook of Vegetable Preservation and Processing, edited by Y. H. Hui, Sue Ghazala, Dee M. Graham, K. D. Murrell, and Wai-Kit Nip, 220–60. Boca Raton, FL: CRC Press, 2005.

Park, K. Y., H. Y. Kim, and J. K. Jeong. "Kimchi and its Health Benefits." In Fermented Foods in Health and Disease Prevention, edited by Juana Frias, Cristina Martinez-Villaluenga, and Elena Peñas, 477–96. London: Elsevier, 2017.

Park, Susan Ji-Young. "Korea." In Food Cultures of the World Encyclopedia: Volume 3: Asia and Oceania, edited by Ken Albala. Santa Barbara, CA: Greenwood, 2011.

Parks, Andrew. "Why Baijiu Is the Liquor You Need to Know." Food & Wine, February 1, 2019. https://www.foodandwine.com/cocktails-spirits/baijiu-chinese-spirit-liquor.

Pasqualone, Antonella. "Traditional Flat Breads Spread from the Fertile Crescent: Production Process and History of Baking Systems." Journal of Ethnic Foods 5, no. 1 (2018): 10–19. https://doi:10.1016/j.jef.2018.02.002.

Pasteur, Louis. "New Process of Vinegar Making." In The Intellectual Observer: Review of Natural History, Microscopic Research, and Recreative Science, vol. 2, 128–30. London: Groombridge and Sons, 1863.

Patterson, K. David. "Lactose Intolerance." In *The Cambridge World History of Food*, edited by Kenneth F. Kiple and Kriemhild Coneè Ornelas, 1057–61. Cambridge: Cambridge University Press, 2000.

Patwardhan, Bhushan, Dnyaneshwar Warude, P. Pushpangadan, and Narendra Bratt. "Ayurveda and Traditional Chinese Medicine: A Comparative Overview." *Evidence-Based Complementary and Alternative Medicine* 2, no. 4 (2005): 465–73.

Pennisi, Elizabeth. "Scientists Pull Living Microbes, Possibly 100 Million Years Old, from Beneath the Sea." *Science*, July 28, 2020. https://www.sciencemag.org/news/2020/07/scientists-pull-living-microbes-100-million-years-beneath-sea.

Pesapane, Filippo, Stefano Marcelli, and Gianluca Nazzaro. "Hieronymi Fracastorii: the Italian Scientist Who Described the 'French Disease.'" *Anais brasileiros de dermatologia* 90, no. 5 (2015): 684–86.

Peters, Achim. "Why Do We Crave Sweets When We're Stressed?" *Scientific American*, February 27, 2019. https://www.scientificamerican.com/article/why-do-we-crave-sweets-when-were-stressed/.

Poelmans, Eline, and Johan F. M. Swinnen. "A Brief Economic History of Beer." In *The Economics of Beer*, edited by Johan F. M. Swinnen, 3–28. Oxford: Oxford University Press, 2011.

Prajapati, Jashibhai B., and Baboo M. Nair. "The History of Fermented Foods." In *Handbook of Fermented Functional Foods*, 2nd ed., edited by Edward R. Farnworth, 1–24. New York: CRC Press, 2008.

Prasad, Sahdeo, and Bharat B. Aggarwal. "Turmeric: The Golden Spice" In *Herbal Medicine: Biomolecular and Clinical Aspects*, 2nd ed., edited by Iris F. F. Benzie and Sissi Wachtel-Galor. Boca Raton, FL: CRC Press/Taylor & Francis, 2011. https://www.ncbi.nlm.nih.gov/books/NBK92752/.

Preserve and Pickle. "Preserving Fruit in Alcohol." Accessed November 2, 2020. https://preserveandpickle.com/preserving-fruit-alcohol/.

Quercus Cooperage. "Kioke." http://www.qcooperage.com/product/kioke/.

Raak, Norbert, Klaus Dürrschmid, and Harald Rohm. "Textural Characteristics of German Foods: The German Würstchen." In *Textural Characteristics of World Foods*, edited by Katsuyoshi Nishinari, 335–52. Hoboken, NJ: Wiley, 2020.

Raukko, Elina. "Fermentation Adds Vitamin B-12 to Plant-Based Foods Naturally." University of Helsinki. https://www2.helsinki.fi/en/news/health/fermentation-adds-vitamin-b12-to-plant-based-foods-naturally.

Reinhardt, Bruno. "Intangible Heritage, Tangible Controversies: The *Baiana* and the *Acarajé* as Boundary Objects in Contemporary Brazil." In *Sense and Essence: Heritage and Cultural Production of the Real*, edited by Birgit Meyer and Mattijs van de Port, 75–109. New York: Berghahn Books, 2018.

Revel, Jean-Francois. "From Culture and Cuisine." In *Cooking, Eating, Thinking: Transformative Philosophies of Food*, edited by Deane W. Curtin and Lisa Maree Heldke, 145–52. Bloomington, IN: Indiana University Press, 1992.

Rhodes, Semetra. "Pawcohiccora (Shagbark) Hickory Soup." *New World Food*, October 7, 2013. http://nativefoodblog.blogspot.com/2013/10/pawcohiccora-shagbark-hickory-soup.html.

Richardson-Read, Scott. "Radicalising the Ancestral Scottish Diet." *Cailleach's Herbarium*, March 2018. Accessed November 12, 2020. https://cailleachs-herbarium.com/2018/03/radicalising-ancestral-scottish-dietary-traditions/.

———. "Sowans (Fermented Oats)—Scottish Traditional Food Recipe." *Cailleach's Herbarium*, August 12, 2018. https://cailleachs-herbarium.com/2018/03/sowens-fermented-oats-scottish-traditional-food-recipe.

Riseley, Charles. "Ceremonial Drinking in the Viking Age." Master's thesis, University of Oslo, 2014. https://www.duo.uio.no/bitstream/handle/10852/40697/Riseley-Master.pdf.

Root, Waverly. "Reaping Those Not-So-Wild Oats." *Washington Post*, August 17, 1978. https://www.washingtonpost.com/archive/lifestyle/1978/08/17/reaping-those-not-so-wild-oats/7cc66f4b-d0c5-4692-b45f-4624359dcc03.

Rozin, Elizabeth, and Paul Rozin. "Culinary Themes and Variations." In *The Taste Culture Reader: Experiencing Food and Drink*, edited by Carolyn Korsmeyer, 34–41. Oxford: Berg, 2016.

Rozpędowska, E., L. Hellborg, O. Ishchuk, et al. "Parallel Evolution of the Make–Accumulate–Consume Strategy in *Saccharomyces* and *Dekkera* Yeasts." *Nature Communications* 2 (2011): 302.

Sabban, Francoise, and Elborg Forster. "China." In *The Cambridge World History of Food*, edited by Kenneth F. Kiple and Kriemhild Coneè Ornelas, 1165–74. Cambridge: Cambridge University Press, 2000.

Saberi, Helen. "Afghanistan." In *Food Cultures of the World Encyclopedia: Volume 3: Asia and Oceania*, edited by Ken Albala, 9–20. Santa Barbara, CA: Greenwood, 2011.

Sagan, Lynn. "On the Origin of Mitosing Cells." *Journal of Theoretical Biology* 14, no. 3 (1967): 225–74.

Salvaneschi, Lenore. "Harvest Time." *The Palimpsest* 65, no. 6 (1984): 207–13.

Sano, Chiaki. "History of Glutamate Production." *The American Journal of Clinical Nutrition* 90, no. 3 (September 2009): 728S–32S. https://doi:10.3945/ajcn.2009.27462F.

Saulnier, Delphine M. A., et al. "Mechanisms of Probiosis and Prebiosis: Considerations for Enhanced Functional Foods." *Current Opinion in Biotechnology* 20, no. 2 (2009): 135–41.

Science Museum. "Joseph Lister's Antisepsis System." October 14, 2018. https://www.sciencemuseum.org.uk/objects-and-stories/medicine/listers-antisepsis-system.

Scots Weekly Magazine. "Christmas." *Scots Weekly Magazine* 1, no. 4 (December 22, 1832): 52–53.

Seeley, Stephen. "The Cardiovasular System, Coronary Disease, and Calcium: A Hypothesis." In *The Cambridge World History of Food*, edited by Kenneth F. Kiple and Kriemhild Coneè Ornelas, 1109–21. Cambridge: Cambridge University Press, 2000.

Sethi, Simran. "The Bittersweet Story of Vanilla." *Smithsonian Magazine*, April 3, 2017. https://www.smithsonianmag.com/science-nature/bittersweet-story-vanilla-180962757.

Seton-Karr, W. S., et al. "Indigo Commission Report." National Archives of India: 1860. https://indianculture.gov.in/archives/indigo-commission-report.

Sha, Shankar Prasad, et al. "Analysis of Bacterial and Fungal Communities in *Marcha* and *Thiat*, Traditionally Prepared Amylolitic Starters of India." *Scientific Reports* 7 (2017): 10967. https://www.nature.com/articles/s41598-017-11609-y.

Sharrer, G. Terry. "The Indigo Bonanza in South Carolina, 1740–90." *Technology and Culture* 12, no. 3 (1971): 447–55. Accessed April 26, 2021. https://doi:10.2307/3102998.

Shockey, Kirsten. "Flower Power: Foraging for Wild Yeast." Fermentation School. Accessed January 4, 2021. https://www.fermentationschool.com/courses/flower-power.

———. "Making Miso with Leftover Bread." Preserving Abundance Virtual Festival, May 2, 2020. https://root-kitchens.com/events/may-2nd-preserving-abundance-virtual-festival/.

———. "Practicing Kraut Non-violence: Pressing Not Pounding." *Ferment Works* (blog), August 14, 2013. https://ferment.works/blog/2013/8/14/practicing-kraut-non-violence-pressing-not-pounding.

Shori, Amal Bakr. "Microencapsulation Improved Probiotics Survival During Gastric Transit." *HAYATI Journal of Biosciences* 24, no. 1 (2017): 1–5. https://doi.org/10.1016/j.hjb.2016.12.008.

Silva, Fabio, Chirs J. Stevens, Alison Weisskopf, Cristina Castillo, Ling Qin, Andrew Bevan, and Dorian Q. Fuller. "Modelling the Geographical Origin of Rice Cultivation in Asia Using the Rice Archaeological Database." *PLoS ONE* 10, no. 9 (2015): e0137024. https://doi:10.1371/journal.pone.0137024.

Skinner, Julia. "Love Beer? Thank the Women Who Made It Possible." Fermentation. Accessed November 10, 2020. https://www.myfermentation.com/beer/women-made-it-possible-zm0z20szwoo.

———. "Mapping Friendship Bread." Google Maps. Accessed November 20, 2020. bit.ly/mappingfriendshipbread.

———. "Put Lemon on Your Fish? Thank Humoral Theory." The Epoch Times, 2019. Accessed November 10, 2020. https://www.theepochtimes.com/put-lemon-on-your-fish-thank-humoral-theory_3025962.html.

Slavery Images. "Indigo Production, French West Indies, 1667." http://www.slaveryimages.org/s/slaveryimages/item/1205.

Slow Food Foundation for Biodiversity. "Khoisan Honey Mead." Accessed November 11, 2019. https://www.fondazioneslowfood.com/en/ark-of-taste-slow-food/khoisan-honey-mead/.

Smith, Lisa. "Medicinal Compounds, Efficacious in Every Case." *The Recipes Project*, January 30, 2013. https://recipes.hypotheses.org/800.

Sorosiak, Thomas. "Soybean." In *The Cambridge World History of Food*, edited by Kenneth F. Kiple and Kriemhild Coneè Ornelas, 422–26. Cambridge: Cambridge University Press, 2000.

Sota, Yamamoto, and Matsumoto Tetsuo. "Rice Fermentation Starters in Cambodia: Cultural Importance and Traditional Methods of Production." *Southeast Asian Studies* 49, no. 2 (September 2011): 192–213.

Sõukand, Renata, et al. "An Ethnobotanical Perspective on Traditional Fermented Plant Foods and Beverages in Eastern Europe." *Journal of Ethnopharmacology* 170 (2015): 284–96. https://doi:10.1016/j.jep.2015.05.018.

Sparhawk, Andy. "Gruit Ales: Beer Before Hops." CraftBeer.com, February 1, 2018. https://www.craftbeer.com/craft-beer-muses/gruit-ales-beer-before-hops.

Spencer, Colin. "The British Isles." In *The Cambridge World History of Food*, edited by Kenneth F. Kiple and Kriemhild Coneè Ornelas, 1217–26. Cambridge: Cambridge University Press, 2000.

St. Pete Ferments. Instagram post, June 4, 2020. https://www.instagram.com/p/CBBlDA8pqX7/?utm_source=ig_web_copy_link.

Steere-Williams, Jacob. "The Perfect Food and the Filth Disease: Milk-Borne Typhoid and Epidemiological Practice in Late Victorian Britain." *Journal of the History of Medicine and Allied Sciences* 65, no. 4 (2010): 530–31.

Steinberg, Maria "Ging" Gutierrez. "Philippines." In *Food Cultures of the World Encyclopedia: Volume 3: Asia and Oceania*, edited by Ken Albala. Santa Barbara, CA: Greenwood, 2011.

Steinkraus, Keith H. "Classification of Fermented Foods: Worldwide Review of Household Fermentation Techniques." *Food Control* 8, nos. 5–6 (1997): 311–17. https://doi:10.1016/S0956-7135(97)00050-9.

Stemler, A. B. L., J. R. Harlan, and J. M. J. Dewet. "Caudatum Sorghums and Speakers of Chari-Nile Languages in Africa." *Journal of African History* 16, no. 2 (1975): 161–83. http://www.jstor.org/stable/180810.

Stephens, Elizabeth A. "Camels." In *The Cambridge World History of Food*, edited by Kenneth F. Kiple and Kriemhild Coneè Ornelas, 467–79. Cambridge: Cambridge University Press, 2000.

Sumich, Jason. "It's All Legal Until You Get Caught: Moonshining in the Southern Appalachians." Appalachian State University, Department of Anthropology, 2007. Accessed November 11, 2020. https://anthro.appstate.edu/research/field-schools/ethnographic-and-linguistic-field-schools/summer-2007-alleghany-county/its.

Sung, Andrea. "Banchan: The Story of the Korean Side Dish." The Migrant Kitchen, October 17, 2016. https://www.kcet.org/shows/the-migrant-kitchen/banchan-the-story-of-the-korean-side-dish.

Super, John C., and Luis Alberto Vargas. "Mexico and Highland Central America." In *The Cambridge World History of Food*, edited by Kenneth F. Kiple and Kriemhild Coneè Ornelas. Cambridge: Cambridge University Press, 2000.

Suzuki, S., et al. "Evaluation of Physiological Functionalities of Amazake in Mice." *Journal of the Brewing Society of Japan* 102, no. 10 (2007): 781–88.

Taape, Tillmann. "Distilling the Essence of Heaven: How Alcohol Could Defeat the Antichrist." The Recipes Project, November 4, 2013. https://recipes.hypotheses.org/1107.

Tamang, Jyoti Prakash. "Animal-Based Fermented Foods of Asia." In *Handbook of Animal-Based Fermented Food and Beverage Technology*, 2nd ed., edited by Y. H. Hui and E. Özgül Evranuz, 61–72. Boca Raton, FL: CRC Press, 2012.

Tanis, David. "Cooking with Kimchi." *New York Times*, January 21, 2015. https://www.nytimes.com/2015/01/21/dining/cooking-with-kimchi.html.

Tanti, Bhaben, et al. "Ethnobotany of Starter Cultures Used in Alcohol Fermentation by a Few Ethnic Tribes of Northeast India." *Indian Journal of Traditional Knowledge* 9, no. 3 (2010): 463–66.

Tarble de Scaramelli, Kay, and Franz Scaramelli. "Cooking for Fame or Fortune: The Effect of European Contact on *Casabe* Production in the Orinoco." In *The Menial Art of Cooking*, edited by Sarah R. Graff and Enrique Rodrgues-Alegria. Boulder, CO: University Press of Colorado, 2012.

Taye, Dereje. "Call for Access and Benefit Sharing of *Rhamnus prinoides*." Ethiopian Biodiversity Institute, July 19, 2016. http://et.chm-cbd.net/news/call-for-access-and-benefit-sharing-of-rhamnus-prinoides-gesho.

Taylor, John. "The Penniless Pilgrimage." In *Works of John Taylor, the Water Poet*, edited by Charles Hindley. London: Reeves & Turner, 1876. https://scholarsbank.uoregon.edu/xmlui/bitstream/handle/1794/5419/taylor2.pdf?sequence=1.

Taylor Sen, Colleen. "Bangladesh." In *Food Cultures of the World Encyclopedia: Volume 3: Asia and Oceania*, edited by Ken Albala. Santa Barbara, CA: Greenwood, 2011.

———. "Nepal." In *Food Cultures of the World Encyclopedia: Volume 3: Asia and Oceania*, edited by Ken Albala. Santa Barbara, CA: Greenwood, 2011.

Teas, Mrs. Don. "Southern Piccalilli." In *Personal Recipes*, 261–62. Lockhart, TX: Christ Evangelical and Reformed Church, 1957.

Thompson, L., J. Sanders, D. McDonald, et al. "A Communal Catalogue Reveals Earth's Multiscale Microbial Diversity." *Nature* 551 (2017): 457–63.

Tine Brunost. "The Story of Anne Hove." http://www.tinebrunost.com/article/the-story-of-anne-hov-copy.

Tomasik, Timothy J. "Fishes, Fowl, and La Fleur de toute cuysine: Gaster and Gastronomy in Rabelais's Quart livre." In *Renaissance Food from Rabelais to Shakespeare*, edited by Joan Fitzpatrick, 25–52. Burlington, VT: Ashgate, 2010.

Tonon, Rafael. "Staying Faithful to Acarajé." *Anthony Bourdain: Parts Unknown*, March 1, 2018. https://explorepartsunknown.com/brazil/bahia-salvador-acaraje/.

Townsends. "Making Mushroom Ketchup." 18th Century Cooking Series at Jas. Townsend and Son. YouTube video, January 29, 2012. https://youtu.be/29u_FejNuks.

Turgeon, Christopher D. "Bacchus and Bellum: The Anglo-Gascon Wine Trade and the Hundred Years War (987 to 1453 A.D)." Master's thesis, College of William & Mary, 2000. https://scholarworks.wm.edu/cgi/viewcontent.cgi?article=5813&context=etd.

Twitty, Michael. *Afroculinaria* (blog). https://afroculinaria.com.

———. "Food and the Book: 1300–1800." *The Newberry*. https://www.newberry.org/10022020-food-and-book-1300-1800.

———. "Inspired by Hercules: Akara." First Chefs: Fame and Foodways from Britain to the Americas, Folger Shakespeare Library. Accessed December 30, 2019. https://folger.edu/exhibitions/first-chefs/recipes#hercules.

Umami Information Center. "List of Umami Rich Ingredients." Accessed November 8, 2020. https://www.umamiinfo.com/richfood/.

Ungar, Peter. "The 'True' Human Diet: From the Standpoint of Paleoecology, the So-Called Paleo Diet Is a Myth." *Scientific American*, April 17, 2017. https://blogs.scientificamerican.com/guest-blog/the-true-human-diet/.

United Nations Educational, Scientific and Cultural Organization. "Kimjang, Making and Sharing Kimchi in the Republic of Korea." Accessed November 11, 2020. https://ich.unesco.org/en/RL/kimjang-making-and-sharing-kimchi-in-the-republic-of-korea-00881.

US National Library of Medicine. "The World of Shakespeare's Humors." https://www.nlm.nih.gov/exhibition/shakespeare/fourhumors.html.

Uyehara, Mari. "The Modern Jang Master." *TASTE*, May 17, 2018. https://www.tastecooking.com/modern-jang-master/.

Vaughan, Theresa A. "The Alewife: Changing Images and Bad Brews." *Avista Forum Journal* 21, no. 1/2 (2011): 34–41.

Vaughn, R. H. "The Microbiology of Vegetable Fermentations." In *Microbiology of Fermented Foods*, vol. 1, edited by B. J. B. Wood, 49–109. New York: Elsevier, 1985.

Velsko, Irina M., and Christina Warinner. "Bioarchaeology of the Human Microbiome." *Bioarchaeology International* 1, nos. 1–2 (2017): 86–99.

Vinepair. "How Wine Colonized the World." https://vinepair.com/wine-colonized-world-wine-history/.

———. "The History of Distilling." https://vinepair.com/spirits-101/history-of-distilling/.

Wacher, Carmen. "Nixtamalization, a Mesoamerican Technology to Process Maize at Small-Scale with Great Potential for Improving the Nutritional Quality of Maize Based Foods." In *2nd International Workshop: Food-based Approaches for a Healthy Nutrition, Ouagadougou, Burkina Faso*, November 23–28, 2003, 735–44. Rome: Food and Agriculture Organization of the United Nations.

Wallace, Pamela S. "Sofkey." Oklahoma Historical Society. Accessed November 1, 2020, https://www.okhistory.org/publications/enc/entry.php?entry=SO003.

Walsh, Eoghan. "The Gruit and the Good—The Enterprising German Brewers Bringing Gruit Culture Back to Its Roots." *Good Beer Hunting* (blog), September 9, 2020. https://www.goodbeerhunting.com/blog/2020/9/8/the-gruit-and-the-good-the-enterprising-german-brewers-bringing-gruit-culture-back-to-its-roots.

Wang, Huiying, et al. "Effect of Probiotics on Central Nervous System Functions in Animals and Humans: A Systematic Review." *Journal of Neurogastroenterology and Motility* 22, no. 4 (2016): 589–605. https://doi:10.5056/jnm16018.

Warinner, C., C. Speller, and M. J. Collins. "A New Era in Palaeomicrobiology: Prospects for Ancient Dental Calculus as a Long-Term Record of the Human Oral Microbiome." *Philosophical Transactions of the Royal Society B*, 370 (2015), 20130376.

Weedeater Documentary. "About." Accessed November 10, 2020. http://weedeaterdocumentary.com/about.

Wholesome Kitchen , The. "Marcella Hazan's Tomato Sauce." May 7, 2020. https://www.twkchicago.com/tag/tomato/.

Wiggins, Jasmine. "How Was Ketchup Invented?" *National Geographic*, April 21, 2014. https://www.nationalgeographic.com/culture/food/the-plate/2014/04/21/how-was-ketchup-invented/.

Wild Colours. "History of Indigo & Indigo Dyeing." Accessed November 12, 2020. http://www.wildcolours.co.uk/html/indigo_history.html.

Wilford, John Noble. "In Ancient Egypt, the Beer of Kings Was a Sophisticated Brew." *New York Times*, July 26, 1996. https://www.nytimes.com/1996/07/26/world/in-ancient-egypt-the-beer-of-kings-was-a-sophisticated-brew.html.

Williams, Allison. "How Germans Are Taking Back Sauerkraut." *Handelsblatt*, December 30, 2017. https://www.handelsblatt.com/english/companies/sour-power-how-germans-are-taking-back-sauerkraut/23573570.html.

Wilson, Christine S. "Southeast Asia." In *The Cambridge World History of Food*, edited by Kenneth F. Kiple and Kriemhild Coneè Ornelas, 1151–64. Cambridge: Cambridge University Press, 2000.

Witt, Lulu. "Tarhana—A Labour of Love." *Pantry Fun*, October 28, 2018. http://seasonalcookinturkey.com/turkish-tarhana-labour-of-love.

Woo, Jiwon. "Hand Taste (*son-mat*), 2016–2017." Jiwon Woo. Accessed May 16, 2019. https://www.woojiwon.com/mht.

Wright, Clarissa Dickson, and Johnny Scott. "Know Your Oats: Grow Your Own Grains." *The Ecologist*, August 25, 2009. https://theecologist.org/2009/aug/25/know-your-oats-grow-your-own-grains.

Wright, Katherine I. "Domestication and Inequality? Households, Corporate Groups and Food Processing Tools at Neolithic Çatalhöyük." *Journal of Anthropological Archaeology* 33 (2014): 1–33. https://www.sciencedirect.com/science/article/pii/S027841651300055X.

Valamoti, Soultana Maria. "Plant Food Ingredients and 'Recipes' from Prehistoric Greece: The Archaeobotanical Evidence." *Plants and Culture: Seeds of the Cultural Heritage of Europe* (2009): 25–38.

Van Esterik, Penny. "Cambodia." In *Food Cultures of the World Encyclopedia: Volume 3: Asia and Oceania*, edited by Ken Albala, 44. Santa Barbara, CA: Greenwood, 2011.

Vos, Stijn, Tim S. Nawrot, Dries S. Martens, Hyang-Min Byun, and Bram G. Janssen. "Mitochondrial DNA Methylation in Placental Tissue: A Proof of Concept Study by Means of Prenatal Environmental Stressors." *Epigenetics* 16, no. 2 (2021): 121–31.

Yang, Yulan. "Pao Jiu Liquor and Its Preparation Method." China Patent Publication Number 1272536. https://patentscope.wipo.int/search/en/detail.jsf?docPN=CN1272536.

Yi, Dang. "What Are the Energies, Flavors and Properties of Other Foods?" Shen-Nong. Accessed November 10, 2020, http://www.shen-nong.com/eng/lifestyles/food_property_food_tcm.html.

Young, Zachary Jordan. "Hildegard of Bingen: Mystic of the Rhine." Master's thesis, San Jose State University, 2014. https://scholarworks.sjsu.edu/cgi/viewcontent.cgi?article=8069&context=etd_theses.

Zabel, Gary. "Hundred Years' War." University of Massachusetts, Boston. Accessed November 12, 2020. http://www.faculty.umb.edu/gary_zabel/Courses/Phil%20281b/Philosophy%20of%20Magic/Dante.%20etc/Philosophers/End/bluedot/100.html.

INTERVIEWS CONDUCTED FOR THIS BOOK

Ayurveda: Carrie and Suresh, Atina Foods

Corn beer: Don Lindgren

Chinese Medicine and Traditional Chinese Medicine: Tsao-Lin Moy

Chinese medicine and Traditional Chinese Medicine: Xinyi Gong

Epigenetics: Dr. Ellen Ireland

Ferments and community; personal fermentation practice: Rich Shih

Fermentation history; fermented foods through history: Dr. Ken Albala

Fermentation history; personal fermentation practices: Dr. Leni Sorensen

Ferments and health; personal fermentation philosophies: Nickawanna Shaw

Fermentation practice; personal fermentation philosophies: Cheryl Paswater

Fish sauce in Chinese culture; fermentation philosophies: Mara King

Home fermentation practices: Claire Thoele

Home fermentation practices: Larri Brady

Home food preservation: Sherri Vinton

Indian ferments; Ayurveda: Nandita Godbole

Indigo dye: Elliot McNally

Kvass: Kristina Razueva

Lahpet thoke: Kirsten Shockey

Lahpet thoke: MiMi Aye

The present and future of microbiology: Dr. Sudeep Agarwala

Pozol: Danielle Gauna

Senegalese ferments: Abdala Faye

West African ferments and fermented foods in the African diaspora: Michael Twitty

BOOKS

Achaya, K. T. *A Historical Dictionary of Indian Food*. Delhi: Oxford University Press, 1998.

Albala, Ken. *Beans: A History*. New York: Berg, 2007.

————. *Cooking in Europe: 1250–1650*. Westport, CT: Greenwood Press, 2006.

————. *Eating Right in the Renaissance*. Berkeley: University of California Press, 2002.

————. ed. *The Food History Reader*. New York: Bloomsbury, 2014.

————. *Food in Early Modern Europe*. Westport, CT: Greenwood Press, 2003.

Albala, Ken, and Rosanna Nafziger. *The Lost Art of Real Cooking: Rediscovering the Pleasures of Traditional Food One Recipe at a Time*. New York: TarcherPerigree, 2010.

Albala, Ken, and Rosanna Nafziger Henderson. *The Lost Arts of Hearth and Home: The Happy Luddite's Guide to Domestic Self-Sufficiency*. New York: TarcherPerigree, 2012.

Anderson, E. N. *The Food of China*. New Haven, CT: Yale University Press, 1988.

Apicius. *Cookery and Dining in Imperial Rome*. Translated by Joseph Dommers Vehling. New York: Dover, 1977.

Ausubel, Kenny. *Dreaming the Future*. White River Junction, VT: Chelsea Green, 2012.

Aye, MiMi. *Mandalay: Recipes and Tales from a Burmese Kitchen*. London: Bloomsbury, 2019.

Bardwell, Genevieve, and Susan Ray Brown. *Salt Rising Bread: Recipes and Heartfelt Stories of a Nearly Lost Appalachian Tradition*. Pittsburgh: St. Lynn's Press, 2009.

Barnett, Richard. *The Book of Gin*. New York: Grove Press, 2012.

Bateman, Helen, Monica Berton, Fiona Doig, Emma Driver, John Mapps, and Selena Quintrell, eds. *Edible: An Illustrated Guide to the World's Food Plants*. Washington, DC: National Geographic Society, 2008.

Battcock, Mike, and Sue Azam-Ali. *Fermented Fruits and Vegetables: A Global Perspective*. Rome: Food and Agriculture Organization of the United Nations, 1998.

Baudar, Pascal. *The Wildcrafting Brewer*. White River Junction, VT: Chelsea Green, 2018.

Bertelsen, Cynthia D. *A Hastiness of Cooks*. Gainesville, FL: Turquoise Moon Press, 2019.

Betzer, Sarah. *Ingres and the Studio: Women, Painting, History*. University Park, PA: Pennsylvania State University Press, 2012.

Beyerl, Paul. *The Master Book of Herbalism*. Blaine, WA: Phoenix Publishing, 1984.

Brillat-Savarin, Jean Anthelme. *The Physiology of Taste*. Translated by M. F. K. Fisher. New York: Vintage Books, 1949.

Briscione, James, and Brooke Parkhurst. *The Flavor Matrix*. New York: Houghton Mifflin Harcourt, 2018.

brown, adrienne marie. *Pleasure Activism*. Sterling, UK: AK Press, 2019.

Brown, Pete. *Miracle Brew*. White River Junction, VT: Chelsea Green, 2017.

Buchanan, David. *Taste, Memory: Forgotten Foods, Lost Flavors, and Why They Matter*. White River Junction, VT: Chelsea Green, 2012.

Buhner, Stephen Harrod. *Sacred and Herbal Healing Beers*. Boulder, CO: Brewers Publications, 1998.

Bury, Lady Charlotte. *The Lady's Own Cookery Book, and New Dinner-Table Directory*. London: Henry Colburn, 1844.

Butler, Rhonda, and Pam Durban Porter. *Cabbagetown Families, Cabbagetown Food*. Atlanta: Patch Publications, 1976.

Byarugaba-Bazirake, George William. "The Effect of Enzymatic Processing on Banana Juice and Wine." PhD diss., Stellenbosch University, 2008.

Carney, Judith A., and Richard Nicholas Rosomoff. *In the Shadow of Slavery: Africa's Botanical Legacy in the Atlantic World*. Berkeley: University of California Press, 2011.

Chang, K. C., ed. *Food in Chinese Culture: Anthropological and Historical Perspectives*. New Haven, CT: Yale University Press, 1977.

Ciezadlo, Annia. *Day of Honey: A Memoir of Food, Love, and War*. New York: Free Press, 2011.

Clarke, H. C. *Clarke's Confederate Household Almanac*. Vicksburg, MS: H. C. Clarke, 1863.

Clayton, Bernard, Jr. *Bernard Clayton's New Complete Book of Breads*. New York: Simon & Schuster, 2003.

Cooper, Geoffrey M. *The Cell: A Molecular Approach*. 2nd ed. Sunderland, MA: Sinauer Associates, 2000.

Crook, Steven, and Katy Hui-wen Hung. *A Culinary History of Taipei: Beyond Pork and Ponlai*. Lanham, MD: Rowman & Littlefield, 2018.

Dalby, Andrew. *Empire of Pleasures: Luxury and Indulgence in the Roman World*. London: Routledge, 2000.

Dalby, Andrew, and Sally Grainger. *The Classical Cookbook , Revised Edition*. Los Angeles: J. Paul Getty Museum, 2012.

Davidson, Alan. *The Oxford Companion to Food*. Oxford: Oxford University Press, 1999.

de Blasi, Marlena. *A Thousand Days in Tuscany*. New York: Ballantine Books, 2005.

Diaz, Von. *Coconuts and Collards*. Gainesville, FL: University Press of Florida, 2018.

Dirar, Hamid. *The Indigenous Fermented Foods of the Sudan: A Study in African Food and Nutrition*. Wallingford, UK: CAB International, 1993.

Egan, Sophie. *Devoured: How What We Eat Defines Who We Are*. New York: HarperCollins, 2016.

Escoffier, Auguste. *A Guide to Modern Cookery*. London: William Heinemann, 1907.

Estés, Clarissa Pinkola. *Women Who Run with the Wolves: Myths and Stories of the Wild Woman Archetype*. New York: Ballantine Books, 1992.

Feiring, Alice. *Naked Wine*. Cambridge, MA: Da Capo Press, 2011.

Fieldhouse, Paul. *Food, Feasts, and Faith: An Encyclopedia of Food Culture in World Religions* (2 volumes). Santa Barbara, CA: ABC-CLIO, 2017.

Foucault, Michel. *Discipline and Punish*. Translated by Alan Sheridan. New York: Vintage Books, 1995.

Freedman, Paul, Joyce E. Chaplin, and Ken Albala, eds. *Food in Time and Place*. Berkeley: University of California Press, 2014.

Gagliano, Monica. *Thus Spoke the Plant*. Berkeley: North Atlantic Books, 2018.

Gaiman, Neil. *Norse Mythology*. New York: W. W. Norton, 2017.

Gately, Iain. *Drink: A Cultural History of Alcohol*. New York: Gotham Books, 2008.

Gebreyesus, Yohanis. *Ethiopia: Recipes and Traditions from the Horn of Africa*. London: Octopus, 2018.

Gordinier, Jeff. *Hungry*. New York: Tim Duggan Books, 2019.

Grainger, Sally. *Cooking Apicius: Roman Recipes for Today*. London: Prospect Books, 2006.

Grumezescu, Alexandru, and Alina Maria Holban, eds. *Nutrients in Beverages*. The Science of Beverages, vol. 12. Duxford, UK: Woodhead Publishing, 2019.

Guy, Kolleen M. *When Champagne Became French: Wine and the Making of a National Identity*. Baltimore: The Johns Hopkins University Press, 2003.

Hachisu, Nancy Singleton. *Preserving the Japanese Way*. Kansas City, MO: Andrews McMeel, 2015.

Hagen, Ann. *A Second Handbook of Anglo-Saxon Food & Drink: Production & Distribution*. Little Downham, Cambridgeshire, UK: Anglo-Saxon Books, 1995.

Hall, Carla. *Carla Hall's Soul Food*. New York: Harper Wave, 2018.

Harlow, William M. *Trees of the Eastern and Central United States and Canada*. New York, Dover Publications, 1957.

Hatfield, Gabrielle. *Encyclopedia of Folk Medicine: Old World and New World Traditions*. Santa Barbara, CA: ABC-CLIO, 2004.

Heinzelmann, Ursula. *Food Culture in Germany*. Westport, CT: Greenwood Press, 2008.

Hess, Karen. *Martha Washington's Booke of Cookery*. New York: Columbia University Press, 1981.

Holder, Judith. *Christmas Fare*. Secaucus, NJ: Chartwell Books, 1981.

Howard, Vivian. *Deep Run Roots*. New York: Little, Brown and Company, 2016.

Hudson, Charles. *The Southeastern Indians*. Knoxville, TN: University of Tennessee Press, 1976.

Hui, Y. H., Sue Ghazala, Dee M. Graham, K. D. Murrell, and Wai-Kit Nip, eds. *Handbook of Vegetable Preservation and Processing*. Boca Raton, FL: CRC Press, 2005.

Hutchens, Alma R. *A Handbook of Native American Herbs*. Boulder: Shambhala, 1992.

Inikori, Joseph E., and Stanley L. Engerman, eds. *The Atlantic Slave Trade: Effects on Economies, Societies, and Peoples in Africa, the Americas, and Europe*. Durham, NC: Duke University Press, 1998.

Ishige, Naomichi. *The History and Culture of Japanese Food*. New York: Routledge, 2011.

Ishikawa, Masayuki. *Moyashimon: Tales of Agriculture* [manga series]. New York: Del Ray Manga, 2004–14.

Jackson, Ronald S. *Wine Science: Principles and Applications*, 3rd ed. London: Academic Press, 2008.

Jaeger, Paul T., and Gary Burnett. *Information Worlds: Social Context, Technology, and Information Behavior in the Age of the Internet*. New York: Routledge, 2010.

Janik, Erika. *Apple: A Global History*. London: Reaktion Books, 2011.

Katz, Sandor Ellix. *The Art of Fermentation*. White River Junction, VT: Chelsea Green, 2012.

———. *Fermentation as Metaphor*. White River Junction, VT: Chelsea Green, 2020.

———. *Wild Fermentation*. Rev. ed. White River Junction, VT: Chelsea Green, 2016.

Knapp, Arthur William. *Cocoa and Chocolate: Their History from Plantation to Consumer*. London: Chapman and Hall, 1920.

Kurlansky, Mark. *Salt: A World History*. New York: Walker and Company, 2002.

Lane, Joan. *A Social History of Medicine: Health, Healing and Disease in England, 1750–1950*. New York: Routledge, 2001.

Langlands, Alexander. *Craeft*. New York: W. W. Norton, 2018.

Laudan, Rachel. *The Food of Paradise: Exploring Hawaii's Culinary Heritage*. Honolulu: University of Hawaii Press, 1996.

Leigh, Meredith. *The Ethical Meat Handbook*. Gabriola Island, BC, Canada: New Society Publishers, 2015.

Leong, Elaine. *Recipes and Everyday Knowledge*. Chicago: The University of Chicago Press, 2018.

Li, Zhengping. *Chinese Wine*. Cambridge: Cambridge University Press, 2011.

Light, Phyllis D. *Southern Folk Medicine*. Berkeley: North Atlantic Books, 2018.

Lopes, Jane. *Vignette: Stories of Life & Wine in 100 Bottles*. Richmond, Victoria, AU: Hardie Grant, 2019.

Lundy, Ronni. *Victuals*. New York: Clarkson Potter, 2016.

MacKenzie, Aggie, and Emma Marsden. *The Miracle of Vinegar: 150 Easy Recipes and Uses for Home, Health and Beauty*. London: HQ, 2019.

Magness, Perre Coleman. *The Southern Sympathy Cookbook: Funeral Food with a Twist*. Woodstock, VT: Countryman Press, 2018.

Malle, Bettina, and Helge Schmikl. *The Artisanal Vinegar Maker's Handbook*. Austin: Spikehorn Press, 2015.

Maloof, Joan. *Teaching the Trees: Lessons from the Forest*. Athens: University of Georgia Press, 2007.

Margulis, Lynn, and Dorion Sagan. *Dazzle Gradually: Reflections on the Nature of Nature*. White River Junction, VT: Chelsea Green, 2007.

———. *Microcosmos: Four Billion Years of Evolution from our Microbial Ancestors*. New York: Summit Books, 1986.

Markham, Gervase. *The English Housewife*. Edited by Michael R. Best. Montreal: McGill-Queen's University Press, 1986.

McGee, Harold. *On Food and Cooking*. Rev. ed. New York: Scribner, 2004.

———. *Nose Dive: A Field Guide to the World's Smells*. New York: Penguin, 2020.

McGovern, Patrick. *Uncorking the Past: The Quest for Wine, Beer, and Other Alcoholic Beverages*. Berkeley: University of California Press, 2009.

McGrath, Maria. *Food for Dissent: Natural Foods and the Consumer Counterculture Since the 1960s*. Amherst: University of Massachusetts Press, 2019.

McLafferty, Clair. *Romantic Cocktails*. New York: Whalen, 2019.

McNeill, F. Marian. *The Scots Kitchen*. London: Blackie & Son, 1929.

———. *The Silver Bough, Vol. 3: A Calendar of Scottish National Festivals—Hallowe'en to Yule*. Glasgow: William McLellan, 1961.

Metcalfe, Gayden, and Charlotte Hayes. *Being Dead Is No Excuse: The Official Southern Ladies Guide to Hosting the Perfect Funeral*. New York: Hachette, 2013.

Minnick, Fred. *Mead: The Libations, Legends, and Lore of History's Oldest Drink*. Philadelphia: Running Press, 2018.

Mintz, Sidney W. *Sweetness and Power*. New York: Penguin, 1985.

Molokhovets, Elena. *Classic Russian Cooking: Elena Molokhovets' A Gift to Young Housewives*. Translated by Joyce Toomre. Bloomington: Indiana University Press, 1998.

Money, Nicholas P. *The Rise of Yeast: How the Sugar Fungus Shaped Civilisation*. Oxford: Oxford University Press, 2018.

Morell, Sally Fallon. *Nourishing Diets: How Paleo, Ancestral and Traditional Peoples Really Ate*. New York: Grand Central Life & Style, 2018.

Morrison, Karl F. *History as Visual Art in the Twelfth-Century Renaissance*. Princeton, NJ: Princeton University Press, 1990.

Mountain, Harry. *The Celtic Encyclopedia*. Vol. 2. Self-published, 1997.

Nabhan, Gary Paul. *Mesquite*. White River Junction, VT: Chelsea Green, 2018.

Nash, D. W. *Taliesin; or, The Bards and Druids of Britain*. London: John Russell Smith, 1858.

Nasrallah, Nawal, trans. *Annals of the Caliphs' Kitchens: Ibn Sayyār al-Warrāq's Tenth-Century Baghdadi Cookbook*. Leiden: Brill, 2007.

National Research Council (US). *Science, Medicine, and Animals*. Washington, DC: The National Academies Press, 2004. https://www.ncbi.nlm.nih.gov/books/NBK24649.

Nelson, Max. *The Barbarian's Beverage: A History of Beer in Ancient Europe*. New York: Routledge, 2005.

Nosrat, Samin. *Salt, Fat, Acid, Heat*. New York: Simon & Schuster, 2017.

Odinsson, Eoghan. *Northern Lore: A Field Guide to the Northern Mind-Body-Spirit*. Self-published, 2010.

Page, Karen, and Andrew Dornenburg. *The Flavor Bible*. New York: Little, Brown and Company, 2008.

Parker, Thomas. *Tasting French Terroir: The History of an Idea*. Berkeley: University of California Press, 2015.

Pendergrast, Mark. *Uncommon Grounds: The History of Coffee and How it Transformed Our World*. New York: Basic Books, 2010.

Phillips, Rod. *Wine: A Social and Cultural History of the Drink That Changed Our Lives*. Oxford: Infinite Ideas Limited, 2018.

Pliny the Elder. *The Natural History*. John Bostock and H. T. Riley, trans. London: Taylor and Francis, 1855.

Pollan, Michael. *Cooked : A Natural History of Transformation*. New York: Penguin, 2013.

Prance, Sir Ghillean, and Mark Nesbitt. *The Cultural History of Plants*. New York: Routledge, 2005.

Quayle, Eric. *Old Cook Books: An Illustrated History*. London: Studio Vista, 1978.

Redzepi, René, and David Zilber. *The Noma Guide to Fermentation*. New York: Artisan, 2018.

Richards, Todd. *Soul: A Chef's Culinary Evolution in 150 Recipes*. New York: Time Inc. Books, 2018.

Risatti, Howard. *A Theory of Craft*. Chapel Hill, NC: The University of North Carolina Press, 2007.

Rose, Anthony. *Sake and the Wines of Japan*. Oxford: Infinite Ideas, 2018.

Rosenblum, Harry. *Vinegar Revival*. New York: Clarkson Potter, 2017.

Ruhlman, Michael, and Brian Polcyn. *Charcuterie: The Craft of Salting, Smoking, and Curing*. New York: W. W. Norton, 2005.

Russell, Malinda. *A Domestic Cook Book: Containing a Careful Selection of Useful Receipts for the Kitchen*. Paw Paw, MI: Self-published, 1866.

Ryall, Rhiannon. *West Country Wicca: A Journal of the Old Religion*. Blaine, WA: Phoenix Publishing, 1990.

Sale, Kirkpatrick. *Human Scale Revisited*. White River Junction, VT: Chelsea Green, 2017.

Schwartz, Arthur. *Arthur Schwartz's New York City Food*. New York: Stewart, Tabori, & Chang, 2004.

Sercarz, Lior Lev. *The Spice Companion: A Guide to the World of Spices*. New York: Clarkson Potter, 2016.

Shephard, Sue. *Pickled, Potted, and Canned*. Simon & Schuster: New York, 2000.

Sheridan, Richard B. *Sugar and Slavery: An Economic History of the British West Indies, 1623–1775*. Kingston, JM: Canoe Press, 1994.

Shi, John, Chi-Tang Ho, and Fereidoon Shahidi. *Asian Functional Foods*. Boca Raton, FL: CRC Press, 2005.

Shih, Rich, and Jeremy Umansky. *Koji Alchemy*. White River Junction, VT: Chelsea Green, 2020.

Shockey, Christopher, and Kirsten K. Shockey. *The Big Book of Cidermaking*. North Adams, MA: Storey, 2020.

Shockey, Kirsten K., and Christopher Shockey. *Miso, Tempeh, Natto & Other Tasty Ferments*. North Adams, MA: Storey Publishing, 2019.

Shurtleff, William, and Akiko Aoyagi. *Amazake and Amazake Frozen Desserts*. Lafayette, CA: Soyfoods Center, 1988.

———. *History of Koji: Grains and/or Soybeans Enrobed with a Mold Culture (300 BCE to 2012)*. Lafayette, CA: Soyinfo Center, 2012.

———. *History of Miso and Its Near Relatives (200 BCE to 2021)*. Lafayette, CA: Soyinfo Center, 2021.

———. *History of Soybeans and Soyfoods in Japan, and in Japanese Cookbooks and Restaurants outside Japan (701 CE to 2014)*. Lafayette, CA: Soyinfo Center, 2014.

———. *History of Soybeans and Soyfoods in South Asia/Indian Subcontinent (1656–2010)*. Lafayette, CA: Soyinfo Center, 2010.

———. *History of Worcestershire Sauce (1837–2012)*. Lafayette, CA: Soyinfo Center, 2012.

Silver, Laura. *Knish: In Search of the Jewish Soul Food*. Lebanon, NH: Brandeis University Press, 2014.

Simard, Suzanne. *Finding the Mother Tree: Discovering the Wisdom of the Forest*. New York: Alfred A. Knopf, 2021.

Simonton, Deborah. *A History of European Women's Work: 1700 to the Present*. London: Routledge, 1998.

Simoons, Frederick J. *Food in China: A Cultural and Historical Inquiry*. Boca Raton, FL: CRC Press, 1991.

Skinner, Julia. *Afternoon Tea: A History*. Lanham, MD: Rowman & Littlefield, 2019.

Smith, Andrew F., ed. *The Oxford Encyclopedia of Food and Drink in America*. 3 vols. Oxford: Oxford University Press, 2013.

Smith, Andrew F. *Pure Ketchup: A History of America's National Condiment, with Recipes*. Columbia, SC: University of South Carolina Press, 1996.

Smith, Morgan. *Bricriu's Feast: An Inquiry into the Diet and Cooking Techniques of the Early Medieval Irish*. Columbia, SC: Traveling Light, 2004.

Sondhi, Amrita. *The Tastes of Ayurveda: More Healthful, Healing Recipes for the Modern Ayurvedic*. Canada: Arsenal Pulp Press, 2012.

Spencer, Judith, trans. *The Four Seasons of the House of Cerruti*. New York: Facts on File, 1984.

Spengler, Robert N. III. *Fruit from the Sands: The Silk Road Origins of the Foods We Eat*. Oakland: University of California Press, 2019.

Snowden, David, trans. *Flans and Wine: A Benedictine Recipe Book from Evesham Abbey*. Evesham, UK: lulu.com, 2015.

Spiller, Elizabeth, ed. *Seventeenth Century English Recipe Books: Cooking, Physic and Chirurgery in the Works of Elizabeth Talbot Grey and Aletheia Talbot Howard*. London: Routledge, 2016.

Standage, Tom. *A History of the World in 6 Glasses*. New York: Walker & Company, 2005.

Steingarten, Jeffrey. *The Man Who Ate Everything*. New York: Vintage Books, 1998.

Stewart, William Grant. *The Popular Superstitions and Festive Amusements of the Highlanders of Scotland*. London: Aylott and Jones, 1851.

Stradal, J. Ryan. *Kitchens of the Great Midwest: A Novel*. New York: Viking, 2015.

Tamang, Jyoti Prakash, and Kasipathy Kailasapathy, eds. *Fermented Foods and Beverages of the World*. Boca Raton, FL: CRC Press, 2010.

Thompson, Ian. *Choctaw Food*. Durant, OK: Choctaw Nation of Oklahoma, 2019.

Tipton-Martin, Toni. *The Jemima Code: Two Centuries of African American Cookbooks*. Austin: University of Texas Press, 2015.

Trentmann, Frank. *Empire of Things: How We Became a World of Consumers, from the Fifteenth Century to the Twenty-First*. New York: HarperCollins, 2016.

Trubek, Amy B. *The Taste of Place: A Cultural Journey into Terroir*. Berkeley: University of California Press, 2008.

Truong, Monique. *The Book of Salt*. New York: Houghton Mifflin Harcourt, 2004.

Toussaint-Samat, Maguelonne. *History of Food*. Translated by Anthea Bell. New York: Blackwell, 1992.

Twitty, Michael W. *The Cooking Gene: A Journey through African American Culinary History in the Old South*. New York: HarperCollins, 2017.

Unger, Richard W. *Beer in the Middle Ages and the Renaissance*. Philadelphia: University of Pennsylvania Press, 2004.

Van Willigen, John. *Applied Anthropology: An Introduction*. 3rd ed. Westport, CT: Bergin & Garvey, 2002.

Wallace, Benjamin. *The Billionaire's Vinegar*. New York: Three Rivers Press, 2009.

Wallach, Jennifer Jensen. *How America Eats*. Lanham, MD: Rowman & Littlefield, 2013.

Walvin, James. *Slavery in Small Things: Slavery and Modern Cultural Habits*. West Sussex, UK: John Wiley & Sons, 2017.

Ward, Christina. *Preservation: The Art and Science of Canning, Fermentation and Dehydration*. Port Townsend, WA: Process Media, 2017.

Watson, Ben. *Cider: Hard & Sweet*. 3rd ed. Woodstock, VT: The Countryman Press, 2013.

Watson, William. *Glimpses o' Auld Lang Syne*. Aberdeen: William Smith, 1903.

Watt, Alexander. *The Early History of Kintore: Extracted from Old Records and Charters*. Kintore: Mrs. Alexander Watt, 1865.

Wellcome, Henry. *Ancient Cymric Medicine*. Edmonds, WA: Sure Fire Press, 1988.

Wells, Lenny. *Pecan: America's Native Nut Tree*. Tuscaloosa, AL: University of Alabama Press, 2017.

Wigginton, Elliot, ed. *The Foxfire Book*. New York: Anchor Books, 1972.

Williams, Victoria. *Celebrating Life Customs around the World: From Baby Showers to Funerals*. 3 vols. Santa Barbara, CA: ABC-CLIO, 2017.

Wilson, Bee. *Consider the Fork: A History of How We Cook and Eat*. New York: Basic Books, 2012.

Wilson, H. L. *Making American Cheese on the Farm for Home Consumption*. Washington, DC: US Department of Agriculture, 1934.

Zimmerman, Jereme. *Make Mead Like a Viking*. White River Junction, VT: Chelsea Green, 2015.

Acknowledgments

First and foremost, I want to thank my publisher, Storey Publishing, who believed in a book that broke from the usual fermentation book format and published it with an enthusiasm for my vision that I am eternally grateful for. My editors, Carleen Madigan and Sarah Guare Slattery, as well as everyone from copy editing to design to marketing, were all a joy to work with and helped shape the book into something far more wonderful than I ever could have achieved on my own.

My agent, Lisa Ekus, deserves endless gratitude for working tirelessly to place my work in the right hands because she believed this book needed to be written. Her belief in me and my work lifted my sails even at times when the seas of writing felt uncertain.

I also want to thank my dearest fermentation friends, many of whom I've had the great pleasure of meeting and working alongside, and some of whom I foster online (and hopefully someday in-person!) relationships with. Their impact is felt throughout these pages and in my daily fermentation practice. The fermentation community is the most inspiring, connective, curious, and truly human group (in the most beautiful ways), and I'm excited to see all the wonderful ways we'll grow from here.

Sandor Katz brought me into his residency at a crucial moment: I applied to his program while contemplating a serious shift in my career and attended after that shift had come to pass, while in the throes of many personal life changes both tumultuous and beautiful. Through the residency, I found a space to return to myself and the places I had overlooked within myself, and I was able to give my curiosity and enthusiasm (about ferments and beyond) safe quarter to be and to be nurtured. Through him, I met friends who have become a constant source of inspiration, joy, comfort, and exciting collaboration.

I am continuously in awe of both the talent and the kindheartedness of so many in our fermentation community, including Kirsten and Christopher Shockey, Cheryl Paswater, Mara King, Rich Shih, Jeremy Umansky, Sean Doherty, Nickawanna Shaw, Mallory O'Donnell, Ken Fornataro, Alana Toro-Ramos, Lyndon Smith, South River Miso, Wade Fox, Myllasa Riggins, Ishita Bhatia, Maya Hey, Annie Levy, Johnny Drain, Arielle Johnson, Pascal Baudar, Harvest Root Ferments, Raquel Guajardo, Jackie Vitale, Tara Whitsitt, Nella Fusco, Nicole Easterday, Claudia Lucero, Jitti Chaithiraphant, Meredith Leigh, David Zilber, Goen Fermented Foods, Connie Chew, Jo Webster, Justin Dean, Alex Lewin, Trevor Ring, and many others.

I am so grateful for my many colleagues in the culinary fields and beyond who enrich my world in a variety of ways, as friends, mentors, and inspirations, and who aided this book, both directly and indirectly, through advice, brainstorms, sharing knowledge and inspiration, or doing amazing work that informs my own. They include Michael Twitty, Cheikh Ndiaye, Joan Galloway, Anne Bramley, Kyle Cassidy, Elliot McNally, Chef Zu, Umi Feeds, Sudeep Agarwala, Adrian Miller, Elazar Sontag, Sylvan Tea, Amethyst Ganaway, Nia-Raquelle Smith, Zosima Castaneda, Allan Jenkins, Cassandra Loftin, Jen Billock, Rebecca Peloquin, Leni Sorensen, Virginia Willis, Amy Rogers, Claudine Pepin, Jill Neimark, Elizabeth Gabay, Deborah VanTrece, Nicole Cooke, Jeff Gordinier, Leah Penniman, Alicia Kennedy, Christine Stevens, Vitus Spehar, Toni Tipton-Martin, Gena Berry, Kat Kinsman, Mercedes Melendez, Taylor Friese, Hardette Harris, Nandita Godbole, Sally Ekus, Scott Alves Barton, Forrest Hyden, Patrick Sweeney, Hart Epstein, Tiffanie Barriere, Asha Gomez, Tim Jamison, Eleana Hsu, Dawn Betts-Green, Lia Picard, Judith Winfrey, Roshara Sanders, Jennifer Booker, Whit Whitire, Serenity Ibsen, Kelly Fields, Andre Brookins, Bethany Barton, Kim Forster, Alphonso Betty, Mark Phillips, Jeanette Flores-Katz, Robin Santos, Emily Contois, Rose McAdoo, Almeta Tulloss, Nicole Bluh, Ethan Frisch, Alexandra Mackey, Rachel Laudan, Quianah Upton, Raghavan Iyer, Eileen Cho, Jenny Dorsey, Fernando Justo, Drew Kitchens, Christian Zabriskie, Emily Maxwell, Cynthia Stevens Graubart, Karl Gorline, Lena Katz, Kelbi McCumber Morris, Clair McLafferty, Richard DeMontmillion, Zack Ramsey, Allison Devers, Von Diaz, Jessica Kerr, Barbara Pires, Natasha Pogrebinsky, Brady Lowe, Doris Inga, Jeremy Fisher, Sarah Baker, Demitrio Lima, Clifton Lawley, Lauren Utvitch, Marlo Mauricio, Taria Camerino, Garima Kothari, Kevin Mitchell, Katherine Spiers, Joe Yonan, Katie Carter King, Julia Fine, Cynthia Greenlee, Elizabeth Young, Jarod K. Anderson, Ligaya Figueras, Nicholas Gil, Jason Wilson, Ashlie Stevens, Wendell David Brock, Bettina Makalintal, Willa Zhen, Karon Liu, Lukas Volger, Iliana Regan, Dianne Jacob, Stephen Satterfield, Esther Tseng, Lea Zeltserman, Ashley Rose Young, John Birdsall, Alexandra Jones, Cathy Erway, Crystal King, Kim Severson, Rosalind Bentley, Joseph Hernandez, Taffy Elrod, Lauren Vogelbaum, Anney Reese, Kathleen Wall, Matt Kohl, Mercedes O'Brien, Emily Rothkrug, Evanye Lawson, Gina Breedlove, Jude Lally, Liz Alpern, Tasha Marks, Taffany Hyatt, Christina Gibson, Gina Lurubbio, Walker Brown, Darra Goldstein, Eric Kim, Anna Brones, Bee Wilson, Corrina Wood, Julia Turshen, The Wondersmith, Carolyn Ladd, Brent Hall, Jiyeon Lee, Don Lindgren, Ashley Rodgers, Hanna Rodgers, Michele Sponagle, Irina Groushevaia, David Ruggerio, Abiodun Henderson, MiMi Aye, Maggie Topkis, Prashant Shukla, Sean O'Keefe, Lisa McCusker, Ash Dawson, Akiko Katayama, Jaime Ladet, Our Friendly Allies, Betsy Gonzalez, Clark Barlowe, Lisa Marie Donovan, Tamie Cook, Simone Johnson, Sadie Hirst, Malou Herkes, Kathryn DiMenichi, and many others.

Ken Albala, who has been a mentor since I first timidly approached food studies in 2008, was the editor of my last book and, much to my great fortune, is my friend as well. Ken's guidance and friendship have helped me feel like I belong in this writing space, and that the work I do matters. We're fortunate to live in a world alongside him, where he's guided countless others to understand the same. I'd also like to thank Chad Cripe, friend and citation editor extraordinaire, who turned my sometimes disjointed citations into a work of art, and my wonderful intern and research assistant, Bhramari Schiff, for scouring through many a dense article and extracting everything useful for the book as well as every bit of humor. She made the last leg of writing not only easier but more enjoyable as well.

My friends and family have built with me an incredible community that supports and nurtures, and I'm grateful for them every day.

Sarah Higgins is a safe port in storms and calm, bright seas alike, asking me to return to myself and my truth and patiently sitting with me as I navigate whatever the seas may hold.

Brandon Sheats is the pinnacle of proud friendship in action, showing up to be with me as I celebrate life's ups and downs, beaming that pride outward in his ever-knowing and friendly way.

Doc Holliday's friendship is one of unconditional love and honesty, and has only deepened as we've both grown into ourselves. Their influence on me, my culinary practice, and my outlook on the world writ large can be seen throughout these pages.

Jessamine Starr and George Long open their home and hearts to friends near and far, are the ideal foraging adventure partners, and navigate the world with gentleness, creativity, and curiosity.

I also want to thank Jes Distad, who always inspires me to adventure; Narinder Elizabeth Bazen, whose wise guidance always soothes and steers the soul toward play and healing; Abdala Faye, whose curiosity, care for community, and passion for art have deepened my resolve in all these spaces; Stephen DeLorme, who is as fun a friend as he is a reliable one; Ellen Ireland, who always amazes me with her smarts and her humor; Lauren Harris, whose deep kindness, curiosity, and love for nature is such a joy to witness and experience; and Kimberly Coburn, who is always there with a good joke and arts-and-crafts support.

That I have such friends is a testament to how good and kind this world can be, but there are many other friends and family to thank: Darcy Lowman-Craig, Bradley Jones, Haley Murphy, Jeffery Darensbourg, Alys Spillman, Sean Crutchfield, Shelby Belfast Jones, Yale Cohn, Nialle Sylvan, Mercedes Draffin, Justin Haines, Nialle Sylvan, Ramona Muse Lambert, Bethany Bennitt, Joyce Lenoir, Justin Denman, Jan Horton, Jeremy Horton, Tonisha Horton, Jameson Horton, Jon Horton, Kristen Schreiber, Mick O'Dwyer, Elli Marlow, Burak Demirkaya, Elisa Rojas Cardona, John Gibson, John Bluhm, Chakura Kineard, Mike Stasny, Maria McDowell, Pru Hardi, Gary Burnett, Kathy Burnett, Tricia Fetters, Joe Sanchez, Jude Lally, Aajay Murphy, Tammy Peppers, Lena Huang, Len Carter Gilstrap, Luther Moss, Katie Denniston, TK Smith, Sarah Creel, Diana Symons, Connie Boyd, Dylan Norden,

Noah Koester, Lenese Colson, Eulene Walker, Noo Nut Kanyaphat, Rosalind Lenoir-Zachary, Jake Broderick, John Randall, Andy Rehm, Kellie Everett, Jon Hollister, Jisue Lee, William Downs, Fredrik Brauer, Michi Meko, Lindsay Schettler, Adam Taylor, Sam Riles, Gavin Bernard, Melissa Mathis, Patrick Hendershot, Andrew Hendershot, Cosmo Whyte, Elizabeth Shores, Vikram Patel, Melissa Gross, Linda Most, Serenity Ibsen, John Kirremuir, and many others beyond this list.

I also want to express gratitude for the memories, love, and guidance of my mom, grandparents, Justin Denman, Justin Rabideau, Darcy Mullen, John Hopkins, Jason Osburn, David Huntley, and many others who are no longer here but whose influence is still felt in these pages, including Gir, my cat who sat with me every day during the writing process.

And finally, I would be remiss in writing a book about fermentation microbes without including an acknowledgment to them as well. As I tell my students often, microbes are among our greatest teachers. Even when a ferment goes awry or what have you, there is always learning to be had from the experience. My hope is that this book will help foster a bit more appreciation for our incredible partners in food and life.

Metric Conversion Formulas

Weight

To convert	to	multiply
ounces	grams	ounces by 28.35
pounds	grams	pounds by 453.5
pounds	kilograms	pounds by 0.45

Volume

To convert	to	multiply
teaspoons	milliliters	teaspoons by 4.93
tablespoons	milliliters	tablespoons by 14.79
fluid ounces	milliliters	fluid ounces by 29.57
cups	milliliters	cups by 236.59
cups	liters	cups by 0.24
pints	milliliters	pints by 473.18
pints	liters	pints by 0.473
quarts	milliliters	quarts by 946.36
quarts	liters	quarts by 0.946
gallons	liters	gallons by 3.785

Length

To convert	to	multiply
inches	millimeters	inches by 25.4
inches	centimeters	inches by 2.54
inches	meters	inches by 0.0254

Index

apple(s)
  apple beer, 92
  Apple Chutney, Fermented
    Squash and, 214–15
  Apple Scrap Vinegar, 209–10
  pomace from, 97
apple cider, 91–92
apple cider vinegar
  Fire Cider, 208–9
applejack, 234
aqua vitae, 94
Aristotelian elements, 202
Aristotle, 201
Arrazola, Sarah, 293
The Art of Fermentation (Katz), 15, 17,
    38, 210, 218
Asia, 128, 129, 149
  fish sauces in, 138–141
Aspergillus, 144–45
  oryzae (koji), 127, 179
  penicillioides, 179
  sojae, 144–45
Atassi, Omaya, 238
Atharva Veda, 37
Awry, Wren, 76
ayahuasca, 191–92
Aye, MiMi, 240, 241
Ayurvedic medicine, 192, 194–95,
    197, 199

B
Baba, Masahiro, 26
bacteria. *See also* acetobacters;
    Lactobacillus; lacto-fermentation
  acetic acid, 19, 96, 210, 264
  biodiversity and, 152
  culture and, 218
  dairy and, 37, 38
  eukaryotes and, 296
  gene trades by, 188
  human history and, 20–21
  lactic acid, 37, 39, 97, 219

lethal, 169
bacterial colonization, 152
Bai, Li, 250
baijiu, 181
bainne clabair, 129
balao balao, 19
banana leaves, how to fold, 156
Banana Vinegar, 115–16
banchan, 42, 123, 236, 238–39
Barber, Dan, 297
barley, 34, 35, 79–80
  Egyptian Beer, Basic, 51–52
Barriere, Tiffanie, 263
Bateman, Helen, 27
Baudar, Pascal, 108, 184
beans, 172
  Amino Sauces, 164–65
beer, 23–29. *See also* corn beer
  apple, 92
  boiling/not boiling water, 153
  Egyptian Beer, Basic, 51–52
  first ferments and, 21, 24–25
  Ginger Beer, Jamaican-Style,
    273–74
  "gruit" beers, 28
  herbal, 180–81
  hops in, 27–28
  India pale ales, 28
  nutrition and, 174, 182
  preserving, 93–94
  "small beers," 174
Beet Kvass, 213–14
Bell Beaker culture, 29
Benedek, Thomas, 200
benefits of fermentation, 19
Berg, Jennifer, 48, 221
Bertelsen, Cynthia, 66, 199
Best, Michael, 28
beverages. *See also specific beverage*
  fermented, 151
  nonalcoholic, 184–86
bexhin/baxhin, 83

cucurbits, 77–78
Cultural Heritage, Intangible, 227
Cultured Butter, 6–7
culture(s), 121–23, 256–58. See also
    butter culture
    bacteria and, 218
    food, 221–22
    living, 44–45
Curtis, Paula R., 262
Curtis, Wayne, 231

D

dairy products, 37–38. See also butter
    culture; cheeses; milk; yogurt
    nutrition, early ferments and, 172
    preserving, 64–69
    type of, flavor and, 129
Dalby, Andrew, 137, 159
Daniel, Jack, 263
dashi, 136
Day, Ivan, 93–94
Dean, Sam, 129
deities, 250
DePalma, Gina, 125
de Villanova, Arnaldus, 252
de Wet, J. M. J., 79, 81
Didla, Noel, 295
digestion, 167, 196, 201, 201–3, 206,
    207
Dinerstein, Rebecca, 68
Dirar, Hamid, 63
discriminations, worldwide, 263–64
distillation, 94–95, 202
divine, ferments and, 96, 187, 246–251
Doherty, Sean, 7, 282
Dornenburg, Andrew, 133, 247
Dorsey, Jenny, 293
dosa, 89, 172
dos Santos Vilhena, Luis, 47
doubanjiang, 123
Drain, Johnny, 297
drinking, community and, 227–236

Dr. Stevens' Water, 198
Dutta, Sumi, 295

E

Egan, Sophie, 234, 235
Egtved Girl, 283
Egypt
    beer/beer brewing, 23, 26, 29, 99,
        180
    Egyptian Beer, Basic, 51–52
    funerals and, 245
    grains and, 34, 80, 83
    lavender and, 11
    wine/winemaking, 32, 177, 228
Eisen, Jonathan, 207
Elmassry, Moamen M., 26
England, 28, 63, 80, 141, 176, 182, 183,
    191, 231, 242–243, 251, 257, 260.
    See also British people
Escoffier, Auguste, 83, 131
Estés, Clarissa Pinkola, 48
Ethiopia, 229
Eubulus, 182–83
eukaryotic cells, 20, 296
Europe
    alewives in, 260–61
    ancient, fermented beverages in, 24
    Appalachian ferments and, 74
    coffeehouses and, 205
    cooking in, changing view, 203–6
    eastern, 40, 222–23, 225, 287
    fermentation worship in, 250
    funerals, foods at, 245–46
    grains in, 34, 35, 83, 88, 173, 174
    Little Ice Age in, 63
    mead/mead drinkers in, 29, 230
    rituals, ferments in, 247
    sauces in, 136–37, 141, 143
    trends and, 236
    view of cooking in, 203–7
    wines, early herbal, 177–79
    yeast in, commercial, 82

Julia Skinner is the founder and director of Root, a fermentation and food history company that bridges the gap between modern people and historic food. Her work has been featured on Vox, Eater, Business Insider, and Buzzfeed, and she is the author of *Afternoon Tea: A History*. She is the first food writer to receive two 40 Under 40 awards in the same year. She lives in Atlanta, Georgia.